HISTORY OF
FRENCH-CANADIAN
LITERATURE

GERARD TOUGAS

History of French-Canadian Literature

Second Edition

TRANSLATION BY

ALTA LIND COOK

THE RYERSON PRESS, TORONTO

Histoire de la littérature
canadienne-française *by*
Gérard Tougas was originally
published in French by Presses
Universitaires de France.

Grateful acknowledgment is made to
The Canada Council which aided in
the translation and publication of
this book.

PRINTED AND BOUND IN CANADA BY
THE RYERSON PRESS, TORONTO

FOREWORD TO THE FIRST EDITION

Europe, having spilled out over all the continents for five centuries, is gradually withdrawing to its starting-point. In the two Americas, in Australia, in Africa, she leaves behind a whole series of nations which more or less derive from her. Some of these nations, late-comers, have finally obtained their independence by means whose effectiveness they learned from Europe not so long ago. But now that it is possible to glimpse a future that will be marked by extra-European colonialisms, the struggle, this time decisive, is joined between the spirits of the old world and the new. Will it be the fate of Europe to suffer a rapid decline or, thanks to its special genius, will it be able to go on renewing itself for a long time to come?

Across the Atlantic something of the essential French spirit is already written into the young French-Canadian literature. And because the French spirit is one of the pinnacles of European humanism, we shall be replying indirectly to our question if we follow, step by step, the acclimatization of that spirit on Canadian soil.

Canada has reached complete political autonomy by travelling the route prescribed by nature: from infancy it went on to adolescence and from adolescence it is finally arriving at the age of maturity. It has never openly rebelled against Europe; at the most, in the course of its history, it has allowed a few signs of dissatisfaction to show through. And so the bonds uniting Europe and Canada are more easily felt here than elsewhere and, above all, less feared because they are better understood. Another fact, one that is signifi-cant, gives Canada a place apart among the nations created by European enterprise across the Atlantic. This nation is made up almost exclusively of white people. Consequently Canada has never had to solve a problem which confronted, or is still confronting, the majority of the Latin American countries and the United States.

The European inheritance which fell to the lot of Canada is grafted onto an American sensibility. The resulting delicate equilibrium among English, French and American elements is what constitutes the essential originality of Canada. The huge presence of the American Republic tends to disrupt this equilibrium by denationalizing ways of feeling and thinking which give a people its identity. It is possible that geography may have the last word; nevertheless, the imprint of Europe on French-Canadian literature will have been determinative.

It would have been tempting to measure this imprint, step by step, to gauge its future. We have not given up speculations along this line, but our aim in writing this *History of French-Canadian Literature* is more modest. Our main concern is to bring to wider attention a literature which already has poets who hold our interest, and novelists of a high order. This desire to inform has led us to examine from a particular angle the role of the critic and of the historian.

Does a young literature call for a special approach on the part of the critic? We believe that it does. New literatures develop in the shadow of glorious traditions. For this reason there is an obligation on the part of the critic to draw attention to what is really original in the literature that is just coming into being. Contemporary structural criticism which tackles the text before anything else is particularly apt to render elementary justice to young literatures. At every step to compare the works under examination with those which have served them as models, or which are superior to them in the mother literature or literatures of other countries, is to betray the impotence of the critic who compares but does not judge.

Textual criticism, however, can do valuable service because it takes one straight to the written page, whatever it may be. It is most valuable in allowing the critic to avoid those too familiar pitfalls of history, sociology and psychology, pitfalls into which any number of even modern-day critics fall headfirst because they are still prisoners of nineteenth-century determinism. The historian of a literature who takes it upon himself to interpret national histories runs a great risk of providing amusement for the professional historian who has experienced the countless difficulties attending any interpretation of the past. And how is it possible in our day to take seriously those summaries of the psychology of a people with which any self-respecting critic was supposed at one time to preface his work? Is it not obvious that such summaries at best risk being needlessly repetitious since literary history is supposed to reflect the synthetic picture—necessarily subjective—which precedes it? Finally, what is one to say of those small-scale psychologists and psychiatrists who draw their inspiration for the interpretation of literary texts from the discoveries of Freud and Jung? While not denying the interest of all these means of enlightenment, along with so many others that could be named, is it not easy to see that once this scholarly task is completed textual criticism must come into its own?

Generally speaking, the approaches just mentioned, which err only when they are given first place in literary criticism, have been ruled out from our *History*. This means that the laymen seeking acquaintance with the political, religious, social or other origins of French-Canadian literature, as much as with the literature itself, will no doubt find it less rewarding to read what we have written than the one who prefers going straight to the texts. Readers who come to us for the sole pleasure of an honest confrontation will have no difficulty in recognizing, beneath the assertions and judgments with which they will not always be in agreement, the substratum invisible to the others.

None the less, we have not been averse to furnishing a few biographical details, at least for Canadian authors of the nineteenth century. These details, like the quotations, become fewer as we draw near to the contemporary period which, more often than not, is given a simple critical comment. This progressive thinning-out is explained by the quality of the texts. For about a century French-Canadian literature was almost exclusively provincial. One would have difficulty in finding any page of prose or poetry which has excited scholarly comment or remained in the popular memory. Obviously it is to this period, however, that we must go for the origins of the literature of the future, that is, of our own day. This is why it is sometimes necessary to examine the authors of the nineteenth century in the light of biography, sociology or a quotation which, while rarely memorable, will reflect its man precisely just because there is nothing profound or original in it. When the writers begin to improve we shall have to give up these easy methods and have recourse to one which will be more suggestive and which will be a starting-point. We believe that the reader will gain a sufficiently good idea of the majority of French-Canadian authors of the nineteenth century and the first quarter of the present one by running through the pages that we have devoted to them;[1] on the other hand it is to the outstanding works of the contemporary period that we must go if we are to appreciate the profound revolution taking place in French-Canadian literature. Making this new literature more easily accessible, while avoiding the accumulation of short-lived classifications, has seemed to us to be the best possible introduction.

In spite of the many facts, published here for the first time, concerning the contribution of writers born in France and the relations between literary France and French Canada; in spite of the importance accorded to Canadian criticism and to criticism whose particular concern is young literatures; finally in spite of our reorganization of the material making up French-Canadian literature, there are some who will be of the opinion that a completely new, even revolutionary approach to this material was called for. To them we would reply: this would mean taking up again, in another form, the quarrel between writers and critics, a quarrel particularly bitter in Canada. Admittedly the most ingenious re-classifications will alter little on a balance sheet that justifies the highest hopes, but which must above all be submitted to a *critical* analysis that has been lacking up to the present. Indeed, without underestimating the works of Camille Roy or of those writers after him who have attempted to make a synthesis of Canadian literature in the French language, it seems clear to us that only the work of Auguste Viatte, *Histoire littéraire de l'Amérique française* (1954) answers the requirements of modern criticism, whose concern it is to emphasize what French-Canadian literature has already created that is original, while preserving a sense of proportion. M. Viatte's *Histoire,* however, conceived in terms of parallel literary movements in Louisiana, the West Indies and Haiti, offers in the Canadian section only a brief outline of the literary history of French Canada. In publishing our own *History* we have attempted to fill a gap, to furnish the educated public as well as university students with a guide which might be useful because of its fuller treatment, easy to consult because of its technical presentation and thought-provoking in its point of view.

It is the fate of all *Histories* to become outdated by reason of the enrichment—particularly swift in our age—of literary traditions. All the more reason, then, why a *History* dealing with a literature whose future will be greater than its past can be of service for only a certain time. Without entertaining any illusions on the future in store for our *History of French-Canadian Literature,* we dare to hope that it will be a modest contribution toward making the best French-Canadian authors known in Canada and abroad.

University of British Columbia
Vancouver, January, 1959

PREFACE TO THE SECOND EDITION

A problem of literary criticism arose as soon as we began the preparation of the present work in response to the reception given our first. Do four years of intense literary activity justify making major changes in our *History of French-Canadian Literature*?

When a young literature is vigorously on the move but when the direction that it is taking remains imprecise or subject to various interpretations, faithful recordings, in the shape of literary history, must take into account that lack of precision which separates literatures in the making from those solidly based on the centuries.

We were careful, therefore, in our first edition, to keep the classifications wide open to the future. If, for obvious reasons, it was not to be expected that there would be any appreciable modification of the nineteenth-century panorama, this was not the case for the present century. It will be seen, for instance, that the importance of Albert Laberge, to which we drew attention four years ago, has been put in a better perspective in this second edition. And while we gave up the idea of grouping the majority of those writers born in France who eventually became Canadian, we thought it useful to make a distinction between two generations of novelists whose recent publications in those last years would seem to indicate coexistence.

We attach no great importance to this new cross-checking in the interests of an easier understanding of a situation that had become increasingly complex. Should we undertake a third edition at some time in the future it is predictable that certain divisions which today seem to us to have significance might disappear.

It is in the same spirit that the names of several secondary writers have been struck out. Those, more numerous still, which have replaced them might well disappear in their turn in a third edition. Of Heraclitian conception, the pages devoted to contemporary literature are essentially designed only to lift from the literary flood some of its most distinguishable manifestations.

Vancouver, January, 1964

ix

CONTENTS

CHAPTER I

THE DIFFICULT BEGINNINGS

Whether or not the writings of the French period (1534-1759) should be considered as belonging to Canada or to France is a controversial subject among Canadian critics. There has always been a great temptation, on the strength of Jacques Cartier's travel notes, to conjure up "four centuries of literary history." In our day, when French-Canadian literature is taking on a more personal character, when a literary tradition does in fact exist, that innocent, if somewhat inflated, conception belongs to an honourable past. Let us recognize that the critic can benefit greatly from the accounts of French travellers[1] for in them he will find the first examples of attitudes to become characteristic of the French sensibility later on: man's wonderment before the grandiose nature of the new world and the power of his religious feeling. To sing the glories of the American continent, it is possible that many writers had found real inspiration in reading the very sober Jacques Cartier.

It is none the less true that all those navigators, colonists and pious souls were only very rarely moved to literary endeavour. How could they have been, coming away as they did with no idea other than to seek great adventures, spiritual or otherwise? Some of them published an account of these adventures afterwards; others established the chronology of outstanding events in New France; others again, like the Jesuits whose *Relations* contain admirable pages, aimed at moving French opinion and enlightening it with regard to the work of the missions. But nearly all of these works, without exception published in France, reveal preoccupations that were outside the literary and so have no place in French literary history proper except as memoirs. It is true that certain of these works exerted influence. Rabelais may have received inspiration from accounts of Cartier's travels. But it is only in this light that the period 1534-1759 can legitimately be embodied in a history of Canadian literature. In this limited sense the Champlains, the

Maries de l'Incarnation, the Charlevoix, whose testimony has been a source of inspiration to Canadian writers, do belong to Canada. The writers of this French period are an umbilical cord attaching the literature of Canada to the great French tradition.

So, let us now resolutely station ourselves at that moment of history when Canada becomes English. The Canadians who, with the exception of the clergy, were soon to be left behind by a large part of the former notables of New France, are now experiencing some of those feelings a people can have only once. Alone forever, facing the nation which had been the hereditary enemy of France for centuries, and unaware of the ferment of Canadianism working within them, some sixty thousand colonists in a short time became Canadians with a real sense of nationality. But by a process easy to comprehend they also began to miss their old masters. The English, whose language they did not understand and whose religion inspired in them the greatest distrust, could only make them forget the wrongs, real or imaginary, suffered under the French.

In the history of Franco-Canadian relations the English Conquest was a great piece of good fortune. Far from wishing to oppose French influences, the Canadian elite was to do everything possible to comfort itself in the warmth of a close contact with French culture. It may be added, however, that for all of the nineteenth century it was to harbour resentment against France for having abandoned it a second time.

For generations the little French-Canadian population lived almost entirely withdrawn unto itself. England, fearing any contact between France and the new colony, for a long time refused French visitors entry into the country.[2] The clergy practically had to give up filling the gaps in their ranks by recruiting priests from the mother country. With the exception of about forty French priests who crossed over into Canada during the Rebellion, members of religious orders were unable to come to Canada until after 1837. Nevertheless, for three-quarters of a century, a very tenuous contact was maintained with France. A few young people were able to go to France to study. French books arrived in Quebec very irregularly by way of London.[3] However, it is in this period that one can place the first stammerings of French-Canadian literature.

The literary production which extends from 1764 to 1830, very curious and instructive for the historian of French-Canadian literature in its beginnings, is all contained in the newspapers of the period. Of these short-lived writings not one merits survival.[4] This sub-species nevertheless did have its little local triumphs and even found critics, surely the first known in French Canada, to comment on it.

The first French-language newspaper to appear in Canada was the *Gazette littéraire* of Montreal, founded in 1778 by Fleury Mesplet. This Frenchman, whom Benjamin Franklin had met in London in 1773 and induced to follow him to America, settled later in Montreal where he became the father of French-Canadian journalism. The first books published in French also came off his presses. As his collaborator, Mesplet took on a compatriot, Valentin Jautard, the first critic of French-Canadian literature.

The fact that both were French underlines the necessity in which French Canadians found themselves of maintaining, for the preservation of their language, all possible ties with France. In a period of general illiteracy the help of a few educated Frenchmen was of course extremely valuable.

It is significant that with the founding of the *Gazette* a small literary polemic should have broken out, setting up the critic Jautard against a budding Canadian poet. Jautard's literary precepts would have been approved by Laharpe. Now our young Canadian author had been so unfortunate as to express himself in imperfect language. Jautard, who did not fail to correct him, brought on himself this reflection:

This man [Jautard] has an utter contempt for Canadian youth: he is their cruelest enemy. He succeeded in disgusting those who presented themselves at the opening of *La Feuille Littéraire* because their Productions did not please him, because he did not consider them to have the degree of perfection necessary to a good piece of work. Do people think that the Canadian, without teachers, should write as flawlessly as if he were a scholar?[5] [*trans.*]

And so the old quarrel between French and French Canadians was resumed, this time on the linguistic and literary plane. In our own day it is still not entirely settled.

When Michel Bibaud in 1830 published the first collection of poetry to appear in French Canada, from among his predecessors he singled out Joseph Quesnel (1749-1809) as being, in his opinion, an authentic poet: "There is no more or less educated Canadian who has not read at least some of the works of the late Mr. Joseph Quesnel, and who has not recognized in them a true poetic genius."[6]

Born in Saint Malo, Quesnel, good Breton that he was, had become a sailor and left for Pondichéry at the age of nineteen. He spent some time in Madagascar, on the Guinea coast and in Senegal. A few years later he was to be found in the West Indies. Then came the American War of Independence. In 1779 he was put in command of a vessel loaded with provisions for the garrison at New York, but was unable to escape the vigilance of an English frigate and was taken to Halifax.

After all his travels did Quesnel feel that he had found in Canada something of his native Brittany? The fact remains that this adventurous man settled not far from Montreal, in Boucherville. Like Mesplet and Jautard, this Frenchman, who seemed to have no particular aptitude for literature, was yet able to play a useful role in Canada. Actually he had only to warm over things he remembered from school and to repeat more or less the versification he had learned before going to sea, to become straight off not a poet, but a "Canadian poet" of the time around 1800.

In a country lacking literary traditions, whose population for the most part is without the most elementary culture, a rhymester can seem to his contemporaries to be a phenomenon as extraordinary as a poet of genius to an old civilization. By his honest devotion to the cause, however, Quesnel gave to a few Canadians a glimpse of what literature can be. In an epistle dedicated in 1804 to M. Généreux Labadie, in all probability a kindred soul, Quesnel felt that he should address himself to posterity. Since only French-Canadians are in a position to let him reach it, perhaps there is a certain spice of justice in quoting him:

> *Pour nous, cher Labadie, dans ce pays ingrat*
> *Où l'esprit est plus froid encore que le climat,*
> *Nos talents sont perdus pour le siècle où nous sommes;*
> *Mais la postérité fournira d'autres hommes*
> *Qui, goûtant les beautés de nos écrits divers,*
> *Célébreront ma prose aussi bien que tes vers.*
> *Prédire l'avenir est ce dont je me pique,*
> *Tu peux en croire enfin mon esprit prophétique:*
> *Nos noms seront connus un jour en Canada,*
> *Et chantés de Vaudreuil jusqu'à Kamouraska.*[7]

For us, dear Labadie, in this rude country
Where the spirit is still colder than the climate,
Our talents are lost to the century in which we live.
But posterity will provide other men
Who, savouring the beauty of our writings,
Will extol my prose and your verse.
Foretelling the future is something on which I pride myself.
So you may trust my poetic vision:
Some day our names will be known in Canada
And sung from Vaudreuil right up to Kamouraska.[7] [*trans.*]

Quesnel, a simple store-keeper of Boucherville and poet in his leisure time, had a large following in the nineteenth century.[8] As these disillusioned lines testify, the writing profession in a young country was unprofitable. So French Canadians who felt attracted to intellectual pursuits were almost always obliged, like Quesnel, to beguile the boredom of a job they hated by exerting themselves to write poetry or history or stories. The scarcity of outstanding names which the nineteenth century has left us must not let us forget this important fact: the humble efforts of these pen-wielders have contributed to the spread, if not to the acceptance, of the idea that a writer, far from belonging to the ranks of the unproductive, is one of the most indispensable elements of a society. When a first group of writers was established in Quebec around 1850, the ever-vigilant clergy were to do their best, through their priest-critics, to guide this new force.

No writer worked harder in the preparation of the first literary flowering than Michel Bibaud (1782-1857) who devoted his entire life to educating his compatriots in this regard. When he founded the *Aurore* in Montreal in 1817 he made an arrangement for copy from *La ruche d'Aquitaine*, a Bordeaux periodical brought into Canada by Henri Mézières,[9] emulator of Fleury Mesplet. In this way Bibaud made it plain that he wanted to keep his readers informed about what was going on in French intellectual life.[10]

It is as a poet that Bibaud deserves our attention. *Epîtres, satires chansons, épigrammes et autres pièces de vers* appeared in 1830. This is nothing but rhymed prose. Attacking the vices and shortcomings of Canadians, he exhorts them to mend their ways and, particularly, to speak better French.[11] This poor verse has its importance in the history of French-Canadian literature for it ushers in what may properly be called the literary phase. Publication of a collection of poems in 1830 was a gamble. It is to be observed also that if this poetry is Canadian in content, in style it is inspired by the satires of Boileau. That French-Canadian poetry should derive from Boileau in 1830, at a time when Romanticism was triumphant in France, says volumes about the difficulties those first writers had to overcome. In an Anglo-Saxon world, with their language threatened, it was inevitable that they should seek refuge in French literary tradition. And these imitations, servile as they may be, must not make us lose sight of their true significance. Through the intermediary of its Bibauds, French Canada was affirming its immense desire to attain an autonomous life of the spirit. Without doubt this autonomy already existed, but it lacked that distinctive sign of life that makes a literature.

In the twelve years following the appearance of the *Epîtres* the first foundations were laid for the novel and for the theatre.[12]

We shall not linger on the subject of French-Canadian theatre, however. Right up to the contemporary period it was less than mediocre. It could hardly be otherwise for theatre must have a cultivated public if that indispensable spark is to fly between actor and audience. It was only in the twentieth century that Montreal became a great cosmopolitan city. Sarah Bernhardt, who played there in 1880, 1891 and again in 1905, came to the conclusion that Canadians were not yet ready for the theatre.

It should come as no surprise that the first works for the stage were written by schoolboys. The *Griphon ou la vengeance d'un valet* (1837) by Pierre Petitclair and, on a slightly higher level, *Le jeune Latour* (1842), a tragedy by Antoine Gérin-Lajoie, lack brilliance but do lend this literary genre more than a century of history. Presented at the Collège de Nicolet, *Le jeune Latour* was a three-act tragedy written in Alexandrines. Bibaud had relied on Boileau for his poetic style; Gérin-Lajoie could do no better than follow Corneille. A Cornelian hero, young Latour is divided between the respect he owes his father and fidelity to the King of France. When at the end of the century we find Fréchette writing his *Veronica,* he will hardly have gone further than Gérin-Lajoie.

The novel was to have a better fate. It was in 1837 that the first French-Canadian novel made its appearance, *Le chercheur de trésors ou l'influence d'un livre,* by Philippe Aubert de Gaspé, son of the novelist of the same name. Then, after an interval of a few years there followed *Les fiancés de 1812* by Joseph Doutre (1844) and *Charles Guérin* (1846) by Pierre Chauveau.[13]

L'influence d'un livre is a very odd novel of special significance. Canadian criticism which has not been favourable to it has preferred *Charles Guérin,* often considered to be the first novel worthy of the name. It seems to us, on the contrary, that the younger Gaspé's[14] weird imagination calls for less critical severity.

When he gave birth to this *roman de moeurs*—not without having destroyed a painful first draft out of artistic concern—the younger Gaspé was twenty-three years old and only a short time before had made the acquaintance of the great Romanticists. It seemed to him a good idea to collect the old superstitions and songs of the Canadian countryside, incorporating them in a slender story-structure in order to make a book.

The hero, Armand, a dreamy individual, goes looking for the philosopher's stone. He finds a way of taking a hand from the corpse of a murderer, referred to as *hand of glory* in necromancy and highly valued by alchemists. His adventures are not to be taken more seriously by us than by the author himself, who makes a few characters sing old songs which have about disappeared from today's Quebec countryside. From this modest book there emerges an air of authenticity which is not without charm.

The character of Armand is symbolic for he belongs to the race of those who would always prefer their dreams to the reality of a money-making America. The will-o'-the-wisps and ghosts in which the Armands put their faith are nothing but the embodiment of the strong intuitions of an entire people.

Why have the critics made so little of this first novel which is so Canadian? Could it be that the homely superstitions, the simplicity, the very credulity of the characters offended later generations who might have wished to think of themselves as having a less simple-hearted ancestry? These same generations, it is true, were unable to see themselves in those fine little churches bequeathed to them by the artisans of the French regime. Perfectly adapted to the needs of their religion, as well as to the requirements of harmonious simplicity, these churches were abandoned for the pretentious edifices with which we are familiar.

Let us remember that when *Le chercheur de trésors* was published the existence of the French Canadians as a people had never seemed in greater danger. The insurrection of 1837/38, the policy of assimilation advocated soon afterwards by Durham and carried out in effect by the Act of Union of 1840, and still other factors were to stimulate French Canadians to get an education in order to better defend themselves. Their understandable desire to have noble origins was gratified by Garneau in his *Histoire du Canada* (1845). Recalling past glories was to give more pleasure than this novel, which was veracious in spite of its whimsical presentation.

More than *Le chercheur de trésors,* Chauveau's *Charles Guérin* merits consideration as a real novel of the social scene.[15] For the first time a study was made of the repercussions of the conquest on French-Canadian society. In 1846 the citizens of Montreal and Quebec found themselves corralled into a few professions, as their forebears had been. Young men who felt no particular inclination to go into Law, Medicine, or Theology nevertheless had no other choice unless, renouncing all ambition, they joined the swelling contingent of the habitants.

Here we have the whole plot of Chauveau's patriotic contrivance. Of the two Guérin brothers, one goes into the priesthood, the other chooses to clear new land. It was for Antoine Gérin-Lajoie to write the first homilies on the clearing of unproductive territories in Quebec. What Chauveau did was merely to indicate this outlet to French-Canadian youth.

Lacking experience and culture, neither Chauveau nor Gaspé Junior, twenty-six and twenty-three years of age respectively when these two novels were published, could have any clear conception of what a novel should be. More hopeless still is the case of Joseph Doutre, author of *Fiancés* at the age of nineteen. Gaspé Junior, whose preface to the *Chercheur* shows some indication that he had at least given thought to some of the problems posed by the novel, had avoided any personal intervention in the story by a description of Canadian habits and customs that was completely exterior. Chauveau, by his distressingly naïve asides and his painful efforts to rise to the level of a lofty style, showed himself less able to conceal his lack of experience. Basically, however, in all three cases the writing is primitive.

In spite of their obvious weaknesses, *Le chercheur de trésors* and *Charles Guérin* are important in the history of French-Canadian literature. In the nineteenth century the Gothic supernatural in the younger Gaspé is equalled only in the work of his father—who just possibly was no stranger to the editing of *Chercheur*—and is surpassed by Pamphile Lemay. As for Chauveau's tearful and grandiloquent style, it constituted a tiresome example that was much imitated in following generations.

With these first novels Romanticism is introduced into French-Canadian literature. Almost all the literature of the second half of the century will belong to Romanticism as well. In poetry the Classicism of a Bibaud will remain a dead issue. Soon the poets will be singing the joys of home, the beauties of their native land and their longings for the past.[16]

In all of this literary output of half a century, imitation will play a great part. All young literatures have to go through a period of dependence on some tradition by which they are nourished. This imitative phase is in the nature of things. In it, nevertheless, there is something special to French-Canadian literature which will become one of its permanent characteristics. A literature in the French language, by the simple fact of having been born in Romanticism, is distinguishable from French literature, whose highest form of expression is Classicism. Romanticism seems to correspond to some secret need in the French-Canadian temperament as fashioned by the American continent. French-Canadian poets, historians and novelists of the nineteenth century will have done more than imitate their French models: in them they will have found themselves.

NOTES TO FOREWORD

Several literary figures to be found in the literary histories of Camille Roy, Berthelot Brunet, Auguste Viatte and Samuel Baillargeon have been left out. These "oversights" are practically all omissions. French-Canadian literature, in proportion to its progress, must unload itself of the mediocrities which will always be a delight to the specialist and to candidates for the doctorate.

NOTES TO CHAPTER ONE

1. In Auguste Viatte's *Histoire littéraire de l'Amérique française* (Quebec: Presses Universitaires Laval, 1954) there may be found a résumé of intellectual activity under French rule, pp. 1-43.
Throughout our *History* we refer the reader only to those works that stem from a true critical spirit or which contain useful documentary material, and do not attempt to be complete.

2. Thirty-two years after the Treaty of Paris, in 1795, the duc de la Rochefoucauld-Liancourt, exiled in the United States, wished to visit Canada. Because of his nationality he was turned back at Kingston. A few years later Count Colbert de Maulévrier, who, as a preliminary measure, had obtained useful letters of introduction, was able to go to Montreal and Quebec. Cf. Armand Yon, "L'Ottawa vue par les Français," *Revue de l'Université d'Ottawa* (1938), p. 386.

3. M. Gustave Lanctot, in an article entitled "Les relations franco-canadiennes après la conquête," *La Revue de l'Université Laval*, Vol. X (March, 1956), pp. 591-599, has attempted to show that Franco-Canadian relations underwent scarcely an interruption after 1760. The contacts that M. Lanctot enumerates indicate that a few privileged persons in each generation were, in fact, able to go to France. It seems exaggerated, however, to conclude that steady communications between the two countries were maintained.

4. M. Séraphin Marion has made a special study of the journalistic period of French-Canadian literature. Cf. *Lettres canadiennes d'autrefois* (Ottawa: Editions de l'Université d'Ottawa). The first volume of the series appeared in 1948.

5. *La Gazette,* February 3, 1779. Quotation by Séraphin Marion, *op. cit.,* Vol. II, p. 170.

6. *Epîtres, satires, chansons, épigrammes et autres pièces de vers* (Montreal: Ludger Duvernay), p. 46.

7. J. Huston, *Le répertoire national* (Montreal: Valois & Cie, 1893), Vol. I, p. 82.

8. Mention should be made of his immediate successor, Joseph Mermet, from Lyon, who, during his stay in Canada (1812-1816), makes the aspirations of French Canadians his own. He writes patriotic poems, notably *La victoire de Châteauguay* (Huston, *op. cit.,* pp. 95-106).

9. Former prefect of Bordeaux under the Empire, Mézières, stranded in Canada in 1818, launched *L'abeille canadienne.* He was to experience the truth of Quesnel's statement that the spirit of Canada is colder than its climate. After a few months he gave up the idea of spreading among the Canadian population *les sciences, les lettres et les arts.*

10. Among other voluntary efforts of this kind we cite *La Minerve,* founded in 1826 by Auguste Morin. Between 1826 and 1844 this paper published extracts from Rousseau, Hugo, Chateaubriand, Lamartine, Béranger and Gautier.

11.   *La paresse nous fait mal parler notre langue*
    Combien peu, débitant la plus courte harangue
    Savent garder et l'ordre, et le vrai sens des mots:
    Commencer et finir chaque phrase à propos?
    Très souvent, au milieu d'une phrase française,
    Nous plaçons, sans façon, une tournure anglaise.
    Presentment, indictment, impeachment, foreman
    Sheriff, writ, verdict, bill, roast-beef, warrant, watchman.
(*Epîtres, satires* [Montreal: Ludger Duvernay, 1830], p. 38.)

12. Joseph Quesnel had had a comedy in three acts, *Colas et Colinette ou le bailli dupe,* played in 1790 in Montreal. This play, like a few other mildly amusing comedies by the same author, for a long time will remain an isolated occurrence in the evolution of the theatre.

13. The literary output of the period was greater than one would suppose from a dry enumeration of titles. Actually, research of late carried out by critics to shed more light on *Canadian pre-Romanticism* seems to reveal the blossoming, between 1830 and 1837, of a real literary movement. For David Hayne the "pre-Romantic generation" is made up of "waves," of which the third may be situated around 1853.

The unearthing of these first writings in Canadian literature is not without its uses since it leads to our fixing with greater accuracy the place of more valid works that appeared around 1860 in Quebec. At any rate it is clear that the patient researchers who, today, would like to open a new chapter in Canadian letters called *pre-Romanticism,* run no risk of conferring on the years 1835-1845 any literary importance whatever. Admittedly, it is somewhat arbitrary to limit one's choice to the names mentioned above. But other authors and other titles might have held our attention without modifying our conclusion on the intrinsic value of these first literary efforts. Interesting details on the pre-Romanticists are to be found in the article by David Hayne, "Sur les traces du préromantisme canadien," *Archives des lettres canadiennes.* Special number of the *Revue de l'Université d'Ottawa* (1961), pp. 137-157.

14. According to Camille Roy, the father of Philippe Aubert de Gaspé collaborated in this work. *Nos origines littéraires* (Quebec: L'Action Sociale, 1909), p. 313.

15. The considerable work of Chauveau is known today only to a few specialists. Maurice Lebel has drawn up a table of studies on the novelist. Cf. "P.-J.-O. Chauveau, humaniste du XIXe siècle," *La Revue de l'Université de Laval* (September, 1962), pp. 32-42.

16. At almost the same moment that Bibaud was publishing his anachronistic poetry, Garneau was rhyming:

> *Le murmure des flots qui blanchissent ces bords*
> *Et la brise du soir cadençant ses accords . . .*

(J. Huston, *op. cit.,* p. 239).

CHAPTER II

THE AGE OF GARNEAU
1845-1865

In the history of French-Canadian literature no work has created a more immediate and wider interest nor exerted a more enduring influence than François-Xavier Garneau's *Histoire du Canada* (1845-1848). Speaking for his generation Abbé Henri-Raymond Casgrain says, "We shall never forget the profound impression produced on us as young students by the appearance of M. Garneau's *Histoire du Canada*. This book was a revelation to us."[1]

Garneau's success is explained by the political climate of 1845 and the high quality of his work.

Durham, in his celebrated Report of 1839, a masterpiece of liberal English opinion in the nineteenth century,[2] had proposed the gradual assimilation of the French-Canadian element by the British, in order to put an end to the rivalries which were setting up the French and English elements against each other. To hasten that end Durham had proposed union of the two Canadas and the adoption by England of a policy of massive immigration which would throw the French Canadians into a fatal minority situation, a prelude to their final disappearance.

The French Canadians have always opposed the idea of their annihilation by imperceptible stages with a vigour and obstinacy never more marked than in the period when Garneau conceived the idea of writing a history of his country. As for the ministers of Queen Victoria, the Canadian problem presented itself in terms that were very clear: England would have to disregard its conquest of Canada, giving complete satisfaction to French Canadians and, by reason of their high birth-rate, hand the country over to them, or assure the triumph of British institutions through the adoption of appropriate measures. In the middle of the nineteenth century it was not possible for England, advanced as she might be along the road of liberalism, to withdraw from the American continent. As

11

well, any move of this kind would have thrown the English Canadians into the arms of the Americans. So it is very fortunate for the destiny of Canada that England, by wisely loosening little by little the bonds which bound her to Canada, did not withdraw completely until assured, once and for all, of the preponderance of the English and, consequently, of Canada's political unity. Reassured on this score, England was to view with a different eye that small French-Canadian people which definitely had no intention of dying. The presence of a strong French-language minority was to appear to the aristocratic Elgin, the Crown's representative in Canada between 1846 and 1854, as an additional guarantee of the solidity of a political framework invented by the English genius. The English Canadians had too often shown him the cloven hoof, *yankee,* for him to feel completely sure of their future sentiments.

But the French Canadians of the time, even more sensitive than they are today, had scarcely noticed that Durham in his Report had found them to have more aptitude for speculative thought, in a word to be more refined, than their English-speaking compatriots. More than anything else they had kept in mind this statement: "They are a people without history or literature."[3] François-Xavier Garneau made a point of proving the opposite.

For the writing of his *Histoire,* Garneau, born in 1809, was sufficiently close to the French regime to be able to make it live again in a manner that was authentic. His youth had been filled with memories of the last battles that France and French Canadians had fought in America:

My old grandfather, bent over by age, sitting on the verandah of his long white house, high up on top of the hill overlooking the old church of Saint-Augustine, with trembling hand would point out to us the spot where the naval battle of the *Atalante* had taken place with several English ships, a battle which he had witnessed himself as a child.
I grew up in the midst of these events, this talk, with a taste for the travel, the incessant movement characteristic in our day of the inhabitant of North America. If circumstance or good fortune did not yet permit me to venture across those lakes, those great rivers that our forefathers had discovered in the New World, to visit that Old France from which they had come, I did none the less promise myself to take the first opportunity to realize at least one of my great desires, to go and bow my head before the cradle of my ancestors on the shores of the Seine.[4] [*trans.*]

With the enthusiasm of youth, Garneau was fired with the desire to write the astounding epic of the founders of New France. Especially he wanted to put in their right perspective both the Seven

Years' War, in the course of which his countrymen had accomplished prodigious feats of valour, and that ensuing period which was so difficult for them.[5] It was one of Garneau's merits that having such sentiments he made himself remain objective and gave to his *Histoire* a maximum of authenticity by backing it up with first-hand documentation.[6] Already, at the age of nineteen, he had visited the places made famous by those battles which ended in the loss of Canada. Then in 1831 he left for England and France. This trip was the necessary complement of the first one that had given him the opportunity of seeing New York, Boston, Buffalo, Niagara, and Kingston. It was indispensable for the future historian to take stock personally of the true character of the English and French peoples. He was able to profit from his stay in Europe.[7] In London he took note of the English genius for commerce as well as the solid bases of British liberties; and like many a French Canadian since, he experienced the joy of landing in France, along with the sober thoughts inspired by the lack of loyalty to their government among the French people and the painful process of adjustment to the world of that day.

After his return from Europe the legal profession for which he had been prepared held little interest for him. It was the Rebellion of 1837-1838, then Durham's recommendation on the advisability of fusing the two races, that prompted him to become the historian of forgotten causes.

Reading through the three volumes of the *Histoire* (1845-1848), it is easy to understand the inevitable reactions of a people as harassed as they were proud. The greatest quality in Garneau is the very one he had admired in Michelet: the power to call up the past. Garneau had considered the drama of French colonization in America as a kind of Greek tragedy. He makes us feel the full significance of the smallest acts, the shortcomings of French colonial policy, which had such consequence for the future. The pre-industrial America he knew allowed him to rediscover in imagination the regions visited by La Salle, Marquette, d'Iberville. And so it is that among his finest pages are those in which his Romanticism—not the wild variety of writers to come after him—leads him to make little sketches to embellish his narrative.

Si la découverte du nouveau monde par les Européans a exercé une influence salutaire sur la destinée de l'Europe, elle a été funeste aux nations qui peuplaient les forêts de l'Amérique. Leur amour de la liberté, leurs moeurs belliqueuses, leur intrépidité, retardent encore à peine d'un jour leur ruine: au contact de la civilisation, elles tombent avec plus de rapidité que les bois mystérieux qui leur servaient de retraite, et bientôt, selon les paroles poétiques de Lamen-

*nais, elles auront disparu sans laisser plus de trace que les brises qui
passent sur les savanes. Nous plaignons leur destinée. En moins de
trois siècles, elles se sont effacées d'une grande partie du continent. Ce n'est pas ici le lieu de rechercher les causes de l'anéantisse-
ment de tant de peuples dans un espace de temps si court que
l'imagination en est étonnée: cela mènerait loin, et ne nous offrirait
que des images tristes pour l'orgueil de l'homme. Nous abandon-
nerons à l'oubli qui les couvre ces hécatombes muettes sur lesquelles
ne s'élève aucun monument, aucun souvenir, et nous tournerons nos
regards vers des peuples dont les grandes actions ne passeront pas,
et dont la hardiesse et le génie, portés d'Europe en Amérique, ont
donné une nouvelle impulsion à la civilisation.*[8]

If the discovery of the New World by the Europeans exerted a
salutary influence on the destiny of Europe, it was fatal for the
peoples who inhabited the forests of America. Their love of
liberty, their warlike customs and their fearlessness delay their
destruction by hardly a day. Once in contact with civilization they
fall more swiftly than the mysterious woods which were their refuge
and soon, in the poetic words of Lammenais, they will have disappeared, leaving no more trace than the breezes that blow over the
savannahs. We pity their fate. In less than three centuries they
have been erased from a great portion of the continent. This is not
the place to look for the causes of the annihilation of so many
nations in a period of time so short the imagination fails. This
would be taking us too far afield and would present us with pictures to sadden the pride of man. We shall leave to the oblivion
that clothes them those silent hecatombs over which no monument
is raised, no memorial, and we shall turn our eyes towards peoples
whose great exploits will not pass away and whose daring and
genius, brought to America from Europe, gave a new impetus to
civilization.[8] [*trans.*]

While not a stylist, Garneau knows how to restrain his effusions.
But any quotation gives only a very imperfect idea of the first real
writer produced by French Canada. Garneau, who had to spend
many a solitary late night to finish his education, never mastered
the written language to perfection. It would be only too easy to
pinpoint his errors, his sometimes uneven and none-too-lucid
sentence construction. In these circumstances how is it that there
have been critics who considered him a writer of incomparable
ability? It is because Garneau lived the grandeur of his subject;
his inner vision often comes through even colourless prose. Garneau's generation, more open to patriotic than to aesthetic considerations, felt itself come alive as it read his *Histoire,* and the
stimulus was such that this work remained a source of inspiration
for more than one writer in the second half of the century.

As in the case of any historian, time has meant that some of

Garneau's ideas are outdated. The contrast he held up between the "phlegmatic races" and the "Gallic temperament" of the French Canadians, which kept them from being assimilated even in Louisiana, seems peculiar in the light of what we now know about sociology. However, almost everybody in the nineteenth century believed in the idea of "race" and Taine was not the least among them.

Garneau belongs to the first half of his century also by reason of his over-simplified conception of the Middle Ages as ignorant, as the Dark Ages, and by his confidence in the perfectibility of modern man. But here again he is in distinguished company.

In his treatment of religious problems Garneau showed an impartiality which, for the wrong reasons, was held against him in his own time. It may seem surprising that he had no understanding of mysticism, which he characterized as "delirium of piety."[9] A William James, far removed as he was from the Catholic tradition, was to define very differently a state of mind which throws such a vivid light on the nature of man.

Finally, one must not forget that Garneau, by placing his *Histoire* within the larger framework of the political West, by emphasizing the new and revolutionary elements heralded by those few centuries, such as the prime importance of trade, saved his work from oblivion. He even takes on the aspect of a prophet if we think about his advice to the France of 1845, busy at that time creating a second empire on the ruins of the first, that it reflect on the lessons of its first failure. But France was to follow another destiny as with her genius and customary lack of foresight she laid across the world the same fragile foundations of her power, contested today, and tomorrow perhaps forever reduced to nothingness.

POETRY

As a poet Garneau is mediocre. By his example he contributed to the spread of French Romanticism in a generation enamoured of the poetry of Lamartine and Victor Hugo.[10] His stay in France came only a short time after the Hernani "ruckus" and the publication of *Harmonie politiques et religieuses.* Under the influence of the new poetry, and particularly that of Lamartine, Garneau, even before his return home, had written an elegy, *Le voyageur,* bolstered with commonplaces liberally borrowed from the Romantic poets: *l'astre du silence, la coupe du malheur, les sombres abîmes, ma paupière attendrie.* Later on when his versification took on firmer shape he was never able to rid himself of *zéphir* or *aquilon,* whether he was evoking the last of the Hurons or the ancient oak, witness of past glories. In the tearful and patriotic path Garneau was to be followed by numerous verse-makers who, though lacking any real talent, can be credited with assuring the continuity of literary production up to the time of Crémazie.[11]

POETRY

Octave Crémazie (1827-1879)

With Octave Crémazie the level of poetry, very low until his appearance, rose perceptibly. Crémazie was the first to convey the impression of an authentic poetry, one with real feeling.

His life deserves consideration almost as much as his poetry for it is the story of the disappointments of many a poet and writer to come after him.[12]

There are two sides to his intellectual and artistic evolution: the first is Canadian, the second French. Between 1827 and 1862 Crémazie completed his studies and was in partnership with his two brothers in a bookstore in Quebec on the Rue de la Fabrique. This period, which was the happiest of his life, was the one he devoted to poetry. Then, as a result of financial difficulties, he felt obliged to leave the country, never to see it again.

The last years (1862-1879), which he spent in France, were almost a blank as far as poetry is concerned. However, as a result of observations which his life abroad led him to make on the state of Canadian literature and on the intellectual and moral climate of his adopted country, he became the unwitting founder, along with his faithful correspondent, Abbé Henri-Raymond Casgrain, of French-Canadian literary criticism. The opinions on France which he set down in his diary at a time when he was sharing with the Parisians the privations imposed by the German siege of 1870-1871, make very curious reading. Here it is possible to look into his state of mind and through him into that of the Canadian writer of the second half of the nineteenth century.

Crémazie is above all the poet of patriotism and of fidelity to the memory of France. His fellow countrymen saw themselves in his poetry, as they had felt a renewal of courage in reading Garneau's *Histoire.* The resumption of diplomatic relations between France and Canada, which took place officially with the arrival of the Belvèze mission in 1855,[13] was the occasion for Crémazie to write his *Chant du vieux soldat canadien. Le drapeau de Carillon,* which he composed soon afterwards, is also a song to the glories of a France rediscovered. Re-reading today these two poems which made Crémazie famous at the time, one can easily see them as nothing but cast-off patriotic trappings of the first part of the century. This poetry in which *glorieux* rhymes with *victorieux, gloire* with *victoire,* is none the less animated by the breath of passion. One would have difficulty, it is true, in quoting two consecutive Alexandrines with any streak of originality. But the whole effect, more important than the details, is one of life.

More original is his unfinished poem, *Promenade des trois morts.* Here there are certain lines with a studied rhythm proving that Crémazie was more than a versifier:

> *Drapés, comme des rois, dans leur manteaux funèbres,*
> *Ils marchent en silence au milieu des ténèbres.*

The death image is not artificial and although all the usual commonplaces can be found in French-Canadian poets of this century, *La Promenade* succeeds in creating an artistic tonality that could not be discovered in Crémazie's predecessors.

It would be fitting to add to Crémazie's list of successes the poem of similar inspiration entitled *Les morts,* which went unnoticed among his compatriots, those "shop-keepers," when it appeared in 1856. Crémazie thought it was the best thing he had done, and if we confine ourselves to the versification, where there is an unusual flexibility, we must admit that he was right.

Crémazie left for France in 1862. His probable state of mind at the thought of going to France—leaving aside his financial difficulties—makes one think of the young Garneau in 1830. As a matter of fact the French-Canadian writer, going to France for the first time, presents a very particular psychological case that would be worth analyzing; this spiritual adventure, if the stay is of any length, conditions his future thinking.

Driven into an inferior position as a result of the Conquest of 1760, French Canadians have always been able to find consolation in the thought that they descended from a nation which was a leader in Europe for centuries and whose civilization is still universally admired. For the French-Canadian writer especially, France has been regarded as a Holy Land. Crémazie was only one of the first among many poets who wrote passionate lines extolling the virtues of a chivalrous France, mother of the arts and beacon for the world. These eulogies, often wildly extravagant, are explained by the wounded pride of French Canadians—a state of mind lasting far into the twentieth century.[14]

Crémazie's stay in France resulted in a paralysis of the poet in him. In this respect he was a kind of precursor, for other writers after him experienced as he did the changes effected by a too complete identification with French life. This phenomenon is explained by the French-Canadian temperament. The French-Canadian intellectual, from birth hemmed in on all sides by an Anglo-Saxon world, achieves an adequate knowledge of his own language only at the price of a real struggle within himself, marked with failures and half-successes.

To protect himself against anglicisms, against the language of his compatriots—which is authentically French, certainly, but impoverished—and against an encroaching commercialism which destroys intellectual and moral values, means that his fate is to be a cripple. Let him come to live in France and that delicate defence mechanism which, after all, makes for his originality, relaxes, then disappears. Instead of rejecting outside influences he welcomes them, happy at last to be in a country where his talent can grow to a full flowering. It is a dangerous euphoria that can kill the writer by turning his face away from the sources of his inspiration.

Crémazie's sterile years can be explained also by the impossible picture of France that he had painted for himself. A pious and simple man, Crémazie was to find himself confused in a France that was at the very centre of modern thought. In his diary he wrote about "the well-beloved France" of his youth: "Instead of that great nation which occupies so large a place in the annals of history, today there is nothing left but an agglomeration of men without principles, without morals or manners, without faith and without dignity."[15] Increasingly disillusioned, Crémazie, an exile in France, no longer had the heart for anything except his own country and the fate of the Canadian writer. In his correspondence with Abbé Henri-Raymond Casgrain he was to found the first French-Canadian literary criticism worthy of the name, before going to die in le Havre in 1879.

CRITICISM

The eternal quarrel between writers and critics has always been particularly lively in Canada. Recriminations easily become abusive since in addition to the countless reasons writers and critics normally have for misunderstanding each other's intentions can be added that of the small amount of space in the cultural eyrie where they must confront each other. Usually the people who create the literature and the people making the professional comments on it are acquainted. Consequently the word, the judgment that would only be irritating from a stranger, can be deeply wounding. Praise is unsatisfactory too, since the unconscious partiality of the judge will be questioned. In this atmosphere, unfavourable to the objective and calm discussion of literature, the writer will be inclined to underestimate criticism that is incapable, according to him, of judging what he writes. And the critic will long for some heady product of the mind finally capable of setting his faculties in motion.

In this quarrel it seems that nobody has ever asked a question fundamental to a literature in the first stages of development. Can criticism raise itself to a position above literature, in a word, be superior to it? Canadian writers who have appealed with all their hearts for some Sainte-Beuve have refused from the start to see what the real problem is. If it can be admitted that criticism may on occasion throw some light on the future, it is the literature being created which provides the impetus in the first place. Criticism will always be closely conditioned by literature itself. Now the writer is relatively free. The novelist, the poet, the playwright can do without criticism in proportion to whatever talent they possess. The best minds in Western literature have paid little attention to the critics, except when scoffing at them.

Criticism tends to go along with the graph of a literature. The more a literature rises the more it calls on the criticism which is complementary to it, without there being any relation of cause and effect between the two. In the history of French-Canadian literature criticism has reflected slow but sure progress over more than a century. The evolution of that criticism is significant, therefore, and worth a pause to consider its beginnings.

Real Canadian criticism goes back to Abbé Casgrain and so to the age of Garneau. There had certainly been literary criticism in the eighteenth century at the time of the Montreal *Gazette littéraire,* but basically it was no more a question of real criticism at that time than it was of literature, the Jautards of the day being teachers with school-boy copies to correct.

Henri-Raymond Casgrain (1831-1904)

Like all of his generation, Henri-Raymond Casgrain came under the fruitful influence of Garneau.[16] He was one of the people whose imagination took fire on contact with an historical work which, at the very beginnings of French-Canadian literature, must have seemed miraculous to him. The very severe ophthalmia from which this young priest was already suffering at the age of twenty-five made the exercise of his ministry difficult and so was the means of directing his energies to study. On his return from a first trip to France and Italy in 1858 he was to find his second vocation. From 1855 Crémazie had been gathering around him in his bookstore the best minds of the time: besides Garneau there were Pierre Chauveau, Etienne Parent, Gérin-Lajoie, Joseph-Charles Taché, the poets Fréchette, Lemay and Alfred Garneau.[17] In 1859 they were joined by Gauldrée Boilleau, the first consul sent to Canada from France. To devote himself to this nascent literature, to create some of its outstanding works, to guide, if need be, the as yet unsuspected talents—all these projects presented themselves to the young *abbé* as worthy of his time and means.

In 1860-1861 Henri-Raymond Casgrain published *Le tableau de la Rivière-Ouelle, Les pionniers canadiens, La jongleuse.* Influenced by writers of the Romantic school, like Charles Nodier, who had been zealous in collecting stories and superstitions from the lips of the people themselves, Abbé Casgrain, as much through patriotism as literary ambition, wrote a few French-Canadian *légendes,* not without first having stylized them to satisfy his artistic sensibility. The result was worse than mediocre. In spite of his recent trip to France, during which he had had the leisure to put himself in touch with the intellectual movement in Europe, Abbé Casgrain had remained resolutely retrograde, isolating himself in the most exaggerated Romanticism. In his *Tableau de la Rivière-Ouelle* the author feels obliged to embellish his story with descriptions of this nature:

It was one of those superb December nights which the waning year seems to sow in its footsteps to greet the year about to be born, and whose marvellous splendour is unknown to the peoples of the South.

On the deep azure of the sky, innumerable stars pour their cool light in silvery tears. They might be tears of gladness that the light bursting forth from the Sun of justice snatches from the dazzled eyes of the blessed.

The moon climbs up the various constellations and takes pleasure in contemplating its own resplendent disc in the mirror of the snows.[18] [*trans.*]

The unpublished pages of the *Influence d'un livre* are attractive in comparison. But for the writers of 1860 Abbé Casgrain's prose was a model to be imitated. When the seventy-year-old Philippe Aubert de Gaspé had some doubts about his *Anciens Canadiens* (1863), quite naturally it was to Abbé Casgrain that he submitted his manuscript.

Fame came early and with it the possibility of influencing the course of literary history in French Canada. Abbé Casgrain was immediately conscious of all that the consolidation of national feeling could owe to an indigenous literature. But for this result literature must set out on the right road, that of the ancestral faith and a convinced patriotism. Here we have the dominant idea in Abbé Casgrain's critical thinking.

In 1866 the Abbé made this prognostication concerning the future character of French-Canadian literature:

If literature, as is incontestable, is the reflection of the customs and manners, the character, the aptitudes, the genius of a nation . . . ours will be serious, meditative, spiritualistic, religious, evangelical like our missionaries, generous like our martyrs, energetic and persevering like our pioneers of long ago . . . But above all it will be essentially religious and truly believing . . . This is its sole condition of being; it has no other justification for existence.[19] [*trans.*]

Nearly twenty years later, in 1884, this priest-critic will observe with satisfaction the *fait accompli* of Canadian literature. On this point he concludes, "our compatriots of English origin would only acknowledge our superiority." As to France, she welcomes this young literature "as a feather in her intellectual cap."[20]

Should one conclude that with the years Henri-Raymond Casgrain had arrived at a less narrow conception of literature? No indeed, for the "feathers" to which this soldier of French-Canadian letters alluded were not among those which France, even right-thinking France, has ever claimed.

Nevertheless, Henri-Raymond Casgrain deserved to be well regarded by his literary motherland. By his example he made a powerful contribution, just as Michel Bibaud had done but with more authority, to the spread of the idea that the writer in his own way exercises an apostleship. Even though his conception of literature was narrow, because of him the profession of writing became a less thankless one.

Should we reproach Abbé Casgrain for his shortcomings as a critic? It seems that he had not made himself familiar with French criticism which, in Europe in the second half of the nineteenth century, was regaining a supremacy lost to the Germany of Herder, Goethe, Kant and the Schlegel brothers. At the most we discover in him some ideas taken from Mme. de Staël and perhaps also from Montesquieu. Obviously Abbé Casgrain's inborn knowledge was adequate for commentary on the works of Gérin-Lajoie. More than that, by the very fact of his shortcomings he was the critic needed at this decisive turning-point in the intellectual and artistic history of French Canada. Even though he may have been lacking in enlightenment, his energy was boundless and he was an admirable catalyst for budding writers.

The publication in 1860 of his first *légende* marks the beginning of a literary movement at whose centre he will always be found, encouraging, criticizing, stimulating his fellow writers. He was a member of two teams who were to publish in quick succession two very important literary reviews: *Les soirées canadiennes* (1861-1865) and *Le foyer canadien* (1863-1866).[21] The year 1863 saw the publication of the very popular *Anciens Canadiens,* with slight alterations made by him. In 1864 *La revue canadienne,* which was to continue into the twentieth century, was founded as well. Then in 1865 Ernest Gagnon, following the precepts of Abbé Casgrain concerning folklore, published his *Chansons populaires du Canada,* a book frequently re-edited since. While saving French-Canadian musical folklore from oblivion, Gagnon brought to light the fact that many an old refrain is sung in the Gregorian tonality. This finding conferred, if there were any need of it, the seal of antiquity on the French-Canadian people and, in keeping with Abbé Casgrain's programme, reinforced in them the feeling of their own originality. It is in part thanks to Abbé Casgrain, to Ernest Gagnon and to folklorists coming after them that studies in folklore, so important in their literary ramifications in music and the other arts, have finally been put on a firm scientific basis by the creation in Laval University in 1946 of the Folklore Archives.

Octave Crémazie

In the history of criticism the names of Abbé Casgrain and Crémazie are indissolubly linked. From the time that Crémazie went into exile in France in 1862 he was to keep up a lengthy correspondence with Abbé Casgrain. Generous by nature and spurred on by the feeling that he was presiding at the baptism of French-Canadian literature, Henri-Raymond Casgrain had planned to set aside a certain sum of money from his private funds to help the poet. In this way, he thought, Crémazie would be stimulated to finish his *Promenade des trois morts.* Too dejected for literary creation, Crémazie, on the other hand, had ample leisure to think about French-Canadian writing.

Did Crémazie bring to literature a more serious preparation than that of his protector? According to legend he had an astonishing erudition. Supposedly, German, Spanish, English and Italian literatures were as familiar to him as French. He was even said to be no stranger to Sanskrit. Sufficient attention has not been given to the fact that it was none other than Abbé Casgrain who made himself guarantor for Crémazie's knowledge.[22] This knowledge becomes immediately suspect, more especially as a reading of Crémazie's letters and particularly of his *Journal du siège de Paris*[23] fails to reveal any great culture and still less an original mind.[24] So we run no particular risk of being mistaken if we put the two men on the same intellectual level. Both of them, in the second half of the nineteenth century, remained impervious to Realism and to the progress of ideas in France and Europe. Nevertheless, Crémazie possessed one advantage over his correspondent, that of having spent an important part of his life abroad. Having endured suffering and privation he was able to see more clearly, and he raised questions in his correspondence that are still unanswered.

Crémazie was one of the first to reflect on the particular difficulties which a very young country, culturally dependent upon a great one, has to overcome if it is to affirm its originality. Struck by the increasing vogue in France of foreign literatures and by the number of translations from Russian and Scandinavian languages, Crémazie—already inclined to pessimism as a result of financial worries and uncertain health—did not predict a favourable future for French-Canadian writing:

Plus je réfléchis sur les destinées de la littérature canadienne, moins je lui trouve de chances de laisser une trace dans l'histoire. Ce qui manque au Canada, c'est d'avoir une langue à lui. Si nous parlions iroquois ou huron, notre littérature vivrait. Malheureusement nous parlons et écrivons d'une assez piteuse façon, il est vrai, la langue de Bossuet et de Racine. Nous avons beau dire et beau faire, nous ne serons toujours, au point de vue littéraire, qu'une simple colonie . . . Depuis vingt ans, on publie chaque année, en France, des traductions de romans russes, scandinaves, roumains. Supposez ces mêmes livres écrits en français, ils ne trouveraient pas cinquante lecteurs.[25]

The more I think about the fate of Canadian literature, the less chance I find of its leaving a trace in history. What [French] Canada lacks is a language of its own. If we spoke Iroquois or Huron our literature would live. Unfortunately we speak and write—in a pitiable way, it is true—the language of Bossuet and Racine. It is useless to say or do anything; from the literary point of view we shall always be a mere colony . . . In France every year for the last twenty years they have been publishing Russian, Scandinavian and Roumanian translations. These same books, written in French, would not find fifty readers.[25] [*trans.*]

These reflections, given a paradoxical twist by Crémazie, have often been noted in French-Canadian criticism. A crucial problem is raised: the excessive dependence of French-Canadian literature on that of France, a dependence accentuated by a common patrimony—the French language. Beyond this bitter fact are the considerations of interest to general criticism.

All the countries which European enterprise has created around the world have experienced some difficulty in ensuring their intellectual independence. Even in our own day the literary personality of former colonies like Australia and New Zealand is not sufficiently formed to enable the foreigner to see in it any distinguishing characteristics. That this personality exists, however, is not in doubt. The United States of America can furnish the example of an independence quickly affirmed and which today has taken solid shape in a self-contained literature. A close examination of the American situation is enough, however, to make one realize that essentially it is very similar to that of the other countries of the two Americas and of Australia.

Has the English language been a hindrance to the literary development of the United States? Inevitably, in the colonial era and in the years following the War of Independence, American writers did copy English models. The first writer to enjoy a European reputation, Washington Irving (1783-1859), was an emulator, by the marked urbanity of his style, of Lamb and of Hazlitt. But after him we have a whole collection of novelists, poets and essayists bursting from the American soil and drawing their inspiration from it: Whittier, Emerson, Thoreau, Hawthorne, Whitman, and many others. It is true that during the nineteenth century England gloated over the American accent and the solecisms and neologisms that became increasingly abundant in the literature of the United States. But little by little, as we have drawn nearer to the Hemingways and the Faulkners, the American version of the English language has taken on dignity.[26] How was this evolution possible? Simply because, after a spectacularly swift expansion that is without precedent in human history, the United States, from being a small country exerting only a modest influence on international politics, became the most powerful nation in the world.

The American language, replete with neologisms and barbarisms, has spread into every corner of the earth and has taken the place of French as the first language in international councils. Moreover, Europe is being invaded with ideas and industrial methods which she frequently accepts along with their American names. The universalization of the English, or rather the American, language is a reminder of a truth that we are inclined to forget just because it is so obvious. Even linguistic victories go to the biggest battalions. The supremacy of the French language and culture in Europe in past centuries, which the French often attribute to the "clarity" of the language and the "French genius," can be explained more easily, alas, by the superior weight of a country which, because of the size of its population, for a long time was the China of Europe.

Did Crémazie ponder considerations of this kind? What could she hope to do, this French Canada, in the year 1867? She had a French-speaking population of merely a million, facing a French Empire with a population nearly forty times greater and enjoying the immense prestige to which her past entitled her. From this observation it was only one step to the conclusion that an autonomous French-Canadian literature was unthinkable. A decision had to be taken and Crémazie put it before the future writers of his country:

Quand le père de famille, après les fatigues de la journée, raconte à ses nombreux enfants les aventures et les accidents de sa longue vie, pourvu que ceux qui l'entourent s'amusent et s'instruisent en écoutant ses récits, il ne s'inquiète pas si le riche propriétaire du manoir voisin connaîtra ou ne connaîtra pas les douces et naïves histoires qui font le charme de son foyer. Ses enfants sont heureux de l'entendre, c'est tout ce qu'il demande.

Il en doit être ainsi de l'écrivain canadien. Renonçant sans regret aux beaux rêves d'une gloire retentissante, il doit se regarder comme amplement récompensé de ses travaux, s'il peut instruire et charmer ses compatriotes, s'il peut contribuer à la conservation, sur le jeune terre d'Amérique, de la vieille nationalité française.[27]

When the father of a family, after a tiring day, tells his many children about the adventures and accidents of his long life, provided that those gathered around him get pleasure and instruction from listening to what he tells them, he does not worry about whether or not the rich owner of the manor knows the sweet and simple stories which are the delight of his own home. His children like to listen to him and that is all that matters.

This is how it must be for the Canadian writer. With no regrets, giving up fine dreams of resounding fame, he must consider himself amply rewarded for his work if he can instruct and delight his countrymen, if he is able to contribute to the preservation of the old French nationality in the young American land.[27] [*trans.*]

This advice is more the result of disillusionment than of critical analysis, by virtue of which Crémazie seems in his own mind to have fixed the limits of the literary aspirations of a small people.

But it is none the less true that he has touched here on a problem of great complexity, that of the reciprocal permeability of literatures. Since Crémazie's time this problem has presented itself to French-Canadian criticism in the shape of a minor literature that has had a rapid growth. Because it is still with us it deserves careful examination.

Reduced to its simplest form, Crémazie's idea is this: since French Canada is in the position of being culturally dependent on France, it must give up any idea of creating a literature for a world audience and be satisfied with cultivating a provincial one. The fact that Canada shares the French language with France and the other French-speaking countries assures its inferiority. This inheritance, glorious as it is, is a stumbling-block on the path to literary honours, for Canadian works will inevitably be compared, and to their disadvantage, with masterpieces of French literature.[28] This comparison will be all the more prejudicial since the French language, as it is spoken and written in Canada, has been impoverished since the Conquest.

It is after acknowledging this that Crémazie comes out with his remark about the Iroquois and Hurons. Many a Canadian critic has made the mistake of taking this half-joking comment out of context and pointing out carefully all the advantages which come from being able to express oneself in French, a language of great culture. Now, in his letter of January 29, 1867, Crémazie adds: "Look at Belgium, which speaks the same language as we do. Is there a Belgian literature?"

Here again it seems that we would be making a mistake in calling up the great names of Verhaeren and of Maeterlinck. Aside from the fact that these two writers enjoyed a great reputation at the beginning of the twentieth century, how can one fail to see that their assimilation to the French Symbolist movement, rather than to the Belgian literary tradition, would prove Crémazie right? Actually, if a few Belgian poets and playwrights have been snapped up by French literature, the majority of them, who make up the Belgian tradition, have not been able to cross the boundaries of a small literature. This is the sense that must be given to the question: is there a Belgian literature? This literature, like the Canadian counterpart, does exist. But who knows anything about it?[29]

Here we are again faced with that problem of criticism which Crémazie could perhaps have clarified. It would seem that small countries like French Canada and Belgium will never be able to claim universality for their literatures, irrespective of their intrinsic worth. In their situation of dependence or relative obliteration they are condemned to suffer outside influences; even at best their literature will be created in a vacuum. That infinitely complex literary phenomenon, the power of attraction between literatures, has never been systematically studied as far as we know.[30]

These few considerations permit us to make a better judgment of Crémazie's critical thought as expressed in his correspondence with Abbé Casgrain. It would be wrong to expect too much from these texts, particularly as Crémazie was unable to say his last word. He had the incontestable merit, however, of being the first to stir up ideas that went beyond the narrow limits of French-Canadian literature. The conclusion to which he had come in 1867 on the attitude becoming the French-Canadian writer was the logical development of his prognosis. Let the writer stop worrying about the reception he will get abroad and contribute to the best of his ability to the glory of the national literature. It is of no importance that his renown should go no further than the narrow circle of the French-Canadian elite. Is that appreciation of no value?

THE NOVEL

The powerful stimulus given to French-Canadian literature by Garneau's great book extends not only to poetry and criticism but also to the novel. The generation that had read the *Histoire du Canada* was ready, around 1860, to create a literature based on the past glories and virtues of the race.

Philippe Aubert de Gaspé (1786-1871)

The most famous novelist of this period is Philippe Aubert de Gaspé,[31] father of the author of *L'influence d'un livre*. Won over by the effervescent patriotism that prevailed in the case of Casgrain and his disciples, this seventy-year-old man, son of one of the oldest and most respected Canadian families, took it upon himself to make a story out of his recollections. Twenty-three years older than Garneau, Gaspé was a survivor of the next generation after the Conquest. But by reason of his upbringing and intellectual training Gaspé was closer to the Old Order than Garneau.

The objectivity of the historian as well as a certain egalitarianism inclined Garneau as much to the future as to the past. His imagination caught fire when he contemplated the immense continent where he had been born, with its limitless possibilities brought to light by the revolutionary activity of the Americans.

Living completely in the past, Gaspé had no appreciation of the democratic innovations of the Americans and English and advised his countrymen, if they wanted to keep the fine title of a noble people, "not to covet the degree of liberty presently enjoyed by our neighbours."[32] Astonishingly young for his seventy-six years, Gaspé had a meticulous memory for the smallest events of his youth, as well as the inestimable quality of a genuinely French sociability, the kind on which an eighteenth-century gentleman prided himself. Conscious, moreover, of his noble ancestry, he perpetuated in his personal life and appearance those virtues which were in danger of disappearing in a "republican" century. Thus equipped to write down significant facts of the past, Philippe Aubert de Gaspé was in a position to compose one of those books written in conversational style which contain the essence of a civilization.

It is with understandable hesitation that Gaspé made his approach to literature. The material of his book was something he carried within himself. As for the shape his recollections would assume, he relied on the style of the times and the prescriptions of that first Canadian Aristarchus, Abbé Casgrain. From these divergent influences came *Les Anciens Canadiens* in 1863.

In his picturesque preface the author warns the reader that he intends to write a work "Canadian in style." It was of little importance to him whether the critics would call his work a novel, memoir, chronicle or hodgepodge. Actually it is one of those innocent adventure novels that the French-Canadian public of the time had a particular liking for. Jules d'Haberville and Archibald Cameron de Locheill, two inseparable friends, were put to a severe test in the Seven Years' War. Blanche d'Haberville, a Canadian heroine, chose honour rather than love, refusing to marry Archibald who was a sore trial to the Haberville family all through the war. The novel, embellished with the most insipid episodes, becomes interesting only when Gaspé enlivens his story with descriptions of Canadian customs and manners of long ago. Such is the quality of these pages that *Les Anciens Canadiens* has become a French-Canadian classic.

Encouraged by the success of his first attempt, Gaspé brought out his *Mémoires* three years later. With inexhaustible verve this seventy-nine-year-old man poured into his work all that his astonishing memory had stored up from the age of three. No longer having to subscribe to the Romantic style—which went against the grain—Gaspé has given us a delightful evening's entertainment. In all of Canadian literature there exists no work that is more "Old France" than these *Mémoires*. The anecdotes handed to us without affectation or false modesty, with the straightforward honesty of a French-Canadian gentleman of the old school, have a merit all the more rare because, in the telling, Gaspé's language is as flavourful as it is precise. Little scenes, cleverly lifted from their past, abound in this reliquary of a Canada still French in his memory of it. The towering figure of the narrator's father, enamoured of a chivalrous code of days gone by; the last of the Récollet friars and the uproariously funny things that happened to them in their disappointments and struggles; in a word, all those characters Gaspé brings to life out of a past already in the long-ago in 1866, give him first place among Canadian story-tellers.

The *Mémoires,* superior to *Les Anciens Canadiens* as a work of art, have nevertheless remained little known. The rudimentary and formal construction of *Les Anciens Canadiens* has seemed to the critics to show more professional skill than the deliberately informal pattern of the *Mémoires.* No thought was given to the fact that an old man could not reasonably be supposed to master the novel form without previous experience, or that he had to have remarkable natural gifts to emerge relatively unscathed from a lesson in composition and good taste conducted by Abbé Casgrain. Left to his own genius—that of discoursing endlessly on a past of which he was a part—from the very beginning this first of French-Canadian story-tellers gave to the *Mémoires* a spontaneity lacking in *Les Anciens Canadiens.* Gaspé, along with his contemporaries, was mistaken about the quality of his second literary effort, which had been prepared for publication only on the insistence of his friends and which, in his own eyes, could have merit only as a complement to the notes of his first work. Today we can reverse the order of values and consider the *Mémoires* as the best stylized banter in nineteenth-century French-Canadian literature.

Joseph Marmette (1844-1895)

From 1860 onward a good many novelists exploited, more or less successfully, the history of Canada.

Joseph Marmette, who was to marry in 1868 a daughter of François-Xavier Garneau, was the first novelist to make systematic use of Canadian history. In 1865, after writing a story, *Charles et*

Eva, based on the expedition led by Frontenac against Schenectady towards the end of the seventeenth century, Marmette became ambitious to win popularity for his country by way of novels featuring mighty deeds in the history of New France. To this end he wrote, with more patriotism than art, *Le Chevalier de Mornac* (1873) and *L'intendant Bigot* (1872).

For his *François de Bienville* (1870), Marmette made a serious effort at documentation on the second siege of Quebec. His talent as a novelist being scarcely creditable, it is of keener interest to the present-day reader to know that a great quantity of Bordeaux wine was consumed in Canada than to follow the fortunes of François de Bienville.

Napoléon Bourassa (1827-1916)

Napoléon Bourassa, one of the founders of the *Revue canadienne,* thought that he should yield as Gaspé had done to the urging of his friends and contribute to the literary movement with a work of his own. From 1852 to 1856 Bourassa had studied drawing and painting in Italy and he gained confidence upon his return from the prestige conferred on him by his stay in Europe.

Jacques et Marie (1865), as he imagines the story, is situated as far as possible from the Roman countryside or the charms of Fiesole. Born in a colony of Acadians, Bourassa wanted to evoke the martyrdom of this people he had learned to love. "The tale I am going to offer the reader," he says in his prologue, "brings together the vague impressions I still have from all those people I heard talking about the Acadians in my childhood." Then he adds: "Never having written the slightest book . . . I have undertaken this one without preconceived ideas on form and without taking any model." This formula, which had suceeded in the case of Gaspé and which is the best one when a primitive art is concerned, was fatal to the literary ambitions of this sketcher. So it is of no use to follow the adventures of the *fiancés,* Jacques Hébert and Marie Landry; they will end up all right, after "the great upset," by reunion in Petite Cadie, Bourassa's birthplace.[33]

Georges de Boucherville (1814-1894)

To the names of Marmette and Bourassa one must add that of Georges de Boucherville, whose cloak-and-dagger novel *Une de perdue, deux de trouvées* appeared in 1864 in the *Revue canadienne.*

Pierre de Saint-Luc, a dauntless sailor who routs the buccaneers of the Caribbean, spends the years of his youth in Louisiana. In his father's will he learns that he was born in Canada, where his mother may still be living. Our hero arrives in the country of his ancestors at the time of the Rebellion of 1837/38. He makes inquiries which bring no results at first, but at last he does locate his dying mother and his two sisters with her—which explains the title of the novel.

Gaspé, then Marmette, Bourassa and Boucherville had made use of Canadian history with varying results. Historical truth, embellished with picturesque asides, is the stuff of the novels of Marmette and Bourassa, with this difference, that the first describes the virtues of the French Canadians in victory, the second in disaster. In Boucherville's case history serves to give some semblance of truth to the episodes of his novel. History as Gaspé understands it is something that he has lived or that at least has come down to him through oral tradition.

These are the trail-blazers of the Canadian historical novel, which would continue, with its by-products—memoirs, chronicles and stories—to be the favourite literary form of the writers and especially of the French-Canadian public.

Antoine Gérin-Lajoie (1824-1882)

The reader lacking information on the evolution of French-Canadian literature would be very much surprised, after reading *Jean Rivard le défricheur,* to know that this unpolished work, published in 1862, remains, along with *Jean Rivard économiste* (1864), one of the most important novels of the nineteenth century.[34] This is because the author was one of the first able to set forth those topics around which future didactic and patriotic novels were to be written. Twenty years earlier, Pierre Chauveau in his *Charles Guérin* had outlined a few of the social problems left to French Canadians by the Conquest. It was for Gérin-Lajoie to point out with practical suggestions the road to salvation. Chauveau had indeed suggested that it was to the colonizing of empty country that his countrymen should turn in their search for work. This solution seemed to the next generation, Gérin-Lajoie's, to be of the greatest importance for the survival of the *race,* for in the meantime had begun the exodus of French Canadians to the United States. It was Gérin-Lajoie's idea to make his own country, rather than the United States, benefit from the superabundance of the vital forces that were French-Canadian. It was in the form of a novel that he revealed his plan of action.

Jean Rivard, in the full vigour of his twenty years and with dauntless courage, would go off with his companion, Pierre Gagnon, to carve a domain out of the virgin forest—a Herculean task calculated to make strong bodies and healthy minds. It was to provide the setting for singing the joys of life in the open, of the creative accomplishment of the French Canadian clearing new land for cultivation. It would show the sceptics all the uses to which an enterprising man could put the redoubtable forest: the burnt stumps would furnish excellent fertilizer, sap from the maples was to become a valuable product. Better still, the French Canadian, instead of exposing himself to the harmful influences of the big city, could find health of mind and body in the life-giving air of the eastern part of the country. He would be contributing also, according to his ability, to the development in America of a French Catholic nation.

To do away with any last doubts about the national usefulness of his programme, Gérin-Lajoie in his *Jean Rivard économiste,* painted an idyllic picture of the temporal and spiritual success of his hero's enterprise. With their land cleared and the first harvests under cover, the farmers, their courage fired by Jean Rivard's dynamism, settled in the same localities themselves and little by little a village grew up, Rivardville, symbol of French-Canadian society.

Gérin-Lajoie's didacticism and clumsiness make his novel of interest only from the historical point of view. But on the other hand it would be impossible to deny the influence that *Jean Rivard* has had on the evolution of the French-Canadian novel. That is, Gérin-Lajoie lacked the professional touch yet recognized intuitively some of the permanent aspects of French-Canadian psychology. The ease with which he set life in the country over against life in the towns rests on a profound, deeply rooted feeling in the French Canadian: between him and nature there is a pact, compelling by reason of his spiritual origins. When Gabrielle Roy, who is closer to our time, makes her cashier, Alexandre Chenevert, feel the joys of a first night in the solitude of the Laurentians, she repeats and confirms what Gérin-Lajoie felt before her.

THE SHORT STORY

In Canada, "a country where the spirit is colder than the climate," the theatre and the novel had a slim following compared with minor literary genres which demand less sustained effort on the part of the writer; this explains the numerous verse-makers, story-tellers and writers of memoirs. Nowhere else is mediocrity of thought and invention more evident than with these pen-pushers. From the beginning of the nineteenth century, in the newspapers and reviews, one can pick up stories relating to some oustanding incident in the past or to customs of the French Canadians. To find the first stories worth mentioning we shall have to wait for the two Gaspés who, by reason of their fondness for digressions in story form, may be ranked as much among story writers as among novelists.

Why, from among all the short-story writers, have so few names come down to us? Doubtless the subject matter does not lend itself to development and leaves the writer little opportunity for personal interpretation. It was the purpose of stories collected from oral tradition to strike the imagination of a population which still observed the custom of the *veillée.* Feeling for religion and the mysteries of nature was the stuff of these rudimentary confections. Have French Canadians kept ribald tales in their traditions? They have, indeed, since even in our own day folklorists are still bringing to light some fairly racy ones; however, austere customs and habits militated against the popularization of a fundamental tendency dating directly back to the *fabliaux,* and so the story-tellers were deprived of a rich vein. Confined to the religious and miraculous, it was difficult for writers of stories to keep from repeating themselves. The younger Gaspé had touched lightly upon the symbol in his *Chercheur de trésors.* This example, if it had been imitated, would have permitted more variety in the Canadian story. From the second half of the nineteenth century we have tales which were a great success around the stove in wintertime but which, with a few exceptions, may be relegated to the literary bric-à-brac of the period.

One writer, Joseph-Charles Taché (1820-1894),[35] was able to hit on the right key for the French-Canadian story. Its principal interest is in the evocation of the collective soul of French Canadians of times past: simple good-heartedness, piety and self-sacrifice, the mixture of mischief and credulity, the struggle against nature in the background—such are its component parts. Carried away like so many others by the wave of patriotism which followed the appearance of Garneau's *Histoire,* Taché, animated by the same sentiments that moved Gaspé to write his *Mémoires,* published *Trois légendes de mon pays* in 1861, and in 1863 *Forestiers et voyageurs,* a work for which he is still known.

Forestiers et voyageurs makes a worthy companion piece to the Gaspé work. While Gaspé evokes the Canada of yesteryear, Taché tells of the adventures of intrepid woodsmen and explorers with whom he had rubbed shoulders. Thanks to the fidelity with which the writer has set down the stories he has lived himself or heard from friends of a night's acquaintance, we can enter into that time past and gone, which, thanks to Taché, has remained astonishingly alive.

Like all story-tellers of this period Taché cannot resist the temptation to dress up his narrative; the awe-inspiring immensity of Canada was an open invitation to do this. And it is this part of his book that has to be rejected. Let him but make his characters talk and the spell is cast again. In his story entitled *La chapelle de Portneuf,* Taché has succeeded in capturing the sublime side of the religious faith of French Canada. Death, which modern man does his utmost to forget in a dizzy round of entertainment, to this French Canadian becomes a subject of ineffable joy. Because he has described to such perfection an essential aspect of the religious feeling of his country, for once in his life Taché reaches the level of true art.

NOTES TO CHAPTER TWO

1. *Le foyer canadien,* Vol. IV, p. 4.

2. Earl of Durham, *Report on the Affairs of British North America.* Edited, with an Introduction, by Sir C. P. Lucas (Oxford: Clarendon Press, 1912) Vol. II. This document is remarkable for the very British objectivity with which the author tackles the problem of the two races and is a fine example of the liberal English attitude of mind.

3. *Ibid.,* p. 46.

4. François-Xavier Garneau, *Voyage en Angleterre et en France dans les années 1831, 1832 et 1833* (Quebec: Augustin Côté & Cie, 1855), pp. 5-6.

5. A good many *Histoire du Canada* were published prior to 1845. In 1744, in Paris, at the end of the *ancien régime,* Charlevoix had published a very useful *Histoire.* Joseph-François Perrault, who had been interested in Garneau, had written an *Abrégé de l'Histoire du Canada* (1832-36), and Michel Bibaud had published in his *Bibliothèque canadienne* (1825), an *Histoire* lacking originality, which he re-edited in 1837-1844.

6. He scrupulously consulted the papers, not known in Canada, which Papineau had brought from France and analyzed, also those that Dr. Edmund O'Callaghan had copied in Paris at the request of the State of New York. He had access to the archives preserved in Canada.

7. Garneau's travel impressions were collected in his *Voyage en Angleterre et en France dans les années 1831, 1832 and 1833,* published in 1855. While very important for anyone wanting to follow Garneau's intellectual evolution, this book, which he tried to have removed soon after its publication, adds nothing to his literary reputation.

8. Garneau, *Histoire du Canada* (4th ed.), Vol. II, p. 135.

9. *Ibid.,* Vol. I, p. 199.

10. Laurence Bisson's thesis, *Le romantisme littéraire au Canada français* (Paris: Droz, 1932), contains useful information on Canadian Romantic poetry. Nevertheless, this work does not escape the usual disadvantage of theses: that of relating everything to the subject under study. Consequently, the tracking down of influences lacks a sense of proportion.

11. In this connection Joseph Lenoir-Rolland (1822-1861) should be mentioned. His poetry, scattered through the reviews of the period, has been collected in one volume by Casimir Hébert: *Poèmes épars* (Montreal: Le Pays Laurentian, 1916). The reader curious about poetry written between 1832 and 1848 may refer to the four volumes of J. Huston's *Répertoire national.*

12. *See: Oeuvres complètes de Octave Crémazie* (Montreal: Beauchemin & fils, 1883); *Lettres et fragments de lettres de Octave Crémazie* (Montreal: Beauchemin & fils, 1886); Abbé Henri-Raymond Casgrain, *Octave Crémazie* (Montreal: Libraire Beauchemin Ltée, 1912); Jeanne Paul-Crouzet, *Poésie au Canada* (Paris: Didier, 1946), pp. 27-55; Michel Dassonville, *Crémazie* (Montreal: Fides, 1956).

13. Cf. pp. 252, 262.

14. Olivar Asselin (1874-1937), for whom the English Canadians are "half-civilized," is a typical representative of the French Canadian of the twentieth century who makes the culture of France his own.

15. Octave Crémazie, *Lettres et fragments de lettres,* p. 285.

16. *See: Oeuvres complètes de l'abbé H.-R. Casgrain* (Montreal: Beauchemin, 1896-1897), 4 vol. Abbé Casgrain's literary theories are to be found in the study he published in 1866 on *Le mouvement littéraire au Canada,* Vol. I, pp. 353-375. The best work on the life and works of Abbé Casgrain is that of Camille Roy, "L'abbé Henri-Raymond Casgrain," *Essais sur la littérature canadienne* (1907), pp. 29-104.

17. These writers are members of the *Ecole de Québec.* This designation, which has become classic, seems to us unsatisfactory. Properly speaking, there was no "school."

18. *Oeuvres complètes,* Vol. I, p. 17. Casgrain's prose as an historian will be much more restrained. Cf. pp. 52-54.

19. *Ibid.,* pp. 368-369.

20. *Ibid.,* Vol. II, pp. 530-531.

21. Members of the first team are: Abbé Ferland, Joseph-Charles Taché, Gérin-Lajoie; of the second: the same, with the exception of Taché, who was to remain editor of *Soirées.* These two short-lived reviews are indisputably important in the history of French-Canadian literature, not only because certain works such as Gérin-Lajoie's *Jean Rivard* were published in them for the first time, but because, with a circulation that was large for the period, they made it possible for the Canadian writer to reach an audience of several thousand readers.

22. *Poésies d'Octave Crémazie,* with a biography by Abbé Casgrain (Montreal: Beauchemin, 1925), p. 15.

23. Published in *Lettres et fragments de lettres d'Octave Crémazie* (Montreal: Beauchemin, 1886), pp. 37-243.

24. Is this judgment too harsh? Only the publication of the entire text of the correspondence, preserved in the Archives of the *Séminaire de Québec,* will make it possible to give Crémazie his due place. The extracts published by Michel Dassonville in his study of *Crémazie* (Montreal: Fides, 1956) do not seem to indicate that we have to wait

for the sudden appearance in French-Canadian nineteenth-century literature of a Crémazie hitherto unknown. At the very most it might be possible to get a glimpse of a mind more open and less exclusively French-Canadian than a reading of the *Journal* would lead one to suppose.

25. Henri-Raymond Casgrain, *Octave Crémazie* (Montreal: Beauchemin, 1912), pp. 56-57. Letter of January 29, 1867. This long letter contains the essence of Crémazie's critical thought.

26. The growth in dignity of the American language and its acceptance, a subject treated summarily here, engaged the attention of H. L. Mencken in a work which, while its conclusions do not always carry conviction, is well documented: *The American Language* (3rd ed.; New York: Alfred A. Knopf, 1923).

27. Henri-Raymond Casgrain, *op. cit.,* pp. 58-59.

28. This idea is implicit in Crémazie's reasoning. Refer to his letter to Abbé Casgrain, dated January 29, 1867.

29. It must be admitted that the term "Belgian literature" lends itself to various interpretations because very complex literary considerations are involved. It seems that the Belgians themselves are reluctant so to label the literary production of their country. In this regard, the title *Histoire illustrée des lettres françaises de Belgique* (Brussels: Renaissance du Livre, 1958), is significant. If we call to mind the case of Belgium, it is for the purpose of following Crémazie's thought to its ultimate conclusions. It is clear, nevertheless, that Crémazie would have done better to turn his attention to French Switzerland. For political, religious, and geographical reasons, the literature of French Switzerland has not been under French influence to the same extent as that of Belgium. Although the Swiss French are not all convinced of the "existence" of a literature of their own, there is no doubt in our mind of its originality. In the literature of French Switzerland Crémazie would have found a more solid basis for his critical position.

30. This is a problem in comparative literature, a field of research whose most recent developments have encompassed considerations of this nature. The Third International Congress of Comparative Literature, held in Utrecht in 1961, was devoted to the minor literatures. The critical problems raised by the meagre impact of lesser literatures was the subject of a number of papers.

31. Philippe Aubert de Gaspé, *Les anciens Canadiens* (Montreal: Beauchemin, 1899); *Mémoires* (Quebec: N. S. Hardy, 1885); *Divers* (Montreal: Beauchemin, 1924).

32. Aubert de Gaspé, *Mémoires,* p. 558.

33. Camille Roy observes in his *Histoire de la littérature canadienne-française* that this novel contains exquisite pages on Acadian mothers (Quebec: L'Action sociale, 1930), p. 109. Could it be the following passage that assured Bourassa his popularity in the nineteenth century and touched the critic?

> Oh! our saintly mothers! how we should admire and bless their heroic lives! . . . Married at fourteen, they were mothers at fifteen, then again every eighteen months to the age of forty-five! Count . . . and I am not even mentioning twins.

(Revue canadienne [1865], p. 457.)

34. Gérin-Lajoie published his first *Jean Rivard* in *Soirées canadiennes; Le foyer canadien* published the continuation from 1864.

In the period when he wrote *Le jeune Latour* (cf. p. 6), Gérin-Lajoie, inspired by the events of 1837/38, composed *Un canadien errant,* which was characterized by a melancholy in perfect accord with contemporary taste. This song is now a part of Canadian folklore. *See*: Camille Roy, *Nouveaux essais sur la littérature canadienne* (Quebec: Imprimerie de l'Action Sociale, 1914), pp. 84-134; Louvigny de Montigny, *Antoine Gérin-Lajoie* (Toronto: The Ryerson Press, 1925).

35. Joseph-Charles Taché was Canada's representative at the Paris World's Fair in 1855. His *Esquisse sur le Canada considéré au point de vue économique* won him the *croix de chevalier de la Légion d'honneur.* Later on he filled various posts in the government of his province. *See*: *Forestiers et voyageurs,* preface by Luc Lacourcière (Montreal: Fides, 1946).

CHAPTER III

TOWARDS THE CREATION
OF A LITERARY TRADITION
(1865-1899)

POETRY

Between 1845, the year when the first volume of Garneau's *Histoire* appeared, and the death of the historian in 1866, the impetus had been given to French-Canadian literature. Four literary genres, history, poetry, the novel and criticism, had found in Garneau, Crémazie, Gaspé and Casgrain representatives who, considering their predecessors, furnished excellent proof that the creation of a national literature was possible since its foundations were already laid. None of these genres, it is true, will gain any glory because of particularly original writers. Nevertheless their initial contribution to Canadian literature will be important for it is a real literary tradition which, little by little, will emerge from their combined efforts. On Garneau's death it would not have been unreasonable to suppose that the few unquestionably fine talents who had found recognition in a first generation of writers would remain isolated cases and that a literature which, contrary to all expectations, had begun to blossom on Canadian soil, would soon fade away. But from 1865 to the end of the century a good number of poets as well as some novelists and critics were to bear witness in their writing to the unsuspected vitality of a burgeoning literature.

Before Garneau's time poetry had already furnished an outlet for the modest ambitions of the first educated Canadians; and it was by means of poetry especially that French-Canadian literature was to live and gain strength in the second half of the nineteenth century.

Louis Fréchette (1839-1908)

Louis Fréchette is the best known of the nineteenth-century poets.[1] Having pledged an unwavering love for France at a very young age, to his contemporaries he was the personification of fidelity to French cultural traditions.

38

Very early he showed an undeniable bent for poetry. The musical quality of his verse is already apparent in *La nuit* (1861):

> *Les farfadets, les gnomes,*
> *Les nocturnes fantômes,*
> *Traînant leurs linceuls gris,*
> *Rôdent, spectres informes,*
> *Autour des troncs énormes*
> *Des chênes rabougris.*
>
> *Le serpent rampe et glisse*
> *Et son écaille lisse*
> *D'un rayon fauve luit;*
> *Les bêtes carnassières*
> *Sortent de leurs tanières . . .*
> *Dormons: il est minuit!*

It was not long before Fréchette felt the influence of Victor Hugo, under whose domination he was always to remain. During a stay of some years in the United States, he saw himself, in Chicago, playing a role analogous to that of the voluntary exile of Jersey. This explains the title of his collection, *Le voix d'un exilé.* On his return to Canada he continued to publish poems that appeared in newspapers and reviews and which he brought together, in 1877, under the title of *Pêle-Mêle.* Later he was to resort to the doubtful stratagem of having collections published under different titles, composed in part of poems already published. This was how his *Fleurs boréales* was put together. Published first in Quebec in 1879, then in Paris in 1881, this collection of what were his best poems up to that time won him an award, *le Prix Montyon,* from the Académie Française.[2] This thoughtful gesture on the part of Academicians well disposed to Canada was a consecration in the eyes of French Canadians.

As a first northern flower, Fréchette chose *La découverte du Mississippi,* often quoted as an example of his best style:

> *Fier de sa liberté, fier de ses flots sans nombre,*
> *Fier des bois ténébreux qui lui versent leur ombre,*
> *Le Roi-des-eaux n'avait encore, en aucun lieu,*
> *Où l'avait promené sa course vagabonde,*
> *Déposé le tribut de sa vague profonde*
> *Que devant le soleil et Dieu!*

Among the sonnets to be found under the title of *Oiseux de neige* in the same collection, *Le Cap Eternité* brings out the oratorical style of which Fréchette is capable:

> *Quel caprice a dressé cette sombre muraille?*
> *Caprice! qui le sait? Hardi celui qui raille*
> *Ces aveugles efforts de la fécondité!*
>
> *Cette masse nourrit mille plantes vivaces;*
> *L'hirondelle des monts niche dans ses crevasses;*
> *Et ce monstre farouche a sa paternité!*

It is by his imagery that Fréchette most often rises to heights of real poetry. When, as a Canadian Romanticist, he pours out his feelings on the traditional themes of his favourite poets, he is often dismally prosaic. His thought is indeed that of Jocrisse at Patmos.

An ever-bubbling imagination and an enthusiasm which he maintained into old age were to result in the epic *La légende d'un peuple*. This is Fréchette's best work, the work which will ensure his reputation.

A poem of more than three thousand lines, its subject is the story of French Canada. After a short dedication to France, the poet addresses himself to a continent still untouched that is called upon to furnish the hope of renewal to the exhausted will of a Europe grown too old. In this First Era in the new world, that of French domination, there would unfold scenes of the mighty feats of a Cavelier de La Salle, or of the grandiose nature of the new land itself. In all these pictures there is the same ardent patriotism epitomized in the first two lines, which have remained famous in French-Canadian literature:

> *O notre Histoire!—écrin de perles ignorées*
> *Je baise avec amour tes pages vénérées.*
>
> O history of our country—jewel-box of pearls forgotten,
> It is with love and reverence that I kiss your pages.

As the episodes of the Seven Years' War and the English rule followed each other (Second and Third Eras), the tie binding these poems of diverse form and inspiration became increasingly slender. The variety of subjects dealt with by the poet, along with the evident disparity of accent, is such that the *Légende* ends up as anything but an epic. Actually, the apocalyptic synthesis of the prologue has its complement towards the end of the poem, in a diatribe against the Orange Order. And a few last preposterous lines recall the damage that Voltaire is supposed to have done to Canada. The versification, too, after a good beginning, becomes increasingly commonplace and calls to mind the rhymed prose of Bibaud.[3]

Like other poets whose ardent desire it was to endow French-Canadian literature with its own *Odyssey,* Fréchette made the mistake of failing to think through the problem of the epic poem. In this connection the reflections of Schelling and the Schlegel brothers are still frequently instructive. The difficulty of sustaining unity of tone for a whole epic, the insuperable difficulty for the contemporary poet of forging a symbolism in an age when rationalism has sapped the bases of myth—these are only some of the pitfalls which interpose themselves between the poet and the realization of his project. A modern epic, conceived in the manner of existing models, simply cannot be realized. Perhaps French-Canadian literature will have its epic some day but when it does, in content and style, it will be like a new art form. Only under these conditions, in which a monumental work creates its own criteria, could it escape unfavourable comparisons and come to be recognized for what it is: the national epic.

In spite of a badly conceived plan, some of Fréchette's best poems are to be found in *La légende d'un peuple,* as for instance *Le frêne des Ursulines.*[4] It is obvious that he aimed too high, but equally obvious that with him Canadian literature made a great stride forward. Would Fréchette have been a greater poet if, perfectly aware of his own weaknesses, he had limited himself to his best verse? It does seem that the high place which no one would deny him is partly due to misconceptions about art which, if flagrant, have none the less been fruitful by virtue of the dream that was a part of them.

Pamphile Lemay (1837-1918)

Quite different is Pamphile Lemay.[5] His *Essais poétiques* which appeared in 1865, two years after Fréchette's *Mes loisirs,* reveal an elegiac soul:[6]

> *Je sais bien que ma plainte est vaine*
> *Je ne demande aucun secours:*
> *Mais je me nourris de ma peine*
> *Et je veux la chanter toujours!*

> Well do I know that my plaint is in vain,
> Nor do I ask for succour:
> It is my sorrow that nourishes me
> And I would sing it forever. [*trans.*]

This melancholy is much more than a vague tribute to French-Canadian literary Romanticism. Admitted to the Bar the same year, Lemay had no intention of giving up his dream of poetry. Surrounded by his numerous children, throughout his entire life he kept before him a high Christian ideal of modesty and self-denial. Less gifted at the outset than Fréchette, Lemay, who was librarian of the Legislative Chamber of his province from 1867, was to grow in ability. His *Essais poétiques,* which include the translation of Longfellow's *Evangeline,* belong to a period of apprenticeship, although he was already twenty-eight years of age. Like Fréchette and nearly all the poets of his generation, Lemay did not forget France. His advice to the "children of the St. Lawrence" was to avenge themselves on France for her indifference by "still loving her."[7]

The very great effort required of him by *Les vengeances* (1875), a cloak-and-dagger novel in verse,[8] doubtless brought him a better understanding of his craft. But these eight thousand or more Alexandrines add nothing to his reputation.

It was a quarter-century later, in 1904 that his most finished work appeared, a collection of sonnets, *Les Gouttelettes.* Moving testimony to what can be accomplished by perseverance allied with a genuine, if limited, talent. His great friend, Fréchette, victim of his own facility and perhaps also of the renown he had won in French Canada, found after his *Légende d'un peuple* that he had nothing more to say. Lemay had more modest literary ambitions and tended to store up his most intimate thoughts. Having retired after 1892 to one of the most peaceful spots in his native province, Saint-Jean-Deschaillons, he revealed in his confession to Abbé Camille Roy that he had never heard of the poet Heredia, to whom he had been compared because of his *Gouttelettes.*[9] What gives value to some of these sonnets, whose craftsmanship marks a considerable advance over the *Essais Poétiques,* is the extreme delicacy of the feelings to which he gives expression. Lemay sings in turn of the joys of home, life in the fields, stirrings from the past, which are on the same plane with his old man's sensibility without disturbing it.

> *Mais qu'importe, ô mes jours! que le ciel vous prolonge*
> *Le monde n'est-il pas un abîme qu'on longe?*

And so it is that towards the end, thanks to the slow artistic journey upward that was characteristic of his life, Lemay wrote his last and one of his most beautiful poems, an epitome of the man and his art:

> *Mon rêve a ployé l'aile. En l'ombre qui s'étend,*
> *Il est comme un oiseau que le lacet captive.*
> *Malgré des jours nombreux ma fin semble hâtive;*
> *Je dis l'adieu suprême à tout ce qui m'entend.*

Je suis content de vivre et je mourrai content.
La mort n'est-elle pas une peine fictive?
J'ai mieux aimé chanter que jeter l'invective.
J'ai souffert, je pardonne, et le pardon m'attend.

Que le souffle d'hiver emporte, avec la feuille,
Mes chants et mes sanglots d'un jour! Je me recueille
Et je ferme mon coeur aux voix qui l'ont ravi.

Nérée Beauchemin (1850-1931)

Only Canada could give birth to the kind of man and poet that Nérée Beauchemin was.[10] Having got his degree as a medical doctor in 1874, Beauchemin settled in Yamachiche on Lake Saint-Pierre. For half a century he lived his life to the rhythm of the returning seasons and the cheerfully accepted demands of the faith. Completely removed from the clamour of the outside world, not even having to give up a local reputation when he started to write poetry, Beauchemin lived till 1931 without in effect ever having left the nineteenth century. His two collections of verse, *Les floraisons matutinales* (1897) and *Patrie intime* (1928), by their inspiration connect him with Pamphile Lemay, though Beauchemin's work is superior.

Les floraisons matutinales, written when he was forty-seven years of age, are late flowerings which give evidence of a craft learned with difficulty and the recollection of old themes dear to Crémazie and Fréchette. However, *La cloche de Louisbourg,* a poem often quoted, is the work of an artist. It is in the direction of a still more finished plasticity, dominated by a sharpened vision of his *patrie intime* that Beauchemin is aiming. *Patrie intime* marks the end of that long and patient effort and, notwithstanding the date of publication, may be considered a high point of nineteenth-century poetry in French Canada. The sixteen Alexandrines of *O Prêtre, auguste ami de toujours* are Beauchemin at his best. The contained feeling is combined with a technique that has become fluid and appropriate.

O Prêtre, auguste ami de toujours, tendre Père,
Pur entre les plus purs, doux parmi les plus doux,
Je m'arrête devant ton cercueil de lumière,
Et, tout tremblant d'émoi, je m'incline, à genoux.

Ta mystique beauté n'est pas anéantie,
Corps sacré qu'illumine encore l'Onction,
Grâce au baiser divin de la divine hostie,
Tu respires déjà la résurrection.

Je vous vénère, ô lys de l'antique ciboire!
Mains jointes dans le rêve et le désir des cieux,
Mains en prière encore, ainsi qu'à l'Offertoire,
Je vous vénère avec des larmes plein les yeux.

Vous que la myrrhe embaume et que l'hysope asperge,
Mains jointes dans l'amour de l'Archange immortel,
Je vous baise à genoux, ô lys de l'aube vierge,
O lys enseveli dans le lin de l'autel.

It can be seen that this new world poetry already has two magnetic poles: patriotism and religion. Onto these two elements, usually inseparable, is grafted a belated *mal du siècle*. All the nineteenth-century poets draw from this double inspiration and that is why they bear such a resemblance to each other. The most outstanding are distinguished by the amount of one or the other of these elements to be found in their poetry. In the case of Fréchette it is the patriotic impulse of Crémazie that finds its best expression; with Lemay the gentler idea of the joys and sorrows of the Christian are associated with the different aspects of Canadian traditions and countryside. Numerous poets will modulate these themes until the advent of symbolism at the beginning of the twentieth century. With the exception of the more gifted ones, almost all of them will founder in the pedestrian world of platitudes, characterized as well by a limping versification and language.[11]

Among the poets who can be relegated to this secondary zone, incontestably the most famous is William Chapman (1850-1917). His *Québecoises*, published in 1876, soars to no greater heights than the poetry of François-Xavier Garneau who, forty years previously, had been the first to imitate Lamartine.[12]

After an interval of fourteen years Chapman published *Les Feuilles d'érable*. For the first and only time Chapman here wrote lines which, while not memorable, were proof that he could observe Canadian nature with the eyes of a poet. Also, his style had changed. Although the three sonnets dedicated to Leconte de Lisle, to François Coppée and to Sully Prudhomme were still poems of Canadian Romanticism, the impassiveness of the Parnassians can be found at the end of his best poem, *L'aurore boréale*. For his treatment of this ultra-Canadian subject Chapman found occasional imagery that redeemed its very imperfect versification. The northern lights were sometimes likened to a

> ... *fluide clavier dont les étranges touches*
> *Battent de l'aile ainsi que des oiseaux farouches*

sometimes again to waves which

> *S'écrasent, et, trouant des archipels d'opale,*
> *Déferlent par-dessus une montagne pâle*
> *De nuages pareils à des vaisseaux ancrés*
> *Dans les immensités des golfes éthérés.*

After a second fourteen-year interval Chapman had his *Aspirations* published in Paris. Meanwhile he had been irked at the fame of Fréchette. Chapman, no doubt, was sincerely of the opinion that Fréchette, to whom he had dedicated dithyrambic verse in his youth, was no longer serving the cause of poetry in Canada. As a result, in an unfair book, *Le lauréat*,[13] he picked out all the imperfections, repetitions, faults of syntax and versification, all the imitations of which Fréchette had been guilty.

Did Chapman imagine that he was doing better when he took his *Aspirations* to Paris for publication? He, too, had the satisfaction of seeing his poems crowned by the *Académie Française,* whose members were revealed as being sensitive to rare homage of this nature:

> *Tes fils t'aiment toujours, ô ma mère, ô ma mère!*

Towards the end of his life Chapman realized that he had underestimated Fréchette's poetry. He made amends in his own peculiar way by dedicating a most extravagant poem to his one-time friend.[14] The two volumes that belong to his old age, *Les rayons du Nord* (1909) and *Les fleurs de givre* (1912) are of an undeniable mediocrity.

Less well known than Chapman, Eudore Evanturel (1854-1919) left us a single collection, *Premières poésies* (1878). In his conventional sadness, Evanturel was a poet very typical of his time. There does exist in him, however, a more personal note, a certain freshness of imagination, a spot of mischief, which distinguishes him from his contemporaries.[15]

HISTORY

Of all the literary genres it is probably history which found the greatest favour with Canadian men of letters. France, a continental power, had not been able to make of New France a sufficiently strong entity to resist the maritime and mercantile genius of England

and the expansionism of the United States. On the other hand, she left to her former subjects a legacy of two centuries so laden with memorable exploits and stories of such sublime dedication that whole generations of French Canadians have drawn from it lessons in pride and perseverance. And here we have the peculiar importance of history in French-Canadian literature. Every people raises its monuments to the past and a people whose existence was to remain precarious for so long could not keep from making living legends of its dead. *Notre maître le passé* (The Past our Teacher) is a phrase which in itself is an admirable explanation of how the study of history for over a century has been supplying the sources of energy for French-Canadian historians, analysts and chroniclers, and, through them, for the entire people.

Garneau's History, first classic of Canadian literature, had not satisfied everybody. The clergy in particular had given a poor reception to the many pages that Garneau had devoted to the spirit of chicanery in the religious orders and to the part played by the clergy in the temporal affairs of New France. The clergy had been particularly scandalized by the idea, often expressed by the historian, that the exclusion of Calvinists from New France, an act of intolerance, had not only been prejudicial to the development of the colony but had helped to bring about the loss of it. During Garneau's lifetime Abbé Jean-Baptiste Ferland made it his business to answer him.

Jean-Baptiste Ferland (1805-1865)

A teacher in the collège de Nicolet, Abbé Ferland held the chair of History in Laval University from 1854 to 1865. His *Cours d'Histoire du Canada* (1861-1865)[16] was published only after lengthy research carried on as much in France as in England and Canada. In Paris Abbé Ferland benefited from the very extensive knowledge of Pierre Margry,[17] at that time the greatest among specialists in the history of the French colonies.

The *Cours d'Histoire du Canada,* which covers only the period of French rule, can never supersede Garneau's work. Ferland's most useful innovation was to give prominence to the Indian tribes with a detailed account of their customs, traditions and dialects. His plan of approaching history "as a Canadian and Catholic" led him to select texts favourable to his personal convictions. So Abbé Ferland was the first ancestor of those numerous French-Canadian historians who, in their historical research, have looked not so much for underlying truths as for material supporting their preconceived opinions. A methodical and conscientious worker, Abbé Ferland remained a prisoner of the precise fact and was unable to give to the drama of New France its true proportions.

One is inclined, however, to accept Abbé Ferland's opinions rather than Garneau's on the subject of Calvinism. When Garneau wrote his *Histoire* it was not certain that the French-speaking group would be able to maintain itself in America. It seemed to him that it would have been good politics to welcome any reinforcements— even Huguenots—who could have given help to New France, either in moving ahead the date when the Anglo-Saxons would take over, or in keeping Canada for France. Although it is impossible to invalidate such a hypothesis, everything would lead one to believe that New France, whose doom was already sealed, had more to gain in preserving the religious and moral unity that would be of such powerful assistance to her later on. Abbé Ferland was sure of it and history has not proved him wrong.

Etienne-Marcel Faillon (1799-1870)

Born in France, in Tarascon, Etienne-Marcel Faillon entered Saint-Sulpice in 1820. His extreme piety and his natural aptitude for study brought him the appointment of director of souls; so it is in this capacity that we find him at the Solitude de Saint-Sulpice in 1837. After publishing in 1841 a biography of M. Olier, founder of the Sulpicians, M. Faillon was called upon in 1849 to make the first of three trips to Canada; Mgr. Forbin-Janson[18] had preceded him more than ten years earlier. The Sulpicians had proudly participated in the founding of Montreal in the seventeenth century and looked upon New France as God's work. With rare energy, and well informed as a result of his research on M. Olier about the history of Canada, M. Faillon took it upon himself to investigate the Canadian archives. At the end of seven years in Canada he was finally able to publish, in 1865-1866, the first three volumes of his *Histoire de la colonie française en Canada*,[19] a work that was never completed.

The historical method of Abbé Faillon is rigorously scientific in the sense that for him history must depend solely on facts authenticated by archives and the most trustworthy authors. Every supposition, every theory not supported by established fact is so much smoke. Unfortunately, Abbé Faillon was convinced that the history of New France was a revelation of the divine plan; consequently his role as historian consisted in digging out of the archives not all the documents relating to New France but the right ones.[20] Yet despite the way his thinking was inclined, his astonishing capacity for work, his probity in using the chosen documents, made it possible for him to accumulate so many precise references and to correct such a great number of statements made by his predecessors, conspicuously by Charlevoix, that Canadian historical studies made a great stride forward. Anyone wanting information on the religious foundations of New France will always benefit from the *Histoire de la colonie française en Canada,* one of the pleasures being its style. Now, a century later, we can gauge what Saint-Sulpice must have been merely by reading this free-flowing prose, which would be borne to its ultimate perfection in Renan.

Finally, Faillon's work is a warning to the historian who might be tempted to fall into the opposite error of explaining the establishment of New France by purely commercial motives or those of personal ambition.[21]

Henri-Raymond Casgrain (1831-1904)

The work of another historian-priest, Henri-Raymond Casgrain, is considerable and covers about thirty years.[22] Among his numerous studies and short treatises dealing with French rule one must point out his very fine work, *Montcalm et Lévis.*[23] Thanks to frequent trips to France, where he consulted the archives in the Ministry of the Marine and Colonies, the Ministry of War, the Archives Nationales and the principal libraries in Paris and the provinces, Abbé Casgrain had provided himself with an imposing amount of documentation. More than that, he was the first to lay his hands on previously unpublished documents, which cast new light on the last years of New France. The diaries of Montcalm and Lévis, the correspondence between the two men, as well as several accounts of expeditions undertaken by more or less obscure soldiers, completed his already very wide knowledge of Canadian history. His imagination, like his passionate patriotism, caught fire when he read these last testimonies of an heroic era. He made up his mind to write the history of the Canadian War (1756-1760).

Very fortunately for him, Abbé Casgrain allowed himself to be guided by his documentation, refusing to yield to his inclination for melodramatic descriptions; not without regret, however, because letting the witnesses speak seemed to him a "repellent" task. As one reads on through the detailed accounts of those five memorable years, one feels the presence of the author who, lost in wonder at the poetry of the events, attains a loftiness of spirit not encountered elsewhere in his work. Here and there he intervenes in the story to comment, almost always justly, on the behaviour of the principal actors on the scene. He explains the veiled hostility between the regular army and the Canadians without putting all the blame on either side. He can understand Wolfe's sensitive spirit and noble inclinations. Finally, he is the one who puts an end to the quarrel about opportunity for Huguenot immigration in the seventeenth century. Charity as well as reasons of State demanded that refuge should be found for these Frenchmen. Abbé Casgrain would have opened wide the doors in Louisiana.

It is clear, however, that the historian is far from being irreproachable. Perfect objectivity was foreign to Abbé Casgrain's disposition. We feel him burning with impatience to add his own comments to those of his main characters. When his true feelings show through, the historian sometimes trips. His conjectures on the fate that would have befallen New France, had it not been for the mistakes of Bougainville and Montcalm, are purely imaginary. One may also be permitted to doubt that the strategy of this fiery priest is always free from miscalculation. Yet these faults, whose seriousness one might properly leave to the historians to assess, do not hinder the course of the story. Abbé Casgrain does not belong to that school whose historians want only to enclose themselves behind a wall of facts. History for him was one of the most noble of dramas. You feel this in his *Guerre du Canada.* And it is thanks to this conception that this writer who, in the beginnings of his literary career had shown a taste for the worst excesses of Romanticism, towards the end succeeded in purifying his style and in writing pages which make a discreet setting for the main action.

Avec la rentrée des troupes dans leurs quartiers d'hiver, la besogne du soldat était finie, mais celle du peuple recommençait. C'était sur lui que retombait le fardeau de loger et de nourrir l'armée, sans autre compensation, on le sait, que dix sous par jour par soldat. Depuis le printemps, les trois quarts de la population valide avaient été enlevés à leurs champs, soit pour le service militaire, soit pour le transport des troupes et des munitions. C'était la quatrième année que le gouverneur avait fait appel à leur patriotisme, et ils étaient accourus sous les drapeaux avec le même élan incomparable. Ils avaient enduré avec la même patience tous les dangers, toutes les privations, toutes les fatigues de la guerre. A leur retour au foyer, ils avaient rencontré la misère à leurs portes. Le peu de semences jetées en terre, récoltées trop tard faute de bras, avaient peu produit . . . Les étables étaient presque vides de bestiaux, et une grande partie des chevaux avaient été tués pour servir de nourriture. Les habitants exposés à se voir enlever au nom du roi,

*comme cela se fit, le peu de grains qu'ils avaient, en étaient réduits
à le cacher dans la crainte de mourir de faim. Jamais hiver ne
s'était présenté sous un aspect plus menaçant. Cependant la
constance du peuple ne se démentait pas; son dévouement et son
courage croissaient avec le danger. Il sentait que la crise suprême
était venue, et il s'apprêtait à l'affronter avec l'entêtement du
désespoir. Le héros qui domine tous les autres dans ce drame, c'est
l'obscur milicien qui n'a ni trêve, ni relâche, et qui va courir
au-devant des balles dans la forêt ou sous les murs de Québec.*[24]

With the troops back in their winter quarters, the soldier's work
was done, but that of the people was just beginning again. On them
fell the load of lodging and feeding the army without compensation,
as we know, other than ten cents per soldier per day. Since spring
three-quarters of the able-bodied population had been taken from
their fields either for military service or to transport men and
munitions. This was the fourth year that the Governor had appealed to their patriotism and they had rallied to the banners with
the same incomparable spirit. In the same patient way they had
endured all the dangers, all the privations, all the weariness of war.
Home again, they had met poverty on their doorsteps. The few
seeds thrown upon the earth, harvested too late for lack of men,
had produced little. . . . The stables were almost emptied of cattle
and a great many of the horses had been killed for food. The *habitants,* likely to see what little grain they had taken from them in
the name of the king, were reduced to hiding it for fear of starving.
Never had winter faced them in more threatening guise. Nevertheless the steadfastness of the people did not fail. They felt that the
supreme crisis had come and they made ready to meet it with the
stubbornness of despair. The hero, above all others in this drama,
is the humble militiaman who knows neither truce nor respite and
who runs to meet the bullets in the woods or under the walls of
Quebec.[24] [*trans.*]

Though Garneau did not always see the people at such close
range, no other Canadian historian makes us participate to this extent in the critical years which decided the fate of the French
Canadians. That he could do this successfully is attributable to the
level of skill to which exaltation had finally brought this Romanticist.

RENEWAL OF HISTORICAL STUDIES

The historian-priests — Henri-Raymond Casgrain, Jean-Baptiste
Ferland and Etienne-Marcel Faillon—had helped to throw light on
certain aspects of the French regime that had been left under cover
or simply passed over by Garneau. Because of their work the re-

construction of the French past, an endeavour that dated back to the beginning of the nineteenth century,[25] was from their period onward complete in its broad outlines. Inventories had been made of the battles and skirmishes as well as of the heroes who had taken part. It was impossible to keep on indefinitely, making the same pilgrimage to the ancestral shrine. This was particularly the case as Garneau's work, to which additions and corrections of detail could be added, ran hardly any risk of being outclassed. Other conceptions of history more in accord with the modern world inevitably were to bring about a reorientation in the study of history. Here the people, multiform or protean heroes, replace the captains and the kings, and economic and sociological considerations are obligatory.

Joseph-Edmond Roy (1858-1913) was one of the first to effect, by his own example, a necessary move in the right direction. Having been made a notary in 1880, he very soon became aware of what could be learned from the notaries' deeds of the French regime. The hidden, personal life of the first colonists, of which there was only slight mention in the Histories of Canada previously published, would come clear with the help of these deeds as if from a photographer's negative. By 1883 Joseph-Edmond Roy had drawn up the outline of his projected new work; it was published in 1897-1904 in five thick volumes, with the title *Histoire de la seigneurie de Lauzon.*

Joseph-Edmond Roy had nothing else in mind than a desire to serve the cause of Canadian history by means of the patient accumulation of facts hitherto unknown or difficult to unearth. Aware of the value of burning the midnight oil, he proclaims: "The thought that every conscientious piece of work is certain to find a small number of unknown friends who applaud it in secret has always kept me from giving up."[26] One would have no right to accuse him of delivering his material unprocessed to the reader because, the way he worked, no detail was too small to be taken into account. His was an inquiring mind and the past he uncovered gives us an intimate and charming picture of Canada. At any rate his work, closer to a compilation than real history, must be classed among tools available to the professional historian, for whom it is especially intended.[27]

Benjamin Sulte (1841-1923) also devoted his life to unearthing the minute facts that make up day-to-day history. Furthermore, he was ambitious to make a vast synthesis of all the works on Canada that had been published previously and to give a whole picture of the French-Canadian people. But to carry through such an enterprise Sulte lacked the indispensable critical sense which would have let him separate the adventitious from the essential; he also lacked a sufficiently well-stocked mind. His *Histoire des Canadiens-français,*[28] which had a very mixed reception even at the time, could not put a span of more than three centuries of history in a different light.

Benjamin Sulte published more than three thousand articles on the history of Canada. This is the only part of his work that holds any interest for today's reader.[29]

THE NOVEL

Laure Conan (1845-1924)

The last quarter of the nineteenth century produced one novelist, Laure Conan. Born in 1845 in La Malbaie, Marie-Louise-Félicité Angers lived the greater part of her life there in an atmosphere wonderfully suited to the contemplative spirit. She was away from her village on only rare occasions: at about the age of thirteen she went to school to the Ursulines in Quebec and much later, in 1893, she sought refuge with the Sisters of the Precious Blood in Saint-Hyacinthe, where she remained until 1896. Towards the end of her life she retired to Sillery.

Two passions sum up the entire work of Laure Conan: religion and French-Canadian patriotism. Very early, in the isolation of La Malbaie, she conceived a lasting admiration for François-Xavier Garneau. The similarities between the studious life of the historian, entirely devoted to the emancipation and advancement of the French Canadians, and her own solitary existence must have seemed to her adolescent imagination to be many. "I have thought a lot about him," she was to say later, "about his great hardships, his lonely upbringing, and out of respect I would like to visit that attic where, without teachers and almost without books, our historian worked away at his education. Oh! what courage he had, what perseverance. . . ."[30]

Laure Conan waited until the age of thirty-three before writing her first book, *Un amour vrai.* Three years later, in 1881, this first attempt was followed by *Angéline de Montbrun,* which she published in the *Revue canadienne.* Her profound religious feeling, her respect for the high moral qualities which a "gentle" people is obligated to perpetuate from one generation to the next, find here their finest artistic expression.

After her disfigurement, Angéline de Montbrun becomes aware that the love of Maurice, her fiancé, is growing lukewarm. In her heart she is unable to accept an imperfect love and from that time on, with a truly Cornelian decision, Angéline will live for God alone. Her resolution brings to bear all the instinctive resistance of her young body. In letter form, *Angéline de Montbrun* with marked restraint tells the story of the struggle between her will, which is sometimes weak, and her unappeased desires.

This novel, very Old France in the conception of honour and religion at its roots, is the first example of the Canadian novel of analysis. We shall have to wait for the contemporary period to find other works of this nature which can be compared with it.

Always attracted to history, Laure Conan sooner or later had to pay her tribute to it. From 1891, the year when she published *A l'oeuvre et à l'épreuve*, a story of the Jesuit, Charles Garnier, she wrote several reconstructions of the Canadian past in story form, among them *L'Oublié* (1900), which was crowned by the French Academy. Her last work, *La sève immortelle* (1924), which she finished on her deathbed, added considerably to her reputation in French Canada. In what might be called a testament, the novelist appeals to her compatriots to return to those virtues bequeathed to them by their ancestors. The main events of the novel, which take place just after the conquest, confront the characters with a difficult choice, which is in keeping with the customary literary behaviour of the author. Can Jean de Tilly, born in Canada, marry Thérèse d'Autrée and go to France without denying his origins and failing in his duty to perpetuate, whatever the cost, the memory of France in America?

Because of the sincerity of tone which characterizes them, the historical novels of Laure Conan deserve a very honourable place in the repository of French-Canadian literature. But intensive reading reveals that this woman, who thought of the novel as a kind of apostolate, was able to write only catechisms.

This is not to say that Laure Conan is unimportant in French-Canadian literature. Her historical novels, which have remained very popular with the conventual population of French Canada, have helped us to overlook her other role as an analyst of the human heart. In this regard her most revealing work, which carries on the theme of *Angéline Montbrun*, is *l'Obscure souffrance* (1919).

This imaginary diary, only about fifty pages long, is too intimate in tone to be anything but the sincere emanations of wounded sensitivity in an unmarried woman who has grown old. The struggle between the flesh and the spirit, whose first phase was announced some forty years earlier in *Angéline Montbrun,* ends only in death. "Solitude of the mind and heart seem to me to be the supreme test," she confessed, after having asked the question, "How can one get used to being without everything that makes up the interest, the sweetness and the charm of living?"[31] And her errant mind begins to dream up the kind of man to whom she would have been willing to entrust her destiny. This paragon of virtue never having existed, she abandons the dream for a contemplation of the ennobling truths of the Christian religion. This last picture of Laure Conan reveals a soul tormented by an ideal too lofty to be lived except in rare and privileged moments. But those moments compensate, in their mystical intensity, for the sorrows accumulated in a life made up of *obscures souffrances.*[32]

Religion and patriotism, to which Laure Conan owes the best part of her talent, can be bad counsellors. Jules-Paul Tardivel (1851-1905) was the first novelist to prostitute these two sources of inspiration and may be regarded as the precursor of the racist and separatist novel. Born in the United States of a father from Auvergne and an English mother converted to Roman Catholicism, Tardivel learned French only after 1868, in the Collège de Saint-Hyacinthe. To the language and religion of his adopted province he pledged a convert's zeal. A great admirer of Louis Veuillot, the French writer most widely admired in French Canada at the time of the Second Empire, Tardivel, after long years devoted to the defence of French-Canadian Catholicism and nationality, wrote a novel with the revealing title: *Pour la patrie* (1895). In his foreword he declared that the French novel "seems to be an implement forged by Satan himself for the destruction of humankind."[33] Convinced that French Canada risked the gravest dangers, Tardivel painted an apocalyptic picture of the Province of Quebec as it might be in half a century, that is in 1945. We are told that "France, worldly, sceptical, mocking, impious and atheist . . . France, the declared enemy of God and his Church, has come bursting into Canada."[34] But all is not lost since Lamirande, doughty knight as of old, will thwart the plans of Free Masons and ministers in Ottawa. His mission on earth accomplished, Lamirande, like Charles V, will go and bury himself in an abbey.

Pour la patrie is the work of a fanatic as sincere as he is lacking in appreciation of the ways of literary art. It will be necessary to wait for Abbé Lionel Groulx for the nationalistic novel to attain the refinements of which it is capable.

CHRONICLES, MEMOIRS, THE
SHORT STORY

Arthur Buies (1840-1901)

In company with novelists and poets such as Laure Conan, Louis
Fréchette, and Pamphile Lemay, who broadened the Canadian
literary tradition, there is Arthur Buies, news writer and geographer.
With Buies we have a breath of fresh air blowing through the
patriotic and religious stuffiness of the nineteenth century.

Buies came into view as a free-lancer at an early age.[35] Born
of a Scottish father and a French-Canadian mother, Buies, like the
poet Nelligan later on, who also had a mixture of traits from two
ancestral lines in his blood, was unable to accept the mysticism
which was so natural to Laure Conan's talent. The majority of
French-Canadian writers had found sufficient inspiration in the
spiritual origins of French Canada. Dynamic by nature, the adolescent in Buies balked at the *vocation* of the *French of America* in
so far as this vocation seemed to him to be static and sterilizing.
Although Buies was a sincere patriot, the severe criticism that he
levelled at all aspects of the intellectual and moral life of his
countrymen scandalized and alienated those people in a position to
be of influence in French-Canadian society. For men of his generation, very much aware of all that they wanted to safeguard in the
French heritage, Buies for a long time seemed like an enemy of the
common interest.[36]

Buies came to literature indirectly by way of journalism. During
his apprenticeship in Paris he had admired the lively enterprise of
the pamphleteer Henri Rochefort. On June first, 1868, the latter
had founded a weekly newspaper, *La Lanterne,* in which the imper-
ial government was violently attacked. Inspired by this example,
Buies made himself the Canadian Rochefort and in the last days of
September, 1868, launched a paper bearing the same name as the
Paris news sheet. He constituted himself the defender of the Canadian Institute and set out to wage war against Mgr. Bourget, whose
blasts had already resulted in leading the majority of the Institute's
members to mend their ways. His cause being lost in advance,
Buies could not hope to make an anticlerical newspaper prosper in
French Canada. In any case, *La Lanterne,* for lack of readers,
made a last appearance on March nineteenth, 1869. In these six
months or so Buies had acquired an unenviable notoriety. At a
time when hundreds of volunteers, on an appeal from Mgr. Bourget,
were going off to defend the terrestrial interests of the Pope, Buies
had written: "The Pope, it appears, says a prayer every day for the

reinstatement of Isabella on the throne. Providence should have spared the Pope this trouble; he cannot say too many prayers if he wants to stay on his own."[37]

Deprived of his rostrum, Buies, who loved reporting, discovered the formula which was to make his reputation as a writer. He travelled across the province tackling less controversial subjects, and in the shape of news reports set down his impressions of the places he had visited. The Canadian public which had given a poor reception to his philippics against the clergy had more appreciation for pieces of this kind on Quebec City:

Les gens de notre bonne vieille ville ont adopté depuis quelque temps une nouvelle spécialité; c'est la mort subite. Tous les jours il y a deux ou trois narquois qui se paient cette boutade aux fils d'Esculape, ce qui varie un peu les faits divers, devenus monotones, d'orteils écrasés entre deux madriers de trottoirs. La boue des rues s'est endurcie depuis hier, de sorte qu'au lieu d'éclabousser quand elle vous jaillit au visage, elle vous casse une dent ou vous crève un oeil; il n'y a que l'embarras du choix. On avait craint beaucoup l'apparition de la petite vérole; dimanche dernier les curés avaient fait les plus vives recommandations sur ce sujet à tous les prônes. Recherches faites, on a trouvé que la petite vérole en question se réduisait à deux cas de jaunisse. Rien n'est tel que de prendre ses précautions.[38]

For some time past the people of our good old town have been going in for a new specialty—sudden death. Every day there are two or three jokers who play this prank on the sons of Esculapius, which gives variety to the increasingly monotonous news items about toes being crushed between two boards in the sidewalk. The mud in the streets has hardened since yesterday so that instead of splashing you in the face it breaks one of your teeth or puts out your eye; you have a wide choice. We had been afraid of an outbreak of smallpox; last Sunday the priests had given the liveliest counsel on this subject from every pulpit. Upon investigation it was found that the smallpox in question could be reduced to two cases of jaundice. Nothing like taking precautions.[38] [*trans.*]

Encouraged by this first success, our reporter published other accounts in the same vein. His *Petites chroniques pour 1877* came to the notice of Father Antoine Labelle.[39] With rare energy, this priest was carrying out the programme advocated by Antoine Gérin-Lajoie, that of clearing Quebec's uncultivated land. Father Labelle had been quick to realize from the quite nationalistic trend of Buies' last news reports that the anticlerical cloaked an ardent patriot. Judging correctly the assistance that Buies was in a position to lend him, Father Labelle cast a spell over him and bound him to himself forever.

Promoted to geographer, Buies experiences a literary renewal. Once he has become the propagandist for Father Labelle's work he plies his craft all the better since it seems to him that he has regained his fiery youth in his explorations of the most inaccessible regions of Quebec. His study entitled *Le Saguenay et la vallée du lac Saint-Jean* (1880) shows up clearly both his good qualities and his shortcomings as a writer and is the story in brief of the second phase of his career.[40]

Buies lacked the requisite knowledge to make his work as a geographer what he wanted it to be. His hypotheses on the origins of the Saguenay, fantastic as they are, could not, it is true, do any harm to his literary reputation. More serious is the poverty of his thought. This swashbuckler of anticlericalism, having come back to the Catholicism which he had never really left, constructs for his own needs a considerably over-simplified religious dialectic.[41] His reflections on the brevity of life and on the foolishness of man are utterly banal.

There remains the landscape painter. It is on this score that Buies is worthy of real consideration, even though his prose is not that of a stylist.

Buies had kept in his memory literary recipes learned at school in France and he rarely rises above this level.[42] Nevertheless, when he abandons lofty reflections on life and death which do nothing but lay bare the limited scope of his mind and when, with habitual good humour, he tackles some characteristic aspect of his native province, Buies succeeds in writing some excellent pages which admirably bring back to life the hopes of French Canada at the end of the last century:

LE LAC SAINT-JEAN

Nous voilà enfin arrivés devant cette petite mer qui est restée en quelque sorte légendaire jusqu'à nos jours, dont le nom frappe encore singulièrement bien des oreilles, et sur laquelle a plané pendant bien longtemps le voile mystérieux qui couvre l'immense solitude du nord. Il y a cinquante ans à peine, personne n'aurait osé croire qu'on pût seulement se rendre jusqu'au lac Saint-Jean; c'était tellement loin dans le nord! Le pays qui l'entourait ne pouvait être que la demeure des animaux à fourrures et, seuls, les Indiens étaient regardés comme pouvant se hasarder dans ces sombres retraites, que protégeait la chaîne des Laurentides et que défendait contre l'homme une nature réputée inaccessible. C'était un préjugé, sans doute, mais avouons que ce préjugé, qui représen-

*tait comme inaccessible à la colonisation et à la culture toute la
région du lac Saint-Jean, avait quelque raison d'être, car cette région
a une physionomie qu'aucun autre aspect du Canada ne rappelle.
Voyez se balancer, s'agiter ou s'endormir, sur son lit de sable et
d'alluvion, cette petite mer intérieure, semblable à un énorme crabe
étendant dans tous les sens ses longues et nombreuses rivières, comme
autant de tentacules, toutes prêtes à saisir les colons et à les attirer
quand même sur le sein du monstre! Elle n'est pas enfouie dans les
dépressions des montagnes comme tant d'autres lacs de notre pays
que ressemblent à des coupes profondes laissées par les eaux en
retraite; mais elle s'étale avec une négligence dédaigneuse sur un
fond sans cesse mouvant, élargissant ou rétrécissant ses limites
suivant les saisons, s'élevant ou s'abaissant sans marée, rongeant ses
rives ou bien les exhaussant par les accumulations répétées de sable
et de terre végétale que lui apportent ses tributaires. Elle n'est pas
enclavée dans un cercle infranchissable, réduite à une immobilité
passive et monotone, mais elle joue librement sur un lit incertain
que les années l'une après l'autre déplacent; elle s'ébat, chante ou
gronde tour à tour sur les molles et grasses rives d'une plaine
qu'elle recouvrait jadis tout entière et qu'elle a laissée dupuis
longtemps à nu, après l'avoir fécondée pendant des siècles; elle a
certaines senteurs propres qui traversent l'atmosphère et vont
s'exhaler au loin dans les bois et les champs; on la pressent aux
fraîches bouffées qui s'échappent de son sein et on croit l'entendre
avant de l'avoir aperçue, dans les échos ranimés, dans les frais
murmures qui emplissent l'air, lorsqu'on arrive enfin au terme du
long et ennuyeux trajet qu'on a parcouru à travers toute le
presqu'île de Chicoutimi.*[43]

And now at last we have come to that little sea which has remained somehow legendary right up to our own time, whose name still has a particularly happy sound to the ear and over which there has hovered for the longest time the mysterious veil which covers the immense solitude of the North. Less than fifty years ago no one would have believed it possible even to get to Lake Saint-Jean, it was so terribly far north. The country all around could not be anything but a place for fur-bearing animals to live in and only the Indians were considered capable of venturing into these dark haunts guarded by the Laurentian chain and protected against man by a Nature said to be inaccessible. This was doubtless an antiquated notion but let us admit that such a notion, which pictured the whole Lake Saint-Jean region as beyond reach of colonization and culture, had some justification, for this region has a physiognomy like no other in Canada. Watch this small inland sea swinging, shaking or sleeping on its bed of sand and alluvium, like an enormous crab stretching out in all directions its long and numerous rivers that are so many tentacles, ready to lay hold on the settlers and, in spite of all, draw them to her monster's bosom. It is not buried in the hollows of the mountains like so many other lakes in our country which look like vast cups left behind by the retreating waters, but it sprawls on its ceaselessly moving depths with a disdainful lack of regard, expanding or retracting according to the seasons, rising or falling, with no tide, gnawing at its shores or raising them by repeated accumulations of sand and loam brought by its tributaries. It is not enclosed in an impassable circle, reduced to passive and monotonous immobility, but plays freely on an uncertain bed that the succeeding years displace. It frolics, it sings or groans in turn on the soft, rich shores of a plain that it covered over long ago and which, for a long time, it has left bare after fertilizing it for centuries. It has certain scents of its own which carry through the atmosphere and are breathed out far away into woods and fields. You know it is there from the puffs of cool air that escape its breast and you think before you see it that you are hearing it, in the echoes, in the fresh murmurings filling the air, when at last you get to the end of the long and wearisome trip that has taken you across the whole Chicoutimi peninsula.[43] [*trans.*]

What place can Buies be given in the history of French-Canadian literature? The life of the man is inseparable from his work. More courageous than shrewd, Buies was the strangest personality in the French-Canadian literary tradition of the nineteenth century. Buies is the first writer of importance to assert his right to freedom of expression, and into the defence of that ideal he put all his sincerity and his tremendous energy. Only in the twentieth century would he have successors.

Faucher de Saint-Maurice (1844-1897)

This uncomplicated man was the soul of honour and capable of devotion. The French intervention in Mexico (1862-1867) gave this Canadian Don Quixote an unhoped-for opportunity to serve the former mother country in a grand, selfless gesture. With dispatches and a letter of introduction handed to him by M. Gauldrée-Boilleau, the French Consul in Quebec, for the Marquis de Montholon, Minister Plenipotentiary of France to Mexico, Faucher de Saint-Maurice found himself in the Mexican capital at the end of 1864. It was of little importance to him what cause he had come to serve; was he not there to fight under French colours? From the twenty-seventh of November, 1864, to his great joy, he belonged to the Mexican expeditionary corps. Taken prisoner near Saltillo by General Negrete's troops, Faucher de Saint-Maurice had a narrow escape from the firing squad in a last-minute exchange of prisoners.

Later on a slight wound, then the increasing distress which he felt at the high altitude, forced him to ask for his final discharge. He had served under the French colours for less than a year.

That he entitled his memoirs *Deux ans au Mexique* is no surprise. Had he not appropriated the *particule* through a feeling that was of the same ilk, that is, a desire to escape from what he found commonplace in Canadian life, if possible by years of action, if necessary by means of the imagination?

Later on Faucher de Saint-Maurice was to write stories and accounts of his travels that were of an extravagance unequalled in the history of French-Canadian literature. But he found accents of sincerity, relatively free of braggadocio, to recall the Mexican campaign.[44] When he took leave of his French comrades-in-arms in New York, what doubt can there be that this separation for all time was indeed a grief?

My trunks were carried into the hold of the whale-boats and when the passengers, one by one, had disappeared through the opening to the main stairway, with heavy heart I clasped the loyal hand of our worthy commander and, in my turn, started down the narrow ladder, turning around once more to salute the officers of the transport ship who were waving their handkerchiefs in good-bye. I could not part without emotion from that tri-colour that my four companions had taught me to love, to defend and to look upon as a bit of my own country. Every stroke of the oars carrying me farther away from it was a blow to my heart, and although in travelling one finally gets used to the continual good-byes that one always has to have on the tip of the tongue, something or other that I cannot explain told me that if I were ever to see it again, never again was I to serve it or hug to myself the noble ambition of being able to die for it some day.[45] [*trans.*]

Basically, Faucher de Saint-Maurice had no more aptitude for literature than many a soldier who, wanting to pass the time in a too-monotonous retirement, has bequeathed us his recollections of days with the army. It may happen, if the narrator has been observant, that this literary by-product makes pleasant reading. And, while it is only too apparent that Faucher de Saint-Maurice had less than a critical spirit, it is impossible to dispute the fact that he had a very good eye for the outward appearance of events and of things.

Le 18 mars . . . une foule énorme encombrait la place de Mixcalco, lieu ordinaire des exécutions à Mexico.

Il était six heures du matin. Le temps faisait plutôt rêver au bonheur de vivre que songer aux tristes mystères de la mort . . .

Soudain un roulement de tambours se fait entendre: les clairons sonnent au champ. Romero, mené sur une charrette du train des équipages militaires, vient d'entrer dans le fatal quadrilatère, suivi de quatre de ses malheureux compagnons.

Deux gendarmes aident le chef à descendre. C'est un petit homme qui marche en traînant de la jambe. Son air est souffrant et abattu: il est tête nue. Un large zarape *s'enroule autour de sa taille bien prise, et laisse entrevoir une chemise très fine et très blanche; son teint est brun olivâtre, sa moustache noire comme l'aile d'un corbeau.*

Les gendarmes le guident vers le poteau en bois de fer: Romero s'y adosse avec calme, mais sans forfanterie, et demande à parler à l'officier commandant:

—Colonel, lui dit-il, je réclame la permission de commander le peloton d'exécution.

—Ce n'est pas le colonel Romero que j'ai l'ordre de fusiller, c'est le bandit Romero, réplique l'autre froidement en retournant à son poste.

Le signal se donne: une détonation déchire l'air, et les cinq malheureux roulent dans la poussière: puis un sergent s'approche, leur donne le coup de grâce dans l'oreille, et toute la brigade défile au pas accéléré, musique en tête, devant ces crânes ouverts, fumants et laissant échapper leur cervelle sur le sable.[46]

On the eighteenth of March . . . there was an enormous crowd filling Mixcalco Square, where executions ordinarily took place in Mexico.

It was six o'clock in the morning. The weather made one think about the joy of living rather than the sad mystery of death . . .

Suddenly there is a rolling of drums; bugles sound. Romero, drawn in a cart belonging to the Army Service Corps, has just entered the fatal quadrangle, followed by four of his unfortunate companions.

Two police help the chief down. He is a small man who walks with one leg dragging. He seems to be downcast and in pain; he is bare-headed. A wide *zarape* is wrapped around a body that is well set up and allows a glimpse of a shirt that is very fine, very white; his complexion is olive brown, his moustache as black as a raven's wing.

The police guide him to the stake; Romero leans his back against it calmly, but without any affectation of defiance, and asks to speak to the commanding officer:

"Colonel," he said, "I beg permission to give the order to the firing squad."

"It isn't Colonel Romero I have orders to shoot, it's the bandit Romero," the other replied coldly, going back to his post.

The signal is given; an explosion rends the air and five luckless men roll in the dust. Then a sergeant comes up, gives them the *coup de grâce* in the ear, and the whole brigade, a military band at its head, quick-steps past those open, steaming skulls, with the brains spilling out over the sand.[46] [*trans.*]

Pamphile Lemay (1837-1918)

In 1837 the younger Gaspé had given some idea of the cabalistic effects to be realized by a Canadian writer when he draws on the stories and legends of his country. Pamphile Lemay in 1899 brought this genre to its highest degree of artistic development in *Contes vrais*. It is as a poet who is himself amused that Lemay describes the reactions of the good *habitants* to the witch, Marguerite-le-boeuf. Whether it is a question of a haunted house, of gypsies or of a patriot of '37 going over old memories, Lemay can admirably bring back to life that fantastic world which, as a result of the fertile imagination of the French Canadians, was the Quebec countryside in the nineteenth century.

Like many writers who have tried the short story as their medium, Lemay sometimes had difficulty in finding an ending which would be neither artificial nor obvious from the beginning. In the manipulation of plot, certain of his stories remind one inevitably of some of Maupassant's more garish exercises. On the other hand, in the way he begins a story, he can plunge us from the start right into the great and melancholy nature of French Canada:

Autrefois, il y avait du poisson dans toutes les eaux, et les ruisseaux les plus humbles voyaient se jouer sous leur mousse blanche, parmi les cailloux, d'alertes familles de goujons. Vous jetiez la ligne et ça mordait. Achigan, truite ou perchaude ne regardaient guère à l'appât, et se laissaient enlever par amour pour le pêcheur. Aujourd'hui, les ruisseaux sont à demi desséchés, à cause des défrichements, et le poisson qui s'attarde encore dans les mares formées par les échancrures de leurs bords ne mord qu'aux hameçons dorés et aux amorces succulentes. Il imite l'homme, son frère.

Il faut s'enfoncer maintenant sous la grande forêt, dans cette région vierge des Laurentides, immense et tourmentée comme une mer en fureur; dans cette région de montagnes ombreuses et de crêtes scalpées qui viennent brusquement s'arrêter au grand fleuve, et lui faire un rempart crénelé qui déchire la nue.[47]

In times past there were fish in all the waters, and the humblest brooks saw families of lively gudgeon playing under their white foam among the pebbles. You would throw in the line and there would be a bite. Achigan, trout or perch hardly looked at the bait and let themselves be caught out of pure love for the fisherman. Today the brooks are half dried up as a result of land-clearing projects, and fish still loitering in the pools made by indentations in their banks no longer bite at anything but golden hooks and succulent bait. They are imitating their brother, man.

Now one must go deep into the great forest, into that virgin territory of the Laurentians, immense and tormented like a sea in fury, into that region of lowering mountains and ridges that look as if they had been scalped as they come to a sudden stop at the great river and make for it a crenelated rampart which cuts straight up through the clouds.[47] [*trans.*]

It is, indeed, when Lemay paints those impressions which especially strike the eye that he becomes the story-teller born and bred. Some of his stories, such as *Le boeuf de Marguerite, Baptême de sang, Le jeune acrobate,* charm the reader in their photographic gaiety with a quality rare in French-Canadian letters. Unfortunately, Lemay, along with most French-Canadian authors of the nineteenth century, has a taste for the didactic. The patriot and the preacher too often pop in, and more than one page which could have been delightfully rakish is spoiled beyond repair.

Louis Fréchette (1839-1908)

Louis Fréchette, long established as national poet, was tempted towards the end of his career by the short story. In publishing his *Originaux et détraqués* (1892) it is worth noticing that he had found a new formula: putting together in one volume twelve stories, each one taking a noteworthy Quebec figure for its subject. Thus conceived, *Originaux et détraqués* had some chance of rising above the anecdotal appearance of the French-Canadian short story. According to Fréchette these exceptional individuals were meant to embody the character of the race.

The portraits which fill this gallery are very unequal and have the weakness of seeming to be alike. However, one remembers Cardinal, an usher in the Quebec parliament. Cardinal deserves to be one of the *originaux et détraqués* because of his language, which he strives to make as distinguished as possible. Not being well enough educated to be ridiculous, this adept before his time of the *Société du Bon Parler* makes us like him in the end. His wrong liaisons and spoonerisms are amusing and at the same time they reveal the scrupulous soul of this humble individual, saved from oblivion by Fréchette.

Fréchette's method is a kind of linguistic memory business. A collector of words by profession, he knows how to show off his most curious finds. As soon as he leaves this path, too narrow for the short story, he is capable of falling flat. In his collection *La Noël au Canada* (1900), only the story entitled *Tom Caribou* escapes mediocrity by reason of its picturesque vocabulary.[48]

Among news reporters and story-tellers[49] worth mentioning are Hector Fabre (1834-1901) and Jules Fournier (1884-1922).

At the time when Notre Dame Street in Montreal was the *rendez-vous* of idlers, Fabre humorously drew attention to the different types that made up the race of strollers and gapers (*Chroniques,* 1877).

The undeniably lively mind of Jules Fournier played on the French-Canadian political scene. It will always be enough to leaf over *Mon encrier,* published in 1922 by his wife, to get a just appreciation of a journalist who has only an indirect interest in literature and who is remembered above everything else for his high moral and intellectual mien.[50]

CRITICISM

From the time of Abbé Casgrain there have been critics in abundance in French Canada. What newspaperman, professor or writer has not wanted to get his fingers in the dough and contribute to the rise of French-Canadian letters?

The level of criticism—we have already made this observation[51] —has a certain relation to the quality of a literature. Between 1870 and 1900 French-Canadian literature, after a good start in 1860, knew a period when it was at a low ebb, prelude to a recrudescence of activity to be centred this time in Montreal, which had become a great city. So for this last quarter of a century it would be all too easy to point out the deficiencies of the writers and of their too numerous commentators.

Following the example given by Abbé Casgrain of merging patriotism and religion and literature, French-Canadian critics let themselves be sucked into this rut, to get only half-way out of it with Camille Roy (1871-1943) and completely out with Louis Dantin (1866-1945). The state of mind which predominated in the last three decades of the century was hardly favourable to the blossoming of authentic talents, for perhaps in no period in French-Canadian history did religious, political and literary conservatism make itself more felt. These years saw the silent struggle that, from

1878, was to set up Laval University against its branch establishment in Montreal, which became independent only in 1923. The clergy, aware of the immense work of conservation which it had accomplished since the Conquest, was omniscient, effecting the overall policing of public morality and reading. The *Institut Canadien,* founded in 1852 by a group of young intellectuals whose desire it was to spread among the population the love of science and literature, incurred the disapproval of Mgr. Bourget, Bishop of Montreal. This prelate, who at the time of the fiftieth anniversary of his ordination was to sit on the throne which had been prepared for the coronation of Charles X,[52] led a furious campaign against the *Institut* which he found guilty of harbouring a library that contained books on the Index. When Joseph Guibord, a member of the *Institut,* died in 1869, he was refused Christian burial. So began the Guibord Affair which impassioned French-Canadian opinion for a whole generation.

We shall know enough about literary criticism during these lean years if we call up the names of Pamphile Lemay and Edmond Lareau.

Pamphile Lemay (1837-1918) is above all a poet. But like so many French-Canadian writers he succumbed to the temptation of criticism. He had intended to join the priesthood but had to give up this vocation for reasons of health. The last twenty-five years of his life slipped away peacefully in Saint-Jean-Deschaillons. His poetry, which is appealing, is that of a man of God. His criticism is situated half-way between Abbé Casgrain and Crémazie.

Lemay takes up again on his own account the theme dear to Crémazie: let us cultivate our literature according to our ability. But Crémazie had formulated this wise programme in 1869, after an exile of seven years during which he had been able to follow the development of Canadian letters only from afar. In a short speech delivered in 1880, on June twenty-fourth, the occasion of the national holiday of the French Canadians, Lemay could point to legitimate reasons for believing in the future of intellectual achievement in French Canada. While advising modesty, he gave his hearers a glimpse into a brilliant future for a literature which would be the reflection of a country to become powerful among the nations of the West:

Nous sommes relégués dans l'ombre, et jusqu'au jour où nos vallées profondes et nos plaines magnifiques seront peuplées d'une foule intelligente, jusqu'au jour où nous serons devenus un grand peuple, nous devons courber le front et attendre dans la résignation.

Mais si l'on nous ignore à l'étranger, il ne nous est pas permis, à nous, de méconnaître nos gloires et de perdre le souvenir de ceux qui nous ont instruits et charmés par leurs récits ou enthousiasmés par leur ardeur poétique.[53]

We are consigned to the shadows, and until the day when our deep valleys and our magnificent plains have a massive and intelligent population, until the day when we shall have become a great people, we must bow our heads and wait in resignation.

But if we are unknown abroad, we ourselves are not permitted to disregard the glories that are ours nor to forget those who taught us and delighted us by their stories or awakened our enthusiasm with their poetic ardour.[53] [*trans.*]

As to the role of the French-Canadian writer, it is essentially that which had been defined by Abbé Casgrain and which the critic-priests, in what amounts to unanimity, have never stopped proclaiming:

Your mission is easy because you are in communion with the truth. Your words are miraculous seeds which spread everywhere and multiply to infinity. You are the force that destroys and edifies. Speak of God with respect, and the nation, reading what you write, will respect God; do not blush when you state your pious belief and the crowd will believe to the point of martyrdom; teach purity of heart and your pages will have the fragrance of chastity.[54] [*trans.*]

EDMOND LAREAU (1848-1890) published in 1874 the first *Histoire de la littérature canadienne.*[55] Were it only for this reason he would deserve honourable mention among nineteenth-century critics. How can he be blamed for drawing up a list of some hundreds of writers, journalists and lawyers when French-Canadian literature was in its infancy? But a more serious charge may be laid against him. When, abandoning biography and statistics, Lareau tries his hand at criticism, the result is unique in the history of French-Canadian literature. Lareau is very much the inferior of Abbé Casgrain, whom he imitates only in style: the critic seizes "with faltering hand the torch of criticism and prepares to go down into the palace of the intelligence, the vast domain which he has found in every nation . . ."[56] Then what does he discover in this "palace"? He thinks he sees a general law applicable to the whole of literature. Here it is: the literary history of every nation experiences a triple evolution, "the beginnings, the zenith, the decline."[57] As for the great literatures of Europe which have condemned themselves to impotence since they have ceased to be Christian, all hope is not lost: "I believe in the reawakening of the national literatures of Europe,"[58] wrote Edmond Lareau.

Let us be fair. Lareau belongs to that big French-Canadian family whose members have wanted to set everything working to ensure the success of the literary enterprise of the house. Several of them are fuzzy-minded. What of it? At the inception of a literature are even the smallest acts of devotion to be treated with disdain?

NOTES TO CHAPTER THREE

1. Born in Lévis, Fréchette at the age of fifteen went to Ogdensburg in the United States where he worked as a labourer in road-building and maintenance. Back in his own country he pursued his studies at the collège de Saint-Anne and at the collège de Nicolet. He began rhyming when he was nineteen and found in poetry a vocation which appealed to him more than the law. Like all his generation he read Lamartine and Victor Hugo. In turn lawyer, journalist, member of parliament, Fréchette was above everything else a poet.

Poetic works: *Mes loisirs* (1863); *La voix d'un exilé* (1868); *Pêle-mêle* (1877); *Les fleurs boréales* (1881); *La légende d'un peuple* (1888); *Feuilles volantes* (1891); *Epaves poétiques* (1908).

See: William Chapman, *Le lauréat* (Quebec: Léger Brousseau, 1894); Camille Roy, *Nouveaux essais sur la littérature canadienne* (Quebec: Action sociale, 1914), pp. 135-215; Henri d'Arles, *Louis Fréchette* (Toronto: The Ryerson Press, 1924); Marcel Dugas, *Un romantique canadien, Louis Fréchette* (Paris: Editions de la Revue Mondiale, 1934); Jeanne Paul-Crouzet, *Poésie au Canada* (Paris: Didier, 1946), pp. 56-78; George-Alfred Klinck, *Louis Fréchette, prosateur* (Lévis: Le Quotidien limité, 1955).

2. On the conditions in which the prize was awarded and the reactions of the [French] Canadian public, cf. pp. 255-256.

3. Lines like these pertaining to the spoken language are numerous:

> *D'ailleurs, c'est entendu, quand l'homme s'émancipe,*
> *On doit toujours sévir pour sauver le principe.*
> *Redresser les griefs, reconnaître son tort*
> *C'est très bien; mais il faut des exemples d'abord!*

(*La légende d'un peuple* [Paris, 1887], p. 243.)

4. It is to be observed that the verses composing *La légende d'un peuple* include a widely variable number of Alexandrines. This is a sign of weakness rather than strength since Fréchette's verse, rarely memorable, needs all the support of a fixed form to escape mediocrity. This is why *Le frêne des Ursulines,* which is in quatrains, the last of them in six syllables, seems to stand out from most of the other poems.

5. Works: *Essais poétiques* (Quebec: G.-E. Desbarats, 1865); *Les vengeances* (Quebec: Darveau, 1875); *Petits poèmes* (Quebec: Darveau, 1883); *Les gouttelettes* (Montreal: Beauchemin, 1904); *Les épis* (Montreal: Alfred Guay, 1914); *Reflets d'antan* (Montreal: Granger Frères, 1916).

6. *Essais poétiques*, p. 317.

7. *Ibid.*, p. 211.

8. The plot of *Vengeances* recalls, in certain respects, Georges de Boucherville's novel, *Une de perdue, deux de trouvées,* published the year

before in the *Revue canadienne*. Léon, kidnapped by a Huron Indian at the age of three, comes back to his family, the Lozets, some twenty years later. Here he finds Louise, a child whom his parents had taken in soon after his disappearance. Only at the end of the novel, of course, will Louise and Léon be able to love each other in all freedom. Meanwhile Léon will have played a prominent part in the Rebellion of 1837/38; the reader gets an intimate picture of customs and landscapes of Quebec at this time.

9. Camille Roy, *A l'ombre des érables* (Quebec: Imprimerie de l'Action Sociale, 1924), p. 31.

10. *See*: Jeanne Paul-Crouzet, *Poésie au Canada* (Paris: Didier, 1946), pp. 91-106; Clément Marchand, *Choix de poésies de Nérée Beauchemin* (Trois-Rivières: Editions du Bien Public, 1950), pp. 9-29.

11. *See: Anthologie des poètes canadiens,* edited by Jules Fournier, rearrangement and preface by Olivar Asselin (Montreal, 1920). Among the poets who wrote between 1860 and 1900, Alfred Garneau should be mentioned (1830-1904), son of the historian.

12. Compare this stanza with Garneau's verse:

> *L'autre soir, je marchais sur la plage déserte,*
> *Perdue sous l'ombre des bouleaux,*
> *Le regard dans les cieux, et l'oreille ouverte*
> *Aux bruits harmonieux des flots.*

(*Les aiguillons d'une rose*)

13. *Le lauréat* (Quebec: Léger Brousseau, 1894).

14. On Louis Fréchette's tomb (*Les rayons du Nord,* pp. 161-166).

15. He was able to renew this poetic exercise, so popular with French-Canadian poets at the time: that of improvising verses on the seasons or months of the year. Under this pretext Fréchette, among others, had lined up verses devoid of the least originality. But here we have this young man straight away finding variants suited to the genre, doubtless light and superficial, and thus setting up a severe test for a poet unsure of himself:

> *Phtisique, et toussant dans la neige,*
> *L'Hiver s'est éteint lentement.*
> *Le ciel pleurait pour le cortége,*
> *Le ciel pleurait pour le cortège,*
>
> *C'est au Printemps à lui survivre.*
> *Il revient en grand appareil,*
> *Non pas en casquette de givre,*
> *Mais en cravate de soleil.*

(*Premières poésies* [Quebec: Augustin Côté, 1878], p. 7.)

16. Published in Quebec by Augustin Côté, in two volumes. The second volume appeared soon after Ferland's death.

17. Pierre Margry (1818-1894). He published, from manuscripts and documents in the Archives of France, his *Découvertes et établissements des Français dans l'ouest et dans le sud de l'Amérique septentrionale* (Paris: Imprimerie de D. Jouaust, 1876-1886), 6 vol.

18. Charles-Auguste-Marie-Joseph de Forbin-Janson (1745-1844). A noted preacher who made a lively impression on his Canadian listeners.

19. Villemarie, Bibliothèque paroissiale. The *Histoire* has reference to the beginnings of colonization up to 1675.

20. It is to be observed that Faillon, in his preface, makes no mention among his predecessors of Garneau, whose work no doubt seemed to

him hardly worth recommendation. Abbé Ferland had at least felt obliged to make a discreet allusion to the illustrious historian.

21. The American historian, Mason Wade (*The French Canadians, 1760-1945*, Toronto: Macmillan, 1955) has sought to "debunk" the religious history of Canada.

22. Among his historical works may be mentioned *Histoire de la Mère Marie de l'Incarnation* (1864). This first historical work is only a literary curiosity today. Taking the declarations of the famous mystic at face value, he writes, *Les sublimes harmonies des neuf choeurs célestes et leurs rapports avec la divinité lui furent en même temps révélés* (*Oeuvres complètes* [Beauchemin, 1896], Vol. II, p. 129).

A disciple of Bossuet, he was confidently to predict: "Here, as in Europe, and still faster than in Europe, Protestantism is dying; broken up into a great number of sects, it is crumbling into the dust and being lost in rationalism. Soon . . . the empire of Protestantism, hard pressed around the Gulf of Mexico and the St. Lawrence, will split in the middle, and the children of truth, flocking from North and South, will embrace on the banks of the Mississippi, where they will establish for evermore the reign of Catholicism" (*ibid.*, p. 64).

Another biography of the saints, *Histoire de l'Hôtel-Dieu de Québec* (1878), is a companion piece to his first historical work. Among his biographies, that of Francis Parkman (1872) throws some light on the profession of historian as Abbé Casgrain understood it. The list of Abbé Casgrain's writings is to be found in the *Bio-bibliographie* of Charles Rogeau, Ecole de bibliothécaires de l'Université de Montréal, 1940, p. 78.

23. Quebec: Imprimerie L.-J. Demers & Frère, 1891, 2 vol.

24. Casgrain, *Oeuvres complètes* (1891), Vol. II, pp. 22-23.

25. Two French-Canadian historians had prepared the way for Garneau: Joseph-François Perrault (1753-1844), self-taught and commonly known as the "father of public education in [French] Canada," published an *Abrégé de l'Histoire du Canada* (Quebec, 1832-1836), 5 vol.; Michel Bibaud (1782-1857) had published in instalments, beginning in 1825, his *Histoire du Canada,* which appeared in three volumes in 1837, 1844 and 1878.

26. J.-E. Roy, *Histoire de la seigneurie de Lauzon* (Lévis: Merder & Cie, 1897), p. v.

27. The work of Joseph-Edmond Roy is considerable (cf. Gérard Martin, *Bio-bibliographie de Joseph-Edmond Roy.* Preface by Antoine Roy. Ecole de bibliothécaires de l'Université de Montréal, 1945). After founding *La Revue du Notariat,* in 1898, he dedicated to his profession an important *Histoire du Notariat au Canada, depuis la fondation de la colonie jusqu'a nos jours* (Lévis: Revue du Notariat, 1899-1902), 4 vol. A member of the Royal Society in 1891, Joseph-Edmond Roy made two trips to France, in 1903 and 1909, after which he published another research tool: *Rapport sur les Archives de France relatives à l'Histoire du Canada* (Ottawa: C. H. Parmelee, Imprimeur de Sa Très Excellente Majesté le Roi, 1911). Three historians had preceded him in this work without having been able to complete it: Abbé Hospice Verreau (1828-1895), who published a report of his mission in 1874; Joseph Marmette (1844-1895), who succeeded in cataloguing 1,200 volumes in manuscript concerning Canada; and finally Edouard Richard (1844-1904), whose researches were published in 1899, 1904 and 1905 in the *Archives du Canada.*

To the name of Joseph-Edmond Roy must be added those of three researchers, Mgr. Cyprien Tanguay (1819-1902), Philéas Gagnon (1854-

1915) and Narcisse-Eutrope Dionne (1848-1917). Mgr. Tanguay is the author of the *Dictionnaire généalogique des familles canadiennes* (Quebec, 1871-1890), 7 vol. This directory is still useful in spite of the numerous mistakes in it. Philéas Gagnon supplied literature with an *Essai de bibliographie canadienné: Inventaire d'une bibliothèque comprenant imprimés, manuscrits, estamps, etc., relatifs à l'histoire du Canada et des pays adjacents avec des notes bibliographiques* (Quebec: privately printed, 1895-1913), 2 vol. Narcisse-Eutrope Dionne finished Gagnon's *Essai* by publishing his *Inventaire chronologique des livres, brochures, journaux et revues publiés dans la province de Québec de 1764 à 1904* (Mémoires de la Société Royale du Canada, séance de juin 1904), which he followed in 1905 with an *Inventaire chronologique des ouvrages publiés à l'étranger dans diverses langues sur la Nouvelle-France et sur la province de Québec, depuis la découverte du Canada jusqu'à nos jours, 1534-1906* (Mémoires de la Société Royale du Canada, séance de mai 1905, section I).

The ancestor of Canadian bibliographers is Georges-Barthélemi Faribault (1789-1866). His *Catalogue d'ouvrages sur l'Histoire de l'Amérique et en particulier sur celle du Canada, de la Louisiane et autres lieux* (Quebec: W. Cowan, 1837), is the very first work of its kind to appear in French Canada.

28. Montreal: Wilson & Co., 1882-1884, 8 vol.

29. M. Gérard Malchelosse has reverently put together Sulte's scattered and unpublished studies after having dedicated to the historian a biography filled with details on literary life at the end of the nineteenth century. Cf. *Mélanges historiques* (Montreal: Editions Edouard Garand, 1918-1934), 21 vol.; *Cinquante-six ans de vie littéraire* (Montreal: Le Pays Laurentien, 1916).

30. Renée des Ormes, *Célébrités* (Quebec, privately printed, 1927), p. 18.

31. L. Conan, *L'obscure souffrance* (Quebec, 1924), p. 17.

32. Certain writers and critics have considered the space we allotted to Laure Conan in our first edition excessive. This is to forget our set purpose, which is relativistic, as explained in the Foreword; *Angéline de Montbrun* shines only in comparison with the mediocre French-Canadian novels of the nineteenth century.

33. J.-P. Tardivel, *Pour la patrie: roman du XXe siècle* (Montreal: Cadieux & Derome, 1895), p. 3.

34. *Ibid.*, p. 19.

35. The study by Charles ab der Halden, *Nouvelles études de littérature canadienne-française* (Paris: F.-R. de Rudeval, 1907), pp. 49-184, remains the most vivid of all those devoted to Buies. Raymond Douville's biography, *La vie aventureuse d'Arthur Buies* (Montreal: Editions Albert Lévesque, 1933), has a useful bibliography in the appendix. The most recent study is that of Léopold Lamontagne, *Arthur Buies, homme de lettres* (Quebec: Les Presses Universitaires Laval, 1957).

36. Raised by two aunts, Buies attended the collège de Nicolet and the collège de Sainte-Anne-de-la-Pocatière. At sixteen years of age he escaped the tutelage of his teachers and in 1856 went to British New Guinea, where his father was expecting him. The latter, who had left Canada when his son was born, was to have a decisive influence on his future. It was agreed that Arthur would finish his studies at the University of Dublin where, in fact, he went. The attraction of France was too strong for him not to succumb, and soon afterwards the boy was found in Paris. With the audacity of youth he introduced himself first to Guizot, who dismissed him out of hand, then to Montalembert, who was more

polite about sending him away. At the end of his resources, Buies found the support he needed in M. de Puisbusque, known as a friend of Canadians. This man of letters put him in touch with Abbé Hamel, future bursar at Laval University, who was then at the Ecole des Carmes. Thanks to the good offices of this priest, Buies entered the Lycée Saint-Louis on the first of October, 1857, where he remained until July twenty-fifth, 1859. It was when he finished his studies that Buies decided to go to Italy, where he enlisted under the banner of Garibaldi. Military discipline being ill-suited to his temperament, he went back to France as early as 1860. It seems that the liberalization of the regime and the example of an irreverent press, at least in comparison with Canadian newspapers, made a great impression on Buies' inquiring mind. In 1862 he sailed back at last to Canada.

In the following years he made one more trip to France, staying only a short while this time. After an unhappy love affair he also went on an escapade to California. As a result of his collaboration in Father Labelle's work, and his marriage in 1887, his last years are cloaked in sober French-Canadian respectability.

37. Quoted by Raymond Douville, *op. cit.,* p. 104.

38. *Chroniques canadiennes* (Montreal: Eusèbe Senécal & fils, 1884), pp. 15-16.

39. Antoine Labelle (1834-1891), called the "King of the North."

40. Among his works devoted to colonization, *L'Outaouais supérieur* (1889) and *La vallée de la Matapédia* (1895) are worthy of mention.

41. "If the soul were not immortal, man could not live; for despair would overtake him at his first steps in the world. How, in fact, could one stand firm in the face of disappointments, injustice, persecutions, wickedness . . . if the certainty of a happier life did not give strength to human weakness?" [*trans.*] *Chroniques canadiennes,* p. 346.

42. Worse than that, as conservative in literature as he was a rebel politically, Buies had a taste for late-blooming Canadian Romanticism. Sometimes he almost equals the effusions of Abbé Casgrain, as witness this description of the moon over Lake Ontario:

> At last, around eleven o'clock, on the horizon we saw her still-hesitant disc emerging from the vast depths; she was three-quarters hidden by the circle of the surrounding darkness. For a long time we saw her on the crest of the clouds, battling to push back their cohorts, piled up and opaque. Finally she appeared victorious, in a heaven that she had liberated and conquered, and her vast globe, in full splendour, seemed like a great chandelier held in boundless space by an invisible hand. Under the gentle and, as it were, maternal splendour of that star that keeps watch over sleeping nature in the bosom of the night, the heavens rapidly lost their wild appearance and Lake Ontario, inclined to wrath, suddenly grew calm and until dawn permitted the caress of the long silver moon-beam floating on its back. [*trans.*] *Récits de voyage* (Quebec: C. Darveau, 1890), pp. 30-31.

This passage may be compared with the one quoted on page 20.

43. *Le Saguenay et le bassin du lac Saint-Jean* (Quebec: Léger Brousseau, 1896).

44. He had first revealed himself to the public in *De Québec à Mexico* (Montreal: Duvernay Frères et Dansereau, 1874). Fortunately he decided to recast and shorten this work and in 1881 published *Deux ans au Mexique* (Quebec: C: Darveau).

45. *Deux ans au Mexique,* p. 219.

46. *Ibid.,* pp. 179-180.

47. *Contes vrais* (Quebec: Le Soleil, 1899), pp. 65-66.

48. The true picture of the prose writer, as reflected in *Originaux et détraqués* and *La Noël au Canada* was completed fortunately by *Mémoires intimes* (Montreal: Fides, 1961). Most of the *Mémoires* had appeared in *Le Monde illustré* of Montreal in 1900.

George A. Klinck, who arranged the text for the *Collection du Nénuphar,* is right in observing in his preliminary remarks that Fréchette reveals here his kindliness and simplicity. These pages, the most modest ever written by Fréchette, may be likened in their charm to Robert de Roquebrune's very similar recreation of the past, *Testament de mon enfance.*

49. In 1946 the librairie Beauchemin published a collection, *Contes d'autrefois,* in which, as well as the best-known stories of Fréchette, there are reprints of stories by Paul Stevens (1830-1882) and the very well-known *Chasse-galerie* of Honoré Beaugrand (1849-1906).

50. Cf. Adrien Thério, *Jules Fournier* (Montreal: Fides, 1954).

51. Pp. 18-19.

52. Mason Wade, *The French Canadians* (Toronto: Macmillan, 1955), p. 357.

53. H.-J. Chouinard, *La fête nationale des Canadiens-français célébrée à Québec en 1880* (Quebec: A. Côté & Cie, 1881), p. 376.

54. *Ibid.,* p. 383.

55. *Histoire de la littérature canadienne* (Montreal: John Lovell, 1874).

56. *Ibid.,* p. 18.

57. *Ibid.,* p. 10.

58. *Ibid.,* p. 16.

CHAPTER IV

THE MODERN PERIOD
(1900-1939)
POETRY

Emile Nelligan (1879-1941)

Poetry, earliest flowering of the literary genres, found its first great poet in Emile Nelligan. His work, begun in 1896, when he was only seventeen, and ended in 1899, is extraordinary.[1] In the history of French-Canadian literature very few poets can be compared with him. For the spontaneity and quality of his imagery he remains unequalled.

The rapid spread of his reputation as a poet and the quality of the criticism which ensured for his name a place apart among French-Canadian poets, are not isolated phenomena having little relation to Nelligan's poetical work. For not only did Nelligan at one stroke modernize French-Canadian literature, which had been lagging at least a generation behind French and European taste, but, to comment on his poetry and explain it, he found at the same time that most eclectic of Canadian critics, and consequently the most receptive to the new aesthetic trend—Louis Dantin. Better still, the valiant efforts of Quesnel and Bibaud, continued more successfully by the poets of the Garneau period, found their supreme justification at last in the birth of a literate public. This public was still limited, certainly, but its existence would henceforth permit the writer or poet to escape isolation.

Of mixed ancestry, like Arthur Buies, Nelligan soon recognized those contradictory attractions to which the adolescent sensibility is exposed. Besides this, aware of the superiority conferred on him by his multiple vision of the world, little by little he withdrew into his dreams, as much through contempt of the Philistines as through necessity. At a time when Fréchette was still writing poems inspired by Victor Hugo and Pamphile Lemay was writing Parnassian verse without being aware of it, here we have this school-boy discovering poets who reveal to him secrets that are *his* secrets: first Baudelaire, then Verlaine, Catulle Mendès, Georges Rodenbach. Melancholy by nature, Nelligan will always remain so, and will not have to go to the Parnassians and the Symbolists for subjects, although at the beginning he borrows from Parnassus.[2] The marmoreal perfection of Parnassian verse echoed some intimate need of this soul tortured by an ideal and remains one of the characteristic features of its brief poetic flight. As early as June of 1897 Nelligan gave this proof of his virtuosity:

MOINES EN DEFILADE

Ils défilent le long des corridors antiques,
Tête basse, égrenant d'énormes chapelets;
Et le soir qui s'en vient, du sang de ses reflets
Empourpre la splendeur des dalles monastiques.

L'heure a versé déjà ses flammes extatiques
Au fond de leurs grands coeurs où bouillent les secrets
De leur dégoût humain, de leurs mornes regrets,
Et du frisson dompté des chairs cénobitiques.

Ils marchent dans la nuit et rien ne les émeut,
Pas même l'effrayante, horrible ombre du feu
Qui les suit sur le mur jusqu'au seuil des chapelles,

Pas même les appels de l'infernal esprit,
Suprême Tentateur des passions rebelles
De ces silencieux Spectres de Jésus-Christ.[3]

What an astounding sonnet for a seventeen-year-old poet! The imagery is not yet the visual creation of the poet that he will become in two years' time; a few lines too commonplace are the price of his inexperience. But the sharpness of the photographic image, the sensuous suggestiveness of the rhythm are undeniable. If the borrowings are obvious, so too is the originality.

A few months before the publication of this poem Nelligan, who was never very socially inclined, succumbed to the entreaties of a young friend and made his appearance in a literary club, known since that time as the *Ecole littéraire de Montréal.*[4] From 1897 this society of young French Canadians brought together future poets animated by the same feelings as those which had inspired the founders of the *Institut Canadien* forty years earlier. Until the Guibord Affair the *Institut* had played an important part in the intellectual life of French Canada. The rapid success which the *Ecole* enjoyed is partly explained by the fact that the new generation had to find a cultural home to take its place. The *Ecole littéraire de Montréal* was soon to attract the most diverse talents and to be identified with the literary movement of the first part of the twentieth century.[5]

In 1897 the *Ecole* was still only a small literary group. The most assiduous of its members, Jean Charbonneau, Albert Ferland, Germain Beaulieu, Arthur de Bussières, Edouard-Zotique Massicotte, all poets, made a select audience for Nelligan, their junior by several years. Nelligan read his poems at gatherings of the *Ecole* and in 1898 and 1899 took part in public meetings held at the *château de Ramezay.* It was at the meeting on the twenty-sixth of May, 1899, that Nelligan knew a brief moment of glory. After reading *La romance du vin* he achieved a personal success matching that of the poem, which has remained famous; for those who heard it that evening, it must have seemed like a miracle. He was escorted in triumph by the crowd right to his door. This public homage rendered to poetry was proof that the French-Canadian people, a people of storekeepers if you like, could become enthusiastic about literature and honour its writers. Three months later, his strength undermined by gloomy apprehensions, walking "on tiptoe" in his "dark youth" (*sa jeunesse noire*), Nelligan at last fell victim to the madness of which he seemed to have had a foreboding.

Nelligan's poetic work, left in abeyance in mid-evolution, is of necessity only a suspicion of what it might have been. Dead to poetry at the age of nineteen, Nelligan had not yet had time to assimilate perfectly the poets who were his delight as a student. He is all the more remarkable since an original inspiration emerges from the borrowings and reminiscences of which his poetry is woven.

A Romantic in feeling, a Parnassian in form, a Symbolist in vocabulary, Nelligan in his best moments effects a fusion of these elements through his gift of imagery. His thought may be too thin, even empty at times, his prosody borrowed, his epithets often plucked from poets he revered—what difference does it make? He looks around him with keen and seeing eye and the image springs forth:

> *Et les rayons, ainsi que de pourpres épées,*
> *Percent le coeur du jour qui se meurt parfumé.*

As if by instinct he finds the right tone, the ideal cadence to make the setting for the delicate impressions of his *Rêve de Watteau,* he who has no knowledge of painting except through an intuitive vision:

> *Puis, las, nous nous couchions, frissonnants jusqu'aux moelles,*
> *Et parfois, radieux, dans nos palais de foin,*
> *Nous déjeunions d'aurore et nous soupions d'étoiles.*

With the most astonishing facility Nelligan was able at the very beginning to master verse technique, whereas all the French-

Canadian poets before him had always had a hard struggle with form. Certain poems of his are fireworks in which he merely exercises his virtuosity. When there is a meeting of the anguish within him and the music of his verse, the effect can be startling, like this reaction as he looks on the *Christ en croix*:

> *Et j'entendais en moi des marteaux convulsifs*
> *Renfoncer les clous noirs des intimes Calvaires!*

Nelligan was to exercise a lasting influence on French-Canadian poetry. Before him there had been hardly any variation in the choice of subjects. The history of French Canada, the joys of the home or of life in the fields, vague sadness in the style of René, these were about the only themes that a French-Canadian poet had been able to employ with confidence. Now Nelligan scorned the so-called Canadian subjects and found his inspiration in Symbolism. By the example of his genius he had proved that the authentic poet seeks his subjects according to rules known to himself alone and that these subjects attain value only through the magic of form. He was to be reproached for not having found his inspiration in Canada yet basically Nelligan is the most Canadian of poets.

Charles Gill (1871-1918)

In 1903 when *Emile Nelligan et son oeuvre* was published by Louis Dantin, the poets of the *Ecole littéraire* recognized the rare quality of that poetry. Paradoxically they were incapable of profiting from it. Doubtless their idea of poetry was too narrow for them to understand that in stubbornly continuing to write Romantic verse they would not be rid of anachronistic imitations. They were more conscious of the musical quality of Nelligan's verse and his precocious technique than of the lesson of renewal that lay in his Symbolist vocabulary and in his subjects.

One of the traditionalist poets was Charles Gill. In his youth Gill had made the trip to Paris and thought at first of devoting himself entirely to painting. A pupil of Gérome, he was in touch with the poets also and must have known Verlaine. He never seems to have become an enthusiast of the new literary schools since for his entire life he pledged his exclusive admiration to Lamartine. For him *Jocelyn* was the height of poetic genius. So it is not surprising that Gill, on his return to Canada, wrote verse which bore much closer resemblance to the academic ideas of his teacher of painting than to Symbolist innovations. Plastic perfection seeming to him the supreme ideal, in 1909 he decided to create a kind of Canadian epic in Alexandrines. In this canvas the Saint Lawrence was to have a part similar to that of the Mississippi in Fréchette's *La legende d'un peuple.* Never completed, *Le Cap Eternité* was published in 1919 after Gill's death.[6]

In his lifetime Gill had enjoyed the greatest prestige among French-Canadian poets and was reputed to be working at an extraordinary poem, from which he would read extracts from time to time to his intimate friends. This relative renown has survived the publication of *Le Cap Eternité.* It is doubtful whether a few more thousands of Alexandrines would have added much to the already great number which make up the more or less legendary poem. But it must be admitted that among the scattered fragments of this unfinished poem there flows an epic breath of real grandeur which, if sustained, would have made of Gill a poet very much the superior of Fréchette.

> *Quand sur le sol Laurentien seront passés*
> *Des jours dont le calcul nous entraîne au vertige;*
> *Sur les sables mouvants quand seront effacés*
>
> *Notre éphémère empreinte et nos derniers vestiges;*
> *Quand nous aurons été par d'autres remplacés,*
> *Et quand à leur déclin, le vent des cimetières*
> *Aura sur d'autres morts roulé d'autres poussières;*
> *Plus loin dans l'avenir, peuples ensevelis,*
> *Quand le linceul du temps vous aura dans ses plis;*
>
> *Après votre néant, quand d'autres millénaires*
> *Sur d'autres vanités tendront d'autres oublis,*
> *Le Cap sera debout sur les eaux solitaires,*
> *Debout sur les débris des nations altières;*
> *Le Cap Eternité dressé sur l'Infini*
> *Sera debout dans son armure de granit.*

Albert Lozeau (1878-1924)

The superior of most poets of his generation, Lozeau,[7] a paraplegic at eighteen, had to endure for his whole lifetime an infirmity which haunts even present day opinion of his work; the romantic picture of an unspeakable affliction as a wellspring of art has become permanently fixed to his name. In *Poésies complètes* is there anything more than an uninterrupted elegy? Reading the poems written at love's dictation, which hold a considerable if forgotten place in his work, one has to conclude that the incomplete notion that criticism has too often left of Lozeau's life has to a certain extent hurt his reputation. Taking into account what French-Canadian poetry was at the beginning of the century, Lozeau, while not truly original, did achieve, in a poem like *Les mots,* an extremely rare freshness and sincerity.

> *Puisque je t'aimerai toujours, malgré le temps,*
> *A quoi bon te le dire en des mots inconstants,*
> *Des mots fervents hier que demain rend frivoles?*
> *Puisque change le sens intime des paroles*
> *Selon qu'un jour est né, selon qu'un jour est mort,*
> *A quoi sert de lier notre amour à leur sort?*
> *Les mots autrefois dits jamais ne se répètent*
> *Sans trahir quelque peu des âmes qu'ils reflètent;*
> *Comme des astres vieux, ils se sont refroidis,*
> *Eux qui brûlaient au bord des lèvres de jadis.*
> *Leur forme ancienne s'est pour toujours effacée*
> *Et l'âme qui vibrait en elle a fui, blessée.*
>
> (*L'âme solitaire*)

Nevertheless—and in this lies the explanation of the hallowed image—because Lozeau does not avoid the conventional in his love poems, even when with exemplary restraint he gives expression to the earthly vision he sees from his window, it is to these last pages, inspired by Canadian nature, that his name will always be linked:

> *Par ces longs soirs d'hiver où, fatigués des livres,*
> *Les yeux suivent l'effet sur la vitre des givres*
> *Dessinant d'un pinceau lent et mystérieux,*
> *Sous l'impulsion des grands vents furieux,*
> *Des jardins, des forêts blanches et toujours calmes,*
> *De fantastiques fleurs et de bizarres palmes,—*
> *Ces soirs-là, comparant l'ombre qui rôde en lui*
> *A la blanche splendeur des choses de la nuit,*
> *Le poète isolé du monde, dans sa chambre,*
> *Rêve à la grande paix des tombes de décembre*
> *Et du linceul d'hermine amoncelé sans bruit*
> *Qui, sous le ciel empli de clair de lune, luit.*[8]

Among the poets whose names appear in the *Soirées du château de Ramezay* (1900) and the *Soirées de l'Ecole littéraire de Montréal* (1925), should be mentioned:

GONZALVE DESAULNIERS (1863-1934): Clever practitioner of the Alexandrine, Desaulniers has remained spellbound in Parnassus. *La chevrette,* which he published in *Les soirées du château de Ramezay,* could have been inserted in *Les bois qui chantent* which appeared at the end of his career in 1930. His vocabulary includes a good bit of tinsel in the manner of Lamartine's Romanticism.

Works: *Soirées du château de Ramezay,* pp. 161-180; *Pour la France,* 1918; *Les bois qui chantent,* 1930.

ALBERT FERLAND (1872-1943): Ferland's profession of poetic faith would have overjoyed Abbé Casgrain: "Create an art that is simple and proud, worthy of an upright heart." ("La Muse te veut seul," *Les Soirées de l'Ecole littéraire de Montréal*). Ferland, whose beginnings in poetry were extremely modest, improved his technique without, however, attaining Desaulnier's mastery or showing himself the equal of Pamphile Lemay, to whom he was close in inspiration.

Works: *Mélodies poétiques,* 1893; *Femmes rêvées,* 1899; *Soirées du château de Ramezay,* pp. 275-285; *Le Canada chanté* (4 vol.): *Les horizons,* 1908; *Le terroir,* 1909; *L'âme des bois,* 1909; *La fête du Christ à Ville-Marie,* 1910; *Montréal ma ville natale,* 1946.

LUCIEN RAINIER (1877-1956): Attracted to poetry at the same age as Nelligan, Rainier, one of the first to be active in the *Ecole littéraire,* bears a slight resemblance to the poet of *Romance du vin* in the easy flow of his verse. His work is scattered here and there in Canadian newspapers and reviews. He published only one collection, in 1931, *Avec ma vie.* Bolder than the two poets above, Rainier obtained his best effects by sympathetic harmony:

> *L'heure sombre se traîne alanguissante et lente*
> *Qui s'envolait jadis en joyeux instants courts;*
>
> (*Saisons mystiques*)

Uneven as a poet, Rainier in his best moments rises above most of the poets in touch with the *Ecole littéraire. See*: Louis Dantin, *Poètes de l'Amérique française* (Montreal: Editions Albert Lévesque, 1934), pp. 73-85.

JEAN CHARBONNEAU (1875-1960): Founder, inspiration and historian of the *Ecole littéraire,* Jean Charbonneau in contrast to Nelligan felt little attraction to the new poetry. He published an indictment of Symbolism with a few very ordinary verses in *Soirées du château de Ramezay.* Like most poets of his generation Charbonneau remained a Romantic, aspiring to Parnassian perfection. Although his first collection, *Les blessures,* published in 1912 (Paris: Lemerre), was an improvement compared with his first poetic efforts, his laboured verse did not succeed in hiding the unshakably commonplace quality of those *blessures* which, half a century earlier, would have appeared out of fashion. When *Sur la borne pensive* was published in 1952, it marked the close of a long poetic career very worthy of respect.

Works: *Les blessures* (Paris: Lemerre, 1912); *Des influences françaises au Canada* (Beauchemin, 1916); *Les prédestinés* (Beauchemin, 1923); *La flamme ardente* (Beauchemin, 1925); *L'ombre dans le miroir* (privately printed); *L'Ecole littéraire de Montréal* (Editions Albert Lévesque, 1935); *Sur la borne pensive* (Paris: Lemerre, 1952).

LOUIS-JOSEPH DOUCET (1874-1959): Having attended school hardly at all before the age of twenty, Doucet spent his youth in Lanoraie with his parents, *habitants,* who were in very poor circumstances. And he always kept the forever-young approach to things, typical of people who have known life on the farm. He had a special admiration for Villon, from whom he borrowed the eight- or ten-line ballad form. Throughout Doucet's copious and patchy work one happens at times on imagery of exquisite subtlety:

> *La cigale chantait l'heure de la moissan,*
> *Et les bons engerbeurs rassemblaient les javelles;*
> *Parafant leur énigme au bord de l'horizon,*
> *Au rêve du couchant passaient des hirondelles.*

(La jonchée nouvelle, 1910)

Works: *La chanson du passant* (Montreal: Librairie nationale Hébert, Ferland & Cie, 1908); *Les palais d'argile* (Quebec: privately printed, 1916); *Feuilles de chênes et nénufars* (Montreal: Maison J. G. Yon, 1926).

Paul Morin (b. 1889)

The spell cast by France made an indelible mark on the poet Paul Morin. From 1763 many a writer has dreamed of leaving the banks of the Saint Lawrence to go and breathe the air of the Ile-de-France; and nearly all who have come back have been able to calculate how dangerous to their talent this greatly desired transmigration of the soul had been. For the soul of the French Canadian is an uneasy one divided between feeling for two things: its origins and the new world. The balance he instinctively seeks could not be Mediterranean. A stay in France can consolidate the personality of the writer if only in permitting him to take a dip into French. Let that stay be prolonged, however, and the inevitable tension between the two poles of his being tends to dissolve. There have to be some exceptions to this rule, however, in which we have a writer finding himself in France instead of losing himself there. Paul Morin is one of those.

A great admirer of the comtesse de Noailles, whose salon he frequented, Morin, who had felt cramped for room in his native land, opened up and became himself in the broader environment of France and Europe. This self-discovery is clearly apparent in his first collection of poems, *Le paon d'émail.* In Versailles Morin did more than bring the period of Marie-Antoinette back to life; he rediscovered a French soul:

> *Mon coeur français et moi nous vîmes ce matin*
> *Le paisible hameau parfumé de fougère*
> *Où Marie-Antoinette en paniers de satin*
> *Rêva d'être bergère.*[9]

The appearance in 1912 of *Paon d'émail* and in 1922 of *Poèmes de cendre et d'or* marks an important stage in French-Canadian letters. Never had such delicately polished poetry been written by a French Canadian. And whatever critics have thought of it, foreign as this first collection may be to French Canada fundamentally, it is nevertheless more Canadian than it appears at first sight.

In the French-Canadian writer the tension to which we have just alluded expresses itself in the style. If the essential problem of the written language for every writer is to reduce as much as possible the distance between the thought and the artistic form in which it takes final shape, how much more must this problem preoccupy the French-Canadian writer who spends his whole life waging a silent war against the encroachments of the English language! It can happen—and the history of French-Canadian letters furnishes some examples—that the writer surmounts this obstacle and manages to achieve a perfect facility in expressing himself. But this is not always the solution of the problem because, having been too long prisoner of a language either incorrect or simply lacking precision, the writer becomes the slave of his own facility. Morin has not escaped this defect, and it is in this respect that *Le paon d'émail* remains, in spite of everything, a French-Canadian work.

With the exception of Nelligan no Canadian poet had succeeded to such a degree in freeing himself from the technical difficulties of poetry. The banal rhymes, the halting and commonplace verse of his predecessors have disappeared. Because he finds himself at last in France, because he is free to wander over Greece, Turkey, North Africa, the poet sings his liberation. Morin borrows his truth as he does the form of his poetry from Leconte de Lisle and from Heredia, and a portion of his vocabulary from the comtesse de Noailles:

> *Il tient de la nature innombrable et subtile*
> *Le secret de la belle impassibilité.*[10]

If there was nothing of the innovator in him at least he succeeded in creating a work of his own when he wanted to convey rapture at the sight of landscapes that supplied the needs of his inner life. His best indeed are his travel poems. *Eternel pèlerin du mystère*, Morin revealed himself completely in *La rose au jardin smyrniote:*[11]

> *O profonde, amoureuse paix orientale*
> *Des cyprès ombrageant un sépulcre exigu,*
> *Vous me garderez mieux que la terre natale*
> *Sous l'érable neigeux et le sapin aigu!*

With love of the Mediterranean countries is mingled the memory of France:

> *Par le rappel toujours présent des jours meilleurs*
> *Je veux, dans un jardin que le croissant nuance,*
> *Qu'émblouissante et noble entre toutes les fleurs*
> *S'effeuille sur ma tombe une rose de France.*

But his facility often betrays him, and the poems in which artifice takes the place of authentic feeling are numerous in the two collections. Thus in *Le prix*[12] the poet lines up words like *Euclée, Thryallis, Eglé, Astra, Myrrhine, Gnathénion, Agallis, Philétas, Synoris, Callisto, Lampas, Phrynée,* a cheap way of achieving the *rime rare.* Elsewhere he does not hesitate at piffle of this kind: *Des paons perchés sur chaque pan,* or again, *La palme est du cyprès si près.* Finally, he did not avoid the tamest banality as he could write, *Son coeur toujours tranquille est pur comme le ciel.*

These weaknesses notwithstanding, Morin remains one of the greatest poets of French Canada.[13] Besides, like Nelligan, but in a different way, he contributed to the liberation of French-Canadian literature. Morin's French and European preferences were bound to bring him sharp reproach in Canada—an understandable reaction in a new country but one which has nothing to do with aesthetics. Stendhal much preferred Italy to his own country: Goethe could not hide the contempt which certain traits in the German nation aroused in him. Great cultures tolerate these defections which are more apparent than real. To the achievements of

Paul Morin must be added that of having proved that the French-Canadian literary tradition was not plotted in advance and that it is for each writer to enrich it by his personal statement.

Lionel Léveillé (1875-1955)

French-Canadian literature lacked a poet capable of evoking the various aspects of French Canada in an accent less serious than that which for half a century had been characteristic not only of poetry but of the whole literary output. Lionel Léveillé[14] was the first to succeed in making light verse without being commonplace or coarse. In his first collection, *Les chemins de l'âme,* he had tried his hand at the kind of thing usually done by the French-Canadian poet: loves unfulfilled (though chaste), the sweet joys of rural life, empty effusions of all kinds. While not original, this poetry held promise in the economy of its execution. Looking for subjects more suited to the nimble octosyllabic line he preferred, Léveillé succeeded finally in creating with *La claire fontaine,* a minor work of art which was very much his own. He was not to abandon, however, the romantic Canadian themes which he treated with increasing skill; but he proved to be truly original only when he forgot his sorrows and pictured the familiar things of his childhood: *la guignolée* on New Year's Day, the experienced smokers of his grandfather's time. This is poetry that kindles joy and longing and, without making Léveillé a great poet, ensures him a place apart in French-Canadian literature. Thanks to a few unpretentious but artistically turned poems, he successfully took up again a theme dear to Crémazie:

> *Il aurait fait du bruit en France*
> *Si l'opiniâtre Providence*
> *—Elle aurait pu tout aussi bien—*
> *Avait daigné l'y faire naître,*
> *Mais il avait la guigne d'être*
> *Un Canayen.*[15]

René Chopin (1885-1953)

Two collections of poems, *Le coeur en exil* (Paris: Crès, 1913) and *Dominantes* (1933), have won their author the esteem of French-Canadian criticism. Grandson of a former captain in the *Grande Armée,* who had left France following the events of 1848,

René Chopin had been brought up to have a great respect for the French language which his father, Jules Chopin (born in Doubs), no doubt believed to be threatened in Canada. His poetry gives the impression of great concern for construction and grammatical correctness. With less skill than Paul Morin, Chopin is superior to most poets of his generation. Poems written in his maturity, in which the themes are shared between pure lyricism and Canadian landscape, are the work of an accomplished poet:

OFFRANDE PROPITIATOIRE

Cygnes effarouchés du chaste hiver qui fond,
Votre vol s'éparpille et déserte ma grève;
Je sens mon coeur s'ouvrir comme une digue crève
Et se répandre ainsi que les grands fleuves font.

Avec mes pleurs votre eau secrète se confond,
O sources dans mon âme, ô printanière sève,
Philtre voluptueux de souffrance et de rêve
Qui jaillit et me verse un bonheur trop profond!

Colombe de la Neige à l'aile pure et blanche
Pour que ma soif d'aimer cette saison j'étanche,
Entre mes doigts émus et d'un geste pieux

Je tordrai ton cou frêle, ô victime immolée,
Et ta chair hiémale et ta plume souillée
Rougiront sur l'autel en offrande à mes dieux.[16]

Louis Dantin (1875-1945)

It is always a great temptation for the critic, of necessity led to a continual rethinking of the bases of art, to be his own alchemist instead of making use of others. Louis Dantin, who exerted a veritable magistracy as a critic, was a mediocre novelist and an excellent poet.

Le coffret de Crusoé (Montreal: Lévesque, 1932) as well as *Chanson javanaise, Chanson citadine* and *Chanson intellectuelle,* published separately between 1930 and 1932, mark one of the high spots in French-Canadian lyric poetry. One must wait for Saint-Denys Garneau to hear again accents that are so personal. The quatrains of *Ame-univers,* skilfully symmetrical, successfully build up to the last avowal:

En mon âme, comme aux enfers,
Vont, rivés, aux squelettes caves,
Des souillures qui sont des fers
Et des remords qui sont des laves.

Canadian poetry was as yet unacquainted with deliberate preciosity as a means of expression. Dantin provides a charming sample in his *Billet doux du carabin*:

> *Jusqu'à ce soir, blonde Lucie,*
> *Je croyais m'être sans retour,*
> *Par miracle d'antisepsie,*
> *Immunisé du mal d'amour.*
>
> *Je croyais, dans mon coeur frigide*
> *Ainsi qu'un marbre d'hôtel-dieu*
> *N'offrir au bacille morbide*
> *Qu'un antipathique milieu.*
>
> *J'en étais sûr, nulle cellule*
> *En moi qui ne fût à l'abri*
> *Du doux symptôme qui pullule*
> *Dans un plasma moins aguerri.*
>
> *Grâce à la vertu souveraine*
> *Des prompts sérums que nous créons,*
> *J'avais mis hors de mon domaine*
> *Les redoubtables vibrions.*
>
> *Hélas! illusion risible!*
> *Sous ton oeil où l'ardeur se peint*
> *Je me revois plus susceptible*
> *Qu'un cochon-d'inde ou qu'un lapin.*
>
> *Devant toi, chère créature,*
> *Mon sang, que sa flamme a trahi,*
> *N'est plus qu'un bouillon de culture*
> *Par mille fièvres envahi.*
>
> *Et ma lèvre, au repli sonore*
> *De ton baiser contagieux,*
> *Sent un fourmillement éclore*
> *De microbes délicieux.*

The poems which make up *Le coffret de Crusoé* are extremely varied, as much in essential thought as in form. Their composition, which was spread over several years, would seem to indicate that Dantin never found the form he was looking for as a setting for his thought. Several of these poems are obviously exercises. Those by means of which he wanted to exorcise the sadness of his loneliness or simply to avow his innermost feelings, reveal the structural weaknesses which veil the poet's profound anguish. When Dantin is most sincere himself, his poetry—and *Chanson javanaise* is one of the best examples—is full of exasperating syncopation, aphaeresis and apocope, which come close to reflecting the language of the ordinary uneducated people, but fall short. This mannerism is betrayed in the beginning by the care with which he respects the syllable count to the detriment of linguistic verisimilitude. What Dantin lacked, to be a great poet, was not knowledge nor fine feeling but simply audacity. It was psychologically impossible for him, the critic considered by the best poets of the era to be the court of last appeal, to offer an example of the *avant-garde* in poetry. Dantin was a severe judge of the new poetry in France: "In five hundred years people will talk about Vigny, Hugo and perhaps Henri de Regnier, but who will remember Gustave Kahn and Jean Cocteau?"[17]

Louis Dantin, because of the relative breadth of his conception of criticism and the variety and high quality of his poetry, is one of the great names of French-Canadian literature in the twentieth century. Peoples small in number nearly always claim tribute of their children, from which obligations only the highly creative minds can free themselves. If Dantin did not escape the general rule, by his example he did enlarge the idea of French-Canadian culture.

Robert Choquette (b.1905)

In *A travers les vents* (1925), Robert Choquette openly attacked rhymesters who give themselves up to the game of *rimes rares*. The French-Canadian people, the poet explains in his foreword, must take its inspiration, because it is young, from the vast nature around it and sing of its hopes in virile terms. Only a nation like France, with a literary history of several centuries, may indulge in a little decadent poetry. Adolescent temperaments require more substantial nourishment. In an explosion of energy, Choquette cries aloud his desire to "live and create."

> *Oh! je voudrais saisir le nuage qui passe,*
> *Pour pétrir de mes mains, dans ce morceau d'espace,*
> *Un rêve passager, humain, et tel pourtant*
> *Qu'il éterniserait ce fugitif instant!*[18]

The poet's abilities did not justify this hope. This first collection, in spite of its noble inspiration, bears the indisputable mark of the commonplace. The original images are rare: *Arrondir la souffrance ainsi qu'une margelle autour de sa pensée intime.* On the other hand, the clichés of the Romantic school (*Le coeur grandit dans la douleur*), the whole legacy of nineteenth-century Canadian poetry, are here in this first work. Nevertheless, the last poem, *Le chant de l'aigle-rouge*, in its twenty-two ten-line verses, reveals a certain power and is a portent of the great poem to appear six years later, in 1931.

Choquette's *Metropolitan Museum* revealed one of the strongest poetic talents that Canada had produced. Throughout his work Nelligan had indeed sown dazzling images. Paul Morin had just brought French-Canadian poetry to a remarkable point of formal perfection. But neither of these two poets had been able to measure up to his own lofty inspiration for any length of time. He is less essentially a poet than Nelligan, less polished than Morin. But while these two are soon out of breath, Choquette succeeds in keeping *Metropolitan Museum* on a high plane for four hundred lines.

One day after a walk through the labyrinths of the famous New York museum, it pleased Choquette to imagine that he could see that melancholy succession of civilizations dead and gone. When he came out of the museum the unique spectacle of gigantic buildings rising to heaven like symbols, standing like revelations of a living world, suggested the subject of his poem. In truth Choquette had only found one of the eternal themes that present themselves to the disillusioned spirit of mankind. That he made a work of art out of it simply underlines more firmly the successful formula to which his skill enabled him to put his signature. One after another are conjured up historic times, Egyptian, Chaldean, Assyrian, Greek, Roman and Christian civilizations. The timid gait of *A travers les vents* gives place here to a versification which, without being bold, satisfies the poet's needs. Between the Alexandrines, whose ample measure is suitable for this synthesis, free verse is frequently inserted. The quality of the thought or of the feeling will determine the number of syllables. This first part of the poem could degenerate into a tedious enumeration of eras gone by; if this danger is not completely avoided, the variety of the rhythms at least keeps the impression from being sustained.

Following the centuries that have passed we have the present and it is when Choquette allows himself to be taken captive by the regenerative forces of America that he carries us along—exuberance suiting him better than the purely cerebral—in an irresistible movement of youth:

> *Et de sentir autour de moi*
> *Se dérouler la Ville Folle*
> *Je ne sais quel aveugle émoi*
> *Quelle fièvre au-delà des paroles*
> *Multipliaient mon coeur en milliers de rayons!*
>
> . . .
>
> *La ville était en moi comme j'étais en elle!*
> *Essor de blocs! élans d'étages! tourbillons*
> *De muraille qui font chavirer la prunelle!*

But this young American is not only an American; he is old by virtue of the faith of his forefathers. And doubtless that is why this hymn to American civilization has to end on a serious note. Of what use will these conquests be without those which are obtained by regenerations of the spirit?

In *Les Poésies nouvelles* (1933) we come to a waiting period. This is because Choquette was beginning to ponder a work of epic proportions on which he was to labour for eighteen years.[19]

Alfred Desrochers (b. 1901)

If it is true that Desrochers unveiled everything in his first two collections, in contrast with Choquette who had grown since his first poetic endeavour, Desrocher's first work placed him very high among Canadian poets. No one has responded better than he to the earthy appeal of the American continent. His strength lay in his close communion with the Quebec soil. The rough spots in his verse, unfortunately, are seldom occasioned by the impetuous course of virile evocations as in *L'hymne au vent du nord*. Because Desrochers had chosen a conventional mould for his poetry, the too-conspicuous imperfections of his technique were a real weakness; without taking from him his due place among French-Canadian poets of the twentieth century, they considerably reduce the positive value of his work.

L'OFFRANDE AUX VIERGES FOLLES

O Vierges folles, vous que maudit l'Evangile,
Soeurs de mon âme, qui voulant trop tôt danser,
Dans un amusement stérile, avez laissé
L'huile se consumer dans la lampe d'argile;

Qui, souples, et sachant tout avenir fragile,
Entrelaçant vos pas d'un rythme cadencé,
Sans souci du moment fugace dépensé,
Avez au lendemain préféré la vigile:

En gage fraternal, je vous offre ces vers,
Où j'ai mis mon passé d'attente et de revers,
Dont mourut sans plaisir ma jeunesse trop sage,

Afin que dans nos ans de désirs, le regret
D'un qui n'a su goûter ce que l'instant offrait,
De par-delà les siècles morts vous rende hommage![20]

BLANCHE LAMONTAGNE-BEAUREGARD (1889-1960): The best-known of French-Canadian women poets prior to World War I very early made a profession of singing the virtues of the Canadian soil and of *la campagne de chez nous*. She was born on the borderland of the

Gaspé and, starting with *Visions gaspésiennes* (1913), proclaimed the attractions of a region more or less neglected by the poets. Her work, very sincere, touching at times, is drenched in the froth of sentimental language. Louis Dantin in *Poètes de l'Amérique française* wrote some of his best pages to save *La vieille maison* and the kind of art practised by Blanche Lamontagne from too-severe criticism. In doing this he raised a question which has a close bearing on the problem of marginal literatures and finds two solutions, according to whichever may be the critic's point of view.

Are writers to be judged positively or relatively? In other words, are French-Canadian writers to be compared with the best writers of France, or still further, with the men of genius in world literature? Or are they to be placed solely in their own context? The first solution would most frequently reduce criticism to silence. The second would at least partially relieve it of its function. To be fair let us say then that Blanche Lamontagne, like nearly all the poets of her generation, expressed herself in a language belonging to too many nineteenth-century French poets to make it possible for the reader to react favourably to epithets and rhymes worn to a frazzle. This judgment would be incomplete and unjust if it were not added that, in the framework of French-Canadian poetry, this kind of repetition has not jarred as it would have in France and has not kept many French-Canadian readers from an intimate appreciation of the poetic feeling in Blanche Lamontagne's vision of the Gaspé. This feeling does exist, undeniably, and means that Blanche Lamontagne has a very honourable place among the poets of the first half of the twentieth century.

Works: *Visions gaspésiennes* (privately printed, 1913); *Par nos champs et nos rives* (Edition du Devoir, 1917); *La vieille maison* (Bibliothèque de l'Action française, 1920); etc.

EVA SENECAL (b. 1905) sang in languid, girlish verse her *Course dans l'aurore* (Sherbrooke: La Tribune, 1929). Prize-winner in 1928 of the *Salon des Poètes de Lyon*, her poetry belongs to the French-Canadian nineteenth century. Her verse is endowed with a nice precision:[21]

JOUR DE BRUME

Une froide, attristante brume
Filtre du ciel opaque et gris,
Et l'espace vague, imprécis,
A la mine d'un toit qui fume.

Tout mouvement est arrêté,
Au lointain royaume des astres;
Les arbres sont les bruns pilastres
Appuyant cet éther ouaté.

ALICE LEMIEUX (b. 1900): There is no reason for quarrelling with the verdict of Robert Choquette who called Alice Lemieux a "pleasant poet." Her two collections, *Heures effeuillées* (Quebec: privately printed, 1926) and *Poèmes* (Montreal: Action canadienne-français, 1929), could have been entitled *A quoi rêvent les jeunes filles canadiennes*.

MERE MARIE SAINT-EPHREM (1889-1921): It is strange that a people as religious as the French Canadians has produced almost no really mystical poetry. If one leafs through the numerous reviews published by congregations for half a century it is plain that the poetry accepted by these reviews comes under the heading of indoctrination and very rarely goes beyond a quite routine conception of dogma. Mother Marie Saint-Ephrem, whose scattered poetic work was put together in 1929 with the title *Immortel amour*, is the only one to have come close to that particular form of art, brought to its highest degree of perfection by the great Spanish mystics. Her language, with little variation or suggestiveness, kept her from creating an artistic form to meet the uprushing of devotion which she so intensely lived. Towards the end of her life, however, when confined to her bed, her sufferings seemed to intensify her ecstasy. She did succeed, by force of will, in writing *Mon sacerdoce, Ma messe quotidienne*, poems which truly expressed at last the ardour of this fiancée of the Lord:

> *Quand je vois monter le prêtre à l'autel,*
> *Je sens que soudain tout vibre en mon âme,*
> *Et mon coeur étroit, fragile, mortel,*
> *Sent d'un grand désir l'embrasante flamme.*
> *Oh! si tu voulais, mon divin Seigneur,*
> *M'octroyer aussi ce droit, cet honneur*
> *D'offrir chaque jour le pain d'allégresse!*
>
>   . . .
>
> *Et pourtant je veux, d'un vouloir ardent,*
> *Offrir au Seigneur quelque sacrifice;*
> *Vers moi, je veux qu'il s'incline pendant*
> *Que je remplirai mon sublime office,*
> *Je connais un glaive, un glaive sacré . . .*
> *Aux flancs de mon coeur, je le plongerai!*
> *Et, savourant ma douloureuse ivresse,*
> *Je pourrai lever mon regard vers Dieu*
> *Et lui dire avec des accents de feu:*
> *"O Maître, voici, recevez ma messe."*

SIMONE ROUTIER (b. 1900), like so many other poets, started with a collection in which there may be found all the verve and noble yearning of youth: *L'immortel adolescent* (Quebec: Le Soleil,

1928). Leaving for Paris soon afterwards, she remained there until the German invasion in 1940. In the meantime she had published *Ceux qui seront aimés* (Paris: Editions Pierre Roger, 1931) and *Les tentations* (Paris: Editions de la Caravelle, 1934), with Prefaces by Fernand Gregh. Her poetry, of a personal nature, is appealing because of its sincerity. When Simone Routier describes the loves of her life, those in her mind or those more carnal which have been disappointed, her unpretentious verse finds the right key. Her return to Canada, and perhaps the future of France, so dark in 1940, seem to have inclined Simone Routier towards religious themes. In *Le long voyage* (Paris: Editions de la Lyre et de la Croix, 1947), after the "show of finery" she asks for "the song of silence." As for *Psaumes du jardin clos* (*ibid.*, 1947), these spiritual exercises are a step backwards, compared with her first style.[22]

Attention should be drawn to the following names among the poets who contributed to the poetic movement between 1900 and 1939 or who, though having published since, belong to an earlier period of French-Canadian poetry:

Albert Dreux (1887-1949), *Les Soirs* (Saint-Jérôme: J.-E. Prévost, 1910), *Le mauvais passant* (Montreal: R. Maillet, 1920); Guy Delahaye, *Les phases* (Montreal: Déom, 1910), *Mignonne allons voir si la rose* (*ibid.*, 1912); Jovette Bernier (b. 1900), *Roulades* (1924), *Comme l'oiseau* (1926), etc.; Emile Coderre (b. 1893), *Les signes sur le sable* (1922), *Bonsoir les gars* (1948); Medjé Vézina (b. 1896), *Chaque heure son visage* (1934); Jean Aubert Loranger (1896-1942), *Les atmosphères* (L. Morissette, 1920), *Poèmes* (*ibid.*, 1922).

HISTORY

The movement in the second half of the nineteenth century in favour of minor history is now seen to be widening as it becomes the preoccupation of a throng of research-workers and of some historians. A century and a half already separated the French Canadians from their favourite era: the French regime. No fact, no custom linked with this side of Canadian history was insignificant; each piece of this mosaic was getting to be a relic, a microcosm of national pride.

Pierre-Georges Roy (1870-1953), brother of Joseph-Edmond, pursued the same task as the author of *La seigneurie de Lauzon* with a method which makes him the master of the minutiae of French-Canadian history.

Powerfully attractive to anyone of more or less philosophic mind is the possibility of reinterpreting the past through original research. Too often, nevertheless, a futile hunt of things of no consequence is substituted for the legitimate curiosity of the historian. Pierre-Georges Roy, conscious of the necessity of avoiding this shoal and of co-ordinating the efforts of the researchers in order to avoid work that had no usefulness, founded in 1895 the *Bulletin des Recherches historiques,* a review which rendered excellent service to French-Canadian historians as long as it continued to appear. By reason of the high quality of his very numerous monographs on the oldest families of the Province of Quebec, of a very useful inventory of the ordinances of the administrators of New France and also of a number of articles of all kinds on French-Canadian history, Pierre-Georges Roy in 1920 was appointed first Archivist-in-chief of the Province of Quebec. And it was then that the historian, with the support of the provincial government, embarked on an important work of conservation.

After the publication of the *Premier Rapport de l'Archiviste de la Province de Québec pour 1920-1921,* an Historical Monuments Commission was set up. This organization, conceived in a spirit very like that present at the creation of the Historical Monuments Commission of France, was to play an important role. In spite of fires, always to be feared in a cold country, several churches and houses which had been built under French rule were still standing. Nearly all these buildings, it is true, had been repaired or had undergone great changes. Their solid construction, designed to stand up to the centuries, gave such a living spirituality to the banks of the Saint Lawrence that it was a matter of the most extreme urgency to protect them from demolition. In the years following, Pierre-Georges Roy published richly illustrated books on the subject of these appealing churches and houses, each more valuable as a means of enlightenment than a library of *les petits faits de notre histoire.*[23] In this way his work has contributed to the appreciation and preservation of these living testimonies to the past.

It was for Antoine Roy (b. 1905) to attempt to synthesize the the vast work of half a century in *Les lettres, les sciences et les arts au Canada sous le régime français.*[24] In the building up of this sum of knowledge the Roy family had played a role of the greatest importance. For a Roy what could have had more fascination than the idea of putting the finishing touches on such an endeavour?

Les lettres, les sciences et les arts au Canada only partially lives up to the intentions of the author. A synthesis presupposes a whole view, an historical method, even though it be that of certain con-temporary historians for whom the supreme refinement is the simple listing of events in their chronological order. Such is not the case here for Roy's work constitutes little more than a compila-tion, albeit a useful one, of historical studies relating to New France. This leads us to a general conclusion regarding the devotees of the minutiae in history.

The most important of them, the three Roys and Sulte, have accomplished—often at the cost of selfless labours that command our respect—a collective work which makes certain aspects of New France completely real to us. When these historians attempted to raise their sights, the sweep of history eluded them because they had too much concerned themselves with its minute details. Pierre-Georges Roy was able to make the best use of historical studies, whose limitations he honestly accepted. In other words, for half a century French Canada produced principally scholars and copyists, not historians.

It is very probable, too, that on one point these scholars deceived themselves. All these voluminous works were in principle designed to help resuscitate the past. Joseph-Edmond Roy, incapable of the effort which is inseparable from the art of writing, had been willing to be the drudge for some future historian who, reading these inventories of an era past and gone, would put life into them by the wave of some magic wand. Now if one admits that the greatest historians have been compelled to perform the same thankless tasks as a Joseph-Edmond Roy, there is no evidence to suggest that the critical analysis involved could have been done by others.

The great living synthesis of Canadian History is still unwritten. If ever it sees the light of day there is every likelihood that its author may have to thank the historian-copyists for having tracked down documents which he, unfortunately, will have to read over again.

THE HISTORIANS OF MODERN FRENCH CANADA

Where is there a people that, having come under foreign domina-tion, can consider its final conquest without too much bitterness? This attitude, nevertheless, is true of the French-Canadian people. This is the story of all the tenacity of the French-speaking group and the relative lenience of the new laws under which it was obliged to live after 1760. So a new field opened up to the historians:

description of the necessary adjustment to the Anglo-Saxon presence.

Garneau had indeed studied the English regime from 1760 to 1840: the Act of Union, the declared purpose of which was the progressive assimilation of the French Canadians; Lord Durham's Report on the causes of the fruitless and humiliating rebellion of 1837-1838; the social antagonism which set English and French Canadians against each other. Briefly, the political and moral atmosphere made it difficult for an historian of French language to tell an impartial story of events. There was another difficulty: the correspondence exchanged between the English governors and the British government, which would have made it possible to make a fairer judgment of London politics, was not to become available to research workers until much later. In these circumstances it was inevitable that Garneau, either through lack of information or national pride, did not always have a complete grasp of this phase of Canadian history.

Thomas Chapais (1858-1946)

Thomas Chapais, Head of the Department of Canadian History in Laval University, is the first French-Canadian historian to have assimilated the parliamentary history of Canada and England. Straightforward and accurate, conservative in religion and politics to the point of astonishing even French Canadians,[25] his *Cours d'histoire du Canada*[26] is one of the high spots in French-Canadian historiography.

Chapais passes easily from the Parliament in Ottawa over to the one in London and succeeds in putting an elegant order into the tangled matter of Anglo-Canadian politics. If impartiality is his ideal, on the other hand he rejects impassiveness, for he is too much at one with the French-Canadian people to tell of its successes or failures without emotion. Here we have the source of his qualities and his defects. Chapais has the gift of bringing life into Parliamentary debates, especially when the fate of French Canada is at stake. Full-length portraits of the two adversaries, Lord North and the lawyer, Dunning, bring to bear on the discussions preceding the promulgation of the Quebec Act the searchlight of actual experience. His analysis of the two English Houses of Parliament of 1774 flows in oratorical prose—it is a lecture after all—which has real distinction although it is somewhat out of date:

The British Parliament of that day was the most eminent and the most important political body in the world. Whatever the constitutional vices of its composition, the shocking inequalities of its representation, the weaknesses and faults of many of its members, on the whole it compelled admiration through intellectual power, political skill, and the oratorical magnificence which distinguished its deliberations. The two Houses held everything that was most famous in the English nation. The House of Lords could boast of having in it Lord Chatham who, while no longer a great minister, was still a great and moving orator. At his side, prominent for their knowledge or their eloquence, were Lord Mansfield, the celebrated legal expert, Lord Camden, his emulator and often his opponent, the Duke of Richmond, as distinguished for his ability as for his birth, Lord Hillsborough, to whom a long career in office gave a special authority, Lord Shelburne, effective in argument, a recognized authority in questions of foreign and trade relations, and many others. The House of Commons, too, had a whole group of gifted members. If you disregard the political mistakes and unfortunate results of his system, the Prime Minister, Lord North, who had been in power for several years, was unquestionably a highly qualified parliamentarian. His tact, his flexibility, his clever repartee, his knowledge of affairs, particularly of finance, made him a debater to be feared. He was surrounded by eminent colleagues in whose first ranks figured . . . Messrs. Wedderburn and Thurlow, the one lucid and persuasive, uniting charm of imagination with strength of logic, the other putting a vigorous and persuasive delivery to the service of nobility of thought. [*trans.*]

Chapais happens to give the impression of being more alive than Garneau. It would be risky, however, to give the preference to one or the other from a literary point of view since, for that matter, their styles are alike even in their inaccuracies. As to the historical work, properly so called, of the two historians, one must prefer Chapais for the period 1760-1840, although he is intellectually inferior to Garneau.

Lionel Groulx (b. 1878)

With the exception of François-Xavier Garneau, no historian has exerted on his contemporaries an influence comparable to that of Abbé Lionel Groulx.[27] The very controversial work of this priest-historian has reached beyond the lecture-room to the intellectuals and then to the French-Canadian community itself. The notoriety of Abbé Groulx is explained by his qualities as man and historian and particularly by the conjuncture, at a decisive moment, of his conception of history and his national feeling.

Lionel Groulx was beginning to teach at a time when the national unity of Canada was compromised. The mute antipathy which had reigned between the two principal national groups from the time of the Conquest, quickened by the execution of Louis Riel, by the loss of the French schools in Manitoba and the various reactions to the Boer War, was keenly felt in the generation of Lionel Groulx. The Great War moved back the date of a necessary reconciliation. The fate of the French schools in Ontario in 1915-1916 was no reassurance to French Canadians regarding the future of French-Canadian culture in Canada. Actually it is not at all surprising that the French-speaking group, obsessed by the war of attrition waged against its forces in Canada, should have considered the recruiting of French-Canadian soldiers to be a national danger. Certain patriots, like Oliver Asselin, silenced their apprehensions because France was threatened. The majority appraised the seriousness of the danger differently.

Abbé Groulx was definitely one of those people who believed that without a vigorous effort at rejuvenation the French spirit in North America was doomed in the long run. This preoccupation can be felt in his historical method. To him history did not appear as dead matter but rather as the living substance of man. One of his main tasks was to make the past live again and especially to draw from it rules of conduct for a people that had become amorphous and destined slowly to disappear.

From the very first, Lionel Groulx rejected as ineffectual the research done by the scribes of the latter half of the nineteenth century, those "masterpieces of mnemonics."[28] As in Garneau's time, the historian had to come down to the people. In the beginning he dreamed of a History of Canada in ten or fifteen volumes. His enthusiasm was to incline in another direction with more immediate and certain yield. For the mass of the people who had become powerless, he would put facts to work, big, suggestive doses of them, which would throw light on what was the very essence of New France and French Canada. This was historian's work, doubtless, but it was also creative, for the truths that he reveals are operative:

From the actions of one's ancestors taken together, from their decisions, from the way they behaved in doing their daily work as well as in the more serious times, a special habit of mind stands out, a long and lasting intention, which is tradition. History takes over this habit of mind; it drops the seed of it into the very heart of each and everyone; it creates the light and the strength which command the innumerable activities of a people.[29] [*trans.*]

In order that the lessons of the past may act on a people, the spiritual unity of this people must be a reality. Very early in his career Abbé Groulx was determined to demonstrate the French-Canadian originality.

God cannot shape a race as he shapes an individual. A poke here and there, a few light touches of the divine hands can suffice for the fashioning of a human soul. The pressures, the stimuli reaching it, are translated into immediate forces of energy, principles of ensuing action. It is quite otherwise with the shaping of the soul of a race, a soul that is enduring, multiple, changeable, diverse. All hope lies in the progressive accumulation of energy, in the slow flowering and in the ideal. God, in works of divine fermentation, begins by kneading and leavening the dough of a first generation. He unleashes against it at times the storms of war, of persecution, the wind of mighty tempests. In the infancy of a people whom he would have great, he multiplies the solemn hours, the superhuman labours. And while these efforts are being buttressed, while wills are stretched and heroism stirs, souls are swept higher and the greater virtues begin to flower in them. A second generation comes, then a third, braving the same scorching blasts, garnering and adding to the heritage of the past. Soon new traits are established, a human type of a superior quality begins to live.[30] [*trans.*]

With Abbé Groulx the determination of a specific French-Canadian personality becomes an intangible principle which serves as a criterion for him in his judgment of the behaviour of the English. This eye-glass that distorts hides from him the real character of Lord Durham and leads him to misunderstand the great value of his Report. As to the evolution of English liberalism in the nineteenth century, Lionel Groulx would have denied the existence of that liberalism in Canada. As early as his first year in the University of Montreal, after making an examination of the constitutional struggles of French Canadians, he had concluded: "Let us put an end once and for all to this historical imposture of a liberal England, a mother England which has treated us like the spoiled children of her empire."[31]

The number of magnifications or deformations to which Abbé Groulx submits the facts throughout his work are so numerous that the reader becomes disheartened in the end. This historian who is so prejudiced has stature nevertheless by reason of his eloquence. His influence is in part explained by the effulgence of a spirit absolutely sincere and capable of raising up followers and stirring hearts. In every literature are found those temperaments so closely bound to the native land that a chasm is created between them and the outsider. Actually, Lionel Groulx takes on the guise of a prophet whose teachings have their origin in some holy inspiration. Consequently it is the accent, very noble at times, that must be listened to, and nothing but the accent:

What distinguishes us from others, or makes us different, is neither the architecture of our houses, nor the system of our roadways, nor the shape of the properties we hold, nor our social group of a type too often indistinguishable from our neighbour's. What is our own, exclusively our own, is that spiritual cavalcade, that procession of Latin crosses with which we have marked, everywhere, our occupation of the land, that procession of steeples you meet everywhere in some form or other, at the crossroads, on the roofs of our schools, of our hospitals, sometimes even on the brow of our mountains. Beginning at the mouth of the river, in that far-away time of the first discovery, that procession has crossed the whole continent from East to West with countless ramifications, gigantic tangents, some ending on the shores of polar seas, and others crossing the southern border, penetrating deep into the heart of the Yankee colossus.[32] [*trans.*]

MODERN CRITICISM

With the first years of the twentieth century a great change takes place in French-Canadian criticism. Up to this time critics had been recruited among journalists, lawyers and a few professors and writers who wanted to further the growth of French-Canadian letters by means of reflections, to which they gave themselves by fits and starts. The need for a more methodical criticism having made itself felt, two clerics, Camille Roy and Eugène Seers (Louis Dantin), took up criticism as a profession, and both made a first appearance with works of high quality. The preface to Nelligan's poetry, which Dantin published in 1904, is justly famous. It was a fortunate circumstance which brought the least dogmatic of critics to comment on the work of the most inspired of French-Canadian poets. In 1907 Camille Roy published his first *Essais* on French-Canadian literature.

Between these two publications there comes the criticism of a Frenchman, Charles ab der Halden. His two works on French-Canadian literature[33] complement the works of Dantin and Camille Roy. After 1907 it will be difficult for a French-Canadian writer to persuade himself that any really well-informed intelligence is not following the movement of ideas and letters in French Canada.

In approaching this phase of French-Canadian criticism it is fitting to examine first of all the thought of Camille Roy. For more than half a century this indefatigable labourer in the field of French-Canadian writing was to exert a direct influence on young minds. The best writers will doubtless make a distinction between the fine analyses of a Dantin and the too frequently over-sweetened pages of the man who, in certain respects, is the continuation of Abbé Casgrain. But Dantin is exceptional and as much outside the tradition of French-Canadian criticism as Camille Roy is its most illustrious representative.

Camille Roy (1871-1943)

When Camille Roy dedicated himself to the study of Canadian literature with the publication of articles in *Nouvelle-France* in 1902, he gained immediate recognition for his sound Greek and Latin scholarship and his intimate knowledge of French literature. In contrast to all the critics who had gone before him, Camille Roy came to criticism well prepared and, more than that, for the whole time that his tenure of authority lasted—until his death—he did his utmost to define in distinct terms what he conceived to be the role of the critic of a young literature. It is for this reason that the thought of Camille Roy, better than that of any other, lends itself to analysis.[34]

When a young man, Camille Roy turned to France to gain experience in critical discipline. Not only did he ponder the writings of Villemain, Nisard, Sainte-Beuve and Brunetière, but at the Sorbonne he was introduced to the severe and sober methods of a Lanson and the eclectic approach of a Faguet. Of an independent mind, Camille Roy had no intention of applying wholesale to Canadian literature the aesthetics of his teachers, but none the less he was profoundly impressed by them.

The *Essais,* a collection of articles published between 1902 and 1907, already contain the critic's essential thought. The study devoted to Abbé Casgrain is a résumé of his method as it is of his literary theories. The influence of Sainte-Beuve is recognizable here:

Family upbringing, the beloved countryside which is the scene of the flowering of childhood, then youth, what is read at school, the teachers' lessons, the fascinating example of our patriotic writers and, finally, the excitement and the instruction of travel: all these various influences mingle and seem to dissolve to shape the historian, the poet, the literary critic which Abbé Casgrain by turns became.[35] [*trans.*]

To this biographical investigation, the critic adds a doctrine after the manner of Brunetière on the evolution of the genres:

If we must be truthful, to become a literary critic in the strict sense of the word, Abbé Casgrain lacked a sufficiently wide knowledge of the history of classical literatures, a certain training in the examination and discussion of texts, enough practice in applying literary tenets. It is necessary to be somewhat accurately acquainted with the human spirit as it makes its appearance through the works which are successive manifestations of its strength and its life; it is necessary also to be acquainted with the constructive laws of literary genres and the conditions of their development and decline, if one is to have any hope of excelling in criticism . . .[36] [*trans.*]

It should not be thought from this, however, that Camille Roy accepts, in order to apply it indiscriminately, Sainte-Beauve's method of using biographical minutiae, nor that he believes in the strict evolution of genres. Later, in 1918, he will make a close study of French criticism in the nineteenth century and will come to the conclusion that the intellectual curiosity of a Sainte-Beuve succeeds more in throwing light on the adventitious aspects of a literary work than on the work itself. As for the evolution of the genres, this notion seems to him to err in its excessive simplification of an extremely complex reality.

It is to Brunetière, however, that Camille Roy is most closely related. In this eloquent and late-coming Catholic he finds a way of appreciating literature which is so close to his own that, when he has finished reading, he cannot avoid being more persuaded than ever of the sublime qualities of *L'histoire des variations* and the *Génie du christianisme*. This is what will make him say, in spite of everything, that Brunetière's thought was "the most substantial, the most fertile, the most laden with judgments and doctrines, the most eloquent and the most heeded of the nineteenth century."[37]

Such an appreciation, little in keeping with the verdict of the twentieth century, is a pointed example of the weak side of Camille Roy. His utter attachment to French Classicism, eternal and sole standard of literary beauty, takes us back to the narrow criticism of the eighteenth century. It should be recognized, at any rate, that the strict discipline of good taste and fine construction that Camille Roy advocated could not fail to benefit a literature scarcely out of its swaddling-clothes. Camille Roy was so firmly convinced of this that he elaborated a whole theory on the transmissibility of the "clarté française" through the blood of one's ancestors. This theory calls for special comment, for what is involved concerns the delayed influence from France on French-Canadian literature, which is more Romantic than Classical in its origins.

The ideal represented by this French clarity was certainly the one that Camille Roy most frequently preached to his followers. For him French classical culture is a discipline designed to make the mind supple, to regulate it, enrich it and contribute to its growth. French Canadians have inherited that mind as a birthright. When confronted with Guy Delahaye's imprecise and obscure poetry, Roy cries out:

Our French spirit is not accustomed to this way of writing: it never will be accustomed to it. Let this be called, if you like, stubborn lack of willingness to understand. Everybody knows this stubbornness to be concern for the clarity which is an essential and inherent strength in the genius of our race.[38] [*trans.*]

It follows that the intellectual kinship between a Frenchman and a French Canadian is such that a French-Canadian book will always resemble a French book[39]—a prognosis that the years have only partially ratified.

It was in pursuance of this clarity—which is a part of the French-Canadian heritage as language and religion are, and which, consequently, every French-Canadian writer should practise—that Camille Roy in respect to Canadianism in literature adopted a position that was preordained.

The contentious question among French-Canadian critics on the subject of this Canadianism in literature was soon raised. In order to be completely original is it not the duty of the French-Canadian writer to stop imitating French models and keep to description of the customs and the landscapes of his own country? To do this is it not right for him to dip into the French-Canadian language, so picturesque in its archaisms, neologisms, even its barbarisms? This temptation must be resisted, for "the French language handled by the skilful Canadian artist will always be supple enough, ample enough, beautiful enough to permit the imprint on this material of a sufficient or powerful originality."[40] To him subject matter is of little import. Rejecting every narrow formula Camille Roy declares that literature must be human before being Canadian.[41]

Usually so indulgent, Camille Roy, for the sake of French clarity, ridiculed the inflated style of French-Canadian orators. Education in French Canada, he concluded, is good only for the making of rhetoricians. "We think that the traditional methods employed in France are much more effective for the shaping of minds and for education in good literary taste,"[42] he declared as early as 1907.

Through his influence Camille Roy helped tighten the bonds with France. Up to the time of the Second World War the schools and universities were strongly marked by French methods. This is because the French-Canadian elite, after having gone to France to finish their education, on their return did their utmost to be French in everything in conformity with the genius of the "race."

For more than half a century Camille Roy exerted a salutary influence on French-Canadian letters. His Classicism would have made it impossible for him, in France, to fully enjoy the latest products of Symbolism. Most certainly, in him Surrealism would have found an enemy. French-Canadian writers themselves took care never to submit his sensibility to so rude a test. His most serious defect, one which would have made a very mediocre critic of him if he had had to judge the greatest works of European literature, is his moralism. In 1901 when the city of Paris put up a statue in the Montmartre cemetery to the memory of Heinrich Heine, Camille Roy opined that the great German poet "certainly is not one of those men who compel the admiration of posterity for long." Why? Because Heinrich Heine was not "an apostle of right ideas" nor of "healthy morality."[43]

In French Canada where writers for a long time have followed the path of national and religious edification which Abbé Casgrain had pointed out to them, Camille Roy's classical dogmatism, like his moralism, led him to commit scarcely any injustices.[44] In a word, to be a judge of his contemporaries, Camille Roy possessed an adequate equipment of culture and high-mindedness.

Convinced that criticism, in a country just being born as far as literature is concerned, must keep from being too severe, he was led inevitably to mask his reserves and without doubt to devote unmerited praise to writings undeserving of publication. It would be wrong to reproach him for Camille Roy only suffered the bondage that weighs heavily on writers and critics alike in a country such as French Canada. To be really fair one would have to avoid dwelling on all his enthusiasms, even those that were sincere. Because he adapted himself to the thought of mediocre authors he went astray in his estimate of some of them, like Pamphile Lemay, whose modest sonnets seemed to him to be authentic works of art. Rather, one must come upon him in a moment when he is his best self, when he has not suffered too much from the confinement in which he normally had to work. More particularly one must re-read that monograph on Abbé Casgrain where, comfortable in his treatment of a subject of which he is clearly the master, he is an excellent critic. Would it be because he had to analyze the work and personality of a priest that he was able with malicious urbanity to put his finger on the intellectual insufficiencies and innocent worldly ambitions of the first French-Canadian critic?

The ascendancy exerted by Camille Roy over the young minds at Laval University, the reputation which he had acquired in French Canada, together with his personality, were to guarantee him followers among the budding analysts of French-Canadian literature. Maurice Hébert (1888-1960)[45] is their most characteristic representative. For the latter, his revered teacher is the incarnation of "the orator in Demosthenes and Cicero, the poet in Virgil, the critic in Brunetière. . . ."[46] Hébert's method is a close copy of that of the author of *Essais sur la littérature canadienne,* which had as a principle that no literary ambition should be discouraged. Therefore, French-Canadian authors were to be subjected to a uniformly benevolent criticism that may give a blurred picture in which originality will be confused with paltry mediocrity. Camille Roy had not always avoided this reef, from which he was to some extent saved, however, by a critical spirit and above all by a language rich in nuances. In this way, without seeming to condemn, he was able to express to the knowing reader the most explicit reservations.

Louis Dantin (1866-1945)

In the shadow of Camille Roy another cleric—the latter unfrocked —followed with the same affection the course of French-Canadian literature. Louis Dantin had started out in 1903 with a remarkable introduction to the poetic work of Emile Nelligan. These pages are among the most brilliant in French-Canadian criticism. For the first time writers of French Canada had reason to feel that they had among them a superior critic, perfectly objective and dedicated besides to the cause of French-Canadian culture.[47] After having gone into voluntary exile in the United States where he spent most of his adult life, Dantin continued to follow closely the evolution of letters in French Canada and published articles on novelists and poets who seemed to him worthy of mention. Because he was less doctrinaire than Camille Roy, in Dantin one finds no system of clearly defined patterns; nevertheless, in his scattered work a few main trends are noticeable, making it possible to give him his place in the criticism belonging to the first half of the twentieth century.

Louis Dantin is free of the moralism which had remained the touchstone of all literary criticism in French Canada since Abbé Casgrain. For Dantin, beauty is manifold, as varied as man himself. Between religion and art there is no essential connection, although the one does not exclude the other. On the subject of *L'offrande aux vierges folles* by Alfred Desrochers, which had apparently offended because of its title, Dantin observes: "It would be regrettable if orthodoxy should count for so much in questions that are pre-eminently aesthetic. . . . It would seem to be better, instead of poetry contests, to set up contests in the catechism."[48]

Louis Dantin's eclecticism takes in theoretically all the literary schools. While French Classicism is the pinnacle for Camille Roy, Dantin considers that good criticism must acknowledge the multiplicity of criteria where art is concerned.

It is generally believed that a critic must always think the same thing. If he is a Romantic, or a Classicist, or a Symbolist, or a Dadaist, well, let him be it; let him judge works according to the theory he has made for himself; let him approve those who conform to it and condemn those who deviate from it; let him have criteria, principles, which show clearly, and beforehand, that a thing is good or that it is not. But that is not exactly my idea of criticism. With Sainte-Beuve, I am of the opinion that there must be a mirror capable of reflecting the beautiful in its most diverse forms, that the soul of the critic must be fluid enough to mould itself frequently to casts that are entirely different. The critic may have opinions, preferences, and he must have them, but the minute they become exclusive they close off all those worlds of art which are not strictly his and make him incapable of sympathetic judgment. Too dogmatic beliefs hinder him from being able to feel. He must be something of a receiving apparatus, an interpreter, suited to transforming himself by turns into whatever he is decoding. He must force himself to understand everything understandable and to admire everything which emits one flash of beauty, to be ready, if need be, to make his doctrines yield before the fact—and the fact is frequently that beauty will strike you in poses that are foreign to the rules or in shapes different from those you recommend. Am I to deprive myself of a beautiful page of Romanticism because I am instinctively inclined to an art that is more real? Am I to hold in disdain an involved page from Victor Hugo, from Zola, because I prefer the spare line from Maupassant, from Anatole France? Shall I never be able to love Gautier and Rodenbach, Rostand and Francis Jammes at the same time? . . . .[49] [*trans.*]

In actual fact the distance separating Dantin and Camille Roy, notwithstanding declarations of this kind, is less than it would seem at first sight. Actually, in placing works, Dantin, too, sometimes unconsciously compares them to French Classicism, the absolute gauge of beauty. No French-Canadian critic has given more importance to form than he has. At the beginning of his career form to him had appeared to be the supreme mark of talent. "It is not trite to recall," he declared, "that art is above all the living splendour of form. In poetry, as in painting, style is not only the whole man, it is almost the whole work."[50] Later on his judgments on the literature of his day exhibit an unrelenting conservatism. "What come to the surface in the shipwreck of all the passing *isms* are those works in which poetic tradition has persevered, has had a second flowering, where the thought, though unexceptional, is succulent, is strong, and is embodied in a form that is the result of skill. In five hundred years they will speak of Vigny, of Hugo and, perhaps, of Régnier; but who will remember Gustave Kahn and Jean Cocteau?"[51]

Like Roy also, Dantin in principle supports the idea that criticism must be generous. Not so much out of fear of discouraging young talents, of being a hindrance to the blossoming of a national literature, as that truth is better served: "I always quote the best; I do this on principle in the belief that the role of criticism is above all to bring out the value of the work, and that the true measure of an author is in his highest flight."[52]

It is obvious that Dantin made his technique more subtle, gave it more variety than did Camille Roy. But here again, as soon as Dantin leaves the realm of theory he can very well be guilty of the same weaknesses when it comes to specific cases. For instance, the pages that he devotes to Blanche Lamontagne do not lack subtlety.[53] They end up, however, in making a poet of the author of *Visions gaspésiennes* by this unconsciously ironic reasoning: "that to be a poet to the people living in the hamlet of Escoumains is to be one from undeniable vocation."[54] Camille Roy would have been satisfied to consecrate another poet and let it go at that. Dantin's mistake is not less serious for having been expressed on a more rarefied plane.

One last comparison between these two critics is called for on the subject of style, which both wanted to be elegant and precise. The intellectual training they had in common is recognizable in the long, sonorous sentences that grace many a sermon. As to correctness, more irreproachable than Dantin, whose prose bears the occasional mark of his long sojourn among the Americans, Camille Roy, who may be considered one of the best prose writers of French-Canadian literature, is still this side of being original. Louis Dantin enhances his style with metaphors which are those of a born writer. The way his quick mind makes his best criticism stand out means that his superiority on this score may be conceded.

Is Dantin the greatest French-Canadian critic? Among those no longer living the only one to be compared with him is Camille Roy. Less dogmatic than Roy, Dantin was unable to show everything that he was capable of because he had to examine authors who were, for the most part, mediocre. Although Camille Roy also was limited to a literary area much too circumscribed for his abilities, it was Dantin who suffered most from being the critic of a young literature. His treatment of Nelligan is sufficient indication that Dantin, with more frequent opportunity to measure his strength against talents as strong as his own, would have given any number of proofs of a superiority which one is obliged to look for especially in his rare declarations of doctrine.[55]

Marcel Dugas (1883-1947)

Criticism was the real objective of Dantin and of Camille Roy; for Marcel Dugas it was often a pretext. From the time of *Le théâtre à Montréal* (1911), he told his own story through Rostand, Henry Bataille, Dumas *fils*. He was an impressionist in the manner of Jules Lemaître and so one must not look to him for a method, let alone a well-defined doctrine.

His first volume of criticism bears the stamp of distinction. In this lies the story of Marcel Dugas and of all those who, like him, have been tempted by Paris. His criticism is essentially only a copy of Parisian theatrical criticisms at the end of the last century, that is, criticism of the extreme right.[56] How he would have liked to provide theatrical news copy in the manner of a Sarcey, a Larroumet! When one re-reads *Le théâtre à Montréal,* taking into account what the criticism of Larroumet and Sarcey was, it is not certain that French criticism would have lost much if Dugas, by some chance or other, had been able to take their place on *le Temps.*

But since Dugas, like Buies before him and those following the path of Parisian ambitions, was indeed obliged to look back to Canada for an audience, in his literary and critical work there are traces of disappointment which are explained by an artistic error. In Dugas the optical illusion consists in applying to French-Canadian writers a style and kind of criticism which would scarcely have been appropriate for the great masters of European literature. Here is the beginning of an article on a French-Canadian poet:

In contrast to other men moulded from coarser clay, M. Albert Lozeau is really a fallen god raised to supreme authority in the domain of poetry. Recalling Olympus, he embraces a world in arms that have been spared by misfortune. Let him raise them, and the world of beauty unfolds with its retinue of goddesses and harmonious elect chanting alternately. From his heart, still trembling from the sounds of divine music, an irrepressible sigh escapes and rises from earth towards the abandoned reaches of Paradise. The muses have nourished his soul, and infinite as are the fallen gods he resembles them through election and through grief.[57] [*trans.*]

Lozeau deserved better than this crazily opulent style and these misplaced metaphors.

There is worse still. Dugas, instead of merely making a criticism of some authors or some work or other, explains his enthusiasms. An essay on Péguy degenerates into an interminable hymn to Jeanne d'Arc;[58] a short study on *L'invitation à la vie* by Roquebrune leaves the reader uncertain about the nature of the work being examined. Are we dealing with a poem, a short story, or a novel? We can never know exactly when criticism takes this turn:

He is drunk, this Roquebrune!
But his drunkenness is nothing but a fanciful challenge to mortal power. O unyielding death, violent and ferocious, I feel you laughing in your filthy, greedy cruelty!
He is drunk, this Roquebrune!
But with what delights! In the mottled net of things, his mouth on fire . . . .[59] [*trans.*]

Despite such extravagances, in all fairness we must give one honourable mention to Dugas. If it is true that he was talking only about himself, the character in every case was exceptional. And by his religious devotion to the cause of French-Canadian literature he provided an example to be followed.

Dugas' prose is not always turgid. Sometimes he happens to strike the right note. Then his eloquence and the musical quality of his phrasing are undeniable. Before Alain Grandbois, Dugas furnished the first valid examples of art prose.[60]

JEAN-CHARLES HARVEY (b. 1891) called himself a man of letters "who does not make a business of flattering and who follows the straight line of conscience and the prompting of his heart."[61] In no wise a theorist, Jean-Charles Harvey wanted to avoid too indulgent criticism by proposing as models for French-Canadian writers the masterpieces of French and other European literatures. Like Olivar Asselin, Harvey recommended retention of solid cultural ties with France. Very conservative when it came to language, he advised young writers to follow a high linguistic and somewhat unreal ideal: "In literature Quebec is a province of France. No more licence is permissible to it than in Touraine or Normandy."[62]

As in his novels, Jean-Charles Harvey fought against the intellectual and moral conformity which he held partly responsible for the mediocrity of writers in his generation. It was in this direction particularly that he exercised a salutary influence by contributing to a healthier artistic atmosphere in French Canada.

CLAUDE-HENRI GRIGNON (b. 1894): From the days of Crémazie and Abbé Casgrain, every time a future poet or novelist turned to literature, set there in front of him were the questions: what language will be my own? shall I be able to be *canadien* and by this means have international appeal? Around these fundamental problems it was Claude-Henri Grignon who stirred up ideas.

Imitation of French models is the source of mediocrity in French-Canadian literature. This imitation, which persists in language and literature, should be outlawed. Better a page stuffed with Canadianisms and Anglicisms—provided they correspond to the linguistic reality—than false eloquence. "So it is for our writers and poets to use a Canadian vocabulary which does not exist anywhere else. It is at this price, and we think at this price only, that we shall establish a national literature."[63]

Claude-Henri Grignon tracks down pitilessly in his fellow writers the masters who are being used as guarantees. Is there a hidden Brunetière in Harry Bernard, a Thibaudet in Albert Pelletier? These too-vague rapprochements, which have the added disadvantage of thwarting direct appreciation of the texts, are a weakness.

SERAPHIN MARION (b. 1896): The excavating that Séraphin Marion has undertaken in the unprofitable soil of French-Canadian literary origins has led him to resurrect quite a number of pen-pushers and several very curious pieces of writing. The so-called criticism of this antiquarian of French-Canadian letters belongs to an honourable past associated with the name of Edmond Lareau. Works: *Sur les pas de nos littérateurs* (Montreal: Lévesque, 1933); *Les lettres canadiennes d'autrefois* (Hull: Editions L'Eclair, 1940-1958), 9 vol., etc.

ALBERT PELLETIER: From being a passionate spectator of literary disputes, Albert Pelletier became a combatant himself. His two collections reveal a spirit of compromise rather than that of a just arbitrator, the ardent defender of an integral Canadianism rather than the critic who has read all the books. *Carquois* (Montreal: Librairie d'Action canadienne-française, 1931); *Egrappages* (Montreal: Lévesque, 1933).

THE CRITIC-PRIESTS

With the exception of Louis Dantin, the numerous clerics who have sought to guide the development of French-Canadian literature have always insisted on the importance of Christian morality as the criterion of art. In the history of Western criticism moralism has played a very important role; several of the keenest minds, like Frederick Schlegel and Schopenhauer, having identified art with religion. In the case of the French-Canadian critic-priests this identification is usually automatic and frequently characterized by a quite dogmatic severity. From Abbé Casgrain to Abbé Dandurand, from Abbé Dandurand to the Redemptorist Samuel Baillargeon, the method hardly varies. According to Dandurand, Flaubert has an "unsound morality." In the contemporary era, Baillargeon accuses offending writers of "moral deviationism."

ALBERT DANDURAND (b. 1899): Making Taine's method his own, Dandurand says: "When it is a question of works belonging to an already distant past, how are they to be understood and soundly judged without the historical criticism which reconstructs the milieu, the period and the condition of the arts in the era in which they were composed?"[64] The works of his predecessors or contemporaries, notably those of Camille Roy, having seemed to him to be insufficient, he devoted conscientious studies to poetry, the novel, and the art of oratory. Dandurand's excessive "historicity" leads him to discover, in his examination of erudite authors, sources which are out of all proportion in number to the importance of the author, whereas in good criticism he would have taken the opposite road. The pages devoted to Nelligan are characteristic. According to him this inspired writer was influenced by art of the Middle Ages, by that of the Renaissance and by Ronsard in particular; Hugo and Rostand are to be found in Nelligan's work as well as François Coppée, etc. This kind of criticism is self-defeating as at no time is the real personal contribution of an author brought out.

Works: *La poésie canadienne-française* (Montreal: Editions Albert Lévesque, 1933); *Littérature canadienne-française. La prose* (Montreal: Le Devoir, 1935); *Le roman canadien-français* (Lévesque, 1937); *Nos orateurs* (Montreal: Editions de l'A. C.-F., 1939).

EMILE CHARTIER (1876-1951): Called in 1927 to lecture at the Sorbonne on literature and art in French Canada, Emile Chartier brought together the essential material of his lectures in a volume entitled *La vie de l'esprit 1760-1925* (Montreal: Editions Bernard Valiquette, 1941). The resultant work, necessarily composite, contains in what may be called the literary section appreciations which are intended for a French audience and are above all popularizations. Although informed about French-Canadian writing, Chartier does not seem to have brought any original contribution to his labours. A résumé of French-Canadian literature written by him is to be found in *La littérature française à l'étranger* by J. Calvet (Paris: J. de Gigord, 1923), pp. 53-75.

HENRI BEAUDE (1870-1930): Having started out in art criticism in 1903, later on Henri Beaudé frequently wrote criticism on Canadian literature. Entirely shaped by French culture, and a convinced Neo-Classicist, nevertheless for his entire life he remained a French-Canadian Romanticist without being aware of it. One has only to read the account, written shortly before his death, of a trip to California for his health, to understand that in him French-Canadian literature found its twentieth-century Casgrain.[65] A stop-over in Chicago reminds him of *La voix d'un exilé*, "où il y a des accents sublimes."[66]

Beaudé's criticism is made up almost entirely of borrowings. On the other hand, clearly his own is the suggestion that French-Canadian literature will not have a *History* worthy of it until its riches are inventoried—not by a single man, since the task would be impossible—but by a team of specialists. It is in pursuit of such a judgment that he concludes: "Ours is the only literature which can complain of never having had its Tacitus or its Titus Livy."[67] The numerous works of Camille Roy were worthy of more than this disapproving silence. But is it not true that Camille Roy himself had exercised the same kind of disdain, with more justification, granted, towards Abbé Casgrain?

MARC-ANTONIO LAMARCHE (1876-1950): This priest-critic was modest enough to admit that "long days of thoughtful hesitation" were necessary before he decided to publish his appreciations of some French-Canadian authors.[68] He makes sensible appraisals of Hémon and Robert Choquette. While relying on France, where "it is suitable at the present time to ask for a large measure of advice and direction,"[69] he condemns, nevertheless, most of the recent productions of the French theatre. His advice is to avoid Bernstein and Bataille who are apt to corrupt the "spiritual health" of young girls.

THE NOVEL

In the great Western literatures since the nineteenth century the novel has attracted an increasing number of writers. But we have to wait until the middle of the present century for this form of literary production in French Canada to match that of France, England and the United States. French Canada's relative isolation and the social set-up of the French-speaking groups have for a long time held back a development which is the inevitable result of the rapid industrialization brought about by two world wars.

The first forty years of the twentieth century may be considered as a period of transition during which the contingent of novelists gradually broadens as it becomes diversified. The contemporary novel, extremely varied, proceeds directly from the 1900-1939 period and, in contrast to the poetry, owes little to foreign models. How is it to be explained that the novel, which was so slow in taking shape in French Canada, seems, more than the poetry— which is on a higher intellectual plane—to be a product of the national temperament? The fact is that literary fashions on the other side of the Atlantic from the days of Realism and Naturalism scarcely fit the character of the French-Canadian society. The first French-Canadian novelists found favour with their readers because they were equally unsophisticated. But things could not keep on this way. After the First World War aesthetes, rebels, or observers less superficial and above all less timid, ensured that there would be a changing of the guard. We witness then the birth of the first works to endure in the history of the novel for other than historical or sociological reasons, since it is taken for granted that no French-Canadian novel in the nineteenth century had an autonomous existence. What we credit it with is tainted, being made up of extra-literary considerations.[70]

It was a Frenchman, Louis Hémon, who put French-Canadian novelists on the right track with the example of *Maria Chapdelaine,* the first Romantic masterpiece of French-Canadian literature. Tying themselves to an old tradition, other writers who had come from France—Bugnet, Constantin-Weyer, Le Franc—were to endow a literature in search of itself with *La forêt, Un homme se penche sur son passé, La rivière solitaire.* And in their turn, Albert Laberge, Ringuet, and Henri Grignon would found a virile French-Canadian realism in complete contrast to the depressed condition of the Canadian novel, which they revived, broadened and made ready to welcome that promising diversity of present-day novelists.[71]

THE CONTRIBUTION OF FRENCH WRITERS

At the beginning of the nineteenth century, at a time when the first French-Canadian writers were dreaming of the creation of a native literature, Frenchmen like Mesplet and Quesnel, by their example, had stirred up literary inclinations and hastened the blossoming of a national literature. Yet the French-Canadian literary tradition was to be shaped without any outside aid in the course of the critical period of the second half of the nineteenth century. France doubtless remained the provider *par excellence* of literary models but its influence, while all-powerful, manifested itself only indirectly. It was necessary to wait for the first years of this century for other Frenchmen to ensure the replacement of Mesplet and Quesnel. The growing interest that France began to show in Canada manifested itself in the number of writers or recognized writers who came looking for subjects in a country linked to the French past.

The most famous of these is Louis Hémon. His influence on French-Canadian letters has been profound. Fame, which is blind, could just as well have favoured Georges Bugnet. But while waiting for the exceptional qualities of this novelist to be more widely recognized, it is not out of place to put Hémon at the head of that phalanx of French writers who belong to Canada as much if not more than to France.[72]

Louis Hémon (1880-1913)

Born in Brittany, in Brest, Hémon was sensitive to the influences of his native soil. Intuitive, he seems to have been very conscious, during his student years in Paris, of all the artificiality of big modern cities. France in particular wearied his spirit and got on his nerves with the affectations of its life, which was too far removed from nature for his taste. More at home in England, Hémon went there in 1903 and remained until 1911. These years were important to him for this was when he broke into the writing profession. He was attracted by sport—that is, by the side of human activity which has its origins in man's primitive instincts—and considered it a training in courage and healthy living. Hence his sporting novel, *Battling Malone,* one of the first of its kind.[73]

Inevitably England, too, would appear cankered by the complications of a world that had become industrialized. So he left for Canada—he had been tempted by Bolivia—in search of rejuvenation in primitivism. This was a happy choice for his Breton atavism would be of the greatest use to him in understanding French Canada. Arriving in Quebec in October of 1911, he spent the winter in Montreal. That city, decidedly too close to Europe, made him wish for more breathing space in the direction of the almost unpopulated open country of the West. His final choice was the region being colonized around Lake Saint-Jean. And it is there, at Péribonka, then at Saint-Gédéon, in a spot reminiscent of the French countryside, that he wrote his novel.

What gifts did Hémon bring to his project of writing the novel of French survival in America? Born in a university family—his father was chief inspector of Education—young Hémon, while at the Louis-le-Grand Lycée, witnessed the final years of Naturalism. Regard for exact and impersonal observations and note-taking was a rule he made his own. To the precision of a clinician he now added the ability to choose the topical, even the poetic detail. Because he had already seen these French-Canadian *habitants* in their cousins, the French peasants, tendencies hidden in the souls of both suggested to him syntheses, abridgments of a truth which constitute real art. When painting the resignation of the landowner in the face of death, he would be depicting not just the death agony of Mother Chapdelaine but a thousand times over that of the tillers of the soil. Some centuries earlier Montaigne had been struck by the apparent indifference of the plague-stricken people of Guyenne to the certain death awaiting them. In Mother Chapdelaine, their distant descendant, the same miracle of renunciation was renewed.

Must there be an explanation of the very restricted place of love in Maria's life? Instead of the pious and squeamish approaches that French-Canadian novelists from the time of Chauveau and Gérin-Lajoie had devised for themselves to soften the realities of the flesh, Hémon tackles the problem head on. Not as a naturalist this time but as a poet who does not retreat before the evidence:

For the second time a young man was speaking to her of love and putting into her hands all that he had to give, and for the second time she listened and remained speechless, embarrassed, saving herself from awkwardness only by remaining motionless and silent. Town girls would have thought her silly, but she was only simple and sincere, and close to nature which is without words. In other times, before the world had become complicated as it is now, no doubt young men, half violent and half shy, would go up to a girl with broad hips and generous bosom, to offer and to ask. And every time, if nature had not yet spoken imperiously in her, no doubt she would listen to them in silence, listening less to what they were saying than to a voice within and getting ready to make some sign that would put a distance between them and protect her against the too-ardent suit, waiting . . . The three men in love with Maria Chapdelaine had not been attracted by clever or gracious words, but by the beauty of her body and by what they knew instinctively of her transparent honesty; when they spoke to her of love she remained herself, patient, calm, silent as long as she could see nothing that should be said to them, and they only loved her the more for it. [*trans.*]

Maria Chapdelaine has exerted a considerable influence on a whole generation of French-Canadian novelists. It is easy to realize why this should be. After a half-century of waiting a gratuitous gift had been bestowed on Canadian literature. Writers were to start peeling away at this evocation of the peasant soul to get at the secret of how it was done.

Hémon's formula, easier to analyze than to imitate successfully, consisted in the first place of seeing the French-Canadian people objectively in one of its essential incarnations, the *défricheurs*, the pioneers: a first difficulty, doubtless, since the picture of French Canada as Hémon painted it offended more than one French-Canadian critic who considered it a distortion. But it was a salutary and indispensable lesson which taught French-Canadian novelists to avoid exhortations to virtue and courage to which they were only too inclined.

It was a lesson in technique as well. Hémon, aiming first of all at truth, had insisted on making his characters speak the language commonly spoken in French Canada. By a judicious alternate use of a sustained style and of French-Canadian words he was able to avoid two dangers: a language over-polished and consequently unreal, or a language exclusively dialectal and incomprehensible to anyone but a French Canadian.

The universal success of *Maria Chapdelaine* was the signal for the appearance of numerous imitations. With each new novel of the soil it became apparent that the lesson had been learned too well. One novelist, abandoning the academic language that in all probability he would have been unable to handle perfectly, would plunge into picturesque dialogues stuffed with Canadianisms and encroaching on the function of the plot; another, making himself the psychologist of the minute and the insignificant, would take delight in calling attention to all the peculiarities of the *habitant*. Only good taste and objectivity were lacking in these lucubrations.

Other novelists, anxious to avoid errors of the past, benefited from these gropings. Laberge, Ringuet, Germaine Guèvremont and Félix-Antoine Savard, each in his own way, have carried on from this success of Hémon: Laberge and Ringuet in furnishing the second part of the *habitant's dyptique,* that of his slow and complete disintegration; Germaine Guèvremont in choosing among the great number of daily doings which make up the life of a farmer those that clearly define him; Félix-Antoine Savard in forging a prose of his own by grafting a selected French-Canadian vocabulary on to a style already personal.

Georges Bugnet (b. 1879)

Coming from Chalon-sur-Saône, Bugnet intended when he entered college in Dijon to teach in some Catholic university. The religious struggles at the end of the century seem to have diverted him from that first ambition. Having married in 1904 he soon left with his wife for Canada, attracted like so many others by the tempting Canadian publicity, and in 1905 came to Saint-Boniface. Judging, perhaps, that Saint-Boniface, at that time the last outpost of civilization on the way west, did not offer sufficient challenge to a man of his dedication and resources, he moved more than a thousand miles farther away, to country near Edmonton, in the very heart of the inaccessible forest. This was the region where Georges Bugnet would live a rare spiritual adventure made up of incessant struggles against an implacable nature and a literary vocation discovered at a late date.

It was at the age of forty, in a winter when the snow made all activity impossible, isolating him completely from the outside world, that Bugnet began to write for his own amusement. Like so many others who have started this game, Bugnet was surprised at first at the discoveries he made about himself. Having an inkling of the fresh contribution that he was in a position to make to the literature of his adopted country, the writer often took precedence over the farmer in the fruitful years that were to follow.

The first thing to come out of this confinement was *Le lys de sang*[74] in 1923. The hero, Henri, is none other than the author himself who, thanks to the roving of an imagination awakened by the Canadian winter, has strange adventures in Africa. A simple first step in the art of writing, this novel is significant only because it opened the way to the works which came after.

It was at this moment in his development that Bugnet became aware of what might be his vocation. Having spent nearly twenty years in the Canadian West, he had seen the end of an era. He had been particularly struck by the sad lot of the Indian tribes. Pushed back towards lands increasingly less productive, these tribes were not yet so far removed from their ancient virtues that a trained eye could not restore them. Their downfall, which had begun according to a pitiless logic that Tocqueville in his *Démocratie en Amérique* had described brilliantly in the preceding century, presented itself vividly to the seeing eyes of Bugnet, spiritual heir of a nation whose civilization had not been baleful for the original inhabitants of America. Here the death of the Crees particularly awoke sympathy in him, all the more so as the French language, still in use among the *métis,* was linked to a grandiose dream of empire that was reduced to nothing in the nineteenth century.

It was in this state of mind that Bugnet conceived his novel *Nipsya.* Born of an Irish father and an Indian of the wilds, Nipsya is the product of two worlds: that of the white man who maltreats nature and fashions it to the needs of his inventive genius, and that of the native who, on the contrary, submits to the promptings of nature and bows before its demands. The conflict growing up in Nipsya's soul would be fatal were it not for the Christianity which reconciles these two opposing worlds. There lies the solution, but how many Indians can avail themselves of it? We see Nipsya's grandmother, symbol of the Cree nation, stiffen in instinctive disdain, addressed alike to the religion of the "black robes" and to the inventions of modern materialism. With rare delicacy Bugnet etched the portrait of this old woman who, unable to adapt herself to the new times, withdrew into the dignity of her ancestral stoicism. The slow death of her race was ensured by the civilization represented by the Englishman, Monsieur Alec.

Bugnet does not make the mistake of falling into a false sentimentalism by condemning the mechanical world while painting a Rousseau-like picture of primitive man. On the contrary, Monsieur Alec is a "gentleman" who, thanks to Nipsya, broadens his conception of the relation between man and his environment. Monsieur Alec, the Anglo-Saxon, represents in his way a very high civilization; but in Bugnet's eyes it is at fault in not replacing those values which it has destroyed in the Cree nation, and consequently in all tribes condemned to disappearance or to degradation. Only the vital Christianity of the *métis* Vital can soften the bitter reality. Through her love for Vital, Nipsya is led to practise Catholicism, at first imperfectly, then to know through a painful discipline the indescribable happiness of a union made possible by Christian self-denial.

Bugnet's realism fails when it comes to making this last metamorphosis probable. The complete conversion of the primitive Nipsya is a surprise to us; as for Vital, no *métis* has ever been like him. One may reproach Bugnet, too, for having preferred in his conclusion a partial truth to the tragic breadth of the American reality, the more so since the optimistic ending of *Nipsya* is a contradiction of his analysis of the evolution of the modern world.

A few years went by which Bugnet used to put his reflections on the twentieth century into *Siraf,* a kind of Canadian *Micromégas.* In his conversations between the Spirit and Twentieth-Century Man we find constants in Bugnet's thought: censure of contemporary materialism and reservations about democracy, especially democracy of the American kind. These thoughts of a recluse belong to a cultivated mind, formed by a France of the extreme Right of half a century ago.

Having exorcised the painful need to philosophize, it remained for Bugnet to recapitulate, in the form of a novel, his long, and, in certain ways, unique experience of the Canadian wilderness. The result is *La forêt,* a strong, true work, and one of the three or four greatest novels in French-Canadian literature. Here the imperfections of *Nipsya* disappear.

In a study published subsequently, Bugnet was to explain the original point of view which led him to write *La forêt*:

Nature in Canada is far from being a simple setting sought by writers to enhance their characters, as it is in almost all other countries; here, without any resort to literary artifices, it takes on an importance, a power, a majesty that it presents nowhere else. For the poet nurtured on the first pages of Genesis, on the Book of Job, on the Odyssey, there is a source of thought, of beauty from which only a Canadian soul can draw abundantly and which would pour into his work the fullness of a flood-tide that is ours, with a truer conception of human actions and also with that distinct national flavour we look for everywhere and which, in my humble opinion, will be found particularly here.[75] [*trans.*]

Endowed with experience going back to 1905, Bugnet was situated differently from Louis Hémon for describing with full knowledge the forbidding Canadian forest. Bugnet's conception of nature is actually what separates him most clearly from Hémon. For the latter, nature is a setting, very important, it is true, enhancing the drama which is Maria Chapdelaine's. In *La forêt,* nature, never a supernumerary, is the determinant factor in the action by reason of her overwhelming presence. Hémon had indeed analyzed the temper of the French-Canadian colonists obliged to face up to the terrible forest. But for lack of having been able to share, except for a brief period, the Spartan life of Lake Saint-Jean, he was not in a position to examine the slow metamorphoses of personality under the imperceptible but decisive pressure of Canadian nature.

Thanks to Bugnet's art we are to see the corrosive effect on a young French couple of a country all the more inhuman because she is clothed for the sacrifice of her victims with allurements to be found nowhere else on earth.

There is a high human resonance, too, in the voice of *La forêt* because in order to write about it the author had to surmount difficulties which mark every page of this diary-novel. Cut off for so long from every contact with French culture, Bugnet had to wage a personal war against the loss of his ability to use words as well as against the dulling of his thought. It was an unequal struggle marked here and there with short-lived defeats in the years of apprenticeship. *La forêt,* which closes the cycle of Bugnet novels, is an artistic and moral triumph. A powerful rhythm pulses through entire pages to make them some of the most poetic in Canadian literature:

Devant les sérénités de ce froid, implacable comme sans haine, de ce firmament immense et énigmatique, de cette énorme forêt qui l'avait faite ici prisonnière, Louise sentit son âme s'emplir de frayeur et de désolation. Si faible, et sans défense, en face de ces puissances à la fois formidables et paisibles, elle frissonnait sous une impression de vide infini. Que servirait de lutter contre ces majestés, calmes, occultes, devant qui l'homme et ses oeuvres ne sont que de brefs et imperceptibles atomes, pullulant un instant comme une poussière animée, puis résorbés, eux et leurs travaux, sous l'épiderme d'un globe infime qui, avant eux comme après eux, suit son propre destin, au long d'une route inconnue perdue dans un espace insondable?[76]

Before the calm of that cold, as implacable as it was devoid of hate, before that immense enigmatic firmament, that enormous forest which had made her a prisoner here, Louise felt her heart fill with dread and desolation. So weak, so defenceless, facing those powers at once formidable and peaceful, she shuddered as she felt the endless emptiness. What would be the use of struggling against those calm and occult majesties to whom man and his works are nothing but fleeting and imperceptible atoms, swarming for an instant like animated dust—then re-absorbed, they and their works, under the epidermis of a minute globe which, before them and after them, follows its own destiny along an unknown road lost in unfathomable space?[76] [*trans.*]

Bugnet's renown has scarcely penetrated beyond a limited circle of French-Canadian and foreign readers. Literatures in the making, more than others, have their lost poets. Will the interest being shown in the world in the nascent culture of French Canada be favourable to the rediscovery of one of its most honest craftsmen?

Maurice Constantin-Weyer (1881-1964)

In 1902, when twenty-one years of age, Maurice Constantin-Weyer left France and roamed America from the Gulf of Mexico to Hudson Bay. For the following twelve years he was cowboy, trapper and lumberman in order to meet the circumstances and, particularly, the demands of the adventure that spelled life to him. When France was invaded in 1914 he felt an imperative call to leave the farm where he had established himself in Manitoba to embark on another adventure, which was to be the climax. Wounded in Macedonia, Constantin-Weyer made a short return trip to Canada at the end of the war but felt no urge to take up his neglected farm again. All he had to do now was to call back to mind in the form of novels a picturesque phase of his life. Between 1921 and 1928 he published his *Epopée canadienne: Vers l'ouest* (1921); *Manitoba* (1924); *La bourrasque* (1925); *Cinq éclats de silex* (1927); *Cavelier de La Salle* (1927); *Un homme se penche sur son passé* (1928).[77] This last book won the *Prix Goncourt*.

A witness, as was Bugnet, to the sad lot of the *métis*, Constantin-Weyer would like to have dedicated a literary monument to the brief resistance they set up against the inexorable Anglo-Saxon advance. *Vers l'ouest* is the romantic restoration of the epic of Louis Riel's father and the happy period when the *métis* had not yet been dispossessed of their fief, the Western plains. This first novel of the *Epopée canadienne* is clearly inferior to *Nipsya*. The descriptions and the psychology of the *métis* are blurred and give evidence of the author's lack of craftsmanship—faults which show up in *Manitoba*. Although among the pictures of Manitoba life one may find good pages, several of them are spoiled by Constantin-Weyer's affectation and superficial asides. The too-ready contrasts of the white man, rapacious and destructive, with the man of nature—contrasts carefully avoided by Bugnet—are all found in *Vers l'ouest* and *Manitoba*.

La bourrasque describes the unfolding of the destructive forces of civilization on the *métis* people. In the holocaust the strange figure of Louis Riel rises to lead his warriors to ultimate defeat. The subject lent itself to one of those broad evocations which novelists in search of the exotic are so fond of.[78] But Constantin-Weyer seems to have been more aware of the ridiculous than of the innocent devotion in Louis Riel's entourage. Consequently his *Bourrasque,* notwithstanding certain convincing passages, has not the power to move us. Louis Riel's love stories smack of the burlesque and would not be inappropriate for a bantering man-about-town. The execution of the rebel is transformed into a sad comedy in which the participants, be they English, French Canadians or *métis,* are equally ludicrous. And finally, for his long descriptive passages, Constantin-Weyer borrows whole pages from his former novel, *Manitoba,* a method which puts him, as far as imagination is concerned, in the same class as Louis Fréchette.

More suited to his talents are *Cinq éclats de silex,* pictures of the Canadian West. Although the repetitions too often call to mind the novels already written, this work is attractive because it is authentic. The good humour of the novelist—a kind of English sense of humour—this time furnishes a mixed accompaniment to his frolics with a native Indian.

Cavelier de La Salle marks a notable change in Constantin-Weyer's style. When he tackles one of the legendary figures of New France his prose is purified of the dross which had disfigured the first four books. His mocking spirit, no longer having any power over men and events long since a part of history, takes on reverence. He, too, although on a more modest scale, had travelled over the savannahs of the South and the snow-covered wastes of the far North. Thanks to this common experience, Constantin-Weyer wrote not only the story of Cavelier de La Salle but his own as well. The result is one of the best Canadian historical novels.

Un homme se penche sur son passé crowns the *Epopée canadienne.* The man who seemed able to face victoriously the combined powers of nature and man confesses himself vanquished. Because he has become humanized and also because his style is remarkably purified, Constantin-Weyer at last succeeds in touching us. In this stylizing of his Canadian experience, etchings like the following are not infrequent:

Le train me débarqua sur la plate-forme déserte, en un aube d'estampe japonaise. Maisons, forêt, étaient des lavis synthétiques à l'encre de Chine, ourlés d'un trait vert sombre, sous un ciel vert clair. A l'est, entre la cime de la forêt et le ciel, un pinceau ferme et délicat avait tracé d'un seul trait cette bande citron qui allait être le jour.[79]

The train put me off on the deserted platform, in a dawn like that of a Japanese print. Houses and forest were synthetic wash-tints in China ink, bordered with a line of dark green under a light green sky. To the east, between the forest tree-tops and the sky, a firm and delicate brush had traced with one stroke that band of yellow which was the approaching day.[79] [*trans.*]

To Constantin-Weyer's Canadian series may be added *Clairière.*[80] A synthesis of innumerable forest dramas taken from life, *Clairière* reveals a narrator of animal stories of great style. The most literary of his novels, *Un homme se penche sur son passé* will nevertheless be preferred because of its spontaneous verity.

The similarities in the careers of Hémon, Bugnet and Constantin-Weyer invite comparison. Without a doubt, Constantin-Weyer is the least gifted of the three. At the beginning of their adult life they had come to Canada in search of the meaning of profound yearnings within them. The confrontation of Canada and Constantin-Weyer could be only short-lived: just one side of him had any interest in this gamble and, once satisfied, for the full flowering of self he needed other sustenance than that which had been emptied of its substance in the using. Here lies the reason for the lack of depth in a work which, in its last phase, redeems itself by an incontestable success.

Marie Le Franc (b. 1879)

It was in 1905, at the same time as Bugnet, that Marie Le Franc became acquainted with Canada. Still closer to Brittany than Hémon, her work is permeated with intuitions and feminine divinations. Very early for Marie Le Franc, Canada became an extension of France, or rather of Brittany. Now in Montreal or in the Laurentians, now in Paris or on the Finistère moors, her journeys were journeys of intercommunication. So it was that in 1927 *Grand Louis l'innocent,* fruit of a sojourn in Brittany, was printed in Canada before obtaining the *Prix Femina*[81] in France.

The formula which had been successful for *Grand Louis l'innocent* was to be developed further in Marie Le Franc's French-Canadian work. It consists in describing the magic of nature in uncomplicated men, fashioned as much, if not more, by sea, mountains or forest as by society. Grand Louis, a simple soul, is a reflection of the dreary and poetic stretches of the Brittany coast. Hélier, his Canadian counterpart, is fashioned by the Mont Tremblant country. Marie Le Franc's whole art consists in the rediscovery, in a new guise, of the Eden revealed to Europe by Bernardin de Saint-Pierre and Chateaubriand. Two centuries of yearnings and dreams of the New World are back of the pages of fine writing which explain the intimate communion between Hélier, the woodsman, and the glorious Laurentian lakes and mountains.

The trouble is that from one book to the other the method remains unchanged. In the end the characters lose themselves in a semi-darkness, made up of foliation always visible beforehand because always alike. On one occasion, nevertheless, Marie Le Franc endowed French-Canadian literature with a novel which will live.

Coming after the works of Hémon, Constantin-Weyer and Bugnet, *La rivière solitaire* gives to Canadian nature a face hitherto unknown. Nature, always threatening in the background in Hémon, something out of which to make a Japanese print for Constantin-Weyer, a measure of all things in *Nipsya* and *La forêt*, provokes here the unforeseen reaction of trust and total surrender. For the first time maternal concern is found in the soil and seasons of Canada.

The story of the colonization of Temiskaming which makes up the plot of *La rivière solitaire* is told—wonder of wonders!—without raising the shades of Péribonka. The hero of the novel will be the French-Canadian people, not idealized but as it really is— capable, if need be, of a collective dedication to the generous "mystique" of which it is the sole American heir; very often capable also of mediocrity and smug complacency towards the stranger. As in the case of Grand Louis and Hélier, the French-Canadian people will find the way intuitively by means of the mysterious but benevolent play of the forces of nature. Marie Le Franc is the only novelist who, instead of painting pictures, registers with a precision that is poetry itself the sensations provoked by a blizzard or by the sight of a burned forest. In this novelist of the instinct, there are pages that neither Bugnet nor Hémon nor Constantin-Weyer, nor, closer to us, Savard would have been able to write because all those cerebral writers sought to depict a nature which would produce in us a shudder of fear or wonder. Entirely submissive to the Canadian earth, Marie Le Franc has surprised it into intimacy. Because *La rivière solitaire* is the faithful account of some of those privileged moments, French-Canadian literature has been enriched by one more novel of the first rank.[82]

GROWING DIVERSITY OF THE FRENCH-CANADIAN NOVEL

Albert Laberge (1871-1960)

The first great French-Canadian novelist, friend of several of the writers and artists who brought renown to the first half of this century and the writer who preceded Louis Hémon in the path of Realism, Albert Laberge exerted no influence on the course of

French-Canadian literature. His isolation is explained by his savage determination to evade official honours. But even had he sought to assert himself silence might have cloaked his work. If Rodolphe Girard's *Marie Calumet,* a novel as innocent as it is inspid, brought down on itself the thunderbolts of the right-thinking, how audacious *La Scouine* would appear to the contemporaries of Mgr. Paul Bruchési!

An imperfect synchronization such as happens sometimes when a writer reaches a very advanced age, has prevented Laberge's emerging from his relative obscurity. At the beginning of his intellectual adventure Laberge was placed in the *avant-garde* of young novelists of his age; at his death the Realism that he had never stopped practising for more than half a century made him old-fashioned. The paternalistic structure of French-Canadian society at the beginning of the century was hostile to the frank explorations of Albert Laberge. The literary revolution which was to follow the Second World War like a tidal wave has rapidly reached, then gone ahead of the undaunted navigator, leaving him to lag behind in the literary movement.

When Laberge was twenty years of age Maupassant seems to have been the great revelation which gave his vocation its whole direction.[83] No importance is to be attached to this encounter beyond that of a sudden consciousness in Laberge of what he actually had within his power to do. The immense desire to write nothing but the truth, to describe Canada as he saw it, found its justification in Maupassant's example. The pessimism of the one came to reinforce and sanction that of the other, persuaded as he was already of the fundamental wickedness of man. Concern for the correct and irreplaceable detail, which entails long preparation, would remain the technique of the French-Canadian novelist. To the formula of Realism Laberge brought a touch of his own temperament. From a demanding and at times morbid sensuality, he came to evince interest in the more unusual manifestations of sexuality, starting with procuring and ending with voyeurism and necrophilia. In his old age, through a keen feeling for nature, he was able to reach the concupiscence of all creatures and attain an olfactory and visual serenity which, not without a show of impudence, he set over against that of believers.

Going into journalism when young, Laberge immediately found the note that would always be his. In 1895, at a time when the French-Canadian public was applauding the insipid exhortations of

Laure Conan, there appeared in *Le Samedi* a page as new, for the times, as this one:

VIRGILIAN SILHOUETTE

An old wooden house, grey, low, sitting by the side of the road.

An ancient ash, scarred, scrofulous, bearing horrible wounds, its foliage turned brown, bent over towards the old ruin.

Nearby in a field without any grass, cropped right down to the earth, three thirsty reddish-brown cows were mooing plaintively.

Every now and then some crows would come over in heavy, uneven flight, flinging caws into the air as they went by as if they were dung.

Out beyond stretched the country, poor, bleak, still.

There was a winding road where almost nobody ever went by.

And a pale autumn sun smiled feebly down on this landscape that was asleep, dead.

The impression was of something that had died away, that was done, that was of another day.

It was Sunday.

The *habitant,* used to working, incapable of resting, closed up in his dwelling, does not know what to do with himself.

The door of the old house is open.

On a bench against the wall five children, the oldest perhaps eight years of age, are sitting side by side, motionless, speechless, patiently waiting. Their legs and feet are bare and around their necks they are wearing red necklaces, made of hawthorn berries strung together.[84] [*trans.*]

To gauge the significance of these lines, one must compare them with the pastorals that French-Canadian novelists were presenting to their readers at that time as faithful pictures of country life. Having firmly decided to break with the formal lie established in French-Canadian literature from the time when Gérin-Lajoie had wanted to drag the young men off to lands about to be colonized, Laberge devoted himself for fifteen years to his novel *La Scouine,* which was meant to unmask the brutish *habitant.*[85]

La Scouine (1918) is to French-Canadian literature what Zola's *La terre* is to French literature, except for this important difference that the French-Canadian novel, with an edition of only sixty copies, was the object of a private scandal. Like the author of *Nana* Laberge was convinced that ugliness goes with the farmer's work. That is why the characters of *La Scouine* are less important than the sordid reality they represent. Marked by incessant and thankless toil, taking cover in a fierce egotism, the same fate awaits these primitive beings: a progressive dehumanizing in the sufferings of old age, always cruel because experienced in isolation. An intolerable monotony, a nameless feeling of being trampled on, are the reward of dedication to the land.

Laberge, who is like no other French-Canadian writer, gets back to writing at a time when most creative people begin to break off from their work. This impenitent pessimist, gay and confident, at the age of sixty-four sets to work on his future. Strong on his legs, with keen eyesight, he goes from one corner of his flower-bedecked little property of Chateauguay to another to distill the most lugubrious prose in French-Canadian literature. The more he is drenched with joy when in contact with the trees that are his divinities and with the heady scent of his flowers, the gloomier his written thought becomes. Is there not a kind of masochistic coquetry in this old man? Never having recovered from his disillusioned analysis of one of the minor branches of the human species, French-Canadian society, he seems to take delight in the not-too-pretty stories of his gay decline, poking his nose out again only to fill his lungs with the good country air and get ready to enjoy a long series of uninterrupted meals, admirably well digested, until he neared his ninetieth year.

The great weakness of the seven collections of short stories which, with *La Scouine,* represent the major part of his work, lies in the artistic *parti pris.*[86] Misfortune, from time immemorial, has furnished the raw materials of world literature. But the calamities still have to be written into the logic of events. Nothing of the kind in the case of Laberge. If the tale seems to be moving him off from a dramatic and painful ending, a pitiless nemesis will see to it that that young woman in whom we were beginning to take an interest will suddenly be burnt alive in a fire that could not have been anticipated, or that some robust farmer will drop dead along the way before our eyes, preferably falling headfirst into a patch of dung freshly deposited there thanks to the foresight of the novelist.

Because old age explains itself and is a preparation for the last bitter act, Laberge will have no difficulty in finding an endless variety of modulations and in sketching for us every capitulation and horror of it. At times he will be satisfied with a simple clinical description of remarkable accuracy:

Assis sur une petite chaise, dans une chambre sombre et sans air,
le Cheval Blanc, son chapeau sur la tête, était là immobile, ses
vieilles mains sur les genoux, des mains déformées, marquées de

grosses veines bleues, des mains couvertes de mouches qui les mangeaient. Chose incroyable, il ne faisait pas un geste pour les chasser. Figé sur son siège étroit, on l'aurait cru paralysé. Et la bave lui coulait lentement de la bouche, glissait sur son menton et jusque sur son gilet. Avec des yeux bleus, de ce bleu que l'on voit aux poupées de faïence, il regardait droit devant lui.[87]

On a little chair in a dark airless room, the *Cheval Blanc,* with his hat on, sat motionless, his old hands on his knees, hands that were deformed, marked with great blue veins, hands covered with flies that were eating at them. Incredibly, he made no move to chase them off. You would have said that he was paralyzed, frozen there on his straight chair. And spittle flowed slowly from his mouth, slid to his chin and right down onto his vest. With his blue eyes, the blue that you see in china dolls, he stared straight ahead.[87] [*trans.*]

More often he would lay bare the mean little attentions with which we surround old men in order to be more easily rid of them. Philorum, shown the door by his brother, has only to find some hole in which to die:

There I am just walking along quietly in the street in front of the boarding-house, when suddenly I see him coming. Like everybody else I know that he has no money left, that he has no place to go and that for him there are only the main roads that lead everywhere and nowhere. Just the same, hypocritically, sanctimonious rascal that I am, like somebody trying to pass a bad coin I ask him in a cordial tone of voice: "Well now, how's everything?" Then, aware that I, along with the whole parish, know the terrible fix he is in, he puts on a good face just the same, swaggers a bit and says with a half-smile, "Not too bad." And he goes off. You can't keep on palavering forever, can you? He, well, he was going where he knew, where he had decided that he was going, where his destiny was taking him and I, satisfied with finishing the interview with so little difficulty, I go on again taking my after-dinner walk.[88] [*trans.*]

The psychological acuity of which Laberge gives proof in his best pages makes him one of the greatest French-Canadian novelists. If it is true that the contemporary novel is inspired by other methods than his, it is none the less true that the lesson of his life is one for today, to owe nothing except to oneself. Laberge laughed at literary fashions as the prescriptions of purists. His language, nearly always vigorous if not always correct,[89] put him in the first rank of French-Canadian prose writers.

Lionel Groulx (b. 1878)

For the historian Lionel Groulx, literature is above all a means to an end. He made himself defender of the traditional virtues of French Canadians, all of which seem to him to be summed up in the idea of *race*. François-Xavier Garneau had attached great importance to the racial factor in order to explain history. But *race*, a word which is vague in the case of Garneau, is wreathed with sacred values in the nationalist mystique of Groulx.

In the manner of French-Canadian story-tellers Groulx evokes the past in *Rapaillages* (1916) and *Chez nos gens* (1920). Notably he brings back the touching image of his grandmother, whose religious faith may well have had something to do with determining his own. His emotion when he describes the memories of his youth is so sincere that certain pages are lit up with it. But it seems that this serene picture of country life became impossible to him after the racial struggles which brought English Canadians and French Canadians face to face during the First World War. Wanting to strike the imagination of the greatest possible number of readers, Groulx tried his hand at the novel, for which he had little aptitude. Around disputes over the schools which were poisoning the relations between Canadians of the two languages, particularly in Ontario, he thought up a story which displayed the bad faith of the majority and the sacred character of the mission of the French Canadians. It is hardly surprising that *L'appel de la race* (1922) is an artistic failure. But the historian-become-novelist had found a formula to please the crowd and the same formula was resorted to in 1932 when he published *Au cap Blomidon*, which he might have entitled *L'appel de la race acadienne*.

Abbé Lionel Groulx is an improvement on Tardivel. His nationalism, intransigent though it is, excludes fireworks, and his style, marked by a relative reticence, comes close to distinction while just falling short of the mark.

Groulx's psychology is that of the propagandist. In this regard there could be nothing more over-simple and more improbable than the way in which Lantagnac in *L'appel de la race,* and Jean Bérubé, the Acadian, allow themselves to become imbued with the regenerative forces of their ancestors. By means of these two novels Lionel Groulx wanted to make it understood that the ideal of race justifies all sacrifices. So Lantagnac, carried away by the casuistry of a priest-adviser, does not flinch before the troubles that he brings to his own family. This is of no consequence when the cause of French influence in Ontario will be saved at the price.

The eternal theme of patriotism does not lend itself well to the novel. On too lofty a plane to be within easy reach, it leads the ordinary run of novelist straight to bathos. It was through devotion to the cause that Lionel Groulx took that road.

Jean-Charles Harvey (b. 1891)

That a society like the French-Canadian was able to develop in the bosom of Anglo-Saxon populations over thirty times more numerous is partly explained by the tightly-knit organization of the French-speaking group. This phenomenon of spiritual airtightness is by no means unknown among peoples and is always accompanied by very strong psychological pressures. For sensitive natures the result of this is a feeling of constraint which at times reaches the point of exasperation and revolt. In the nineteenth century, before the exodus to the cities, French-Canadian literature was the spontaneous product of a conservative "mystique" against which only a few hard-heads had rebelled. The First World War, which was conducive to industrial growth in Canada, provoked profound changes in French-Canadian society. The rapid metamorphosis of Canada, which has become one of the great industrial nations of the world since 1939, is actually based on that first transformation at the beginning of the century. The growth of the proletariat in French Canada, the size of which can be measured in the contemporary novel, had already made itself felt betwen the two wars.

Jean-Charles Harvey, spiritual heir of Arthur Buies, was one of the first in the twentieth century to want to awaken his compatriots out of their patriarchal dream. In the interests of the cause he became in turn novelist, journalist and literary critic.

Jean-Charles Harvey's novels provide some of the heaviest reading in French-Canadian literature. In his enthusiasm this writer, who rightfully took issue with the moralism and nationalism of the French-Canadian novel, was guilty of the contrary, or, should one say, the same fault since he, too, in his own way is a preacher. In *Les demi-civilisés* (1934), free love ostentatiously replaces the chaste and unreal loves of the past. A severe religious upbringing, far from benefiting *Sébastien Pierre* (1935), makes him an American gangster. *Les paradis de sable* (1953), more pamphlet than novel, explains what it costs to belong to the "Party."

Jean-Charles Harvey has better served the cause of French-Canadian letters by way of the newspaper. When Cardinal Ville-neuve (1883-1947) forbade his flock to read *Les demi-civilisés*, the novelist-reformer had to leave *Le Soleil* as editor, but not until after saying publicly just what he thought. Later Harvey founded *Le Jour*, which had a longer life than *La Lanterne* of Buies. During the war years *Le Jour*, the best-edited of French-Canadian news-papers of the day, made an effort to maintain the very French tradition of a liberal newspaper.

Pierre Dupuy (b. 1896)

André Laurence, Canadien-français,[90] Pierre Dupuy's only contri-bution to the novel, thoughtfully goes back over the intellectual and moral road taken by the French-Canadian writer before 1939. As we have seen, ever since the Conquest France had had an irresistible attraction for the best minds of French Canada. Every budding writer had one ambition above all others—to go to Paris. Had Nelligan not contemptuously pushed aside the suggestion that he should be published in Montreal? André Laurence is the prototype of the French-Canadian writer who leaves college fired with literary ambition and without knowing how to cope with the material prob-lems which stand in the way of his career. On this score Pierre Dupuy's novel is not unusual since the theme of a young writer having to defend his ideal against the hard realities of life has had any number of interpretations in all literatures. But this traditional background material has been handled with considerable talent. Pierre Dupuy was able to give this novel an unaccustomed ring which came from a consideration of the personal difficulties against which the French-Canadian writer traditionally has had to struggle.

Will André Laurence succumb to the urgent appeals of a woman with whom he is in love in favour of the solution dictated by his bourgeois upbringing? Pierre Dupuy has solved this problem, at once artistic and national, in an elegant and original ending. Actually André Laurence has little real aptitude for literature, having almost no will to get down to work. So his going to Paris is a mistake. Nevertheless he is giving in to a noble dream. Literature will gain nothing by his decision to leave everything else. But will not the example he offers and the false hopes born of it be of service in keeping the sacred fire burning from one generation to the other?

Pierre Dupuy's departure for Paris was amply justified by *André Laurence, Canadien-français*, one of the rare French-Canadian novels between the two wars that is still relevant. At the same time *André Laurence* brings to a close a chapter in the cultural relations between France and French Canada. The intellectual independence towards which it is heading will tend to make Montreal the centre of the literary aspirations of every French-Canadian writer. For a long time Paris will remain the desired goal but no longer the only one as in the case of André Laurence. Inevitably, and very fortunately for the future of French-Canadian literature, it is in Montreal that the literary reputations of tomorrow will be made, the role of Paris now being to ratify and make known abroad the verdict of the Canadian Paris.

Rex Desmarchais (b. 1908)

The novel of analysis is a formidable test for the young writer. Not only must he make himself a clinical expert on the heart, but in addition, in order to express himself, he must strip thought and style to a fine point that few novelists can lay claim to without long and patient effort. Tempted by the genre which had been practised in a small way by Laure Conan before him, Rex Desmarchais published in succession *L'initiatrice* (1932) and *Le feu intérieur* (1933) —two failures in which the author's inexperience makes it impossible for him to rise to the level of moralist in order to write knowledgeably about his love for Violaine or to explain to us the reason for the pointless relationship between Robert and Marthe in his second novel.

La Chesnaie (1942) is the retrospective diagnosis of the uneasy years which came before the war of 1939-1945. While not a profound work, in the nationalistic tradition of the novel *La Chesnaie* takes first place. Tardivel's thin tale, *Pour la patrie,* and the *reductio ad absurdum, L'appel de la race* by Abbé Groulx, are partisan and consequently false interpretations of the Canadian racial problem. The latent antagonism between Anglo-Saxons and French Canadians that was established by the Conquest of 1763 finds at least in *La Chesnaie* a possible literary expression. Hughes Larocque, the strong man who dreams of leading his countrymen to independence, is too close to the ideal that was being forged in those sad years by the most enlightened among the unemployed for this work to be without documentary if not artistic value.

Claude-Henri Grignon (b. 1894)

The name of Claude-Henri Grignon stands out between those of
Louis Hémon and Philippe Panneton, whose *Trente arpents,* published in 1938, after a quarter of a century brings to a brilliant close
the monotonous series of *Maria Chapdelaines.*[91] While Hémon
and Panneton through the characters are interpreters of French-
Canadian farm people, Grignon is the creator of Séraphin Poudrier,
the eternal miser. In part owing to the radio adaptation of the
novel, French Canada has acknowledged *Un homme et son péché*
as a French-Canadian classic. This is a deserved reputation based
on the book's acute analysis, the truth of its dialogue and the
accuracy of language that is resolutely French-Canadian. Grignon,
however, has not been able to escape the snares of his quite conventional theme. The miser plunging his hands into his sack of
gold coins was already a hackneyed subject in the seventeenth
century. Even though this demonstration of the "sin" does correspond to truth, as Grignon assures us in his foreword, the trouble
with it is that, like the last picture of Séraphin perishing in the
flames with his savings beside him, it belongs to the continued-story
class.

Philippe Panneton (1895-1960)

In 1938 *Trente arpents* came on the scene, a novel as important
in its way as *Maria Chapdelaine.* For its sons the French-Canadian
soil will remain an inexhaustible source of feeling and ideas; writers
of the future will vary in their own way and according to their
temperaments the manner in which they sing its praises or dis-
parage it. Ringuet, however, runs no risk of being outdone in his
interpretation of the effects on the French Canadian of his marriage to the land. This is because *Trente arpents,* which is the
crowning point in the efforts of a generation of writers to give
artistically valid shape to the rustic novel, is the reflection of a
world that is ending. The exodus towards the Montreal area and the
industrial centres of Canada, starting at the beginning of the century, has spread decisively in the years following the publication of
Trente arpents. The increasingly general mechanization, the rapid
comings and goings because of the car, radios in farm homes and
in our day television, bring the *habitant* into closer contact with the
town-dwellers, if not with the proletariat. The drama of the break-
up of a farmer's family is still something that takes place today but

no longer does it happen in the circumstances of which Ringuet objectively took note.

Contrary to so many others who, from Hémon's time, have chosen only the themes dear to the recluse of Péribonka, Ringuet takes us into the grandeur and decline of a dynasty of the land, the Moisan family. Under heavy pressure from Euchariste, prototype of the peasant-farmer, as pitiless towards his own family as he is towards himself, and of a corrosive North American materialism, a family of a century-old French-Canadian tradition on the land disintegrates and vanishes when it comes into contact with the modern world.

Hémon and Ringuet, whose novels are separated by a quarter of a century, can usefully be compared. In this French and French-Canadian diptych the French panel stands out because of the finish of the form and sharpness of detail, while the French-Canadian panel, in spite of certain imperfections, is moving because of its authenticity. If faithful likeness were the only criterion by which to decide between these two great novels, *Trente arpents* would belong to a higher order. If it is true that Hémon did not fail to paint the inhuman side of colonization around Lake Saint-Jean, his conclusion, which makes *Maria Chapdelaine* a kind of French-Canadian Jeanne d'Arc, borders on pathos. Nothing of the kind occurs in the case of Ringuet, since Euchariste, far from his fields, ends his days in the murkiness of a little industrial town in New England.

Because Ringuet established a boundary mark in the history of the French-Canadian novel, he has had almost no imitators. After *Trente arpents*, novelists, too, will desert the land for that great field of observation, Montreal, which opens to them.[92] Is it not significant that in our day Germaine Guèvremont, who has remained faithful to the country, brings her analysis to bear on the qualities of the *habitant* that are lasting and outside of any historical and economic contingencies? From this one must not come to the conclusion that the best French-Canadian novelists, those to come to light in the literary growth of the last twenty years, will have forgotten the ideal of the man who clears the land, the pioneer. It seems to us that deep in the majority of French Canadians there sleeps a rustic dream which is not unrelated to the high religious ideal that has come down through generations. Is it not true that *Alexandre Chenevert*, that impenitent city man, resembles all those Montrealers of small means who undergo a change on contact with the virgin forest, even when they must soon return to the ant-hill?

ROBERT DE ROQUEBRUNE (b. 1899): *Testament de mon enfance* (1951) is more representative of the real talent of Robert de Roquebrune than his historical novels. Nearly a century after *Les anciens Canadiens* and the *Mémoires* of Philippe Aubert de Gaspé, Roquebrune continues a prized tradition of French Canada, that of the gentleman-writer. If the author's display of numerous genealogies with all the names involved is irksome at times, this drawback is inevitable, doubtless, in this kind of work. Roquebrune does not have Aubert de Gaspé's colourful language; on the other hand he has restraint. In these touching recollections there is a certain dated charm, precisely what this memorialist of French Canada before twentieth-century industrialization wanted to evoke. The death of Sambo, the faithful Negro servant, is moving in its simplicity and is a picture of a profoundly humane civilization of which all French Canada is heir.

The historical novels of Robert de Roquebrune are in the already-established tradition of the nineteenth century with fewer improbabilities and vulgarities. His first novel in this category, *Les habits rouges*, is representative of his reconstructions of a past into which he has not succeeded in breathing life as he did in his *Testament*.

Works: *Les habits rouges* (Paris: Monde nouveau, 1923); *D'un océan à l'autre* (Paris: Monde nouveau, 1924); *Les dames Lemarchand* (Paris: Le Monde moderne, 1927); *Contes du soir et de la nuit* (Montreal: Valiquette, 1942); *Testament de mon enfance* (Paris: Plon, 1951).

ADJUTOR RIVARD (1868-1945), a co-founder in 1902 of the *Société du Parler français*, poured into his two principal works, *Chez nous* (Quebec: l'Action sociale catholique, 1914) and *Chez nos gens* (*ibid.*, 1918), his wide collection of words belonging to the soil. When the collector forgets himself, the story-teller can bring back to life some departed figure of the French-Canadian countryside in prose which is not lacking in appeal. Rivard joins Roquebrune in recreating the legendary alms-gatherer of his youth. Where idleness is given a respected place the commercial spirit cannot reign supreme. The alms-gatherer, head high, sure of his rights as a free man and generally well regarded, is the product of a civilization at the opposite pole from the dehumanizing ant-hills of our day. Rivard's best pages, like Roquebrune's, are filled with a sense of quiet and repose which have not yet entirely disappeared from French Canada.

GEORGES BOUCHARD (1868-1945): Much less talented than the two above, Bouchard is the author of *Premières semailles* (Quebec:

l'Action sociale, 1917) and *Vieilles choses, vieilles gens* (Montreal: Beauchemin, 1926).

DAMASE POTVIN (b. 1878): With more diligence than talent, Damase Potvin made himself French-Canadian guarantor of Henri Pourrat, poet-novelist of Auvergne. His works are variants on the well-known themes of country labours and the new influence of modern civilization on the younger generation.

Works: *L'appel de la terre* (Quebec: l'Evénement, 1919); *Le Français* (Montreal: Garand, 1925); *La rivière-à-Mars* (Montreal: Les Editions du Totem, 1934); *Sous la signe du quartz* (Montreal: Valiquette, 1940), etc.

ERNEST CHOQUETTE (1862-1941): Choquette's three main works, *Les Ribaud* (Montreal: E. Senécal & Cie, 1898), Claude Paysan (Paris: Casterman, n.d.) and *La terre* (Montreal: Beauchemin, 1916), belong in their poverty of invention to the French-Canadian novel of Gérin-Lajoie's period. Choquette escapes mediocrity because of his landscape painting.

ADOLPHE BASILE ROUTHIER (1839-1920): The name of the author of *O Canada! terre de mes aïeux* should not be entirely forgotten among novelists. If he attempted the impossible in wanting to produce an apologia in story form (*Le centurion*, Quebec: l'Action sociale, 1909; *Paulina*, Quebec: Imprimerie des franciscaines missionnaires, 1918), at least he succeeded in expressing himself in precise, almost elegant language, in a period when French-Canadian prose was still turgid and incorrect.

RODOLPHE GIRARD (b. 1879): All Rodolphe Girard's novels have fallen into oblivion except *Marie Calumet* (1904). At the time of its publication this insipid *Clochemerle* caused a small scandal which was the means of its survival. *Marie Calumet* was republished in 1946 with a preface by Jean Richepin (Montreal: Editions Serge Brousseau).

HARRY BERNARD (b. 1898): One of the most prolific of French-Canadian novelists, Harry Bernard did his utmost through his writings to teach lessons that would be useful. Two of his first novels, *L'homme tombé* (Montreal: Lévesque, 1924), *La maison vide* (Montreal: l'Action Française, 1926), are based on the idea that the fate of the married man is in the hands of his wife. The man accomplishes what he is capable of or, on the contrary, finds himself reduced to absolute mediocrity according to whether or not the wife is willing to say nothing about her own requirements of life. There is an underlying social criticism in these novels: the

French-Canadian woman, influenced by American customs, looks for her happiness outside of the affection and respect of the family. This is a conception which resembles the role of the woman in *La terre vivante* (Montreal: Bibliothèque de l'Action Française, 1925), since Marie does not succumb to the lures of the city but marries a worthy *habitant*, in accordance with a tradition less and less respected. In *Dolorès* (Montreal: Lévesque, 1932) and *Les jours sont longs* (Ottawa: le Cercle du Livre de France, 1951), the setting in the Laurentians indirectly suggests the superiority of life in the great outdoors to the unnatural life of the big city.

From 1924 there is no distinguishable development in Bernard. The love story with which the novelist has dressed up *Les jours sont longs* is worthy of the tradition which, for nearly a century, characterized the not very high level of the French-Canadian novel.

NOTES TO CHAPTER FOUR

1. Everything of biographical importance on Nelligan may be found in Luc Lacourcière's preface to *Poésies complètes* (Montreal: Fides, 1952), pp. 7-38.

The pages devoted to Nelligan's art by Louis Dantin, at the beginning of the century, are still relevant: *Emile Nelligan et son oeuvre* (Montreal: Editions Beauchemin, 1903). In a penetrating analysis of French-Canadian poetry Gérard Bessette has submitted the poet's work to a searching and useful examination: *Les images en poésie canadienne-française* (Montreal: Beauchemin, 1960), pp. 215-274.

The publication of *Emile Nelligan: Sources et originalité de son oeuvre* by Paul Wyczynski (Editions de l'Université d'Ottawa, 1960) recently brought to a brilliant conclusion more than half a century of studies on Nelligan. It will no longer be possible to speculate on the spiritual and artistic origins of this inspired poet. Although Wyczynski at times indulges in pure hypotheses on the origins of poems, and though his erudition is given full play in what are sometimes minor considerations, his study remains a model of intellectual integrity.

2. In the excellent critical edition obtained through Luc Lacourcière, see Nelligan's first poems composed in 1896 and 1897. We owe to this edition the poems quoted and their chronology.

3. Nelligan's swift development may be judged from this same poem, *Moines en défilade*, which he altered entirely before becoming mentally ill in 1899.

LE CLOITRE NOIR

Ils défilent au chant étouffé des sandales,
Le chef bas, égrenant de massifs chapelets,
Et le soir qui s'en vient, du sang de ses reflets,
Mordore la splendeur funéraire des dalles.

Ils s'effacent soudain, comme en de noirs dédales,
Au fond des corridors pleins de pourpres relais
Où de grands anges peints aux vitraux verdelets
Interdisent l'entrée aux terrestres scandales.

136. *History of French-Canadian Literature*

> *Leur visage est funèbre, et dans leurs yeux sereins*
> *Comme les horizons vastes des cieux marins,*
> *Flambe l'austérité des froides habitudes.*
>
> *La lumière céleste emplit leur large esprit,*
> *Car l'Espoir triomphant creusa les solitudes*
> *De ces silencieux spectres de Jésus-Christ.*

4. More than the *Ecole de Québec,* which never existed, the *Ecole littéraire de Montréal* deserves the name because from its inception the School was known to its founders by this name. The drawback to this title is that the School, after all, was only one of emulation, made up of the most diverse talents. At the time it was created, in 1865, it was indeed a school in the limited sense of the word, since its members found themselves under the strict necessity of completing their education by assiduous and regular study of the dictionary; later the School was to count among its members not only poets but historians, novelists. story-writers and literary critics. In short, the School grew to the point of becoming literature-in-the-making. It could not be otherwise since the School, having no literary doctrine to defend, could not have any direct intellectual influence. The *Ecole littéraire* was the outward manifestation of the desire to perfect themselves, felt by French Canadians at different stages of their literary history; at the time it was called *Ecole littéraire de Montréal.* Cf. *L'Ecole littéraire de Montréal,* Archives des Lettres canadiennes (Montreal: Fides, 1963), Vol. II.

5. *See: Les soirées du château de Ramezay* (Montreal: Eusèbe Sénécal & Cie, 1900); *Les soirées de l'Ecole littéraire de Montréal* (Beauceville: L'Eclaireur Limité, 1925); Jean Charbonneau, *L'Ecole littéraire de Montréal* (Montreal: Editions Albert Lévesque, 1935).

6. *Le Cap Eternité suivi des Etoiles filantes.* Preface by Albert Lozeau (Montreal: Editions du Devoir, 1919).

7. Works: *L'âme solitaire* (Montreal: Beauchemin, 1907); *Le miroir des jours* (Montreal: Le Devoir, 1912); *Lauriers et feuilles d'érable* (Montreal, Le Devoir, 1916); *Poésies complètes* (Montreal: privately printed, 1925-1926), 3 vol.

8. M. Yves de Margerie has been good enough to put together for us the main results of research which he has been carrying out over a long period of years concerning Lozeau and his work, a considerable portion of which remains unpublished (cf. Appendix One). Publication of M. de Margerie's doctoral thesis would very likely give a new dimension to Lozeau, as it would appear that emotional involvement with the opposite sex played as great a role as physical pain in determining his intellectual and artistic development. But once the over-romanticized Lozeau of past criticism has been brought into better focus and the scattered writings are known, will Lozeau emerge with greater stature? If literary criticism stands to profit greatly from more complete documentation on this poet, it still seems unlikely that we shall have to modify radically the judgment made of him in our first edition, which we have slightly upgraded in the meantime.

9. *Le paon d'émail* (Paris: Lemerre, 1912), p. 104.

10. *Ibid.,* p. 72.

11. *Poèmes de cendre et d'or,* pp. 207-211.

12. *Le paon d'émail,* p. 64.

13. The publication in 1960 of *Géronte et son miroir* (Ottawa: Cercle du Livre de France), a collection of poems Morin wrote mostly for his own amusement, which masks with a veil of sadness the last years of a man who was a poet and who left us with a pitiful grimace.

In 1961 *Poèmes de cendre et d'or* and *Le paon d'émail* were put together in one volume through the good offices of Jean-Paul Plante: *Paul Morin, Oeuvres Poétiques* (Montreal: Fides).

14. Lawyer and journalist by turns, Léveillé seems to have sought his real profession in poetry. Works: *Les chemins de l'âme* (Montreal: Daoust & Tremblay, 1910); *La claire fontaine* (Montreal: Beauchemin, 1913); *Chante, rossignol chante* (Beauceville: L'Eclaireur, 1925); *Vers la lumière* (Montreal: Librairie d'Action canadienne-française, 1931).

15. *Vers la lumière*, p. 52.

16. *Dominantes* (Montreal: Editions Albert Lévesque, 1933), pp. 29-30. *See*: Louis Dantin, *Poètes de l'Amérique française* (Montreal: Albert Lévesque, 1934), pp. 57-72.

17. *Poètes de l'Amérique française* (Montreal: Albert Lévesque, 1934), pp. 101-102. *See*: Gabriel Nadeau, *Louis Dantin: Sa vie et son oeuvre* (Manchester, New Hampshire: Les Editions Lafayette, 1948).

Through the good offices of Gabriel Nadeau there was published in 1962 *Poèmes d'outre-tombe* (Trois-Rivières: Editions du Bien Public). To three *Chansons* out of print, unpublished poems have been added, confirming the judgment made above.

18. Works: *A travers les vents* (Montreal: Edouard Garand, 1925); *Metropolitan Museum* (Montreal, 1931); *Poésies nouvelles* (Montreal: Albert Lévesque, 1933).

19. Cf. pp. 206-208.

20. Works: *L'offrande aux vierges folles* (Sherbrooke: privately printed, 1928); *A l'ombre de l'Orford* (Sherbrooke: La Tribune, 1929). A portion of the poetical work of Desrochers was republished in the Nénuphar collection (Montreal: Fides, 1948).

The rapprochement suggested in our first edition between Choquette and Desrochers must be recognized with the publication of *Retour de Titus* (Ottawa: Editions de l'Université d'Ottawa, 1963). The illusion which may have guided Choquette in *Suite marine* ought to have made it possible for Desrochers to avoid the same reef. The Alexandrine, if it is not redeemed by a stylized vocabulary, can be practised only with difficulty in our day. This kind of conservativism is all the more surprising since French Canada has a group of young poets to be found in the forefront of contemporary French-language poetry.

21. *See:* Louis Dantin, *Poètes de l'Amérique française* (1934), pp. 161-179.

22. *Ibid.*, pp. 129-145.

23. Antoine Roy has made a critical bibliography of his father's work in *L'oeuvre historique de Pierre-Georges Roy* (Paris: Jouve & Cie, 1928). For the works published between 1928 and 1943, see: Rollande Dorais, *Bio-bibliographie de M. Pierre-Georges Roy* (Ecole de bibliothécaires de l'Université de Montreal, 1943). Preface by M. Victor Morin.

Among the most important works of Pierre-Georges Roy should be mentioned *Les vieilles églises de la province de Québec* (Ls-A. Proulx, Imprimeur du Roi, 1925) and *L'île d'Orléans* (Quebec: Proulx, 1928), a work crowned by the *Académie Française* in 1929.

24. *Les lettres, les sciences et les arts au Canada sous le régime français* (Paris: Jouve & Cie, 1930).

Among the historians who, between 1880 and 1940, participated in the school of research workers with which the name of the Roy family is so intimately associated, there should be mentioned: Auguste-Henri Gosselin (1843-1918), historian of the French-Canadian church: *L'Eglise au Canada depuis Monseigneur de Laval jusqu'à la conquête* (Quebec: Typographie Laflamme & Proulx, 1911-1914), 3 vol.; *L'Eglise au Canada après la conquête* (Quebec: Imprimerie Laflamme, 1916-1917), 4 vol. Amédée Gosselin (1863-1941) examined in all its details public education under French rule: *L'instruction au Canada sous le régime français, 1635-1760* (Quebec: Typographie Laflamme & Proulx, 1911). Edouard-Zotique Massicotte (1867-1947) published: *Montréal sous le régime français.* A list of the decrees, edicts, mandates, ordinances and regulations preserved in the archives of the Montreal Law Courts, 1640-1760 (Montreal: G. Ducharme, 1919); *Faits curieux de l'histoire de Montréal* (Montreal: Beauchemin, 1924). Aegidius Fauteux (1876-1941): *Bibliographie de la question universitaire Laval-Montréal 1852-1921* (Montreal: Arbour & Dupont, 1922); *Le duel au Canada* (Montreal: Editions du Zodiaque, 1934); *Les chevaliers de Saint-Louis en Canada* (Montreal: Les Editions des Dix, 1940), etc.

25. Before devoting himself entirely to history Chapais had spent seventeen years in journalism, becoming editor-in-chief of the *Courier du Canada* in 1884. In 1892 he put his readers on their guard against dangerous books in the following terms:

> We read in *Le Monde*:
> The *Bibliothèque française*, which has such pleasant memories for the well-read class of our population, is to reappear shortly, considerably improved, revised, corrected and enlarged, as they say in prospectus phraseology.
> This is what the management promises us:
> Every month there will be a publication containing one complete novel by one of the best-known authors in France, and it will reproduce the works of the most eminent writers of the century.
> All the works published by the *Bibliothèque française* will be "of indisputable morality and will be available to all."
> If the past is any portent of the future, here we have a new danger to the Canadian public.
> This *Bibliothèque française* has published and thrown into circulation a mass of immoral works:
> Novels by Georges Ohnet, Octave Feuillet, Alphonse Daudet, etc.
> — this publication has popularized all these dangerous books.
> Here it is appearing on the scene again. We are on the watch for it.
>
> But meanwhile, we cry: "Take care!" [*trans.*]

26. Published in four volumes in Quebec by Garneau between 1919 and 1923, then in four more by Valiquette in Montreal between 1932 and 1934. Chapais had made his beginning in history by publishing works of high quality relating to French rule: *Jean Talon, intendant de la Nouvelle-France* (Quebec: Imprimerie de S. A. Demers, 1904); *Le marquis de Montcalm* (Quebec: J.-P. Garneau, 1911).

Mlle. Julienne Barnard in *Mémoires Chapais* (Fides, 1961) has collected an imposing lot of documents concerning the considerable role played by the Chapais family in the nineteenth century.

27. Principal works: *Nos luttes constitutionnelles* (Montreal: Le Devoir, 1915-1916), 5 instalments; *La naissance d'une race* (Montreal: Bibliothèque de l'Action Française, 1919); *Lendemains de conquête* (Montreal: *ibid.*, 1920); *Notre maître le passé* (Montreal: Action Française, 1924); *ibid.* (3rd ed.; Montreal: Librairie Granger Frères, 1937-1944), 3 vol.; *L'enseignement français au Canada,* Vol. I: *Dans le Québec*

(Montreal: Editions Albert Lévesque, 1931); Vol. II: *Les écoles des minorités* (Montreal: Librairie Granger Frères, 1935); *Histoire du Canada français* (Montreal: L'Action Nationale, 1950-1952), 4 vol.

Professor of rhetoric in Valleyfield College from 1901 to 1906, Abbé Groulx continued his studies, first in Rome, where he obtained his doctorate in Philosophy and in Theology, then in Fribourg, Switzerland. Back in Canada in 1909 he lectured at Valleyfield again until he was appointed in 1915 to the Chair of Canadian History in the University of Montreal, affiliated at the time with Laval University. It was from that time that his name became known outside the country. Director of *l'Action Française* from 1920 to 1928, then deputy-professor in France from the University of Montreal in 1931, he lectured on Canada at the Sorbonne and at the Paris Catholic Institute. On December thirteenth, 1946, at the historian's residence, *l'Institut d'Histoire de l'Amérique française* was founded. Its *Revue*, dedicated to "the French fact in America," continues to be a valuable source for research workers. The goals that the Institute assigned to itself are set out in detail in the first volume of the *Revue*, pp. 152-159.

28. *Notre maître le passé,* 3rd ed., Vol. I, p. 16.

29. *Ibid.,* p. 20.

30. *La naissance d'une race,* 2nd ed., pp. 173-174.

31. *Nos luttes constitutionnelles,* lecture, April 12, 1916, p. 21.

32. *Nos responsabilités intellectuelles,* Secrétariat général de l'A.C.J.C., 1928, p. 39.

33. *Etudes de littérature canadienne-française* and *Nouvelles études de littérature canadienne-française* (Paris: F.-R. de Rudeval, 1904, 1907).

34. Among numerous works of Camille Roy: *Essais sur la littérature canadienne* (1907); *Nos origines littéraires* (1909); *Nouveaux essais sur la littérature canadienne* (1914); *La critique littéraire au XIXe siècle* (1918); *Regards sur nos lettres* (1931), etc.

35. *Essais sur la littérature canadienne,* p. 56.

36. *Ibid.,* pp. 95-96.

37. *La critique littéraire au XIXe siècle,* p. 177.

38. *Erables en fleurs,* p. 20. Quoted by Auguste Viatte, *Histoire littéraire de l'Amérique française* (Presses Universitaires Laval, 1954), p. 171.

39. *Regards sur la critique,* p. 226.

40. *Ibid.,* pp. 235-236.

41. *Ibid.,* p. 224.

42. *Essais sur la littérature canadienne,* p. 328.

43. *Nouvelle-France,* February, 1902, p. 97.

44. He will reproach the poet Emile Coderre, author of *Signes sur le sable* (1922), for having "paganized" his pessimism and "for having suggested, like Alfred de Vigny, that heaven is deaf as a stone and an impassive witness of our mortal anguish." (*Regards sur nos lettres,* p. 60). On the subject of *L'homme qui va* (1929) of Jean-Charles Harvey: "It is useless for the author to stud with stars the alcoves of free love; they are still bad places in the eyes of decent people." (*ibid.,* pp. 180-181).

45. Works: *De livres en livres* (Montreal: Carrier & Cie, 1929); *Et d'un livre à l'autre* (Montreal: Lévesque, 1932); *Les lettres au Canada français* (Lévesque, 1936).

46. *De livres en livres,* p. 45.

47. The poet Charles Gill summed up general opinion after the publication of *Émile Nelligan et son oeuvre* (Montreal: Beauchemin, 1903), by stating that Dantin's criticism was "the most impartial and the most equitable ever made by a French Canadian on French-Canadian poetry." Quoted by Charles ab der Halden, *Nouvelles études de littérature canadienne-française* (Paris: F.-R. de Rudeval, 1907), p. 347.

48. *Poètes de l'Amérique française,* p. 112.

49. *Ibid.,* pp. 161-162.

50. *Emile Nelligan et son oeuvre,* 1925, p. xxiv.

51. *Poètes de l'Amérique française,* pp. 101-102.

52. *Ibid.,* p. 125.

53. *Ibid.,* pp. 66-84.

54. *Ibid.,* p. 69.

55. Principal critical works: *Poètes de l'Amérique française* (Louis Carrier & Cie, 1928); *ibid.,* (Editions Albert Lévesque, 1934); *Gloses critiques* (Lévesque, 1931); *ibid.,* 1935.

Yves Garon in his thesis, *Louis Dantin, sa vie et son oeuvre* (Laval University, 1960), has thrown light on the important role that Dantin played for a whole generation of writers. Robert Choquette, Alfred Desrochers, Rosaire Dion-Lévesque submitted their poems to the Boston exile and more often than not followed his advice. In the last years of his life, between 1938 and 1942, Dantin turned to American literature. His signed articles for *Le Jour* testify in their variety to a spirit open to art in all its forms. In its exhaustive documentation and the new biographical elements to be found in it, the thesis of Yves Garon is seen to be an indispensable means to the understanding of Dantin's work.

Gabriel Nadeau published part of the correspondence of Dantin in his *Louis Dantin, sa vie et son oeuvre* (Manchester, N. H.: Les Editions Lafayette, 1948).

56. In addition to his royalist preferences Dugas makes a display of very Old France sentiments: "M. Henry Bataille belongs to that group of artists who, to the sound of bugles and the sighing of the flute, are leading France to the abyss." *Le théâtre à Montréal* (Paris: Henri Falque, 1911).

57. *Apologies* (Montreal: Paradis-Vincent, 1919), pp. 13-14.

58. *Versions* (Montreal: Maison Francq, 1917).

59. *Littérature canadienne* (Paris: Firmin-Didot, 1929), pp. 144-145.

60. In the virgin forest, raised in the fashion of a rustic god, moulded from clay, lifted up by the rhythm of the solitudes and the will to live, there was an august peasant, the father of us all. According to our vicissitudes we have pretended to forget him but he holds us by the secret roots of our soul. In spite of our present anxieties we shall not suppress those qualities of his which flow in our own veins like inexhaustible sap. But he must be less severe than those people who, on all sides, cry out to his fatherhood. I like to think that his form rises over our day's work and that he looks at us with the eyes of faith and love. Perhaps, indeed, the imagination which was alien to this virile mason of our national and human existence does not constitute in his eyes a contemptible game, and perhaps, too, in his rugged eternity he smiles at our literary preoccupations. This hope, in any case, is flattering to our plans; and may we be pardoned in

the presence of this magnificent ancestor who, in the long ago, carved out the sod of our plains, for making a rough-hewn start with words and pictures in this other country of the mind that all of us men of today are asked to found. From our very differences that are the variety of life there will be born, tomorrow, perhaps, the ideal unity. [*trans.*] (*Apologies*, p. 10.)

61. *Art et combat* (Montreal: Editions de l'Action canadienne-française, 1937), p. 9.

62. *Ibid.*, p. 48.

63. *Ombres et clameurs* (Montreal: Albert Lévesque, 1933), pp. 191-192.

64. *Le roman canadien-français* (Montreal: Albert Lévesque, 1937), pp. 7-8.

65. *Horizons* (Montreal: Librairie d'Action canadienne-française, 1929).

66. *Ibid.*, p. 25.

67. *Estampes* (Montreal: Bibliothèque de l'Action Française, 1926), p. 201.

68. *Ebauches critiques* (Montreal: Adj. Menard, 1930), p. 7.

69. *Ibid.*, p. 15.

70. The *Mémoires* of Philippe Aubert de Gaspé, more a novel than history, would be an exception.

71. *See*: Henri Tuchmaïer, *Evolution de la technique du roman canadien-français* (Laval University, doctoral thesis, 1958). In this study, the most exhaustive which has been devoted to the French-Canadian novel, the author brings out the intimate connection between French-Canadian society and the lot of the novelist. According to Tuchmaïer the growing chasm between the *élite* and the Americanized and degallicized population of the big cities is destined to isolate tomorrow's novelists.

72. In our first edition a distinction had been maintained between the writers born in France and their French-Canadian counterparts. On consideration this dissociation has seemed to us to be valid up to 1939 only. Hémon, Bugnet, Constantin-Weyer and Le Franc, whose contribution to French-Canadian literature is disproportionate to that of French-Canadian novelists before the Second World War, deserve a place apart. Since then the very rapid rise of French-Canadian letters has made this distinction superfluous, as those French writers who participate in the French-Canadian literary movement today disappear amongst the multitude of talents.

73. Published later under the title of *Battling Malone, pugiliste* (Paris: Grasset, 1925). Hémon had already begun to write articles on sport before his arrival in England. A list of these articles and the details relating to the London phase of Hémon's life will be found in the thesis by Allan McAndrew, *Louis Hémon, sa vie et son oeuvre* (Paris: Jouve & Cie, 1936). See also Louis-J. Dalbis, *Le bouclier canadien-français* (Montreal: C. Déom, 1925), pp. 73-205; Louvigny de Montigny, *La revanche de Maria Chapdelaine* (Montreal: Editions de l'A. C.-F., 1937).

74. Works: *Le lys de sang* (Montreal: Edouard Garand, 1923); *Nipsya* (Edouard Garand, 1924); *Siraf* (Montreal: Editions du Totem, 1934); *La forêt* (Editions du Totem, 1935); *Les voix de la solitude: Rhythmes en vers, précédés de quelques réflexions sur la poésie* (Editions du Totem, 1938). Towards 1934, Bugnet altered *Le lys de sang*. The manuscript, entitled *Téhôm-la-noire,* comprising 194 pages and an appendix, has remained unpublished.

75. *Les voix de la solitude* (Montreal: Editions du Totem, 1938).

76. *La forêt,* p. 138.

77. All these books were published in Paris, by Rieder, with the exception of the first one, published by Editions Renaissance du Livre.

78. Before Constantin-Weyer, J. Poirier had been tempted by the same subject. His novel, *Les arpents de neige,* published in 1909, was published again in 1931 under the title: *La tempête sur le fleuve* (Paris: Jules Tallandier).

The Vicomte de Vallonges, a recent arrival from France, will be the author's spokesman. Because of the rebellion of the half-breeds there is a revival of the high feats of arms which mark the end of French rule in the eighteenth century. Vallonges throws himself body and soul into the fight on the side of the Riels and La Rondes, for whom the name of France remains sacred. In spite of a very elementary psychology, Poirier, out of fellow-feeling, makes the agonies and the fleeting triumphs of the *métis* live again.

79. *Un homme se penche sur son passé,* p. 129.

80. Paris: Stock, 1929.

81. Seven years before, in 1920, Marie Le Franc had brought out a book of verse, *Les voix du coeur et de l'âme* (Montreal: La Compagnie d'Imprimerie Perrault), which would perfectly fit into the French-Canadian literary tradition. Cast in a very customary mould of Alexandrines and octosyllabics, this melancholy and colourless poetry would have suited *Soirées de l'Ecole littéraire de Montréal.*

82. Canadian works: *Hélier, fils des bois* (Paris: Rieder, 1930); *Au pays canadien-français* (Paris: Fasquelle, 1931); *La rivière solitaire* (Paris: Ferenczi, 1934); *La randonnée passionnée* (Ferenczi, 1936); *Pêcheurs de Gaspésie* (Ferenczi, 1938); *Visages de Montréal* (Montreal: Les Editions du Zodiaque, 1934); *Le fils de la forêt* (Paris: Bernard Grasset, 1952); *O Canada! Terre de nos aïeux. Nouvelles* (Issy-les-Moulineaux, La Fenêtre ouverte, 1947).

83. "And I remembered another evening, when I was between nineteen and twenty years of age, at the Fraser Institute, when the reading of *Contes du jour et de la nuit* by Guy de Maupassant had revealed to me the genius of that writer and of French literature, and had made one of the strongest impressions on me that I have ever felt in my life." [*trans.*] (*Peintres et écrivains d'hier et d'aujourd'hui,* p. 150.)

84. In 1942, Laberge reproduced this passage as well as a second one of the same kind, entitled "Silhouette macabre" in *Scènes de chaque jour,* pp. 9-12. Acutely aware of his role of precursor, he writes: "without having undergone any influence, from the time I could hold a pen I have been a Realistic writer. I was born a Realist." (*Ibid.,* p. 9.)

85. "The task lasted from fourteen to fifteen years. One year I would write sometimes two or three chapters, another year, just one. Years would even go by during which I was unable to add a single page to my manuscript. I had to have perseverance to finish this little novel." [*trans.*] (*Propos sur nos écrivains,* p. 103.)

86. The complete works of Laberge comprise fourteen volumes, all published by the author, in limited editions. Queen's University (Kingston) acquired the complete series in 1962.

Volumes devoted to youthful memories contain valuable testimony on the *Ecole littéraire de Montréal* and on intellectual life at the beginning of the century. Laberge's literary criticism reveals a mind more generous than perspicacious. *See: Anthologie d'Albert Laberge,* Preface by Gérard Bessette (Montreal: Le Cercle du Livre de France, 1963).

Works: *La Scouine* (1918); *Visages de la vie et de la mort* (1936); *Quand chantait la cigale* (1936); *Peintres et écrivains d'hier et d'aujourd'hui* (1938); *La fin du voyage* (1945); *Charles de Belle, peintre-poète* (1949); *Le destin des hommes* (1950); *Fin de roman* (1951); *Images de la vie* (1952); *Le dernier souper* (1953); *Propos sur nos écrivains* (1954); *Hymnes à la terre* (1955).

87. *La fin du voyage,* p. 190.

88. *Ibid.,* p. 249.

89. It was without hesitation that Laberge gallicized several English words currently used in French Canada: *un canistre, un tombleur,* etc. Dialectical expressions are numerous in his stories (*si à bonne heure*) or simply spelling that corresponds to French-Canadian pronunciation (*greyer* for *gréer*). This spirit of independence is in contrast to the touchy conformism of those who condemned the inclusion of words of this category in the recent *Dictionnaire canadien* (1962).

90. *André Laurence, Canadien-français* (Paris: Plon, 1930).

91. Works: *Le secret de Lindbergh* (Montreal: Editions de la Porte d'or, 1928); *Un homme et son péché* (Montreal: Les Editions du Totem, 1933); *Le déserteur et autres récits de la terre* (Montreal: Les Editions du Vieux Chêne, 1934).

92. Ringuet will be the first one ready to bear witness to the rise of a new *bourgeoisie* in *Le poids du jour* (1949). Although his analysis of the awakening of the French-Canadian people and of its desire for maturity does not lack insight, the great tragic picture of the abandonment of the countryside is not there to make his Montreal novel powerfully evocative. (See the first edition of our *Histoire de la littérature canadienne-française,* pp. 184-186).

CHAPTER V

THE CONTEMPORARY PERIOD

THE NOVEL

A century of experimentation seems to have been necessary before we come to *Bonheur d'occasion* (1945), a novel which, in revealing Gabrielle Roy to her amazed and enthusiastic readers, was the starting signal for the first generation of French-Canadian novelists. For this novel, aside from its intrinsic value, marks an important turning point in the evolution of French-Canadian literature.

Little by little, while neither readers nor writers were aware of what was happening, the requisite conditions for the creation of a market for French-Canadian books were established around 1945. Almost all of the important French-Canadian novels which had appeared from time to time between *Maria Chapdelaine* and *Trentes arpents* had been unable to make any decisive impact because of the lack of a flourishing publishing business, which is the outward sign of a large and well-informed public. Without the complete change promised by *Bonheur d'occasion*, the sparks would have produced no explosion; without the revolution which had just taken place in French-Canadian publishing, *Bonheur d'occasion* would have had the same fate as the most authentic works of the past. Therefore, in order to understand the extremely rapid rise of contemporary French-Canadian letters it is important to analyze the dramatic changes which took place between 1939 and 1945 in the literary atmosphere of French Canada.

THE STATE OF FRENCH-CANADIAN PUBLISHING

Following the Crémazie era a reading public had been painfully established. But even in 1939 this public was still too limited to make it possible for the few French-Canadian publishing houses to look forward with any confidence to the publication of a manuscript, even one bearing the mark of genius.

144

Then in 1940 the almost complete reduction of activity in the publishing business in France produced a great need for French books throughout the free world. In Europe French Switzerland, through the enterprise of clearsighted and sometimes courageous publishing houses such as Editions de la Baconnière, ensured indispensable relief. Thus at a time when it was suffering a dangerous eclipse the free expression of French thought was maintained. But the *Confédération,* situated in the heart of a continent at war, could hardly supply the rest of the world. Among the countries open to French culture, such as Lebanon, Egypt and North Africa, proximity to the fields of battle precluded the possibility of making any useful contribution to the cause of French books.

There was Canada, however, and a unique occasion was offered for contributing in a small way to the safekeeping of spiritual values that were threatened. Publishing houses came into being, capable of reducing the disastrous consequences of the silence imposed on Paris.

Arrangements already in existence permitted the swift build-up of a real Canadian market in French books. In the nineteenth century the Beauchemin publishing house, founded in Montreal in 1842, was recognized as the most important publishing business in Quebec.[1] From 1871 its *Almanach du peuple* found its way into many homes. Beauchemin served French-Canadian letters effectively by publishing the best authors of the time—Fréchette wrote stories for the *Almanach*—and by promoting the growth of reading habits among the more humble elements of society. More important still, the decision to print books suitable as awards, a decision taken in 1910 and which in 1914 meant the distribution of one hundred and twenty-five French-Canadian book-titles, was a significant step towards the establishment of present-day publishing houses.

Eugène Issalys, literary director of the Beauchemin publishing house in 1911, who became director of publishing in 1929, was one of the guiding spirits behind this enterprise. In 1942/43 when he founded the *Société des Editeurs canadiens du livre français,* Canada was on the way to being able to supply, to some extent at least, the need for French books in a large part of the world.

Three years after the fall of France French-Canadian publishing houses began to bring out for the first time some of the great classics of the nineteenth century: Hugo, Maupassant, Verlaine, Rimbaud. Among contemporaries Duhamel, Mauriac and Gide appeared. Expatriates like Jacques Maritain and Henri Focillon, as well as others who followed them to New York or Montreal, were published in Montreal also. In 1939 French-Canadian firms had brought out two hundred and sixty-nine French titles.[2] In four years' time the number almost doubled, going from two hundred and sixty-nine to five hundred and sixteen. In 1943 about one hundred works with copyrights belonging to Paris firms were republished. Five years later, when Paris had recovered its pre-war clientele, this contribution to French-Canadian publishing disappeared, falling off in 1948 to twelve French authors. In that same year Canada succeeded in publishing only three hundred and ten titles in French, thus reverting, after a spectacular rise, to a level hardly higher than that of 1939.

The prosperity of the years 1943-1946 was followed by a lean period that was of short duration. The majority of the firms established during the war that depended for a living on sales to South America and the United States were soon obliged to close. The more active among them had been the Editions de l'Arbre, Variétés, Parizeau, Pascal, Brousseau, Valiquette and Pony. *The Institut littéraire du Québec* survived along with firms established before 1940: Beauchemin, Granger, Les frères des Ecoles chrétiennes, Fides and Editions du Lévrier.

The stimulus of the war years had benefited not only the publishers. The existence in Montreal of numerous publishing houses had permitted the most dynamic ones for the first time to encourage young writers. In an extremely short period a decisive impetus was given to French-Canadian literature. Between 1944 and 1948 novelists who rank among the best that French Canada has produced were able to get their start, thanks to publishers soon to be out of business. Robert Charbonneau, Director of Editions de l'Arbre, showed judgment in publishing Roger Lemelin's *Au pied de la pente douce* (1944) and *Contes pour un homme seul* (1944) by Yves Thériault. The following year Gabrielle Roy made her conspicuous appearance with *Bonheur d'occasion* (Société des Editions Pascal). Editions Variétés brought out in succession *Félix* (1947) by Jean Simard and *Au-delà des visages* (1948) by André Giroux.

To these manifestations of literary life were added the reviews. *La Relève*,[3] to become later *La Nouvelle Revue*, which bore the mark of the influence of Maritain and of Mounier, made a rostrum of quality. Other periodicals, with *Amérique française, Les gants du ciel*,[4] in the first rank, would bring to the French-Canadian intellectual world an unaccustomed excitement.

With the progressive disappearance of publishers and reviews must one conclude that the literary and cultural activity of the war years had been almost entirely dependent on factors outside present-day French Canada? Towards 1949/50, at the worst moment of the recession, some had come to the wry conclusion that the familiar doldrums of French Canada were about to return with a vengeance. Recovery took place speedily, however, and was soon a recognized fact in what was a veritable revolution in literary habits. To such an extent was this the case that the rich years of the war seem today to have been only the prelude to the broad development which followed and whose effects make themselves felt more positively every day.

THE COMING OF AGE OF
FRENCH CANADA

The war years brought to an end the cultural isolation of French Canada and at the same time were a revelation of its importance in the French-speaking world. The expansion of French-Canadian publishing, far from having been produced artificially, had been made possible only by the slow conquests of preceding generations. Actually French Canada had reached that stage, well known in under-developed societies, at which cultural investments at last bear abundant fruit. The hopes raised, first in Quebec in Crémazie's time and later in Montreal at the beginning of the century, had not materialized because the structure of French-Canadian society still did not admit of any rapid literary or cultural development. About forty years later, that long winter of the spirit to which Quesnel had alluded in 1804, came to an end. The irresistible strength of the movement may be gauged by the current situation in French-Canadian publishing. Arrested for a time in its expansion, ten years later the publishing industry had changed. In 1961 the *Association des Editeurs canadiens*[5] took part for the first time in the International Book Fair in Frankfurt.[6] This success encouraged it to make the *Quatrième Salon du livre de Montréal*, held in April of 1962, the first great meeting place of publishers of French-language books.[7] As for the activity of French-Canadian publishers, this is comparable in quantity if not yet in quality to that of French publishers.[8]

The ferment of the years 1940-1950, which continues to work in the body of French-Canadian society, has made possible the realization of numerous achievements comparable to those that took place in the sphere of publishing.

The Second World War, by opening wide the doors to foreign influences, gave French-Canadian intellectuals a unique occasion for

expressing themselves. Paul-Emile Borduas (1905-1961), a surrealist painter, was to point the way to several young writers of his
generation in his condemnation of French-Canadian society. It was
at the moment when the painter's talent opened out in *La cavale
infernale* (1943) and *L'île enchantée* (1945)—paintings of genius
which preceded his descent to the uninspired canvasses he was to
execute a short time before his death, which occurred unexpectedly
in Paris—that Borduas published his *Manifeste des automatistes*
(1948), known under the title of *Refus global*.[9] The challenge of
those persuasive words was to incite quite a number of poets to
throw themselves into the surrealist adventure which rent asunder
the traditional framework of French-Canadian poetry.[10]

On another level the establishment in 1944 of the French-Canadian Academy was allied to the formation of a collective consciousness of which Borduas seems to have been one of the instigators.
For Victor Barbeau, its founder, the movement which he and his
friends set up is not explained so much by a specific decision on
their part as by "a crystalization of a long succession of psychological and social influences".[11]

Simultaneously and for the first time good theatre was being
successfully and permanently grafted onto the life of Montreal. The
crowds who came to applaud Emile Legault's *Compagnons* and who
saw themselves in Gratien Gélinas' *Tit-Coq* would remain faithful to
the companies that were to be created later on and which have
since made Montreal an active centre of theatrical life.

So we are witnessing a vast, spreading cultural movement, of
which writers will be the beneficiaries. Not only is an increasingly
affluent public, with more leisure at its disposal, preparing to welcome any talented novelists, but more than that, far-sighted publishers are setting out to create a favourable milieu by bringing all
modern means of persuasion into play. Literary prizes grow in
number and importance. The *Prix du Cercle du livre de France*
soon became the *Prix Goncourt* of French Canada.[12] Its founder,
Pierre Tisseyre, who came to Montreal at a time when the future
of French-Canadian publishing seemed less than assured, makes a
correct analysis of the receptivity of the French-speaking group.
The success of his enterprise is not unconnected with the healthy
state of Quebec publishing today.

Finally the establishment in 1957 of the Canada Council, the
country's Maecenas, in all sectors of Canadian public life is pro-
ducing something like an insurance against the risks of artistic
creation. The formula admits of the obvious danger of making a
free gift to mediocrity: nevertheless the results are convincing. The

Canadian book industry has found itself reinforced and it has often been possible for the best manuscripts of recent years to be published thanks to Council subsidies. The review *Ecrits du Canada français,* whose high quality does honour to French-Canadian letters, could not subsist without the direct aid of the Canadian government.

THE FIRST GENERATION OF NOVELISTS

The convergence of all these favourable factors was to allow the example of Gabrielle Roy to be followed immediately by a considerable number of novelists, so that it is fitting to distinguish them as a group from their predecessors. The latter, scattered here and there, wrote most frequently in isolation.

When Ringuet signed the death warrant of the novel of the soil by unmasking in masterly fashion the falsity of the legend perpetuated by Gérin-Lajoie's *épigones,* all that was left to the novelists was to turn towards the industrial reality of Montreal. Gabrielle Roy was not the first to notice the working man. But before *Bonheur d'occasion* no novelist had really turned to account the theme provided by the proletarianizing of the French-Canadian masses. To the wealth of material that Gabrielle Roy handed to the novelists of her generation there was added the lesson of intellectual and artistic independence. The novel of the soil depended on conventional ethics from which Laberge was one of the rare writers to depart. Here we have Gabrielle Roy examining the new French-Canadian society objectively while clothing her observations with her inimitable charity. From now on a people of city-dwellers, French Canadians, subject to all the pressures of Anglo-Saxon civilization, would offer to novelists a mine of new material: not burdened with a mortgage to nationalism and religion, it gave hope of liberation for the French-Canadian novel.

Lemelin, whose *Au pied de la pente douce* had made its appearance in 1944, soon became one of a group of writers who were at last creating the modern French-Canadian novel by subjecting their own city of Quebec to a humorous analysis. André Langevin, Jean Filiatrault, Eugène Cloutier and Jean Simard constituted themselves the sharp critics of a society which, far from appearing to them to be less touched than others by the moral maladies of contemporary man, seemed in their eyes to be suffering from hardening of the arteries and decay, and consequently deserving of censure. Yves Thériault vigorously dared to investigate sexual problems. Others like André Giroux were to attempt a thorough study of the meaning of the Christian inheritance of the French Canadian by giving to their research a more complicated technique than that of any before them. Robert Charbonneau would make himself the theorist for all of them by pointing the way to an autonomous French-Canadian art.

Today this generation, which freed the French-Canadian novel from some of the worst aspects of its bondage, is no longer in a position to affect the course of literary history. With the exception of Jean Simard all these novelists have shot their bolt. Gabrielle Roy was the first to show that the sources of inspiration had dried up (*La montagne secrète*, 1961). Jean Filiatrault has slipped into the melodramatic mawkishness of *L'argent est odeur de nuit* (1961) and runs faint risk of redeeming himself. In *Malgré tout, la joie* (1959) Giroux makes it apparent that his course is run. While Langevin, Lemelin and Elie observe a silence that is burying them, Savard and Desrosiers continue to preach to a deaf audience, the former on a key which remains lofty and noble, the latter assuming a tone of a kind that would put an end once and for all to the novel of religious edification. Finally, Yves Thériault, like a drowning man, is flailing his arms about aimlessly.

If it is too early to calculate the direction that will be followed by Jacques Godbout, Claire France, Diane Giguère, Claire Martin, Marie-Claire Blais and all the young novelists of today who, benefiting from the experience of their elders, are going off on their own, it is at least possible to state briefly the meaning of the great mopping-up operations of that first generation.

The French-Canadian novelist is free. His enslavement to a few great themes linked to the French survival has never existed, moreover, except in his mind. If it is true that certain novelists like Rodolphe Girard and Jean-Charles Harvey have incurred the vengeful displeasure of their milieu for having sought other solutions, who would dare to say that French-Canadian literature, because of the interference of narrow-minded people, has been dangerously impoverished? More serious would be the calculated indifference that has surrounded the work of Laberge. Aside from the fact that his daring seems tame enough today, is it not obvious that he is at last coming into his own?

From now on all subjects are permissible. Montreal, an international city, hides under the hum of daily business the most prodigious literary activity, while those who still think of themselves as shepherds of the flock are preoccupied, and rightly so, with more serious problems than the latest naughty novel.

The great quarrel over language and grammar, while not entirely exhausted, has become extraordinarily simplified in the last fifteen years. French-Canadian literature counts among its writers some good stylists who can stand comparison with quite a number of the best French prose writers of our day. At the same time the vernacular has taken up a permanent place in the novel. The evidence is that talent carries more weight than mere structural correctness. It will be the burden of the future to complete the collective experience of the first generation of novelists by allowing writers to assume with confidence the risks of a French language that has been enriched from the alluvium of French Canada.

Gabrielle Roy (b. 1909)

Until the middle of the twentieth century French-Canadian writing remained a provincial literature, known beyond its borders only to a few men of letters. Since then it has been making a modest appearance abroad. Several writers today are contributing to this growth away from provincialism, and not one of them more so than Gabrielle Roy. Some twenty years after its publication, *Bonheur d'occasion*—even more perhaps than *Alexandre Chenevert*, which is a work of greater finish—stands out as the French-Canadian novel *par excellence*, a reflection of the vitality of French-speaking Canadians, and of their spiritual and linguistic isolation.

From the first pages Gabrielle Roy asserts her superiority over all other French-Canadian novelists in the subtlety and keenness of her psychology. The way she broaches her subject, brilliantly conceived, is less significant, however, than the dark threat surrounding Florentine, sales-girl in a department store, when she comes under the increasing influence of Jean Lévesque:

Une espèce d'hébétude parut dans son regard. Sur ses traits enfantins fortement maquillés, se superposa à cet instant l'image de la vieille femme qu'elle deviendrait. Aux commissures des lèvres le pli se devina dans lequel coulerait le modelé, la grâce des joues. Et par les yeux fixes, rétrécis, semblaient s'échapper la vie, la jeunesse, la confiance, en laissant derrière elles le vide. Mais il n'y avait pas que la redoutable échéance qui surprenait le visage de Florentine; la faiblesse héréditaire, la misère profonde qu'elle perpétuait et qui était aussi partie de l'échéance, semblaient sourdre du fond de ses prunelles éteintes et se répandre comme un voile sur la figure nue, sans masque.

She had a kind of stunned look. On her childish features, heavily made up, at that moment was superimposed the image of the old woman she would become. Where her lips were joined there was the suspicion of a wrinkle where the lovely outline, the charming grace of the cheeks would drain away. And through eyes that were fixed, narrowed, life and youth and confidence seemed to be escaping, leaving emptiness behind them. But it was not the dreadful outcome which had caught Florentine's face unawares: the hereditary weakness, the profound misery which she was perpetuating and which was also part of that inevitable outcome seemed to well up from the very pupils of her lacklustre eyes to spread like a veil over her naked, helpless face. [*trans.*]

The main characters will be intimately revealed in their weaknesses and the things they care about: Azarius, Florentine's erratic father, vain and incompetent, suffering intensely because he was unable to get his family out of the infernal poverty enclosing them; Rose-Anna, sublime mother, the truly typical French-Canadian woman of the propagandists who comes to life at last before us; Jean Lévesque, in too much of a hurry to escape from poverty to be seriously interested in Florentine, whose love might just possibly drive him into mediocrity.

Cleverly as the plot is built up, the great subject treated of by Gabrielle Roy, which she has progressively plumbed more deeply in subsequent novels, dominates the sad experiences of the Lacasse family; suffering separates us from each other more effectively than indifference. Want and illness become great silent murderers sowing discord among men. There is nothing theoretical in this analysis which is based entirely on the most perfect objectivity. Mutual understanding, which is never quite realized in practice, produces a sadness which, in the end, becomes the most outstanding characteristic of the work of Gabrielle Roy.

Bonheur d'occasion, in which a total rendering of existence meets with the keenest eye to be found in the French-Canadian novel, remains a great novel in the universal sense. The background of the 1939-1945 war has doubtless grown somewhat dim. But that is only a secondary aspect of a work that throbs with disappointments that are understood or shared or pondered in solitude. The occasional impropriety and the awkwardness of a sometimes inadequate language are not enough to break the charm. Are these imperfections not the sign of French-Canadian manufacture, an extra guarantee of authenticity? More serious perhaps is the awkwardness if not the unreality with which the sexual confrontation of Jean and Florentine is reluctantly described. This passage is too reminiscent of the modest concealments and misleading silences of former times. But this, too, is a superficial fault for it is in the effects of our acts and in their hidden significance that the author is interested, not in the acts themselves.

La petite poule d'eau (1950) represents a break, a pause in the development of Gabrielle Roy. There is a universal sympathy for men and beasts in this delightful watercolour from which the anxieties of the first novel have been banished for the time being. In a far-off corner of Manitoba where they share their lot with immigrants from central Europe, the prolific Luzina and her husband Hippolyte lead a life punctuated by the plaintive cry of the marsh hen. Imperceptibly in this ill-matched population generous America works the miracle of fraternal union in diversity. Although the successive pictures of Manitoba life are tied together by only a thin thread, they are bathed in the unifying light of a relative optimism, which Gabrielle Roy seems to have wanted to grant herself in order to be worthy of a return to serious truths already partially exploited in *Bonheur d'occasion.*

One lesson emerges from the first two novels: from the first that in entering the field of political or historical speculation, through her characters, the novelist sacrificed too much to present-day reality, which is the beginning of artistic death; from the second that the analysis of human distress and brief joys vastly increased her powers of expression. To create the great work that she had in mind it was obvious that Gabrielle Roy must find a subject sufficiently anchored to the present to touch us, but with ballast for its most conspicuous earthly chains. At the same time this subject must allow full scope for her unequalled gifts as clinical examiner of the human heart.

Once again it was Montreal which furnished the appropriate setting. Anxious to do something new, after having made herself the interpreter of Rose-Anna and Luzina, did she not have to describe this time the psychology of masculine suffering?

A simple bank clerk is the hero of *Alexandre Chenevert* (1954). Everything leads one to believe that Gabrielle Roy did actually lead the life of bank teller before unburdening herself, in literary form, of this intensely lived experience. From this maturation there came her best novel, the greatest perhaps in French-Canadian literature.

Alexandre Chenevert is a man of limited potential but of great heart. The human beings who are dear to him—his wife, his daughter, his lifelong friend, Godias—are hidden from him by their sufferings, to which are added the complications of modern life. References to current events intervene only sporadically through newspaper headlines and radio broadcasts. The stirring of the contemporary world makes a brief incursion into the domestic worries of Alexandre Chenevert, who will find himself closed in on every side when he begins to be tortured by cancer. With exemplary discretion Gabrielle Roy follows his downward path to destruction. These pages take on symbolic value and bring to the French-Canadian novel a masterpiece.

The superiority of *Alexandre Chenevert* over *Bonheur d'occasion* is in the form. From the beginning, in her first novel, Gabrielle Roy was successful in the difficult test of compassion. Having reached from the very first that privileged zone in which the author communicates directly with the reader, it remained for her to give to this conversation the advantages of a stylized and very classical restraint. The teller with the small salary, typical of millions in the ant-hills of the nuclear age, escapes his own nationality to take on all nationalities. Nevertheless, the closed circle of his life is explained by one particular city, Montreal. It is in this successful ambivalence that *Alexander Chenevert* parts company from *Bonheur d'occasion,* in which the formula, suffering from details somewhat too specifically French-Canadian, has less chance of literary survival. The treatment, which is restrained and consequently in harmony with the seriousness of the subject, guarantees that *Alexandre Chenevert* will have the approval of the connoisseurs if not of the general public.

Did Gabrielle Roy, after her first three novels, feel a need to renew herself? There are several places in *Rue Deschambault* (1955) which hint at an introspective, more personal art. The best chapters, *Le puits de Dunrea* and *Les déserteuses,* give evidence of a poignant and delightful humanity. A mischievous and somewhat unexpected humour makes its appearance, thanks to the religious observances of French Canada which are analyzed with benevolent perception. The narrator's mother comes to Brother André, whose holiness has won him a reputation among the people for accomplishing miracles, to ask if she, the mother of a family, has not committed a sin in leaving her own people without her husband's authorization. The holy man replies solemnly: "Pray earnestly to Saint Joseph, do not drink too much coffee and be optimistic, always optimistic."

It does seem that reminiscences other than personal ones may have slipped into this work. The great shadow of Marcel Proust hovers over the composition of *Rue Deschambault* to the extent that one chapter, *La voix des étangs,* recalls irresistibly *A la recherche du temps perdu.* And so a doubt is cast on these poeticized memories. Like the "I" in *Côté de chez Swann,* Gabrielle Roy has a presentiment of the direction she must take to fulfil her "vocation." But the fact that the problem is so clearly posed indicates that 1955 marks a milestone in the novelist's development, a turning point confirmed in 1961 in *La montagne secrète.*

The years separating *Rue Deschambault* from *La montagne secrète* have been turned to account by the author to think about the art of writing. The search for a new course, evident in *Rue Deschambault,* ends in this very inferior work. It has a poor plot that the writer, too good a judge to believe in it, gives up half-way through, so that the retrospective quality of the ending comes as no surprise. Before coming to the point of her confession, which is presented without artifice and is moving in its sincerity, Gabrielle Roy displays the inferiority of the only long descriptive passages that she has ever written. Her style, never dazzling, reaches a kind of transparency in *Alexandre Chenevert.* Deprived of its psychological support that style, when it is a question of reproducing the colours and sounds of the Mackenzie and Ungava, produces nothing but an ordinary lithograph.

La montagne secrète remains significant, though, in that it contains autobiographical asides by one of the greatest of French-Canadian novelists. After her trip to France Gabrielle Roy came back to her own country, keenly aware of her unshakable Canadianism. Here I am what I am, she confides, without illusions. And what is there left for her to accomplish in life? "Dogs, at the end of the day when they have been pulling since morning, must not stop. They must not; the impetus they have acquired is now their only driving power."

Yves Thériault (b. 1915)

The discreet eclipse of Gabrielle Roy is brought about at the same time as Yves Thériault's smashing departure. So they both leave us in their own way.

There are two main sources of Yves Thériault's sensibility and thought: naturism and a sharp criticism of French-Canadian society. In this regard Yves Thériault is very representative of the first generation of novelists, often impatient when confronted with the impediments to modern sensuality set up by a religion which subdues the flesh and by a conservative society.

Thériault makes liberal use of the symbol to represent the liberation of instinct in his main characters. His *Contes pour un homme seul* (1944) heralds the entry into French-Canadian literature of a whole current of eroticism whose very numerous representatives in France and the United States include Jean Genêt and Henry Miller. If it is true that there is practically no real pornography in Thériault and that his most suggestive pages are indeed innocent if compared with the imaginings of Jean Genêt, everything seems to indicate that the ambient atmosphere of materialism will be responsible for finding more daring successors to Thériault.

His language, deliberately popular and tough, is the expression of a reality made up of carnal desires and murders, which are used as expressions of sexuality. In the *Contes* Thériault is trying to produce a style to match as closely as possible the primitive sensations he wants to evoke; but it betrays him too often.

La fille laide (1950) is more successful. A murder and a marriage, which satisfy the demands of primitive instincts, consecrate the union of Fabien and the ill-favoured girl. It is a picture of integral naturism.

Le dompteur d'ours (1951), Thériault's third work in his first manner, heralds the social criticism of the novels that follow. Hermann, the bear-tamer, the man with the muscular body, makes the village women dream when he decides to come and live there. We see the confusion that his presence, symbol of sexual delight and personal liberty, brings to the village people: Lubin, the adolescent, who comes to maturity in a single day; Geneviève Cabirand, who throws herself to no avail into the arms of this handsome male; Adèle, who grows vegetables and who succeeds where the village women fail because she asks nothing in return for her ready love. Finally the bear-tamer is outdone when the whole village assembles to see him in single combat with a bear. Liberty admits of no bondage.

All through *Le dompteur d'ours* one feels the condemnation of a society which torments man in his instincts. It is by this expedient that Thériault doubtless came to the point of bringing to trial a section of the clergy, too inclined, according to him, to wield its influence. Leaving the symbol for the time being, the author makes a direct attack on abuses of all kinds which, according to him, would corrupt the moral and political atmosphere of his native province. Instead of the hearty Rabelaisian jesting that Thériault would like to have produced in *Les vendeurs du temple* (1951), we have only a poorly fashioned and unconvincing work, inferior to the first attempt of the kind in Canada, Rodolphe Girard's *Marie Calumet*.

Brought back after this failure to the symbolist novel, Thériault writes his *Aaron* (1954) and succeeds finally in effecting the difficult junction of life and symbol. This time by means of a thin plot which brings on stage the Montreal Jewish community, Thériault sets forth the sorry choices offered to any minority. In other words his criticism becomes more objective. For the first time also his use of the symbol loses the stiffness of the theorem, giving to the anguish of Jethro, a Jew of the old school, a feeling of deep tragedy, universal in the way it is developed. Between Jethro and his son-in-law there is the same chasm that widens between all the minorities in the world, those who remain faithful to the old beliefs and those who belong to tomorrow.

Still more than *Aaron* it is *Agaguk* (1958) which furnishes proof of the artist in Thériault. In this latter novel he succeeds, according to the old formula, in making something out of nothing. The plot consists of showing the effect produced on an Eskimo by the very relative sophistication of his wife. To keep the reader's curiosity alive Thériault varies his tempo with remarkable skill. The searching study of the male, charmed and uneasy at the unsuspected talents of his wife, stays in one's mind for a long time. There is one doubt, however: has the Eskimo mentality not been too easily adapted to our modern tastes? Does Agaguk not react a little like a white man when Iriook, his wife, leads him on along the path of sexuality?

In 1958, Thériault, the most prolific of French-Canadian novelists, was beginning to be established in the role, new in French Canada, of the master capable of weakening and falling below his own standards, but whose development, whatever it might be, could not fail to have an influence on the course of the novel. What demon took possession of this bear-tamer to prompt the disastrous words of advice which go by the names of: *Ashini* (Fides, 1960), *Cul-de-sac* (Quebec: Institut littéraire du Québec, 1961), *Les commettants de Caridad* (*ibid.*, 1961), *Le vendeur d'étoiles* (Fides, 1961), *Amour au goût de mer* (Beauchemin, 1961)?

Ashini is nothing but a caricature of *Agaguk.* The conventional portrayal of the White Man, destroyer of Indian tribes, furnishes the theme of this sermon in story form. *Cul-de-sac* reveals another side of this moralizer, a role that does not fit Thériault and makes the heroine, Fabienne, unbearable. *Le vendeur d'étoiles,* a dreary collection of stories the author ought to have left in the drawer where they gathered dust, is unworthy of the man who breathed so much life into the French-Canadian novel after the war. Finally, as if to prove that the sacred fire of the first years has not gone out completely, Thériault gives us *Les commettants de Caridad.* In a so-called Spain one witnesses the development of the irresistible male. All he needs to do is wink to have every woman his, unless, unleashed, she swallows him whole. In spite of the fact that Heron has to take on the appearance of a palm tree with his "two metres and more," it is of no importance; the Spanish women react to this man, even taller than Charles de Gaulle, as if he were the incarnation of all the seductiveness of a Casanova. "We are made to enjoy," is the conclusion of the widow Inez. Can it be that the novelist is desperately trying to evoke his vigorous past? Worse still, Thériault affects a contrived and archaic French which he simply does not have the scholarship to reproduce successfully. The false linguistic note underlines the mediocrity of this French-Canadian lesser *Decameron*.

Thériault will have left to the novel two strong works, *Aaron* and *Agaguk,* symbolizing one of the great victories of his generation. The savage energy with which he has been trying to maintain his creative powers since 1958 is certainly to his credit; but it is doubtful that he will add much to his stature in the years ahead.

Roger Lemelin (b. 1919)

In the evolution of French-Canadian literature Lemelin represents a tardy invasion of Americanism. By this is meant the tendency to reject Europe in resounding fashion in order to affirm the national characteristics, whatever they may be. American literature has gone through a period of national delectation. A Mark Twain—casting his eyes over a Europe showing signs of decay, then coming home again to his own people to celebrate the robust virtues of his own nation, not too refined, doubtless, but with a great future awaiting it—is a picturesque and necessary figure in the evolution of a young literature. If French Canada is going through a parallel development at this late date it is because the Franco-Canadian elite, after the surrender in 1763, turned instinctively to France for its cultural survival. But French-Canadian nationalism, which is essentially American, was sooner or later to inspire writers with thoughts of breaking with Europe. By the vigorous proclamation of his French-Canadian personality Roger Lemelin illustrates better than any other novelist a trend that has become inevitable in French-Canadian letters.

What new element does he bring to the novel? Action, particularly. The irrepressible desire to be himself, to owe nothing to others, is obviously a sign of youth. Lemelin's popularity did not come by chance; his compatriots have recognized themselves in his characters. The sudden deaths, the miraculous cures, the crazy laughter that turns to sobbing—these are some of the things that make up the world in which the ordinary people of Quebec City move. This vision, melodramatic to begin with, usually undergoes a caricatural expansion; not to be taken seriously, it adds to the crazy attraction of the ups and downs of the characters invented by the author and gives the effect of a Punch and Judy show.

Au pied de la pente douce (1944), Lemelin's first novel, remains typical of his work. Characters and events follow each other in a devil-may-care rhythm, and only towards the end of the novel does the reader find out where he is in the imbroglio. Lemelin's very imprecise and less than grammatical language is an added complication. Nevertheless, from this muddle there emerges Denis Boucher, whose ambition is to write a world-shaking novel. This very young man is not only an intellectual. Very proud of his muscles, he cares for his body with an eye to an approaching manhood that dazzles him. Denis, who is only one face of Lemelin, will appear again in *Les Plouffe* (1948).

This second novel is the subject to which *Au pied de la pente douce* will have served as introduction. Feeling surer of himself Lemelin paints a picture of the daily life of the Quebec people. The Plouffes are symbolic of the French-Canadian family with its faults and virtues. When light is thrown on this scene Denis has a minor role and remains more or less outside the plot, acting as he likes, while the members of the Plouffe family are victims of their surroundings. Madame Plouffe, resigned to being the servant of a large family and doing what the *curés* tell her; Ovide, her son, a kind of seminary student on the loose, who, in a mad moment of abandon, dares to lay hands on a young woman; Father Folbèche, mouthpiece of the lower clergy and defender of his flock against the poison of Protestantism; Guillaume, the great baseball player on whom the hope of Quebec baseball depends—such are the supernumeraries of a sentimental comedy not lacking in verve.

Was Lemelin sensitive at this time to criticisms which had been made about the imperfections of his style? In any case he did think it would be a good idea to do his homework, which may be called *Fantaisies sur les péchés capitaux* (1949). In this collection, with the exception of the short story which tells of the eventual paralysis of the hero, Lemelin hardly rises above an honest mediocrity. His prose, however, has improved, and one feels that he is ready for *Pierre le magnifique* (1952).

The clowning of the first two works has disappeared but there remains the action, the art of linking up little concentric dramas

which keep the reader in suspense. It is true that the plot early
turns into the improbable, but at any rate how far we are from
the former works! Pierre's inordinate ambition, his desire for the
absolute, his lively intelligence, make us like him. Pierre tells Abbé
Loupret about the vocation that had lost its appeal for him; we
are touched, and this proves that Lemelin is a thoroughbred among
novelists.

But basically this is not the main interest for the reader who,
beyond the aesthetic value of the work, perceives the essential
novelty of this story that is both Canadian and American. Because
Lemelin is intensely aware of the abundant energy of the new
world, he has been able to create the astonishingly real character,
Willie Savard, the very wealthy industrialist. Lemelin seems to be
saying to us: here is a real French Canadian. And in what country
in the Western world would one find, as easily as in French Canada,
a Willie Savard, struggling between a Priapism healthy as the
mighty North and an intense religious faith? Only the energetic
Lemelin could invent the picture of that old satyr having himself
cared for by the good sisters after a drinking bout—one that would
have killed anybody but a *Canayen*.

Over *Pierre le magnifique* floats some sort of latent promise for
the future which could be the preserve of French-Canadian literature. A huge world of mysterious power—far removed from any
French tradition—is involved in a work of this kind. Roger Lemelin
appears in French-Canadian literature at a crossroads. For the first
time a path of unsuspected wealth is pointed out. Others already
are beginning to follow. Whatever may be the relative value of
Lemelin's novels, they will have had the particular merit of furnishing a healthy lesson in literary independence.

André Langevin (b. 1927)

Evadé de la nuit (1951) has the value of a working design. In a
novel teeming with energies still not clearly defined, the Langevin
of the future already reveals a sense of the dramatic, a taste for
unusual situations which lay bare violent creatures dominated by
the desire to escape an anonymous fate. At twenty years of age
Jean Cherteffe, in his conversations with Roger Benoit from whom
life has taken everything material in ten years, is looking for the
course to follow. Benoit, too, had had a great dream, but he will
commit suicide, in this way escaping the rehabilitation attempted
by Jean Cherteffe. The perfect love which could transcend life will

also be denied Cherteffe, fated very soon to follow his sweetheart into death.

Langevin's romantic conception is close to classical tragedy. Great passions lead to expiation willed by the gods. Langevin by disposition instills into his characters a will of iron which leads them to a solution resembling the proof at the end of an equation. Jean Cherteffe's vision is too big to allow for success in life and when he falls he will drag down with him all those who have come too near.

As often happens with young novelists Langevin has poured into *Evadé de la nuit* the superabundance of his talents. This first work contains the faint tracings of many roads to be taken in different directions. Which ones will be followed to the end in the novels to come?

Having taken his pulse Langevin was prepared, after *Evadé de la nuit,* to dam up in carefully constructed novel form the too-powerful current of the multitude of tempting ideas in his head. Two original works, *Poussière sur la ville* (1953) and *Le temps des hommes* (1956), have made Langevin the younger comrade-in-arms of Thériault, since the latter, too, will have left a rich legacy of two novels.

The lack of unity in *Evadé de la nuit,* which left characters and dialogue in suspense, disappears to give place to the compact drama of *Poussière sur la ville.* What still lives from one novel to the other is the magnetic action, in opposite directions, of the lesser characters. Fate makes its presence felt from the first pages of a Langevin novel. Given a certain situation, a certain exceptional man, the tragedy which follows is to be expected and can surprise one only in its breadth.

The little town of Macklin is the scene of an unusual drama in the life of a married couple. Alain Dubois, the wronged husband, stands aside when confronted with the adultery of his wife, Madeleine. Alain loves his wife and perhaps she loves him in her own way. But she acknowledges only one bondage, that of the senses. So Madeleine is like Jean Cherteffe and does not hesitate in her frantic course to crush anything standing in her way. Fascinated by a fop called Richard Hétu, she will become infatuated and be bold enough to choose her husband's house for her frolics. As a lucid spectator Alain Dubois watches himself being made a cuckold. His endurance, in which there is a mixture of the masochism to be found in Dostoievsky, would mean that he is nobler and, particularly, more humane than the *curé,* a rough-hewn peasant who judges according to a code as traditional as it is implacable.

Alain Dubois will respect to the very end the only thing left of his love—his wife's determination to be independent—by waiting until the last minute to intervene, if the combined powers of the *curé* and the hostile population of Macklin threaten the destruction of Madeleine and of the only hope left to him, that of an eventual reconciliation. But Madeleine escapes his vigilance by pretending to go to her mother's. She tries to kill her lover, whose formal betrothal to a childhood friend she has just heard about through the *curé*. Failing in her attempt, she kills herself in a last arrogant gesture, showing her scorn for the spiritual values which have the force of law in Macklin. Alain Dubois comes out of this test a bigger man. A doctor, he will devote himself to the little town that will never forgive him for his incomprehensible neutrality, insulted as he was in his role of husband.

Alain Dubois is one of the strong character creations of the contemporary French-Canadian novel. When one looks back on that long line of cuckolds who have adorned French literature since the *fabliaux,* is it possible to pick out a single one who is not ridiculous? A few centuries of autonomous living have been enough to give the French Canadians a different reaction to problems of the flesh. In his morbid heroism Alain Dubois does not belong to a Latin literature but indeed to something which is being worked out, between the Soviet Union and the United States, in the country of the too-long winters.

Le temps des hommes is hewn from the same massive block from which the two preceding works emerged. To accentuate the scope of it Langevin situated the action in the solitudes of Quebec. Nature is equal to the intense emotions which shake Dupas, the unfrocked priest. A blizzard is incorporated into the background of the race against destiny which he volunteers to run. Having given up the priesthood through conviction, Dupas none the less continues the search for salvation. And here we have a murderer, Laurier, putting him in the way of a possible atonement. If the man of God can bring Laurier to the point of contemplating his real misery, of gaining redemption by giving himself up to the police after a second murder, the priest will be justified in his own eyes. So Dupas follows Laurier; he will be his shadow, his conscience. But in vain. Laurier is killed accidentally. Logically the only thing left for Dupas to do is to commit suicide.

Le temps des hommes shows a falling off which is attributable to the haste with which it was written. Langevin has yielded to the classic temptation, all the more formidable when the writer is conscious of the full extent of his powers. Pressed by his awareness of all the different directions he is capable of taking, how can he keep cool, choose a single course and be free to follow it to the end of the road? The solution of the problem of facility can become fatal when the author rashly relinquishes all his subjects. The fact that Langevin has since turned to the theatre could mean that two novels so teeming with reality have deprived him of any possibility of renewal.

André Giroux (b. 1916)

French Canada remains—but for how much longer?—one of the rare countries where the Catholic conception of sin, the one prevailing all through the great centuries of Christianity, still exists. If we re-read the chronicles of a Joinville we see that the religious atmosphere is not too far removed from that which reigned in French Canada until the quite recent coming of industrialization. And if it is true that in French Canada blasphemers have never had their ears boxed after the fashion of the inhabitants of the *château de Joinville* in the thirteenth century, at least blasphemy and oaths have always been denounced right from the pulpit.

This conception of the public sin is only one aspect of the profound religious feeling of French Canadians. Most significant for the literary historian are the reactions of the French-Canadian writer to evil, reactions which go all the way from anguish to marked enjoyment. The poet Saint-Denys-Garneau, as his diary and his work reveal him to us, in this respect has been an authentic French Canadian filled with anguish. But the Christian existentialism to which he is related must not let us lose sight of the essentially French-Canadian quality of his inner struggles. Now here we have André Giroux, creating in his two novels, *Au-delà des visages* (1948) and *Le gouffre a toujours soif* (1953)—novels which make one take a look at the distance separating French-Canadian contemporary literature from the stammerings of less than a century ago—the characters of Jacques Langlet and Jean Sirois, who reflect the religious aspirations of a whole people.

By means of a technique whose possibilities had been demonstrated by Gide in his *Faux-monnayeurs,* Giroux is able to lay bare the tragic personality of Jacques Langlet. Although the latter never appears before us, we learn through characters who come into the story that he is particularly fond of music, Mozart especially, that friendship such as he conceives it is more real when nobody knows anything about it; and finally that the world in which he lives the daily round, encrusted in a nameless social and religious conformism, is a hell for him. Up to this point there is nothing very original about Langlet. That he should have kept his virginity to the age of twenty-three makes him a being more or less exceptional; but the extraordinary thing is that when he finally does forfeit it in a hotel room the newly acquired knowledge does more than upset him, it destroys him. Suddenly, before the dreariness of the flesh he experiences a savage collapse. He feels the loss of grace to be so terrible a blight that, beside himself in what appears to him a revelation, he accomplishes the only act which seems one of expiation. He kills his companion. The only thing left for him to do is to face the less complicated justice of man. Before his condemnation he will have found in the person of his confessor, Father Maurice Brillart, a man who, having understood his mystic indignation, will be the means of bringing peace to his soul.[13]

More moving than *Au-delà des visages, Le gouffre a toujours soif* requires our attendance at the slow death of a man who has cancer, Jean Sirois. Haunted also by the thought of the Beyond— not as Langlet, who is an exceptional case, but no doubt in somewhat the same way as his compatriots are—Sirois touches us precisely because his death is one with which we are familiar. His reconciliation with God, while predictable, is not, in the case of Giroux, a demonstration of the efficacy of Catholic dogma; rather, this is a Christian death in the natural order of things. Because the hard-headed people of Quebec often return to the religion of their fathers, and because any other solution would have seemed almost against nature, the writer's concern is brought to bear almost entirely on the suffering of a man, a very ordinary man who, by reason of the successive breakdowns of his body, noted in detail by Giroux, worries us like a portent.

Giroux can claim the same right as Thériault to be considered among the best novelists of his generation. His membership in the two-novel club is no longer in doubt since the publication of *Malgré tout, la joie* (Quebec: Institut littéraire du Québec, 1959). Unreality, absurdity or simply vulgarity characterize the majority of the short stories of this collection. *Le mari parfait* contains a few innovations which fail to compensate for the weaknesses in *L'étranger,* whose moral preoccupations seem caricatural.

Félix-Antoine Savard (b. 1896)

When *Menaud maître-draveur* was published in 1937 it was clear that French-Canadian literature could from then on count among its ranks a stylist, if not a novelist.

Inspired by Louis Hémon's evocation Savard takes up again on his own account the message that the inner voices breathed to Maria Chapdelaine: "We came three hundred years ago and we have stayed here." Menaud is thinking about that lesson in tenacity again when, at the beginning of the novel, he has his daughter Marie read his favourite passages. The problem Menaud has on his mind is that of the progressive buying up by the lumber companies of the wooded region near La Malbaie where he was born. The encroachment on the native soil of "foreigners" is a challenge for this intrepid man, trustee of ancestral values. In vain he will set his face against the arbitrary demands of the financial world and will end by losing his mind.

The leitmotifs of this first novel derive in great part from *Maria Chapdelaine*. The novelty of *Menaud* is in the polish of the workmanship, in a style which places Félix-Antoine Savard in the first rank of French-Canadian prose writers.

Professor of Canadian literature, Félix-Antoine Savard has been led to seek a solution to the problem of style which every French-Canadian novelist has to face: how to melt down in a novel expressions and words of the country and of the written language and make of them an artistic whole. Some generations of novelists had already gone astray by emptying their whole bag of Canadianisms into their works. Louis Hémon had found the first valid solution in asking of the French language, as it is spoken in Canada, nothing but what was required for the appearance of reality and truth. He wrote *Maria Chapdelaine* in a restrained, precise style and studded his dialogue with the Canadianisms best calculated to bring out the psychology of the character. Canadianisms in his case are never unprovoked or numerous enough to make the text less comprehensible.

What constitutes the originality of Félix-Antoine Savard is that he created a language of his own, as far removed from that of his predecessors as from that of Hémon. The line of cleavage between the sustained style and the Canadianisms disappears. This result could be obtained only by an exhaustive knowledge of French and by an intuitive feeling for the dynamics of the French-Canadian vocabulary. So *Menaud* is more than anything else a painting in which the subject is of less importance than the execution.

This artist's skill was carried to its highest point of development by Savard in *L'abatis* (1943). The author, wanting to record the story of the years he had spent in Abitibi among the men who cleared the land, the *défricheurs,* was of the opinion that the bare narration of his experience would hide the significance of the colonizing work in which he had participated. Rejecting the formula of the novel, Savard chose the more tractable form of poeticized memories.

L'abatis is the work of a strong personality developing in response to the call of colonization. Man and poet, they gain from this experience:

J'assiste au balancement de la forêt sous le vent. Je suis comme au bord de la mer dans une pleine et sonore ambiance de force, dans une délicieuse dilation de moi-même. Le souffle roule autour de moi la verte masse élastique, et compose de feuilles battantes, de bois qui craquent et sifflent une épaisse et ronde rumeur.

Voici les clameurs végétales et toutes les orgues et flûtes de la terre, et voici que les sons secrets, en toute fibre enfermés, éclatent.

Foule tumultueuse et puissante!

Le vent visible, le souffle sans élocution demande à mon coeur les mots de sa puissance. Que je balance de mes mains le rythme! que je dirige le cours de ces turbulentes musiques, et chante, et jette des comparisons marines à la forêt toute flottante dans le vent!

Que je lui attribue comme à la mer les beaux textes liquides et lui dise: "Dieu aime tes élans admirables, le balancement de tes forces! Il aime l'essor, le désir, le battement de ton coeur dans la lumière et cette louange qui monte de la profondeur de tes pieds jusqu'à la bouche de tes derniers bourgeons![14]

I see the forest swinging in the wind. It is as if I am at the seashore, part of a mighty, sounding strength, in a delightful expansion of myself. The blast of the wind wraps me in the green elastic mass and out of pelting leaves and wood splitting and cracking, it makes a deep, full-throated roar.

Here the growing things give voice, all the organs and flutes of the earth; here the secret sounds confined in every fibre are suddenly vocal.

Crushing, mighty and tumultuous throng!

The wordless breathing of that visible wind appeals to my heart for words to express the strength in it. Let me catch its swinging rhythm with my hands! Let me lead that turbulent music and sing and toss marine comparisons to the forest floating in the wind!

Let me assign beautiful fluid pages to it as to the sea, and say: "God loves your wonderful outbursts, the swinging of your strengths! He loves the soaring, the desire, the beating of your heart in the light, and that praise rising from down in your feet right up to the life of your latest buds![14] [*trans.*]

From this prose Savard can draw clever effects. Alone among the numerous clergy in the ranks of French-Canadian literature he has been able, by the magic of his style, to make us share his joy in the simple, hard-working life of the farmers and the men who clear the land.

Would it be from listening to the counsels of the Evil One, whose spirit poisons the main characters in *La minuit* (1948), that Savard returned to the novel? His third book shows a very sharp step backward if we compare it with the two that went before. It is unnecessary to mention the plot, thin in his novels when not completely artificial. What is more serious is that the style has become impoverished to the point where the born writer finds only a colourless prose, very close to the commonplace, to evoke the confusion into which simple souls are thrown by Corneau, who personifies the spirit of the century.

La minuit bears marks of a spiritual lassitude which might be partly explained by the very definitive proletarianizing of the French-Canadian people. It was when in touch with the peasant soul that Savard wrote his best pages. When he preached return to the land in the years before the Second World War, the industrialization of French Canada had not yet become as widespread as it is today. *La minuit* reflects some kind of uneasy disappointment. It is in vain that Christmas celebrations put people back onto the right path; a few doubts persist, the doubts of Savard himself.

About ten years will go by during which the very logic of a life tuned to French-Canadian nature will lead to *le Barachois* (Fides, 1959). The teaching of the northern forests, always implicit in anything that Savard writes, becomes insistent with age. Witness and trustee of the qualities of the *défricheurs*, Savard turns with love and compassion to their brothers, the Acadian fishermen. With the broad and sonorous evocation of the harmonious *entente* established between men and tides, one is made aware of the anxiety which had burst the artificial limits of *La minuit,* and which it no longer even tries to dissimulate. *Le Barachois* now becomes a confession and testament.

The advice urgently given to the youth of his country by this incomparable prose writer will not be followed, for the century has taken on the task of dragging it off at a dizzy pace towards other destinies. Like Maurice Chappaz, cantor of another world coming to an end—that of the high and untouched valleys of Switzerland—Antoine Savard will have been the chronicler *par excellence* of the magnificent ancestral virtues of the French Canadians. The crusade that he preaches, holy and respectable as it is, will not be heeded for the machine will soon accomplish, and how much more efficiently, the centuries-old labours which shape the soul of a people. That the young men are "deserting" is proof not only of the fatal attraction of the cities but of the scarcely disguised repugnance felt for the kind of slavery which it is permissible for the poet to sanctify. Nevertheless, as the saddened narrator of *le Barachois* rightly observes, so many strong and life-giving lessons could not be lost forever. The feeling of a lost innocence, ravished by a world foreign to it, sets up in the heart of French Canadians a permanent yearning for their origins. By means of his art Savard has succeeded in recapturing, in pages that will endure, the best moments of a common patrimony.[15]

ROBERT ELIE (b. 1915): Robert Elie is the heir, among other contemporary novelists, of the French tradition of the novel of analysis. If others have practised this difficult art before him—both Laure Conan at the end of the nineteenth century and Rex Desmarchais between wars attempted it—Robert Elie is the first to distinguish himself in it.

La fin des songes (1950) is a surprising work. Murders and suicides become increasingly frequent with French-Canadian novelists and doubtless this fact alone says a good deal about the profound changes going on in French Canada. At a closer look, however, these extravagant acts often have something artificial about them or at least lack profound conviction: Langevin and Giroux have crimes that seem most unreal. Now the suicide of Robert Elie's Marcel is a real suicide. That is, this heartfelt explanation of a very modern ailment to which symbolic meaning has been attached, strikes the reader as something actually experienced.

Marcel and Bernard at the same moment in their friendship ask themselves the same question: where does life take us? Bernard will be lost in the narcosis of the Pascalian *divertissement*; Marcel, more demanding, will die by his own hand. The dialogues, which appear unreal only because they are placed at the level of consciousness of the characters, permit Elie to see into the real Marcel. Boredom and despair seep through from these pages and also from the diary of the man who is to commit suicide. Marcel, the first godless man in French-Canadian literature, is nevertheless of his country. Having experienced sensual enjoyment he will react like Saint-Denys-Garneau in *Après les plus vieux vertiges*, like the Jacques Langlet of Giroux. Marcel is a Christian agnostic.

La fin des songes belongs to a literature which is coming into its majority. Elie has universality through the keenness of his analysis of modern man, an analysis all the more honest since in this novel it concerns a recognizable variant of the species, a French Canadian.

Did Elie grant himself a respite of seven years between *La fin des songes* and *Il suffit d'un jour* (1957) or did he give up the novel provisionally, to come back to it later? In this second novel one does find the inner dialogue, a certain refinement of the analysis. But the failure is noteworthy. The reason may be imputed to an error in technique.

The novel, which depends primarily upon the symbol, can almost never live by that symbol alone; without firm ties to life it becomes a bloodless representation with no connecting links to reality. Among the great contemporary novels, *La Peste* of Camus is a perfect illustration of this literary truth. The extremely keen analysis which makes the plague real in our eyes is at the same time replete with symbolic overtones. Yves Thériault, in his *Aaron*, has furnished an excellent example of the novel on two planes. Now, Elie is wrong in being concerned with the symbol to the detriment of reality. Too many characters pass before our eyes in too few pages for them to be anything but values with labels attached. A *diable boiteux*, Elie breaks into the midst of people who live in the village of Saint-Théodore, looking for a human synthesis.

The theme of misunderstood youth is well delineated: Charlie, the voyeur, and Jeanne, the old maid, would never be able to penetrate the circle of emotions experienced by Elisabeth and Yves. As to the murders which bring to an end *Il suffit d'un jour*, they are not so much unexpected as on another plane. The result is that the symbol, because it is not enriched by life, remains nothing but a formula.

ROBERT CHARBONNEAU (b. 1911): Robert Charbonneau is the author of a single book, *Ils posséderont la terre* (1941). Three attempts at renewal, *Fontile* (1945), *Les désirs et les jours* (1948) and *Aucune créature* (1961), point to a progressive creative deterioration and hardly allow for any foreseeable recovery of the high note struck in the beginning.

During the war years Charbonneau played an important role among young French-Canadian writers. Publisher, critic and novelist, he has been one of the outstanding figures of literary Montreal—promoted by the temporary eclipse of Paris to become the world centre of French publication and particularly the home of an autonomous cultural expansion. Few Canadian novelists have given more thought to the art of writing and to the possibility of creating an original literature in French Canada. On this subject, engaged in a controversy which set him against Jérôme and Jean Tharaud, Charbonneau rose in rebellion against their conclusions as expressed in 1947 in *Figaro*:

Nor in Paris would it be possible to look unfavourably on the emergence, in Montreal or in Quebec, of a great and strong literature which would have its roots in the old Gallic soil. On the contrary, this autonomous, original literature would be magnificent proof of the vitality of our spirit.[16] [*trans.*]

The Tharaud brothers, incapable of measuring the breadth that the anti-colonial complex was to take, doubtless had no inkling that in French Canada the expression "our spirit" might get a poor reception. Charbonneau found only "lack of comprehension and complacency" in this fraternal and flattering way of thinking.

Robert Charbonneau's four novels set about proving that the Tharaud brothers are right in the sense that they are highly suggestive of a Latin world. The friendship between André and Edward in *Ils posséderont la terre* reflects an inaccessible ideal which will be taken up again in the two novels that follow. What is best in us, Charbonneau explains in *Fontile,* we owe to the purity and grandeur inspired by the friendship of youth. Respectful in his interpretation of friendship, of the individualism of André and Edward, of Julien Pollender and Georges Lescaut, or of Auguste Prieur and Pierre Massénac, respectful also towards life itself, which is not a blessing to be squandered but a loan, Charbonneau unknowingly plunges his roots down into something removed as far as possible from Anglo-Saxon morals or manners. The best pages of *Ils posséderont la terre* are perfectly French-Canadian—and French.

Aucune créature, by dint of frankness, contains a few moments of intensity. "So what is to keep me from writing a major work, from outstripping all the quaint, sooty characters who have held me back until now?"

JEAN FILIATRAULT (b. 1919): Among the novelists who distinguished themselves between 1950 and 1960, not one has had a more obvious fall than Filiatrault. After three promising novels—*Terres stériles* (Quebec: Institut littéraire du Québec, 1953); *Chaînes* (Le Cercle du Livre de France, 1955); *Le refuge impossible* (*ibid.,* 1957)— which laid bare the family hatreds common to Latin peoples, Filiatrault seemed destined to polish his art to the point of reaching, in his maturity, the classic nudity, of which something already could be seen in *Le refuge impossible,* his strongest work. The novelist has disproved this assumption, however, for the years between this novel and *L'argent est odeur de nuit* (*ibid.,* 1961) have brought him to pity. He invites us to a melodrama of poverty centred around Rose and George and their brood. This theme, which is Gabrielle Roy's by right of conquest, shows up all the more plainly Filiatrault's indiscreet encroachment.

RODOLPHE DUBE (b. 1905): French-Canadian literature has no writer whose temperament is more clearly defined than that of François Hertel. From a first collection of poetry, *Les voix de mon âme* (1934), to *Claudine et les écueils* (1954), a play that takes in one whole aspect of his development, François Hertel (Rodolphe Dubé is his real name) has become increasingly involved in the question of human personality, nobly affirmed when confronted by the demands of a world in which the State ideal tends to replace that of the individual. Hertel has set forth his doctrine in a trilogy with the three titles: *Leur inquiétude* (1936), *Pour un ordre personnaliste* (1942) and *Nous ferons l'avenir* (1945). Like one of his heroes, Gombauld, Hertel has some difficulty in confronting reality and is easily deluded when faced with the future of French Canada. *Pour un ordre personnaliste*—the best of these three studies—owes too much to Thomist theology and to certain French aestheticians such as Abbé Bremond for it to be a really original work. In spite of this reservation Hertel is shown here to be a dialectician of incontestable vigour and skill.

French-Canadian nationalism, exacerbated in the years of economic crisis before the Second World War, had been an auspicious atmosphere for the creation of a series of works of which the writings of Abbé Groulx and *La Chesnaie* by Rex Desmarchais are characteristic. It was in this period that François Hertel wrote his novel about *l'énergie nationale: Le beau risque* (1939). Although everything in this novel is French Canadian—the pilot of souls, Father Henri Berthier, the repressed aspirations of the students, the high ideal which is the by-product of this hothouse living—everything has the recognizably Latin flavour that is to be found in the *Déracinés* of Barrès. These are affinities to be expected and of which Hertel has made a good, if not brilliant, analysis.

To explain what he means by individualism grafted on to the improvement of the inner self, Hertel found the happiest formula in whimsical and caustic autobiography. In the dual character of Anatole Laplante and Charles Lepic, Rodolphe Dubé explains his object:

On certain evenings when love is in the air, in spite of shabby surroundings, and when weak souls melt into a childish mawkishness which is favourable to soft surrender, the sufferer in spirit needs to live further away and higher up. He has only one chance of saving the moment which would otherwise be lost: he must soar.[17] [*trans.*]

In order to "soar" Anatole Laplante must listen to the entreaties of his *daimôn*, Charles Lepic. He will yield to the life of the spirit, the only one that counts. The three tales *Mondes chimériques* (1940), *Anatole Laplante curieux homme* (1944) and *Journal d'Anatole Laplante* (1947) are an introduction to the Hertel method. The literary critic has little chance of appreciating this new form of art as he always finds the writer offensive. No matter, he, Dubé, has only one preoccupation: to live according to conscience. And this is a difficult programme, all the more so as asceticism easily degenerates into a cult of self. The best remedy is banter. Dubé makes a wag of himself in order to stay pure and it will be the roguish side of his nature that will sound the truest note. It is a new note as well, for when Dubé is the philosopher he is apt to fall into the commonplace. There is a great distance between *Barrabas*, a humorous little picture of a kind not to be found anywhere else in French-Canadian literature, and the numerous pages in which Hertel is decidedly offensive.

In *Un Canadien errant* (1953), Hertel takes up again his usual themes which he ponders with his "forty readers" in mind. In spite of the repetitions and banalities there is an indefinable feeling of sadness in this work. A century later than Crémazie and all the French-Canadian writers who followed him into the bittersweet exile of Paris, we find Hertel, too, writing his diary, not about the diocesan centre of Paris this time but about his isolation. Isolated he is in effect, for who will read his rambling reflections if not those French Canadians to whom he is inevitably referring? These uneven pages contain all of the character that Hertel created for himself. Clown and philosopher by turn, this French Canadian who strayed onto the borders of the Seine is capable of being a real writer. His *Cul-de-jatte* is an admirable short story, a little masterpiece of the genre. The absent-minded and at times queer pages in which he was careful to wrap this affected story should not put us off. This bohemian is capable of anything. Has he not already given proof of it in *Six femmes, un homme* (1949)? These short stories devoted to the eternally unrealized love of the artist are very ordinary with the exception of one: *Le solitaire*. The fifteen pages or so which tell the delightful and laughable story of a Parisian hermit—in this case François Hertel—appear as if by miracle at the end of this dull collection.

EUGENE CLOUTIER (b. 1921): In 1953 Eugène Cloutier had attracted attention to himself by his entry into French-Canadian literature with *Témoins*. The formula of this first work has great originality. François has just killed his wife and her lover, Claude. The different facets of François' personality will be endowed with a life of their own and become the "witnesses" of this drama. These witnesses, who are the intellectual, moral, sensual and adolescent sides of the murderer, indirectly make up the case against contemporary French-Canadian society.

Fascinated by the possibilities in compartmentalizing the thoughts of the protagonist, Cloutier has been unable, in *Les témoins,* to conduct the various dialogues with equal success. Actually the different witnesses who testify for François all speak much the same, and at times very conventional, language.

Much more promising is *Les inutiles* (1956), one of the outstanding novels to appear since the Second World War. In a steady, suggestive style this work goes beyond the framework of the city of Montreal where the action takes place. The two heroes, Jean and Antoine, are unable to adapt themselves to the manners and customs of the ant-hill. Having escaped from a mental hospital, that is, one reserved for men of intelligence and feeling, Jean and Antoine do their best to save a friend, Julien, who will say to them, "There is no longer any conversation possible from man to man." The only thing left to these two heroes is to go their own way alone with this thought, which is the very antithesis of the popular American way of thinking: the only freedom is the freedom to suffer.

LEO-PAUL DESROSIERS (b. 1896); Léo-Paul Desrosiers has given French-Canadian literature some of its best writing. After *Ames et paysages* (1922), a collection of short stories, Desrosiers owed it to himself to write his *roman paysan. Nord-Sud* (1931) is a subtle examination of the struggle going on in Vincent Douaire: the attraction of the *South*—in the circumstances the California of 1849 where gold has just been discovered—will win out over the smile of Josephte and the tranquil happiness it promises. The French-Canadian countryside is studied in detail and described in strong, precise language. The poet is already in a contest with the novelist and Desrosiers will gradually leave the conventional novel and turn to a vision of nature which is personal. A few commonplace short stories, *Le livre des mystères* (1936), and two novels devoted to the virtues of the race, *Les opiniâtres* (1941) and *Sources* (1942), belong to his first phase.

Les engagés du grand portage, published in France in 1938, is the reconstruction of the conflicts which broke out some generations after the Conquest between the big fur-trading companies. Much more than a recital of the adventures of the *engagés,* this novel is a *tour de force.* Writing almost entirely in the present tense is a method which heightens the rough simplicity of the passions and the setting; the short simple sentence gives this work a quality of primitive art which can only be the result of deliberate styling. Nicolas Montour, sly and dishonest, is a French-Canadian Ganelon. It is phrases such as *Longues sont les vagues* which recall the famous *Halt sont li pui* and contribute to the unity of tone in *Engagés*.

L'ampoule d'or (1951) is much more a prose poem than a novel. Freed at last from the obligation of concocting a plot, Desrosiers gives epic proportions to the growing spirituality of Julienne, his heroine. This ascension is only sketched and much reinforced by references to holy books. A hybrid work, *L'ampoule d'or* contains some of the most beautifully rhythmic pages in French-Canadian writing. Because this long poem assumes the exterior form of the novel and because the psychology of the characters is subordinated to a dream of spiritual purification, the artistic result is something between the two and is wearisome in the end.

Desrosiers created for himself a novel form which runs no risk of having imitators. As a novelist he belongs to that small number of French-Canadian writers for whom plastic beauty is such a living reality that it can surpass what is true reality. In his case it is not so much a question of conscious effort towards art as of a subtle revenge that the French language takes on French-Canadian writers who use it as he does, with a familiarity and facility unknown to their predecessors. All great European languages have their intrinsic poetic qualities. French, however, not as close to life as Russian, German, or English, gives way to no other Western language in the number and variety of its prose writers. But below the rank of Montaigne, Pascal, Bossuet, Voltaire, Renan and Valéry stand the simple virtuosos who, deceived by the quality of their instrument, have believed that they were hearing harmonies of their own. To juggle with words and sentences, which have become iridescent from polishing and careful use by the creators of the language, is the temptation of every writer in French. The result is often a rarefied and anaemic art.

At the approach of old age Léo-Paul Desrosiers is turning to the novel of religious edification. *Vous qui passez, Les angòisses et les tourments, Rafales sur les cimes* (Fides, 1958-1960), would have filled Abbé Casgrain with delight. According to a well-known psychological process beautiful and noble sentiments, when presented so plainly, only serve to turn the reader away from what was intended. Is it possible that Léo-Paul Desrosiers is the last respectable representative of a genre that no longer exists?

GERMAINE GUEVREMONT (b. 1896): Guardian in the contemporary period of a tradition which goes back to Philippe Aubert de Gaspé, Germaine Guèvrement recreates the life of the French-Canadian tiller of the soil. After Louis Hémon, Ringuet and Claude-Henri Grignon it was not easy to avoid repetitions but *Le survenant* (1945) and *Marie-Didace* (1947) nevertheless have an independent life of their own and take their place immediately quite close to *Maria Chapdelaine* and *Trente arpents* and beside *Un homme et son péché*.

With *En pleine terre* (1942) Germaine Guèvremont finds the formula which she will perfect later on. In successive strokes the Beauchemin family takes shape. The *survenant*, the man who comes by chance, is the catalyst who will stir up the good qualities and the defects in Didace, in Alphonsine and in her weak husband, Amable. With the departure of this unexpected one, this *survenant*, a curse will seem to weigh on the destinies of the Beauchemins.

Le survenant and *Marie-Didace* show the scope of the novelist's talent and its limitations. The great merit of Germaine Guèvremont's art is in the juxtaposition of short photographic chapters which lay bare the working of her characters' minds, which are at once rudimentary and complicated. The exactness of the design she traces, in great part made up of racy dialogue which fits the actors to perfection, is remarkable. Less skilful when weaving a plot, Germain Guèvremont has made the artistic mistake of inventing a series of misfortunes which strike the Beauchemins, seemingly at random. Perhaps influenced by Ringuet, Germaine Guèvremont has allowed herself to slip into the convention, dangerous for her, of the novel that chronicles a generation. The death or madness which came unexpectedly to Didace, his son-in-law and his daughter belong to a commonplace conception of the novel and blemish the otherwise high quality of the diptych.

JEAN-JULES RICHARD (b. 1911): The blunt introduction of his subject and the stenographic style that the American novel has made fashionable go with Jean-Jules Richard's temperament.

His first novel, *Neuf jours de haine* (1948) is the only French-Canadian war novel which comes to the point of suggesting, by its linguistic impressionism, the killings of the Second World War. The subject lent itself to the way the author deals with the story; for three hundred pages it has bombs bursting and soldiers being machine-gunned. Unfortunately, since all conflicts of this kind are alike, it would have been difficult for even the most talented of novelists—once the form was accepted—to hold the reader's attention. More serious than this, though, the verbal acrobatics of Jean-Jules Richard too often are nothing but clumsy trial shots. Did he seek a surrealistic effect in writing *La rage chez Noiraud périclite sa haine. Sa haine du caporal dont le flair s'est prouvé si mièvre.*[18]? Not at all. Jean-Jules Richard belongs to that category of painters who, never having learned to draw, straight away tackle big subjects. Generally these artists will never be anything but people daubing on canvas or making dirty marks on paper. Of course Jean-Jules Richard is not one of those. *Neuf jours de haine,* however, contains too many experimental pages for it to gain any wide recognition.

The elliptical and sensorial style of Richard has brought good results in the reduced framework of the short story. *Ville rouge* (1949) contains some excellent pages that only Richard could have written. *Servilités,* the report of the opening day of an art exhibition, and the short story which gave its name to the collection, clearly indicate by their suggestive conciseness that Richard's writing could become the vehicle for a strong and original work.

Le feu dans l'amiante (1956), however, is not that work. Drawing his inspiration from a conflict which broke out between the Catholic union and the owners of the asbestos industry, centred in the Province of Quebec, Jean-Jules Richard tried to make a case against the interacting forces of the church, the provincial government and American capitalism. The result is a French-Canadian *Germinal* which did not come off. Obliged to explain how the French-Canadian miners were betrayed and to follow chronologically the different stages of the strike, which has remained famous in the history of employer-employee relations, the author ventured into the path—fatal for the success of his work—of prose that is carpentered according to logic and, consequently, of traditional syntax. Roger Lemelin proved that syntax can be learned. But Jean-Jules Richard is too far in arrears to aspire to a similar accomplishment.

ANNE HEBERT (b. 1916): More structured than *Le torrent, Les chambres de bois* (Paris: Editions du Seuil, 1958) is still close to poetry. But while *Le torrent* lived as a work of art only by virtue of the underlying current of poetry, *Les chambres de bois* belongs frankly to the dream novel as Alain-Fournier understood it. Catharine is the same girl who had evoked her suffering in *Les songes en équilibre,* less painfully in this instance, however, as she has had a glimpse of that *reflet d'aube* to which allusion had been made in *Le tombeau des rois.* This *Chambres* is a fine work, written in a style that is both firm and suggestive. Will Anne Hébert be able to find in the novel the same possibilities of expression as in poetry? The quality of this novel at least makes the question justifiable. It seems more probable, nevertheless, that poetry is more responsive to the demands of a talent which must put a veil over everything in order to be understood.

ROBERT CHOQUETTE (b. 1905): For the French-Canadian man of letters radio and television are a pit into which he throws his ideas, his best inspirations, without being able to claim anything but monetary return. Journalism by comparison is a finishing school. Robert Choquette's novels, with the exception of one youthful work, *La pension Leblanc,* suffer from having been conceived in response to popular demand. *Le curé de village* remains without doubt the work which reveals the most humour and the most searching psychology. But the reader still has to imagine that he is hearing the same voices to restore to these radio novels their ephemeral life.

Works: *La pension Leblanc* (Montreal: Louis Carrier & Cie, 1927); *Le curé de village* (Montreal: Granger Frères, 1936); *Les Velder* (Montreal: Bernard Valiquette, 1941); *Elise Velder* (Montreal: Fides, 1958).

ALAIN GRANDBOIS (b. 1900): Two biographies in story form are the contribution of this great poet to a genre that adds nothing to his reputation. *Né à Québec,* which tells the life story of Louis Jolliet, is inferior to *Cavelier de La Salle* by Constantin-Weyer. Between history and poetry, Constantin-Weyer had no hesitation in choosing the first, while putting into it everything that his own experience could suggest to him. Grandbois, because he felt obliged to follow the historians closely, produced two works which, while not exactly belonging to history, are not poetry either. Every time the poet bursts into the text there is a flagrant lack of harmony between the effect sought and that which results from remaining too faithful to sources.

Works: *Né à Québec* (Paris: A. Messein, 1933); *Voyages de Marco Polo* (Montreal: Bernard Valiquette, 1941).

RENE OUVRARD (b. 1894): René Ouvrard's reputation without a doubt will rest on one of the best novels published after the war, *La veuve* (Les Editions Chantecler, 1954). His first romantic work, *Débâcle sur la Romaine* (Fides, 1945), following the pious recipes of the nineteenth century, was in no way a forecast of the powerful evocation of the thirty-year-old woman that was to follow. It must be admitted, too, that the recent *Fauve* (Beauchemin, 1961), which traces the mental and moral development of a deformed child, is confined to the narrow limits of a special medical problem and does not awaken the reader's concern for the painful existence of the central character.

On the ragged theme of poverty among families farming unproductive land, Ouvrard has superimposed the eternal one of the mature woman who is unattached. The widow Orpha owns the best land of its kind. What she lacks to make her happy is a man to take over the management of her property and to satisfy her sensual longings. Deprived of love over a long period, Orpha starts making eyes at Alidor Larose, twenty-two years old, the eldest in a poverty-stricken family. Alidor is the image of the powerful young male, made to reward the frantic yearnings of the woman no longer young. All the guile of this thirty-six-year-old farm woman and the complicity of Alidor's family are required to bring this reluctant bull to terms. The marriage is contracted and consummated but is too much against nature to fail to produce the inevitable drama of its progressive dissolution, marked by the cynicism and infidelities of Alidor.

This realistic novel stands comparison with *Trente arpents* and *La forêt,* yet Ouvrard's writing, not as convincing as Ringuet's nor as much a work of art as Bugnet's, keeps *La veuve* from being a really great work.

FELIX LECLERC (b. 1914): The ability to communicate directly with life without recourse to bookish reminiscences is the rare quality of Félix Leclerc. The spontaneity and youth of his outlook are already apparent in *Adagio,* a collection of short stories and sketches. His inspiration springs from an instinctive understanding of the hidden humiliations and the noble ideal of work and self-sacrifice in French-Canadian country life. This innate perception may be found on occasion in charming fables that bring together flora and fauna which are transparent symbols of the country as it is today. Such are the fables assembled under the title of *Allegro,* whose leitmotif is the firsthand advice given to a gathering of the animals: "Do not believe in a paradise without effort. Let us remain ourselves. I want no imitators in the country."

Unfortunately, because the thought is the same throughout, Leclerc remains frozen in a primitivism that becomes tedious in the end to the most well-disposed readers. His memories, *Moi, mes souliers,* with a preface by Jean Giono and prepared for a French audience, cruelly underline the fragility of an art that cannot live outside of the circumscribed conditions from which it sprang. Félix Leclerc belongs to the race of rustic poets whose thought can rise only out of the native soil and cannot be fully appreciated away from it.

Works: *Adagio* (Montreal: Fides, 1943); *Allegro* (*ibid.,* 1944); *Andante* (*ibid.,* 1944); *Pieds nus dans l'aube* (*ibid.,* 1947); *Dialogues d'hommes et de bêtes* (*ibid.,* 1949); *Théâtres de village* (*ibid.,* 1951); *Le hamac dans les voiles* (*ibid.,* 1951); *Moi, mes souliers* (Paris: Amiot-Dumont, 1955).

JEAN VAILLANCOURT (1923-1961): The rapid development of French Canada, accelerated by two world wars, has found partial expression in the war novel. In his *Canadiens errants* (Montreal: Le Cercle du Livre de France, 1954) Jean Vaillancourt is revealed, along with Jean-Jules Richard, as the best historian of the French-Canadian soldier. In the nineteenth century Faucher de Saint-Maurice had recorded, sometimes in pages of fine writing, a series of episodes of the Franco-Mexican war of 1862, and before his time stories had been written which called to mind the heroes of the Rebellion of 1837-1838.

Aiming higher, Vaillancourt has wanted to leave a memorial to his generation which lived, on the roads of France and Germany, one of the great moments of modern history. Richard Lanoue, Dubuc, Lanthier and others represent French-Canadian youth as it was shaped by the Second World War. The pathetic experiences of these young men have the ring of truth and make *Canadiens errants* a work of great merit. In certain ways *Les neuf jours de haine* of Jean-Jules Richard is a more original novel, particularly more intense. Vaillancourt, while offering no surprises in his traditional presentation of an old subject, does not lose himself on the other hand in somersaults of a style that will not live.

AIME PELLETIER (b. 1914): Although Aimé Pelletier[19] has tackled the detective novel and the war novel it is only in the role of censor of Quebec manners and morals that he pulled himself up for a time to the level of a Jean Simard or a Roger Lemelin.

Louise Genest is a wife married too young who, when she understands the nature of the sacrifice that French-Canadian society demands of her, refuses to offer herself as this sacrifice in a marriage that has become meaningless. On a less serious note Pelletier approaches the political passions in *Saint-Pépin, P.Q.* His humour is curiously like Roger Lemelin's; events, characters, failings and funny habits are enormously blown up.

The crude jokes that Lemelin and Pelletier allow to slip into their works are the very antithesis of the humorous understatement of the English or French, made up of reticence and subtlety. Pelletier and Lemelin belong to that family of American humourists who get their comic effect through burlesque.

Works: *Louise Genest* (Montreal: Le Cercle du Livre de France, 1950); *Deux portes, une adresse* (*ibid.,* 1952); *Saint-Pépin, P.Q.* (*ibid.,* 1955); *L'assassin dans l'hôpital* (Montreal: Le Cercle du Roman policier, 1956).

PIERRE BAILLARGEON (b. 1916): Pierre Baillargeon is the first moralist in French-Canadian literature. After having explained in *Les médisances de Claude Perrin* what his complaints are against the system of education as it is conceived in French Canada, and having advocated the kind of upbringing advised by Montaigne, Pierre Baillargeon finishes his diary with a literary profession of faith. For him French Classicism offers the noblest intellectual and artistic lesson. Going from precept to example in *Commerce*, in which the protagonist, Claude Perrin, is his mouthpiece, Baillargeon, in a series of imaginary conversations, keeps talking to us about the same subjects treated in *Médisances*, with this difference that his thoughts have been put together in the form of proverbs.

There does not seem to be any very well defined doctrine in Baillargeon. His thoughts find honey where they may, often coming to rest on literary subjects. It is to ethics that he owes his best maxims: "The lazy man dreams that everything becomes dear while costing him nothing"; "There are no beautiful lives, there are only beautiful souls," and so on.

One novel, *La neige et le feu,* in which the hero is a reincarnation of Claude Perrin, is only a variant of *Commerce* and *Médisances.*

Works: *Hasard et moi* (Montreal: Beauchemin, 1940); *Les Médisances de Claude Perrin* (Montreal: Parizeau, 1945); *Commerce* (Montreal: Editions Variétés, 1947); *La neige et le feu* (*ibid.,* 1948).

MARCEL TRUDEL (b. 1917): *Vézine* (Montreal: Fides, 1946), Trudel's only novel, is the result of long observation of peasant ways. Mélida, pitiless censor of the least slip in the moral behaviour of the parishioners of Saint-Narcisse, is one of the most successfully drawn figures of the French-Canadian country novel, to be ranked with the Séraphin of Claude-Henri Grignon. The dialogue is of a picturesqueness rarely equalled in novels of the kind.

ROGER VIAU (b. 1906): *Au milieu la montagne,* suffers from having appeared six years after *Bonheur d'occasion.* Today *Au milieu la montagne* furnishes counter-proof of the importance of Gabrielle Roy's first novel.

Works: *Contes en noir et en couleur* (Montreal: l'Arbre, 1948); *Au milieu la montagne* (Montreal: Beauchemin, 1951).

CHARLOTTE SAVARY (b. 1913): Social criticism and a vague sense of messianic mission of the Laure Conan type are the component factors of two unconvincing novels by Charlotte Savary, *Isabelle de Frêneuse* (Quebec: Institut littéraire du Québec, 1950), *Et la lumière fut* (*ibid.,* 1951).

GERARD MARTIN (b. 1911): His novel *Tentations* (Quebec: Librairie Garneau, 1943) is an unconvincing religious melodrama in which the main characters—in contrast to the good Joinville who would have preferred infinitely to commit a mortal sin rather than contract leprosy—would not hesitate, as between sin and leprosy, to choose the latter.

ADRIENNE CHOQUETTE (b. 1915): Can a very attractive woman simultaneously disturb the souls of four boys to the extent that they bear the mark for the rest of their lives? This is the experience that Adrienne Choquette attempts to describe in *La coupe vide* (Montreal: Pilon, 1948). Short stories collected under the title of *La nuit ne dort pas* (Quebec: Institut littéraire du Québec, 1954) give evidence of a more credible realism.

CLEMENT LOCKQUELL (b. 1908): *Les élus que vous êtes* (Montreal: Variétés, 1949), the story of the spiritual progress of a teaching-brother, is inferior to the *Beau risque* of François Hertel.

CLAIRE MORIN (b. 1918): For once, pure love brings French-Canadian literature a healthy book, *Les enfants qui s'aiment* (Beauchemin, 1956). Claire Morin[20] has evoked in striking and true fashion the first love of André and Annick. Reconstruction of the enchantment of a feeling as powerful and as delicate as the attraction that impels two young things towards each other presupposes uncommon talent for analysis.

Et le septième jour (Beauchemin, 1958), diary of an Atlantic crossing on board the *Ile de France*, is worthy of mention only because it is a first novel that is far removed from the twaddle of the author's second one. In 1962 Claire Morin won a French provincial prize, *Le grand prix du Maine*, for *Autour de toi, Tristan* (Flammarion), a novel which pictures French Canada through the life of four families.

ADRIEN THERIO (b. 1925): *Les brèves années* (Fides, 1953)—the comparison with *Grand Meaulnes* is unwarranted—is an honest evocation of the author's childhood and adolescence. The indispensable poetry which Robert Roquebrune was able to create in the rediscovery of his past is scarcely to be found here in this first work. Is it possible that old age is more favourable to a reconstruction of our brief span than the age of around thirty?

Perhaps, too, the lack of sufficient perspective accounts for the fact that Thério has failed to make the main characters in *La soif et le mirage* (Le cercle du Livre de France, 1960) entirely real to us. This novel, based on a sojourn of some years in an American university milieu, succeeds in making one realize the spiritual vacuum in which the student, and the woman approaching the menopause, live and move and attach themselves to the narrator. In coming into contact with the United States, so far removed from the world that he is seeking to bring back in *Les brèves années,* Thério for the first time realized his French Canadianism. The outline of a criticism of American society is written into the best pages of this autobiography in story form.

It is significant that of all the short stories put together under the title of *Mes beaux meurtres* (Le Cercle du Livre de France, 1961) it is *Le chat sauvage* which remains alive in the memory. The indispensable years—those which cut in between reality and memory—have gone by and Thério is successful finally in bringing back to life the brutish father and the unhappy child which haunt his subconscious and which, described with reserve and true art, do touch us at last.

Le printemps qui pleure (Les Editions de l'Homme, 1962) has completed what will no doubt be the first phase of Thério's development. Once again the theme of adolescence is examined. We witness the awakening of sexual awareness in pimply boys and in girls unconsciously provocative. Thério treats this subject with a convincing realism which does not exclude occasional moments of dreaming.

Probably unable to return to his childhood in future works, Thério will find himself in the dilemma of all the writers, and there are many of them, in whom the imagination does not seem capable of catching fire unless there is a generous recourse to autobiography. The single exception in which he is not autobiographical is *Mes beaux meurtres,* wherein the most purely fabricated crimes are the least successful. Will Thério be able to raise this mortgage in the years awaiting him?

MAURICE GENEVOIX (b. 1890): Maurice Genevoix[21] was only mildly inspired in devoting a diary and two works of fiction to Canada after having lived in the country a few months.

Eva Charlebois, with a title too reminiscent of *Maria Chapdelaine,* is a novel which makes use of the notes of a touring lecturer of the *Alliance Française.* Eva Charlebois, after marrying an *Anglâ,* Reuben Jackson, goes to live with her husband in Field, British Columbia. Ontario would have done just as well to prove the theorem that follows, but what would the author have done with all those impressions gathered on his trip from Quebec to Vancouver? Eva, who speaks hardly any English, will finally feel drawn back to her own people. Her husband will die opportunely to justify the hope that she will not end her days on foreign territory.

Maurice Genevoix sought to paint a picture of Canadian nature —he was greatly impressed by the wild and untouched aspect of it —a picture to correspond to the strong feeling it had left in him and which he was no doubt glad to call to mind in a tragic moment in the history of France. Accurately and with delicacy Genevoix has reproduced the special atmosphere of the Rockies. His plot, unfortunately, is too manifestly superficial, his dialogue too little like the French-Canadian speech to make it possible for *Eva Charlebois* to count among novels like *La rivière solitaire* or *La forêt* which, written by Frenchmen, will always be part of the cultural inheritance of French Canada.

More modest but more successful is the short story *Laframboise et Bellehumeur.* The roving instinct of the French Canadians and the spirit of adventure that still possesses the most daring among them have been observed with remarkable awareness by Maurice Genevoix. His *Nazaire Laframboise,* young in spite of his fifty-odd years, stays in the memory for a long time. The novelist—who had written his fine study of big game hunting, *La dernière Harde,* just before leaving for Canada—was psychologically prepared to understand, with a minimum of actual contact, the French-Canadian trapper.

PIERRE HAMP (b. 1876): Pierre Hamp's French-Canadian novel, *Hormisdas le Canadien,*[22] is a sign of the times. After the rediscovery of Canada by France at the end of the nineteenth century there followed a golden age of Franco-Canadian relations. Here and there a legend based on the reality of a common linguistic and ethnic heritage has been kept alive by writers, lecturers and politicians. The common practice of trips to France among well-to-do French Canadians, and the arrival in Canada of thousands of French immigrants, have contributed since 1946, however, to some reappraisals of the Franco-Canadian bond.

Evidently Pierre Hamp found the reality too different from what he had imagined on leaving France and felt some bitterness. It can be said for him that he wanted to hide nothing and to describe French Canada according to his experience of it.

Disregarding pastoral evocations of the past, he sets himself at the middle of the present century and makes us witnesses to the uprooting of Hormisdas, the French Canadian. The latter, deprived of his land by the Canadian war industry, sees his fields of wheat transformed into a vast enclosed area for a factory and its outbuildings. The arrival of thousands of workers and the permanent establishment in the heart of French Canada of a mechanized and foreign enclave is pitilessly analyzed. Hormisdas' son, Claude, leaves for Montreal where he will learn the art of wood-carving under the benevolent eye of Guillemain. This dyed-in-the-wool Parisian has wandered onto the shores of the St. Lawrence, allowing the author to unburden himself of what is in his heart. What is laid bare is all of the rough, obscurantist side of French Canada. These half-truths—together with a picture of English Canada, depending on the wildest imagination for its information—make one hope that other French writers who wish, as did Pierre Hamp, to see and tell everything, will bring to French-Canadian writing more evidence of serenity and, particularly, of art.

MARCEL CLEMENT (b. 1921): The disorderliness of French politics and the collective forgetfulness of an indispensable national solidarity seem to have pushed Marcel Clément towards French Canada, which published his *Esquisses sur l'homme* (Montmagny: Editions Marquis, 1945). This work was the result of his reflections on the human condition and the German occupation. The sketches, devoted to some of the great names of history—among them Jeanne d'Arc, Rembrandt, Richelieu, Louis XIV—are bound together by an *Introduction à la politique de l'esprit*. Conceived after the event, the *Introduction* suffers from a resounding title not at all in keeping with what is only a collection of biographies, lacking any connecting links. As compensation, however, the sketches reveal a very real gift for writing. While not acceptable to the professional historian, they belong to history in story form. Clément has succeeded in giving life to the rare qualities of a Richelieu, or a Louis XIV, precisely those figures about whom the modern world has increasing difficulty in forming any exact notion. Of what importance is it to us if the political policy of Louis XIV is defined as beneficent?

ROGER BULIARD (b. 1909): This missionary lay-brother, in a work at once autobiographical and ethnographical—*Inuk* (Paris: Editions Saint-Germain, 1949)—becomes part of a tradition dating back to the *Relations* of the Jesuits. His story contains strong, beautiful pages about the Eskimo attitude towards death, about the inhuman yet ennobling life of the many evangelists who left France to blaze trails over the barren territories of the great Canadian North.

In the previous generation Louis-Frédéric Rouquette (1884-1926), a journalist by profession, had set down in his *Epopée blanche* (Paris: Ferenczi, 1926), his impressions of the Canadian West and had told the story of the noble deeds of those great French missionaries who are now remembered in Alberta place-names: Grouard, Lacombe, Falher, Leduc, Millet, Végreville.

Jean Simard (b. 1916)

The strong personality of Jean Simard, already perceptible in his first novels, comes out into broad daylight in the two works of his maturity, *Les sentiers de la nuit* (Le Cercle du Livre de France, 1959) and *Répertoire* (*ibid.*, 1961), in which he laid bare his soul. Of all the important novelists to appear since *Bonheur d'occasion* Simard is the only one who has grown considerably and who, ten years after the novels of his apprenticeship, reveals himself at last for what he is.

At the start, in *Félix* (Editions Variétés, 1947), and *Hôtel de la Reine* (*ibid.*, 1949), Simard had made himself the caustic critic of French-Canadian society. The failings of his compatriots, which Lemelin was also to poke fun at, were subjected to ridicule by Simard: "Everywhere else there are seven deadly sins. In Quebec there is only one—one only—that of the Flesh . . . which people dream of committing, are afraid of committing, agree to commit, commit, have committed, regret having committed and commit again."

Feeling an increasing concern for the social structure of his country Simard abandons his grim humour to become the Public Prosecutor in *Mon fils pourtant heureux* (Le Cercle du Livre de France, 1956). Family and religion are subjected to pitiless analysis. A churlish father, a mother devoted to her child, and Marie-Thérèse Valouris, the tyrannical grandmother, represent the infernal circle to which too many children are subjected. The church school, instrument of an omnipresent religion, completes the destruction of the individual by handing him over to life, forever burdened with complexes.

In a firmer style than that of the two preceding works, *Mon fils pourtant heureux* was no preparation for the revelation that came with *Les sentiers de la nuit* (Le Cercle du Livre de France, 1959). To gauge the significance of this novel it is fitting to refer to *Répertoire* (*ibid.*, 1961). Although this notebook appeared subsequently it contains all the themes the author had been turning over in his mind for years and on which he would draw for the composition not only of *Les sentiers de la nuit*, but also for the charming transcription, *L'ange interdit* (*ibid.*, 1961), a play in three acts without change of setting.

Jean Simard is certainly not the first to question the position of the French-Canadian writer. Saint-Denys-Garneau, Robert Charbonneau and others have given themselves over to reflections inseparable from their work. What makes Simard stand out from those before him, however, is the lucid acceptance of his historical situation. Jean Le Moyne will arrive at a more stylized autocriticism in *Convergences.*

But precisely because Simard has sought before all else to find his place in relation to literature generally, without claiming to reach any lofty conclusions, the modesty of his diagnosis permits us to take the temperature of French-Canadian literature as it is today. "When a European writer takes up his pen," concludes Simard, "it is a tool heavy with years and experience, still slightly warm from the thousands of lettered hands that have manipulated it before him. Whereas ours have held only the axe! We are the first intellectuals in a nation of wood-cutters."[23]

A considerable portion of *Répertoire* is devoted to the subject of painting, which Simard uses to arrive at personal conclusions about artistic creation. We are listening much more to a conversation than to a display of a kind likely to lead to new theories of art. So the importance of *Répertoire* lies in the explanation of a temperament and not in the elaboration of a theory of aesthetics, which would have the drawback of depending on commonplaces.

Simard's most significant avowal is perhaps this: the French-Canadian writer, when he has honestly come face to face with himself, is aware of the fact that he is absolutely, specifically himself and rather far removed from his French colleague. Were it necessary to find a counterpart for him, he would be Nordic. Let Simard react to the Canadian winter, or to a picture painted in Paris by a compatriot, and he will see in it the same glacial significance. Now it is to a demonstration of this truth that we are led in *Les sentiers de la nuit.*

There are two novels in this work. The first one reconstructs the amorphous life of an English Canadian, Godley Roundabout. Irremediably crushed by a puritan upbringing that leaves him no margin for imagination, Godley is the counterpart of Simard's French-Canadian characters. A subtle irony, more detached than that of *Hôtel de la Reine,* is indicative of the distance covered since *Félix.* Simard seems to say to us that man, in whatever ethnic group he belongs, is more often than not only a small island, subject to a whole series of humiliations which await the privileged as well as the Godley Roundabouts.

The second novel, describing in detail the supreme suffering of Godley, who has gone blind, sets before us the most hopeless pages in French-Canadian literature. Albert Laberge is the only one to have employed words like these in following, step by step, the distracted course of his tortured creatures under sentence of death. To Simard, who is a witness to contemporary holocausts, suffering and evil become malevolent divinities to whom he gives himself in a kind of masochism. In *Répertoire* torture has an important place for, as Simard sees it, man, born sadistic, became clearly defined at Buchenwald and Belsen. Godley's symbolic cries of pain represent our lot; they belong to the repertory of the refinements of cruelty from which man does not even seek to rid himself:

Toutes notions confondues, le Désespoir planté dans le crâne, G. G. (Godley) n'est plus qu'un supplicié à bout de forces. Vidé, fini, désintégré. Un condamné longtemps incarcéré, affamé, torturé jour après jour, avec une inflexible minutie. Insulté, giflé, roué de coups. Le visage et les doigts écrasés, tuméfiés, les côtes, le diaphragme, les testicules. Il connaît la morsure des électrodes, de l'épouvante. Ses boyaux se sont liquéfiés au-dedans de lui. Il n'est plus qu'une plaie. Il a pleuré, gémi, supplié. Il a hurlé de douleur, s'est traîné comme une bête aux pieds des bourreaux, dans le sang et le vomi. Il n'en peut plus, implore qu'on le tue, qu'on l'achève, que ça finisse enfin! Il a perdu la raison. Il n'a plus rien d'humain.

Simard's pessimism does not come from that realism of which contemporary literature offers any number of examples. Rather is it explained by a Nordic spleen which exudes from his being. In a background of dark spasmodic forces there is the ugliness of North American cities, covered over with a thick layer of dirty smoke-laden snow. *Les sentiers de la nuit* thus joins the works of Langevin and Lemelin in its promise of a new literature. Having arrived at this point in his development, will Simard be the French-Canadian Strindberg?

Gérard Bessette (b. 1920)

It is not surprising that Bessette has sought to write the novel of the French-Canadian people's aspirations in *La bagarre* (Le Cercle du Livre de France, 1958). As a critic, in a remarkable thesis Bessette had taken in the entire poetic production of French Canada.[24] It was the best possible preparation for his telling of the hopes of Jules Lebeuf, prototype of the young French-Canadian of today, as conscious of his exceptional situation in North America as he is of the immense practical difficulties which hamper the unfolding of his own personality. His preoccupations are, without doubt, in part those of the author; they take concrete individual form in the main characters of *La bagarre*. Jules Lebeuf, who would like to write a major work, is confronted with the linguistic difficulty. Augustin Sillery sums this up succinctly. In language polished to an exaggerated extent he only proves how incapable he is of throwing off the psychological pressures that he analyzes very lucidly:

Que nous parlions mal ou bien, reprit Sillery, ne change rien à ce principe général. Si nous parlons bien, nous nous sentons différents des autres et souffrons de cette originalité de mauvais aloi . . . d'autre part, messieurs, si nous parlons mal, notre conscience nous avertit que nous devrions parler bien. Dans les deux cas, nous nous trouvons dans un état de "facticité existentielle".[25]

That we may speak bad French or not, replied Sillery, does not change this general principle in any way. If we speak good French we feel different from the others and we suffer from this oddity which hasn't a genuine ring . . . on the other hand, gentlemen, if we speak bad French our conscience tells us that we should be speaking good French. In both cases we find ourselves in a state of "existential artificiality."[25] [*trans.*]

Weston, a young American student who has come to Montreal to do sociological research on the French Canadians, takes part in this discussion. Bessette comes very close to the thesis novel here and chooses the easy way out by exposing the characteristics of the French-speaking group in a round-table discussion. Very fortunately it is in Lebeuf's subsequent behaviour, that is, in a way consistent with the art of the novel, that Bessette delivers his conclusions. Lebeuf, because he is better educated than the men he works with, feels responsible for his own people and is unable to refuse them the co-operation which will lead to the loss of his ambitions as a writer. Must we conclude that life and its day-to-day problems, as delineated by Bessette in the last few pages, will gradually destroy Lebeuf's unrealistic ambition? The novelist is right in leaving us in the dark on this question. The fact that it remains unanswered allows us to think there is hope. For this thought to be confirmed it will be enough that every generation produce its Lebeufs: "The important thing is to raise the intellectual level. The rest will follow."

The analytical spirit, indispensable to the novelist, becomes detrimental when it seems to be the source of the characters and of the plot, which must keep the illusion of being independent of it. Bessette comes to the novel with greater clarity of vision than impetuosity. Fortunately in *Le libraire* (Paris: Julliard, 1960) he found the ideal subject for his inclination to abstraction.

The "problem" is reduced to a demonstration of how impossible it is for a free man to make a pact with guardians of morality in a French-Canadian town. The modest propositions of this long short story have allowed Bessette to dispense with the complications of a plot and concentrate all his attention on the occult powers which he wants to unmask. Because he failed to appreciate the laws of the genre, Jean-Charles Harvey, in the previous generation, had never written anything but mediocre novels. Wishing to denounce the abuse of power to which the French Canadian may fall victim, Harvey had fallen into the role of prosecutor. Conscious of the difficulty, Gérard Bessette preferred an objectivity tinged with irony.

Hervé, the narrator, finds employment at Léon's book store. The unofficial censorship of the clergy soon makes itself felt. As we watch the steady advance of the repressive power represented by *Monsieur le Curé's* direct intervention, a second adventure—this one in the interests of *l'amour*—unfolds to its anything but common-place end. This second theme is in perfect harmony with the first since Hervé braves the censorship of what, in the French-Canadian milieu, is called illegitimate love. It is neither out of passion nor self-interest that this very odd lover eventually shares his bed with Rose, his landlady; rather is it out of unconcern:

Comme je l'ai indiqué, les petits ébats amoureux qui ont suivi la soirée de cinéma ne m'avaient pas déplu. Evidemment, je ne suis plus très jeune. Je n'ai plus l'allant d'autrefois—qui n'a d'ailleurs jamais été bien spectaculaire. Peu importe. J'étais en somme satis- fait. Je tenais la preuve que j'étais encore (si l'on peut dire) viril. Ce n'est pas, je le sais bien, un talent exceptionnel, mais c'est quelque chose. Toutefois, je ne tenais pas à répéter l'expérience. Du moins, pas de longtemps. Aussi fus-je désagréablement surpris, le dimanche suivant—tôt le matin j'étais encore au lit—de voir entrer Rose dans ma chambre. Elle était, comme on dit, en simple appareil: un kimono vert à ramages, transparent, qu'elle quitta aussitôt pour se glisser entre les draps, près de moi. En un sens, c'était gentil. Je ne le nie pas. Je ne suis pas un sauvage.

Ensuite, j'ai dû m'exécuter. Au début, j'ai cru que je ne pourrais pas. La migraine me vrillait les temps et je n'avais pas encore avalé mon sel Safe-All. De plus, j'ai découvert que Rose avait un bourrelet de graisse, une espèce de pneu dans la région de l'épigastre. En tout cas, tel que je suis, je ne devrais pas chicaner sur un bourrelet de graisse. Mais c'était plus fort que moi. Il me fascinait. Pour faire diversion, je me suis mis à parler des films que nous avions vus ensemble. Malgré sa surprise, Rose a répondu d'un ton assez naturel. Elle ne manque pas de tact. Ensuite, de fil en aiguille, j'ai oublié le bourrelet et j'ai pu m'exécuter. Ce fut une heureuse suprise. Je ne suis pas trop rouillé.

Le libraire is full of shortcuts from modern anxieties with the extra spice of Bessette's mischievous impertinence. If the tone is ironical the intention is never far from an implied seriousness. This little masterpiece pleads eloquently for a liberalizing of the spirit of French Canada.

It was tempting the devil to explain, by means of a third novel, another French-Canadian problem. The title alone, *Les pedagogues* (Le Cercle du Livre de France, 1961) seems to make one think just a little of a laboratory label. In seeking to unmask what lies at the base of the education problem, the author has made a sacrificial offering to a subject of current interest without finding in it any artistic compensation. There is every indication that Bessette has tried to make use of clinical lecture notes which were put together after the event. With the exception of Abbé Béchard all the characters speak the same language in this novel, which is as colourless as it is badly written. Without doing violence to his feelings one might observe that Bessette would now be in a position to write a fourth novel, *Les prêtres*.

For so gifted a writer the mistake of *Les pedagogues* could be very salutary. Will Bessette turn to the essay stylized by his caustic intelligence? Or shall we be seeing the erotic and off-beat novel as outlined in *Le libraire?*

THE NEW FRENCH-CANADIAN NOVEL

It was inevitable that the novel as it was employed by Michel Butor, Nathalie Sarraute, Alain Robbe-Grillet and Françoise Sagan should influence the development of the French-Canadian counterpart. After the poets the novelists were next to declare their independence of the past. Will this contempt for traditional chronology and clearly fixed characters enrich the novel? Claire Martin and Jacques Godbout have already given proof that French-Canadian novelists move comfortably within the new novel. Shaking off the obligation of rhyme has allowed a generation of poets to express themselves. It is very possible that the inner monologue, the juxtaposition of planes of consciousness, may be of benefit to novelists.

It would be a mistake to conclude that French-Canadian novelists are being sucked into an imitation of foreign models such as cursed them until the very recent past. Boredom, produced by the industrialized societies of the West, can as readily be observed in French Canada as in France and Italy. When Catharine in *Quand j'aurai payé ton visage* observes, "I suddenly wanted to yawn," Claire Martin, who recalls Moravia at this point, may well never have read him.

The new novel represents something different in Canada from what it does in France. Take the question of the novelist Nathalie Sarraute, or the poet Francis Ponge or the critic Maurice Blanchot, and in each case we are witnessing the creation of a link in the chain which is extending the literary history of France. Nothing of the kind is to be found in French Canada where the novelists are seeking not a new way of recreating reality—a concern which is naturally a part of an ancient and illustrious tradition—but simply a flexible means of expression allowing them finally to show what they are like. In all probability we are about to see a whole crop of novelists hurling themselves madly into the unknown country of the amorphous novel for the same reasons that the disjointed poem, open to all the tropisms, reigns authoritatively today. But freshness, spontaneity, sincerity—qualities one expects to find in a young literature—are not enough to make one forgive awkwardness or, what is infinitely worse, borrowed elegance. It would be better, consequently, if the novelist were to cast off his moorings and try to mould in his own way the shapeless clay of the experimental novel. This is certainly an easy solution but one which, in the circumstances, makes good sense for the French-Canadian novelist.

Influenced by French university criticism, most French-Canadian critics have been persuaded of the prime importance of vocabulary and style. An inheritance from rationalism and aestheticism, this conception of art has hardly been favourable to the full development of French-Canadian writers. What value is to be attached to a novel in which the author seems to be incapable of any idea of structure or expression in a French that is grammatical, if not elegant? This is a pseudo-problem used by too many French-Canadian critics as an argument to be wielded like a bludgeon. Léo-Paul Desrosier's last novels, logically constructed and written according to grammatical rules advocated by the purists in classical colleges, neverthless remain exhortations to virtue, having no connection with life. Among the good novelists of the preceding generation only Félix-Antoine Savard was able to forge a style of his own. Gabrielle Roy, Yves Thériault, André Langevin, Roger Lemelin have sustained an unequal struggle with language. Nevertheless, they have succeeded in enriching French-Canadian literature with new blood, though their uneven breathing becomes audible and makes one realize the effort.

For some time to come, French-Canadian novelists will have to hack their way through. The new novel, adapted to their needs, could very well lead more speedily to that clearing towards which they are headed and where some day they will finally be quite surprised to find that they have accomplished a great deal in a short time.

Jacques Godbout (b. 1933)

L'aquarium (Paris: Editions du Seuil, 1962) gives the best idea of the possibilities of renewal offered to the French-Canadian novelist by experimental techniques. While the vague despair which runs through the works of Diane Giguère, Claude Jasmin and Marcel Godin is being learned by the young writers of Stanley Street who have nothing else to do, Jacques Godbout has been able to reconcile perfectly a lack of narrative coherence with an aimless world none the less endowed with intense life.

By chance the narrator finds himself at the centre of a group of men of different nationalities who are stranded in an African town. The miasma of the rainy season gets the better of their will power which goes to pieces in a world that is absurd, not far from that described by Camus. But because Godbout is French-Canadian this spiritless world offers a variant which is not negligible if viewed in relation to *L'étranger* and *La peste*. If the murder committed by Mersault seems to be explained by a sort of logic of the incongruous, and if Rambert in spite of everything finds a reason for living, the French Canadian, perhaps precisely because he has left the quiet life of his own country, joins a human zone bordering on vegetable life, beyond the bite of nothingness. Existence from that time onward can no longer be qualified as absurd, which would represent too lofty an ideal, because it is still human. The characters float in this aquarium like dead fish whose slow movement is the only activity. The encounters, the deaths, the announcement of a palace revolution are unreal and viscous. "Life is not absurd: it is," Godbout concludes.

The success of this little novel is partly explained by the harmony established between the visceral reality held up by Godbout and its exact transcription. The decay of matter thus conceived is felt rather than explained, while the juxtaposed levels of "events" and frequent interruptions of thought combine to produce in the reader the aquatic conditioning sought by the author.

There is no real obstacle to a direct comprehension of this short tale. By reason of his relative conservativism, then, Godbout is an essentially French-Canadian novelist, effecting the junction between his own vision of the world and a conception borrowed from France.

Claire Faucher (b. 1914)

Quand j'aurai payé ton visage (Le Cercle du Livre de France, 1962) is an indication that Claire Martin[26] has arrived honestly at the novel in which plot as such is largely absent. A first collection of twenty-seven short stories, *Avec ou sans amour* (*ibid.*, 1958) had been her means of establishing the theory that the short story, reduced to three or four pages, drives the writer to try to be witty or to knock the reader senseless. This is a difficult formula which accounts for the partial failure of this first attempt in which, in the best pages, a very shrewd feminine psychology is discernible. *Doux-amer* (*ibid.*, 1960) tells the story of the two-way lover who establishes himself between an editor and his protégée, Gabrielle. The biting tone and an inclination to use the percussive phrase afford an opportunity of seeing the direction in which Claire Martin is going. Embarrassed at having to manufacture a plot, on this problem of the heart, however, Claire Martin will already have put the imprint of her ironical conception of the relations between men and women. In order to express herself directly she has now only to get rid of a cumbersome chronology.

Freed of the irksome necessity for making up incidents, Claire Martin, in *Quand j'aurai payé ton visage,* has found the style suited to her turn of mind. Being no longer obliged to standardize her analyses in the old way, she enters right into the complications of Catharine's life. The latter believes herself to be in love with her husband's brother. Successive soliloquies make the life of the three together come alive, whereas a logical presentation of so many overlapping and mixed feelings would have appeared less convincing. By means of the confusion which gradually takes possession of these hearts, as much as by the boredom that Catharine drags around with her, this excellent novel escapes from the narrow setting of the Province of Quebec to take its place in that of the world of today.

Marie-Claire Blais (b. 1939)

After two novels, *La belle bête* (Quebec: Institut littéraire du Québec, 1959), and *Tête blanche* (*ibid.*, 1960)—in which the most obvious gifts of the writer do not quite make up for the contrived perverseness of the main characters—Marie-Claire Blais has recently contributed to the French-Canadian novel *Le jour est noir* (Les Editions du Jour, 1962), the most poetic work of the new school.

The world of Marie-Claire Blais is made up of people who are ill-loved. What child reproaches her parents for being too much concerned about her happiness? In these first two attempts at explanation which depict monstrous parents, one feels the exaggeration born of a judgment still not too sure of itself. Having reached maturity, Marie-Claire Blais, instead of attacking her parents, a family imposed by a cruel fate, turns more profitably to herself.

In a drifting world Yance looks for authenticity. She says of Josué, her childhood friend, her lover, her husband, "I have had a companion in discoveries, father of my first woman's anguish, and now, a lover at last and in this love, a son." In the discovery of her maternal solicitude, Yance serves her apprenticeship to others. Instead of condemning, as she does in her two preceding tales, Marie-Claire Blais turns her attention to the mystery of living. "I do not see myself as important enough to weigh the thought of my life's companion."

Around the lives of Josué and Yance spring other destinies, those of Roxane and Jessy, of Marie-Christine and Raphael, which mean the experience all over again on another key of lives interlaced but cruelly separate. Conversations are jumbled according to the methods to which every self-respecting anti-novelist is expected to conform. Marie-Claire Blais makes moderate use of this fashionable counterpoint. Her language, precise and direct, avoids commonplaces. In spite of the vague outlines demanded by the genre, *Le jour est noir* lives particularly because of the classic restraint of its execution.

DIANE GIGUERE: *Le temps des jeux* (Le Cercle du Livre de France, 1961), belongs to all of those works published since the Second World War which make a hero of boredom. On this score, Céline, the "ill-loved" daughter of Jeanne, seems to owe too much to foreign models to be convincing. When she has incited her mother's lover to murder and her mother has lost her mind, Céline, who disappears "around the corner," takes on very much the appearance of a stereotype.

CLAUDE JASMIN: The technique of *La corde au cou* (Paris: Robert Laffont, 1961) is superior to the content. The narrator, who suffers from his French-Canadian upbringing, drowns his friend Suzanne. By means of tail-ends of conscience that are juxtaposed, the main character reviews his past and his present. Ruled by the exigencies of the new novel, Claude Jasmin has been particularly successful in demonstrating its conventionality.

MARCEL GODIN: The only interest of the clever short stories that make up *La cruauté des faibles* (Les Editions du Jour, 1961) lies in the author's intention. The detachment of Camus' *étranger* before the death of his mother remains a startling image of modern man. But the reactions described in *Ces Trois Jours-là*, which are quite wanton, have no other object than to provoke a feeling of surprise in the reader. Far from shocking, however, these pages are just one more proof that all subjects are good subjects provided that art endues them with life. Could it be that the *twisters* for whom the novel appears intended, have a harder crust than their predecessors?

JEAN-LOUIS GAGNON: It is natural that French-Canadian writers should extend their horizons to include the two continents of the new world whose rhythm they live to some extent in spite of themselves. *La fin des haricots* (Editions du Jour, 1961), a rollicking tale of imaginary and real adventures which the author makes us experience in Brazil and New York, reveals an attractive and unaccustomed cosmopolitanism and, at the same time, an indisputable talent. The success becomes more evident on reading *La mort d'un nègre* which, however, does not escape the false sentimentality which too often surrounds the racial problem in the United States.

POETRY

Very largely Romantic in inspiration, French-Canadian literature is predominantly a literature of poets. Today the novelists are close on their heels yet are only beginning to express themselves in a universal language, while the best poets are modern without effort.

Just as Nelligan gave us the first great French-Canadian poetry by drawing his inspiration from European Symbolism, Saint-Denys-Garneau, too, by his nascent genius, effected the junction of the French-Canadian soul with contemporary anguish. For this reason it is legitimate to place the poetry of today under the sign of a poet already dead, since it is *Regards et jeux dans l'espace* which prepared the way for the fruitful innovations of the present day.

For the past fifteen years the most dynamic among the practitioners of the new school of poetry have taken on a personality. Having buried the centuries-old laws of versification these poets have become intoxicated by their own discovery. The resulting joy has liberated creative forces, previously dammed up by the rigidity of Classicism or imitation. At the same time the poets are rethinking

196. *History of French-Canadian Literature*

the French language, preferring to submit it to their pressing needs than merely to do honourable service to it. Several of them betray their lack of craftsmanship by verbal audacities in no way justifiable. Others, because they can carry out what they want to do only in disjointed words, are successful in this by sheer strength of what is in them. When Maurice Beaulieu, exploding with energy, cries out to us, *J'effluve la doucer arbreuse du matin,* the irradiation is immediate.

In 1954 the *Editions de l'Hexagone* was founded. Under the dynamic impetus given by Gaston Miron and his friends this establishment became the inner sanctum of the new poetry. In this shrine poets met for the first time and, conscious of their number and especially of the great adventure they were living in common, they wanted to explain and show their different reactions to it. The outcome was the collective *prise de conscience* that is *La poésie et nous* (Hexagone, 1958).[27]

The real French-Canadian poetry is that of the innovators, those who dare: Paul-Marie Lapointe, Jean-Guy Pilon, Réginald Boisvert, Claude Fournier, Fernand Ouellette are in the front rank, while on a high level are Roland Giguère, Gaston Miron and Theodore Koenig.

Then come the avant-garde of the army of enthusiasts. Having set out on the intoxicating path of the automatic, magic-spell kind of poetry—going off in all directions at once, very often wasting their energy on mad experiments—they furnish the best idea of the vitality of French-Canadian poetry. Sudden flashes of beauty are not rare in Claude Haeffely and Claude Gauvreau, while Alain Horic and Roch Carrier have their moments of inspiration before foundering in *prose-prose.* Among the latest arrivals, Gatien Lapointe and Guy Robert, both starting off with childhood memories, might possibly be brilliantly able to come to terms with the present.

Finally, because art admits of all definitions, one of the greatest French-Canadian poets, Alain Grandbois, by the fusion of discipline and liberty accomplishes a personal synthesis. To the same family belong Rina Lasnier and Anne Hébert.

Saint-Denys-Garneau (1912-1943)

The poetic work of Saint-Denys-Garneau was accomplished between 1935 and 1938: *Regards et jeux dans l'espace* and *Solitudes,* posthumous poems. A *Journal,* with entries from 1935 to 1939, permits us to place Saint-Denys-Garneau's poetry in relation to his intimate thoughts and fills out our picture of him.[28]

As it has often happened in literary history, Saint-Denys-Garneau, soon after making the decision to put his thoughts down in writing, in his *Regards et jeux dans l'espace*, became aware that this activity was a check on his spiritual progress as well as on his weaknesses. Because he was an exceptional soul his testimony is incontestably original. In the history of French-Canadian poetry his work stands quite apart, both in material and in form.

First of all the poet sets out to establish a propitious mood:

> *O mes yeux ce matin grands comme des rivières*
> *O l'onde de mes yeux prêts à tout refléter*
> *Et cette fraîcheur sous mes paupières*
> *Extraordinaire*
> *Tout alentour des images que je vois.*[29]

These few polymorphous lines already express a vision that is very personal. Nelligan had made us feel the breath of something new at the end of the nineteenth century by his imagery, cast, it is true, in a half-Parnassian, half-Symbolist mould. Saint-Denys-Garneau, somewhat in the manner of Péguy, puts an imprint, in lines long or short according to his inspiration, on a poetry which is the experience of the moment.

But soon he is haunted by thought of the Beyond which brings a special note to his thinking. We have here "Two landscapes." The composition of the first is two hills with a stream in the valley flowing between them, which is Life. In this stream a fish is struggling—Man—unable to see more than a fly.

The second landscape, in a somewhat surrealistic transposition, shows us the anguish of the fish (now dead) pleading for water to drink. This dead thing does its utmost to quench its thirst at different springs where "maid-servants" give it to drink.

> *Celle-là cueille par l'argent des prés lunaires*
> *Les corolles que ferma la fraîcheur du soir*
> *Elle en fait un bouquet bien gonflé*
> *Une tendre lourdeur fraîche à la bouche*
> *Et s'empresse au maître de l'offrir.*[30]

That one over there in the silver of moonlit meadows plucks the corollas that were closed by the cool of the evening; she makes of them a round bouquet, a delicate sultriness, cool to the mouth, and offers it eagerly to the master.[30] [*trans.*]

But in vain because, forever unsatisfied, the dead thing will see itself when morning comes *percé de rayons comme une brume* and will then really die.

From the general scene Saint-Denys-Garneau comes to his own case. Life's melancholy becomes an existential weariness, a "grief" in a "closed house." Wasted with fever, he seems to have an obscure feeling, as Nelligan had had, that destruction is close. Death is already gnawing at him:

> *Je suis une cage d'oiseau*
> *Une cage d'os*
> *Avec un oiseau*
>
> *L'oiseau dans sa cage d'os*
> *C'est la mort qui fait son nid.*[31]

I am a bird cage, a cage of bones with a bird in it; the bird in its cage of bones is Death making its nest.[31] [*trans.*]

He will not know the death that purifies without travelling a very difficult upward path, strewn with setbacks. With Death lying in wait, he will succumb. This temporary victory of natural instinct brings to the soul of Saint-Denys-Garneau a desperate sadness. Because he is a poet he will write *Après les plus vieux vertiges,*[32] certainly one of the most beautiful poems in French-Canadian literature. Out of this deep disgust Saint-Denys-Garneau, just a short time before his death, will reach the light which takes shape in two poems unequalled by his predecessors.[33]

Les regards et jeux dans l'espace and *Solitudes* raise French-Canadian literature to a pinnacle. There had to be more than a century of poetic endeavour before the birth of a work which is the expression in artistic wrapping of the drama of a true spiritual experience. It is significant that it is at a time when the French-Canadian writer is expressing himself in complete freedom that his poetic message should correspond to an act of submission, not of revolt.

How is Saint-Denys-Garneau's place to be clearly defined in relation to the contemporary poetic movement? We ask the question not so much because it seems likely to throw new light on Saint-Denys-Garneau but rather because French-Canadian criticism is faced with this inquiry.

There is no innovation, strictly speaking, in Saint-Denys-Garneau's poetry. The poet does not seem to have exerted himself to any extent to compose regular lines, like a Mallarmé, before creating his own means of expression. Between some stanzas in which the versification is traditional and others which are only prose, Saint-Denys-Garneau succeeds most often in creating poetry entirely his own and indisputably musical, which could never be reduced to rules of precise versification. It is on this score that he is completely modern. His originality began at the point where he was able successfully to fuse supple expression, which softens his verbal imperfections, with an exceptional sensitivity, which might be called anachronistic. Setting this poetry up against that of twentieth-century Europe, one runs the risk of falsifying the comparison from the beginning. Is it not more profitable simply to admit that here we are confronted with a vital personality, attesting to the strength of a young literature?

Alain Grandbois (b. 1900)

In *Les îles de la nuit* (1944) Alain Grandbois attained the plastic perfection rarely realized in Saint-Denys-Garneau. In its artistic unity this collection is one of the most impressive in French-Canadian poetry.

At first sight the verse of Grandbois may appear strange. Modern, rich and harmonious, when analyzed it is revealed to be strongly articulated.

> *Avec ta robe sur le rocher*
> *comme une aile blanche*
> *Des gouttes au creux de ta main*
> *comme une blessure fraîche*
> *Et toi riant la tête renversée*
> *comme un enfant seul.*[34]

Along with the moderns Grandbois rejects the necessity of rhyme although he is not against assonance, interior rhyme, and, occasionally, rich rhyme. But at no time does he break with the essential of eight centuries of French poetry — the syllabic line. Grandbois keeps this respect for number, whatever the arithmetical combinations. So it is natural enough that he should at times indulge in a more traditional poetry:

> *Le rêve s'empare de son doux visage de morte*
> *Un miraculeux brouillard l'élève et la transporte*
> *Au-delà des régions dévorées par le temps*
> *Cet invisible et tendre feu plus vivant que le sang*
> *Elle le nourrit de sa paix la plus profonde*
> *Ses doigts ont écarté l'épouvante du monde*
> *Et baignée de songes ainsi que l'Archange sacré*
> *Elle sourit enfin d'un sourire délivré*
>
> *Ah si le grand rivage absorbe ses petites mains charnelles*
> *Ah si le flux de la mer balaie ses larmes mortelles*
> *Ah si l'éclair aveugle jusqu'au sable de la nuit*
> *Ses blessures nous échappent comme un cristal attendri*
>
> *Car elle est le coeur et la vie et la porte*
> *Du secret retrouvée dans son refuge de morte.*[35]

The theme of death is the one Grandbois has treated most successfully. His second collection, *Rivages de l'homme* (1948), bears the inscription of this thought from Tolstoy: "If man has learned to think, it is of little importance what he thinks about; always at the back of his mind there is the thought of his own death." More polished than *Iles de la nuit, Rivages,* without adding anything to the mainstream of Grandboisian thought, is also more tormented. When Grandbois takes to witness the *lents martyrisés de cette époque,* he produces this piece of shorthand:

LE TRIBUNAL

Le tribunal de nos bras
Tout était plein de fleurs
Tout étincelait comme un feu de joie
Elle venait comme si le temps
Ne chassait pas ses pieds nus
Elle venait avec le sourire
Des hautes notes de l'octave
Pourtant ce vol d'oiseaux
Ce péché blanc
Cet éclair lisse
Au fond droit de l'horizon

Le sable instantané
Le parfait trésor
Le rappel d'hier
Et pour cet abandon
La suprême illusion
Des crépuscules perdus
Car elle savait sourire
Ou peut-être le savait-elle
Ses doux doigts des muguets
Houles moirées de la mer
Qui nous rouleront plus tard
Au gel des étoiles décédés[36]

The poet's weariness shows in *L'étoile pourpre.* With *Noces*[37] which will figure in all the anthologies of the future and is proof that Grandbois is a great universal poet, there is *Le sourire,* a verbose adaptation of the same poem published in *Rivages de l'homme.* And affectation makes its appearance unexpectedly in *Le sortilège.*

The striking success of Alain Grandbois comes from a subtle mixture of old and new poetic methods. Because the quality of his inspiration is nearly always kept at a high level, some see him as the greatest French-Canadian poet of this century.

Does his poetry not present a trap to all those who, very good at detecting sentimental feelings in the traditional poets, are defenceless when confronted with the same sentiments in different dress? While we do not deny that Grandbois belongs in the first rank of French-Canadian poets, he seems to us less likely to withstand the verdict of time than Saint-Denys-Garneau. The lyricism of Saint-Denys-Garneau is rough in comparison with the marble perfection of Grandbois, but because of this very quality is more personal and, particularly, closer to the French-Canadian sensibility.

Rina Lasnier (b. 1915)

Among the women poets, Rina Lasnier is the one whose work is furthest removed from the commonplaces to which men are accustomed to resort when explaining the other sex. As much as the extraordinary evidence of intuition, incisive rhythm and male vigour characterize her poetry.

After her first collection, *Images et proses* (Saint-Jean: Editions du Richelieu, 1941), Rina Lasnier, attracted by religious subjects, exercised her talents on the thankless and artificial subject of *Madones canadiennes* (Montreal: Beauchemin, 1944). In the same vein, but infinitely more successful, is *Le chant de la montée* (Montreal: Beauchemin, 1947), published in a volume which does credit to French-Canadian publishing. Taking her theme from the Book of Genesis which tells the love story of Jacob and Rachel, Rina Lasnier was able to create a poem whose most striking quality is its aesthetic unity. The prose-poetry alternates with poetry that is more traditional in the poems ending each of the fifteen cantos.

Escales was published in 1950 (Trois Rivières: Le Bien Public, 1950). By her verbal sleight-of-hand and by the sharpness and suggestiveness of her imagery, Rina Lasnier puts herself in the front rank of those French-Canadian poets who seek their originality within the bounds of discipline and good taste rather than by temerity.

In *Présence de l'absence* (Montreal: Editions de l'Hexagone, 1956), a poem like *Les opales* in sonnet form, furnishes proof that the old forms, so much decried by young poets, can be brought back to life. Here is an old Mexican superstition "sonnetized"—a superstition which made the abode of priests and wizards out of precious stones:

> *Brumes de larmes, larmes de lune, lait fol,*
> *Le jeune sang aveugle défie ton méfaire*
> *Et inscrit son sort entre tes feux vénifères,*
> *Opale blanche au doigt de la malemort.*
> *Alvéoles poreuses assaillies de couleurs,*
> *Reflets irrités de lumière trop forte,*
> *Pierre embellie du vide comme une note,*
> *Opale meillée, touche du guérisseur.*

> *Incendie de sang aux mains friables des prêtres,*
> *Feu vivipare des dieux durs de la légende,*
> *Veines et voeux noués en cabochons de braises,*
> *Corps sacrificiel, opale flamboyante:*
> *Opales, bris de verre épelant la lumière,*
> *Douleurs denses sublimant l'amour sous la cendre.*

Taking a moment for reflection, Rina Lasnier was overcome by intimations of the world that is felt but invisible and which she first recorded in *Miroirs* (Les Editions de l'Atelier, 1960), prose pieces preparatory to *Mémoire sans jours* (*ibid.*, 1960).

Neither Alain Grandbois nor Anne Hébert nor, among the younger ones, Paul-Marie Lapointe, could ever compare with Rina Lasnier in the expression of simultaneous enjoyments of the senses. The wind from the open sea, the vast cosmic space which Alain Grandbois brought into poetry, are to be found again in *La Malemer*; the cleansing solitude of Anne Hébert holds sway in the composition of *Silves,* and Paul-Marie Lapointe's precise and suggestive vocabulary makes possible the recreation of voodoo-like rhythms in *Poèmes haïtiens.* Religious subjects, treated with restraint, add still another dimension to a work spreading out in different directions at once.

Like a virtuoso Rina Lasnier makes music in all keys. Is the sound of her voice weakened because of its dispersal? A thorough knowledge of the resources of verse has not always been enough to keep her from being trapped by mysticism or even by banality. Her best inspirations have come to her from a combination of her own sensitivity and the original manifestations of North-American cultures. And the splendour of the metaphors gives back to us the very essence of her experience:

LE TAMBOUR NOIR

Sur la peau tendue du silence, ountogni,
pulsion solitaire sans paix ni appel,
progression placide du seul pas du son,
pas des arbres piétinant la forêt,
socle du son insulaire au centre de la solennité,
passe rocailleuse dans la liquidité d'une fête.

Secret serein de la durée par le bris sonore du temps,
insistance horizontale de la corde raide tendue aux dieux,
sommation sans surcharge de signes, d'exil ou de transes;
mailles du filet neuf aux genoux écartés du tambourineur,
et sous ses paumes, étoffe vaste de l'ombre indivise;
césures blanches avant le coloris impur du chant,
os dur du son sans oscillations de plumages;
voix égale des morts sans écho sépulcral,
sonorité du sang lié au sang, levée processionnelle de la négritude.[38]

Anne Hébert (b. 1916)

Les songes en équilibre (Montreal: Les Editions de l'Arbre, 1942)
is the first statement of an original temperament in search of a theory
of poetry. Apparent technical reminders in the form of slightly
modified echoes recall Saint-Denys-Garneau and, through him,
Péguy, source of the method of incantation. Anne Hébert's[39] sensibility, given an over-sharp edge by a very early experience of suffering, already leads her to highly suggestive imagery.

MA DOULEUR

L'on ne sait pas,
L'on ne saura pas,
Au juste quand
Elle est venue.

Gratuite
Comme la Grâce
Et la nuit,
Ma douleur
Est venue.

Depuis longtemps,
Sans doute,
Elle avait creusé là
Sa place en nous.

Présence invisible,
Présence qui pèse
Sans encore se nommer
Puis quel est ce mal,
Cette souffrance centrée
Qui se découvre
Un jour tout établie?
Sans connivence,
Libre et nue,
Sans conscience,
Elle travaille en nous.

Elle n'a pas de figure
Monstrueuse,
Ni griffes,
Ni cornes;
Elle est plate,
Telle une bête à bois
Dans le bois,
Entre les chairs,
Confondue au bois,
Mêlée aux chairs.

C'est le signe de sa perte
Et de son désintéressement,
Ce grugement aveugle
Dans le bois;
Plus elle avance,
Moins elle est sûre
D'en jamais sortir.

Quand je dors, j'entends
Ma douleur qui veille.
Ma douleur ne dort pas,
Elle n'entend pas;
Elle veille.

Lorsqu'elle sera devenue
Si grande,
Plus grande que moi,
Que je ne serai plus moi,
Qu'elle ne sera plus elle,
Lorsqu'il ne sera plus nécessaire
De lui prendre la main
Pour avancer,
Laquelle des deux
Sera reconnue
Au bout des chemins?
Laquelle des deux
Pourra plus justement dire:
"Me voici, Seigneur"?

An interval of some ten years, during which Anne Hébert published poetic prose sketches, *Le torrent* (Montreal: Beauchemin,
1950), separates *Les songes en équilibre* from *Tombeau des rois*
(Quebec: Institut littéraire, 1953). A careful examination of the
second collection reveals the immense refining process that had
been at work. The imprecision that is characteristic of the least
successful poems of 1942 disappears to give way to lines that would
be bare if it were not for the flashing brilliance of a swift synthesis
or symbol.

UNE PETITE MORTE

Une petite morte s'est couchée en travers de la porte.

Nous l'avons trouvée au matin, abattue sur notre seuil
Comme un arbre de fougère plein de gel.

Nous n'osons plus sortir depuis qu'elle est là
C'est une enfant blanche dans ses jupes mousseuses
D'où rayonne une étrange nuit laiteuse.

Nous nous efforçons de vivre à l'intérieur
Sans faire de bruit
Balayer la chambre

Et ranger l'ennui
Laisser les gestes se balancer tout seuls
Au bout d'un fil invisible
A même nos veines ouvertes.

Nous menons une vie si minuscule et tranquille
Que pas un de nos mouvements lents
Ne dépasse l'envers de ce miroir limpide
Où cette soeur que nous avons
Se baigne bleue sous la lune
Tandis que croît son odeur capiteuse.

The foreshortening is supported by discreet rhyme, often placed
at the beginning and at the end of the poem. Since the image
usually takes up scarcely more than thirty lines, the chord struck
at the beginning is heard to vibrate through to the end where it is
resolved. In short Anne Hébert has not broken with the past any
more than has Alain Grandbois. The proof is that hope is not
excluded from her world:

Quel reflet d'aube s'égare ici?
D'où vient donc que cet oiseau frémit
Et tourne vers le matin
Ses prunelles crevées?

These lines herald the decisive choice apparent in *Poèmes* (Paris:
Editions du Seuil, 1960). Not one among the great French-Canadian

poets shows us two faces so different from one collection to another. Not only does poetry become a *solitude rompue* but the language of the poetry itself, still too bare in *Le tombeau des rois*, has been broadened to include the complicated associations of the senses and the affirmation of a possible happiness. Who could have predicted that Anne Hébert would try her hand at *Printemps sur la ville?* Strength is everywhere evident in this *Mystère de la parole*. Starting as she did with dreams centred on deep distress, it is now a good omen that Anne Hébert is creating happy intervals for herself. Obviously *Mystère de la parole* is like an interlude. The great challenge would seem to lie ahead.

ROBERT CHOQUETTE (b. 1905): Well before the Second World War Robert Choquette had acquired the reputation of being one of the two or three best poets of his generation. The publication in 1953 of *Suite marine*—which marked the appearance, when poetry was at its most exciting, of an imposing volume of verse composed partly in classical Alexandrines—necessitates a review of his career.

Suite marine, completed over a long period, is the most ambitious work in the history of French-Canadian poetry. Has Choquette realized the wish expressed by Louis Dantin after reading *Metropolitan Museum?* "I almost wish we could have from him some *chanson de geste*, some rhapsody in twelve cantos in which the instinct that draws him to the epic would have full sway . . . and which would make for its author a lofty and lasting reputation."[40]

Suite marine is the grandiose amplification of a leitmotif in Choquette's thought. That tremendous desire felt by the poet at twenty years of age to attain the absolute, which desire he had expressed in *A travers les vents*, is the substratum of these same six thousand lines, Alexandrines for the most part. Although Choquette has given a symbolic mantle to his thought it is possible, taking his evolution into account, to decipher the meaning of the poem.

In the prologue the poet and his companion, Iseut, from the top of a rock look out on the sea. As the different scenes unfold—*La maison sur la mer, La plage, Le village* and *La figure de proue*—the symbolism linked to certain key words becomes clear. The sea in its ceaseless motion is all of nature from which the writer draws his inspiration. Iseut is the incarnation of beauty, that beauty which confers on art a kind of immortality. Iseut, however, is an ideal never attained, to which the poet can at the very most swear to remain faithful.

A sense of anxiety is perceptible in the poem, anxiety to capture if only for one instant *plus rapide cent fois qu'un reflet de la bague d'Iseut,* the inexpressible impression of beauty.

> *Quelques rares humains, emmurés dans la cloche*
> *Ont visité la mer vers le grands fonds, assez*
> *Pour qu'au retour là-haut, par l'extase oppressés,*
> *Ils ébauchent des mots . . . Mais quel mot nous rapproche*
> *Du spectacle inouï qui vibra dans leurs yeux?*
> *Balbutiants de joie, ils cherchent le mot rare,*
> *Etincelant et sombre, entre tous merveilleux,*
> *Qui serait à la fois plus dur que le carrare*
> *Et fluide, flexible, élastique, soyeux,*
> *Mais, des mots fabriqués par les fils de la terre,*
> *Le verbe le plus vif est un reflet pâlot*
> *S'il faut représenter le royaume d l'eau.*[41]

But once glimpsed, this beauty *plus belle qu'elle-même* counsels the poet to abandon his pursuit. Stunned for the moment the poet collects himself and in a gesture of defiance proclaims what he feels himself capable of:

> *Commander à mes bras les hauts travaux d'Hercule;*
> *Poursuivre, dans la mer où mon ombre bascule,*
> *La monstrueuse main qui s'attache aux récifs,*
> *Et hisse vers le ciel des serpents convulsifs;*
>
> *Dans l'antre inviolé d'où le soleil recule,*
> *Affronter le dragon dont la langue articule*
> *Un jet de flamme et d'or et, les yeux excessifs,*
> *Endormir dans ses yeux ses transports agressifs;*
>
> *Confondre par un mot le Sphinx, brûlante épreuve;*
> *Capter le vent, forger l'éclair, dompter le fleuve:*
> *Tout cela, s'il le faut, pour prouver mes amours!*[42]

The poem ends on a less optimistic note. Since it is impossible to create the works of which Iseut makes one dream, let the poet at least remain forever faithful to her for she has been his inspiration.

In the history of French-Canadian literature there is perhaps no poetic creation to which it is more difficult to do justice. Young French-Canadian criticism gave a very bad reception to *Suite marine,* finding something sterile and old-fashioned in it. This *auto-da-fé,* which Robert Choquette's reputation will survive, raises a fundamental question: can an artist lift himself to the level of great art by borrowing everything from those who went before him? Robert Choquette practises the Alexandrine with such conservative deference that he goes back to the seventeenth century more readily than to the nineteenth. How can one keep from being uneasy, too, with a vocabulary whose key words (*azur, or, ciel bleu,* etc.) are among the most hackneyed in French poetry of the last century? The very philosophical structure of this poem has a slightly musty smell about it. In a word this *Suite marine,* so impressive in scope and intent, has been executed in circumstances which, at best, could only lead to partial failure. A poet with less skill would have capsized completely in such a venture.

Robert Choquette will remain the creator of the more modest but less flawed *Metropolitan Museum* which belongs to an era that has gone by in French-Canadian letters.

ROSAIRE DION-LEVESQUE (b. 1900): His inspiration like his talent puts him half-way between Pamphile Lemay and Nelligan. More complicated than Lemay, less of an artist than Nelligan, the writer of sonnets in *Oasis* does not differ essentially from the French-Canadian Romanticists of the nineteenth century. That the poet could put himself on such an antiquated poetic plane is doubtless explained by the situation of Nashua, the little New Hampshire town where *Oasis* was written. In the United States what possible defence is there against the pervasive influence of the American language? The astonishing thing is that Rosaire Dion-Lévesque, from his first poetry, has never stopped growing in stature, as witness this modest little poem:

L'ENTERREMENT DU PETIT OISEAU

Il est mort durant la nuit,
Dans sa boîte matelassée,
L'oiseau hier accueilli
Avec l'aile brisée.

Une cassette à bijoux pour cercueil,
Et puis, l'âme en deuil,
Une fosse creusée
Dans le hallier;
Deux bâtons en croix
Et quelques fleurs des champs.

Alors il dit, fixant la tombe:
"Les oiseaux vont-ils en paradis?"
Et se ravisant: "Mais oui,
Le Saint-Esprit
Y est, la Belle Colombe!"

Dès le lendemain matin
Il court voir si le serin
Est vraiment parti pour le ciel!
Et voyant la tombe non dérangée,
Il a fallu expliquer
A son âme neuve et perplexe
Le mystère infiniment complexe
De la chair et de l'esprit!

Works: *En égrenant le chapelet des jours* (Montreal: Editions du Mercure, 1928); *Les Oasis* (Rome: Editions Desclée & Cie, 1930); *Petite suite marine* (Paris: La Caravelle, 1931); *Walt Whitman,* translation of *Leaves of Grass* (Montreal: Les Elzevirs, 1933); *Vita* (Montreal: Bernard Valiquette, 1939); *Solitudes* (Montreal: Chantecler, 1949); *Jouets* (*ibid.,* 1952).

RODOLPHE DUBE (b. 1905): Like Rosaire Dion-Lévesque, Rodolphe Dubé was first of all a nineteenth-century Romantic poet. Changing his mind after the publication of *Voix de mon âme* (1934), Dubé fell under the influence of Claudel. The religious poems *Axe et parallaxes* (1941) furnished proof that the *verset* is not to be imitated. These attempts resulted in the more regular poetry of *Mes naufrages* and finally in the very classical *Jeux de mer et de soleil* (1951). Thus the circle of Dubé's poetic experience is closed. Though having returned to the Alexandrines of his beginnings, the poet, in *L'âpre solitude,* was no longer the man who sang of the Laurentians and of his favourite town, Trois-Rivières. Notwithstanding his numerous appeals for death to come, the desire to live was far from extinct in him, if one is to judge by the erotic visions which are so plentiful:

> *Homme pétri de boue, ô monstre déplorable,*
> *Vampire incestueux, créateur de Satan,*
> *Masturbe ta chair noire, et jaillis, déplorable!*

Or again:

> *A jamais enlacés dans leur rêve de joie,*
> *Les amants ont perdu leur âme au bord du ciel;*
> *Nul geste n'est trop vif lorsque l'amour l'octroie:*
> *L'étreinte a mis en fuite, un moment, le réel.*
> *L'absolu est conquis, la terre est mon empire.*
> *J'ai découvert un monde en l'absence du moi.*
> *Je me plonge, infini par mon vaste délire,*
> *Dans l'éternelle extase où l'homme se conçoit.*

A generation before, Louis Dantin, also a cleric, had thought he should publish such verse in a little booklet for his friends alone. *Jeux,* of course, was published in Paris.

Works: *Les voix de mon âme* (Montreal: Lévesque, 1934); *Axe et parallaxes* (Montreal: Editions Variétés, 1941). *Strophes et Catastrophes* (Montreal: l'Arbre, 1943). *Cosmos* (Montreal: S. Brousseau, 1945); *Quatorze* (Paris: Ed. René Debresse, 1948); *Mes naufrages* (Paris: Editions de l'Ermite, 1951); *Jeux de mer et de soleil* (*ibid.,* 1951); etc.

CLEMENT MARCHAND (b. 1912) has expressed his longing for the open-air life and his discontent as a city-dweller in *Les soirs rouges* (Trois-Rivières: Editions du Bien Public, 1947).

Paul-Marie Lapointe (b. 1929)

The year 1960, which saw the publication of *Arbres* by Editions de l'Hexagone, already stands like a milestone in the history of French-Canadian poetry. Paul-Marie Lapointe becomes the first and so the only great nature poet that French Canada has ever produced. What canker has clung to the tongue of thousands of poets deep in this land of rivers and forests to have struck them all with verbal impotence? Gill and Desrochers at the most have brought a few flashing passages into their wonder-struck transcriptions. Savard has been the only prose writer really to open the tremendous dialogue. To the critic who had reproached Bibaud for not making him *see* Canada, Paul-Marie Lapointe replies one hundred and thirty years later:

j'écris arbre
arbre pour l'arbre.

bouleau merisier jaune et ondé bouleau flexible acajou sucré
bouleau mérisier odorant rouge bouleau rameau de
couleuvre feuille-engrenage vidé bouleau cambrioleur
à feuilles de peuplier passe les bras dans les cages
du temps captant l'oiseau captant le vent bouleau à
l'écorce fendant l'eau des fleuves bouleau fontinal
fontaine d'hiver jet figé bouleau des parquets cheminée
du soir albatros dormeur.

aubier entre chien et loup
aubier de l'aube aux fanaux

Each variety is transformed into fireworks with unexpected sparks. An unequaled wealth of imagination, served by rich and accurate vocabulary, creates a splendid isolation for *Arbres,* the only poem to serve as preface to the discoveries of future explorers of these untouched regions.

Very young, Paul-Marie Lapointe had shown signs of a rare virtuosity in *Le vierge incendié* (Mithra-Mythe, 1948). It is with cracklings and phosphorescences and implications of eagerness that Lapointe tackles poetry without knowing, in this juvenile collection, whether he will reach his destination or not. This is of no importance. The main thing is to react to that overwhelming flood of energy.

In the preceding generation, in *A travers les vents,* Robert Choquette in his inexperience had sought to explain logically the causes of that conflagration within him. In words that were too timid he had let only his intentions show through. Lapointe was right to give himself over without reservation to pure sensation in *Le vierge incendié.* Having set no limit to his lunatic course, Lapointe in this way learned to swim in an open sea of lava. Carried along in a turmoil of uncontrolled forces, he whirls around with no purpose beyond that of just following a movement. In the years to come Lapointe will keep the essential in this experience which makes the incantations of *Arbres* rise up from the powerful ground swell within him. Meanwhile more knowledge, a necessary intellectualizing of the divinatory *processus* will come to clarify for the reader what otherwise might remain a boiling magma. Balance, so rare between instinct and reason, has given birth to *Choix de poèmes. Arbres* is promise and despair for future poets.

Jean-Guy Pilon (b. 1930)

Jean-Guy Pilon[43] dares to base some hopes on man and writes an opulent poetry, modern in its refusals and, at the same time, traditional in its acceptance of an intrinsic music.

Death, a subject admirably treated by Saint-Denys-Garneau and Alain Grandbois, finds in him a new interpreter. For Saint-Denys-Garneau death is a haven that he dreads but hopes to reach, because in it alone is there calm after storm. Alain Grandbois, less involved in the religious mystery, has conferred on the theme a sonorous plasticity which does not exclude a macabre kind of pleasure or a touch of pathos. Jean-Guy Pilon, brought by the example of René Char, who wrote the preface to *Cloîtres de l'été,* to the point of casting off every vestige of sentimentality or of rhetoric, at the first attempt shows himself a master:

COMMANDE

Commande à l'attente
Tu verras la vague renaissante
Des amours mêlées à la mort
Invention ce n'est que répétition effroyable
Notre geste était expiré avant son prolongement
Ce baisser sur les lèvres
Contient le consentement d'être
Et la soumission au départ inévitable
Mystère
Je le dis je le crois
Je voudrais que tu ne saches pas le lire
Et que tes yeux ne devinent jamais
La moitié de ton coeur reprise par l'ombre
Ni la suave nostalgie de la terre foulée

Notre vie à retenir le poids de la mort à dépasser

Not everything in *Les cloîtres de l'été* is of this quality. There are already fewer rough spots in *L'homme et le jour*. But whether it is a question of prose-poetry or simply of poetry bearing the seal of rare and discreet rhyme, the diversity of tone, the subtle rhythms and the new underlying hope make it one of the pinnacles of French-Canadian contemporary poetry.

Having reached the age of thirty, Jean-Guy Pilon affirms in *La mouette et le large* first acceptance, then lucid, passionate and sometimes sorrowful possession of country and of self. With no technical innovations this collection represents a halt on the threshold of maturity. The poet here seems not so much in search of something as simply to be establishing where he stands as a man in order to have a better knowledge of the road that he will be travelling. From this self-examination come some very fine pages, strong above all in the choices animating them. For Pilon Canada is a mistress never tamed who allows her lovers some hope in her pursuit as this can lead to ultimate revelations. Meanwhile his wife and children help him to grow by giving him in happiness the opportunity for discoveries which will enrich and expand the prophetic poems of today, making them the new creations of tomorrow.

PIEDS ET POINGS LIES

Terre de mes premiers gestes
De mes désirs inavoués
Devenus maintenant saines réalités
Je te salue du toit de ma liberté
Belle idole et santé
Maîtresse
Tour à tour complaisante et rebelle
Lumineuse et fulgurante
Ta durée est la mienne
Malgré tes visages changeants
Je sais te reconnaître
A travers les pluies les neiges et les brouillards
O mon enfance gâchée

. . .

Terre des naissances prochaines
Et des douces découvertes
J'oublie les tombeaux de glace
J'accueillerai ici
Les orages et les arcs-en-ciel

Fernand Ouellette (b. 1930)

In a thin booklet, *Ces anges de sang* (Editions de l'Hexagone, 1955), Fernand Ouellette presents a summary of a few of the most promising aspects of current poetry. The verse, broken into a thousand flashes, calls for a reconstruction which will at the same time retain its inherent qualities. Without denying the past, Ouellette is creating an ambivalent poetry, made up of known methods and new syntheses.

NOS YEUX DANS LE VENT

Nos yeux vigies au bout des vents
cinglant les phares raillant les escales
oh!
ces récifs de rêves au creux des auges assoupis.
Nos yeux nomades au dos des vents traqués
comme de lourds baluchons gorgés de violence
vrillant des chemins vierges
dans les filets d'espaces crevassés.
Nos yeux soleils qui envahissent le vent
      comme une marée dévorante de blé
Nos yeux rivières glissant dans la brise
gonflant les urnes des mains broyées.

Does Ouellette risk losing his fantastic balance to come a cropper in an absolutely airtight world? His *Séquences de l'aile*[44] contains *Passeport des étoiles*:

Femme au sang obscur qu'un germe habite
   comme une élégie de laine:
Ta pure extase est passeport des étoiles.

Quand dans ton corps les forêts courent
   et les archipels de muguet,

Aucune piqûre de vent, ni l'audace ténébreuse de l'homme
   ne sonderont la clairière de ton ange.

Vive est ta matrice de longs rêves arctiques.
   Et fraîche de galaxies-fougères.

Aux muscles humides de boisson blanche
   s'alimente le mal de vivre.[45]

This is a reassuring passport as it indicates that the poet can suggest without casting off all his moorings.[46]

Pierre Trottier (b. 1925)

Remaining resolutely apart from all trends, Pierre Trottier has been
able to make his presence felt by *Poèmes de Russie* (Editions de
l'Hexagone, 1957). While most of his colleagues are trying either to
understand or to resign themselves to nothingness, Trottier, quite
detached, presents an imagery which can be unexpected and even
roguish. Then comes a powerful bereavement and his facility in
finding the convincing metaphor makes it possible for him to write
the remarkable poem which is *Au salon de la dernière saison*. After
Saint-Denys-Garneau, Alain Grandbois and Jean-Guy Pilon, on this
endlessly renewable theme of death Trottier offers a new variant
composed of heartbreak and dark irony.

AU SALON DE LA DERNIERE SAISON

Enfin la mode acclame la robe linceul
L'aveuglant décolleté qui dégage
La plus séduisante des gorges décharnées
Enfin la mode acclame le souple drapé
Qui accuse la ligne du squelette
Et qui chante les charmes funèbres des os

Ah le beau mannequin à l'agonie
Qui montre aux invitées de ce caveau mondain
La robe de mariée dernier cri de la vie

Robe à la page robe à la dernière page
Ornée d'un bouquet d'âmes embaumées
Tu donnes tant de charme à ce sourire amer
Du mannequin qui sait qu'au lieu de sang de vierge
Un peu de poussière d'os souillera seule
Les craps de satin blanc de son grand lit-cercueil

Robe à la page qu'on détache de la vie
Robe de noce qui ne dure qu'un matin
Mensonge ultime tenant à un seul fil
Que le Oui de la mort et du mourant
Coupe aux acclamations des défuntes beautés
Du salon de cette dernière saison
Pour le triomphe de la mode la plus pure
Et le beau désespoir des couturiers ruinés
A l'instant où commence la lune de miel
Sans fin qui mène à complète nudité
Des squelettes en robe éternelle de nuit[47]

Réginald Boisvert[48] is one of the most representative of those who cry aloud their disgust at the modern world:

> *Nous mourons au dernier acte,*
> *et nous voici tournant les pages par ennui,*
> *n'osant fermer ce livre qu'on a mis*
> *entre nos mains*

Le temps de vivre, written between 1949 and 1955, reveals an incontestable talent which, seen through a partially closed-in world allowing glimpses of diversified poetic reality, could lead to strength.

With Claude Fournier[49] the despair like the poetic prose seems to correspond to an untaught truth and consequently is closer to touching us. After this preface—"What's the use? They started the fashion of the right to live in twisted old iron and kept the reasons to themselves. The last door of hope has closed without a sound, like a friend lowering his eyes."—Fournier succeeds in writing some of the best poetic prose of the new school:

Nous marchons côte à côte, sans nous reconnaître, dans la marée du silence qui nous soulève vers l'espace. Dans cet abîme éclairé d'étoiles et peuplé de rocs altiers, gouffre sombre découpé d'ivoires, dont la mâchoire inférieure devait être notre planète. Mais il n'importait plus de savoir le chiffre et la dimension des choses. Sans fatigue que cette mauvaise sensation de nos corps légers comme un duvet d'oiseau, à laquelle nous n'étions pas encore habitués, nous allions lentement, agrippés aux parois profondes de l'existence.

Nous aurions voulu parler, mais les mots s'agglutinaient en pâtes arrondies, roulaient sourdement dans la gorge. Un monde progressait lui aussi, comme nous, gagnant pas à pas, sans douleur, l'immense terrain perdu par les hommes de tous les siècles. Un monde dont il était possible de recueillir l'haleine tiède et caressante sur nos nuques. Chacun de nos souffles larguait les mystères diaphanes qui ont tourmenté l'univers depuis le début. Le moindre éclat les eût déchirés en chiffons, menaçant l'existence de la barque sur laquelle enfin nous remontions vers la source originelle.

Des ivoires encore plus blancs et lisses, stèles géantes plantées en espalier, annonçaient déjà par la pointe le moment de l'arrivée.

Je connus alors l'urgence de ne jamais terminer ce voyage, de fixer mes os éternellement dans cette mer inorganique. Je tournai la tête. J'étais seul. Le monde avait aussi sombré. Et avant même le retour, je palpai sur moi une solitude bienfaisante, immuable, comme si j'étais entré dans la chaîne froide des pulsations stellaires.

The atomic future finds its interpreter in Jacques Godbout. In *Carton-pâte* (Paris: Seghers, 1956), there is already a sign of the uneasiness which will be crystallized in the anguished anticipation

of *C'est la chaude loi des hommes* (Editions de l'Hexagone, 1960).
Before becoming the most representative of the French-Canadian
poets to deal with this theme, which has of necessity become a
universal one, Godbout had published a short "Poème," *La chair
est un commencement* (Ecrits du Canada français, Vol. V, 1959),
in which the technique, suitable to the novel, is the herald of
L'aquarium.

Although the prose-poetry of Roland Giguère[50] is perceptibly
far removed from any kind of music and appears at first sight to
have no colour, in comparison with Jean-Guy Pilon's rich lines, it
gains on re-examination. Loaded with symbols, what it loses in
euphony it gains in suggestion.

Originality for its own sake can always be attained. It is Théodore
Koenig's weakness to have succeeded too easily. Doubtless it is a
success to have effected in *Le jardin zoologique*[51] a close affiliation
between Conrad Tremblay's surrealistic sketches and the lines
which explain them or are a comment on them. But the verbal
clowning, appropriate as it may be to the fabulous creatures evoked,
becomes tiresome in the end. The trouble with the formula, very
attractive as it leads one immediately to an art full of surprises, is
that it is unable to renew itself; it condemns the poet to silence
after a first flight.

Guy Robert's first steps are *Broussailles givrées* (Editions Goglin,
1959); that is, out of the tangle of sensations and stylistic experiences there come poems whose form, sufficiently clear to be *givrée*,
is still without the flash of suns glimpsed by the poet. Leaving
behind him a childhood wrapped in cotton wool, but deceptive,
Robert confronts his destiny:

> *Mais je préfère à un bonheur*
> *vague et tiède et qui s'ignore*
> *le dur contact d'un malheur*
> *que j'attaque et qui me dévore*

Demanding all the freedoms, Robert admonishes himself:

> *forge l'outil de ta liberté*
> *à la pointe de ton sexe*
> *à la racine de ta vie*
>
> *que ta jeunesse flambe!*

Will the numerous possible directions of this poetry take Guy
Robert to a meeting with his immediate predecessors, Jean Guy
Pilon and Fernand Ouellette?

Gatien Lapointe also takes leave of his childhood but contrary to Guy Robert, who gains satisfaction from the sharp disappointments of the adult, Lapointe turns back with nostalgia towards the perfection of landscapes seen in his mind's eye. Not that he repudiates the present: he takes himself back to the past so that he may be able to face the future, to believe that *le monde est ce chant dans la main.* After two disappointing collections, *Jour malaisé* (1953), *Otages de la joie* (Editions de Muy, 1953), Lapointe has got rid of the false novelties with which he had thought it necessary to adorn his first verse.

The sifting process has allowed him to assert himself in *Le temps premier* (Paris: Grossin, 1962), *Prix du Club des Poètes,* 1962. Because *dire c'est revivre dans l'unité et souverainement se souvenir,* as he expresses it, Lapointe gets nourishment from the past in order to come to an understanding of man. *Le temps premier* is attractive in its simplicity. Feelings expressed without affectation, metaphors chosen with as much modesty as tact, win him appreciation. From now on, sure of himself, Lapointe shoulders responsibility and takes a close look at what it means to be a French Canadian in *Ode au Saint-Laurent* (Montreal: Les Editions du Jour, 1963).

If poetry had to be reduced to the precious gift of inventing metaphors, Suzanne Paradis would have no rival among her young colleagues. *La chasse aux autres* (Trois-Rivières: Editions du Bien Public, 1961), a pictorial horn of plenty, has splendour on every page.

> *Je suis le nouveau jour, l'innombrable dimanche*
> *bondi de la dernière étoile du ciel clos;*
> *je retarde la mort d'une feuille à la branche*
> *je mets la mort du monde en échec d'un oiseau.*

Too many riches set in implacably regular rhymes make one wish for an opening to the choice for which there could be no replacement. Such as it is this collection is much superior to *Les enfants continuels* (1959) and *A temps, le bonheur* (1960).

Among the poets who have succeeded in making for themselves an already recognizable identity and who could bring fame to the French-Canadian poetry of tomorrow, mention should be made of: Gilles Constantineau (*La pêche très verte,* 1954); *Simples poèmes et ballades* (Editions de l'Hexagone, 1960); Louise Pouliot, whose *Portes sur la mer* (*ibid.,* 1956), borrows from vocabulary of the sea to suggest her deeply felt anguish. Olivier Marchand (*Crier que je vis, ibid.,* 1958); Alain Marceau (*A la pointe des yeux, ibid.,*

1958); Michel van Schendel, who transposes in America his experience of Flanders and tries, in his *Poèmes de l'Amérique étrangère* (*ibid.*, 1958), to take an adopted country for his own; Yves Préfontaine, for whom *L'antre du poème* (Trois-Rivières: Editions du Bien Public, 1960) becomes a mysterious and fertile place where the matrixes of art are mingled; Maurice Beaulieu, fraternal and growing like a young tree, prophet of his "Amerindian" land (*A glaise fendre*, 1957); *Il fait clair de glaise* (Editions de l'Orphée, 1958); Jean-Paul Filion, who, after *Du centre de l'eau* (Editions de l'Hexagone, 1955), has been able to find in *Demain les herbes rouges* (*ibid.*, 1962) accents of a beautiful sonority.

Certain poets who work alone, outside of the great modern currents, succeed in bringing themselves to our attention just because they are there. The Gilles Hénault of *Totems* (Editions Erta, 1953) and of *Sémaphore* (l'Hexagone, 1962) is one of these.

The rare poems published by Gaston Miron[52] make one wish to have from the man who is the active force behind Editions de l'Hexagone a creative activity to correspond to the fine impetus he has given to a whole generation of poets.

HISTORY

Guy Frégault (b. 1918)

Among the historians who have acquired a reputation since the Second World War, Guy Frégault[53] is the most eminent. In the space of about ten years his impressive historical work has set him apart from his contemporaries. His method, like the orientation of his thought, makes him an initiator.

M. Frégault is one of the first French-Canadian historians to owe his training to the United States. From Garneau's time all French-Canadian historians have dreamed of continuing their studies in Europe, particularly in France. Here is one French-Canadian historian who draws his inspiration from methods in favour in American universities. One need look no further for the origin of the reorientation that M. Frégault, by his own example, aims to establish in historical research.

Although there is no "American method" that can be set up against a "French method" to bring out the differences between two national ways of approaching history, it is nevertheless true that anyone acquainted with American and French historians could not fail to establish, through the multiplicity of temperaments and methods, significant national resemblances. It is undeniable that in France the historian generally feels the necessity of expressing himself clearly and, if possible, with some degree of elegance. Especially is it expected that the myriad facts he has collected will be presented in such a way as to suggest their assimilation into some general theory of philosophy. Nothing is less pleasing in France than a dry enumeration of facts which the historian, for want of a critical commentary, does not seem to have in his grasp. In the United States, on the other hand, historical studies and scholarship as such even in our day still bear the mark of the Germanic spirit which influenced so strongly the development of American universities in the second half of the nineteenth century. The American professor has only to be so inclined to end up like his German colleague, in an exhaustive bibliography and an in-folio. American learning is playing too important a role in Western culture for it to be possible to underestimate the valuable advantages that its scholarly output procures for the researchers of the whole world. How can one keep from observing, however, that if superficiality is too often the result of the instinctive desire of the learned Frenchman to reconcile aesthetics and truth, the sense of history can just as well escape the historian who refuses to spare the reader the least crumb of information?

M. Frégault's first works, *La civilisation de la Nouvelle France* and *Iberville le conquérant* are still affected by this mania for the least crumb.[54] Nevertheless, intention and method which the historian will not be long in perfecting, are discernible through the quotations.

Like Abbé Groulx, M. Frégault seeks to demonstrate the early formation of a French-Canadian personality, already a reality under the French regime. To this end a method will be practised which is the very opposite of the one operative in the working out of *La naissance d'une race,* the examination in depth of the years 1713-1744. The resulting synthesis is convincing, as is the conclusion: "The whole people became a moral entity, a complete being, a new nation, leaning on a past whose indomitable power projects it into the future."[55]

In 1944, too, M. Frégault published *Iberville le conquérant.* His object was to release the hero from the legend. M. Frégault, because he remains set on the method, blames his predecessors for having embroidered history, for having preferred the picturesque detail to the more prosaic one which is the fruit of patient research. It is undeniable that French-Canadian historians have often allowed themselves to be led astray by the pathos of their history. So M. Frégault's intervention is salutary.

What will become of the heroes or the gravediggers of New France when scrupulous documentation makes it necessary to take a second look at them? Two personages more famous than familiar, François Bigot and the Marquis de Vaudreuil, emerge from the eighteenth century very much alive. Moreover, the accumulation of evidence from the period gives a very precise idea of the French colonial administration. In the light of these facts there is nothing of the Lucifer about Bigot, and Vaudreuil recovers from Montcalm part of the glory which is his due.

Like many French-Canadian writers of history Frégault does not escape an exaggerated patriotism. Usually the bias of French-Canadian historians is directed against the English or English Canadians. At a time when young nations are rejecting what Europe has brought them, M. Frégault, two centuries after the event, attacks European colonialism and that of France in particular. *François Bigot, administrateur français* is an indictment.[56]

The preceding works would have been enough to give M. Frégault first place among historians since the war. He was only preparing himself, however, for his first great work, *La guerre de la conquête*.

Freed at last from university methodology, Guy Frégault is ready to be wholly the historian whose main function is to "correct systematically the tradition according to which a human group is ordering its life."[57] Now, the bloody period of the war of conquest which sealed the fate of the French-Canadian nation has never been truly understood. The orators of French-Canadian history have covered over with their floral wreaths a sad reality—the final defeat of a nation. Consistent with his method of stripping the glamour from important facts, Guy Frégault re-examines the last years of New France. The famous battles are relegated to second place to throw light upon the real drama—the struggle for world supremacy between France and England. The historian's reliable documentation, too conspicuous in his first works, serves to perfection his intention, which is to follow the graph of public opinion in France, in England and in America. For the first time a French-Canadian historian seeks the explanation of the remarkable victories won by a New France in its death throes, in the internal structure of the American provinces and French colonies. In so doing his anti-colonialism is attenuated in the interests of serenity.

By its conclusion *La guerre de la conquête* is an innovation in French-Canadian historiography. A well-established tradition, particularly with the priest-historians, would have it that the conquest was providential since the church came out of it relieved of its burden of gallicanism and, after a difficult interregnum, more powerful than ever. Another benefit would be that the deleterious influences of the French Revolution did not reach as far as Canada. The historian rejects this optimistic view to conclude that a conquest breaks up the fundamental structure of a nation and that it never recovers in the end from the injury done to it. The conquerors, no matter how benevolent, precisely because they are conquerors will have been worse for the French-Canadian people than the French *soudards.* It is to this unexpected conclusion that Guy Frégault's nationalism leads.

Like the work of Abbé Groulx, that of M. Frégault calls for reservations, although to a lesser extent. It would be impossible, however, to deny the success of an historian who has created in so short a time a new school of Canadian History. One may presume that if he tackled the two centuries following the conquest the result might be a deeper knowledge, a new conception of the French-Canadian personality.

Robert Rumilly (b. 1897)

Coming from France in 1928, Robert Rumilly has made for himself a place among historians comparable to that of George Bugnet among novelists, with this difference that he soon became well known. These two Frenchmen, from a society of the extreme right in France, found their true vocation in Canada.[58] That both have been able to play a very useful role in the development of French-Canadian letters is not explained simply by the evident filiations between a traditional French Canada and conservative elements in France. The fact is that a collaborator of *La Croix* and a *Camelot du Roi* with difficulty escape sectarianism. In French Canada, perceiving that their programme is largely realized here already, these same men have only to devote themselves wholeheartedly to the French survival in America. Purified, so to speak, through the Canadian experience, a Bugnet and a Rumilly put to the service of French-Canadian culture precious gifts which would have been left unused in France.

M. Rumilly's first writings were only a preparation for the really masterly work with which his name will remain principally connected, the *Histoire de la Province de Québec.* Although M. Rumilly in 1941, in his preface to the third volume of his *Histoire,* explained his method, this comes out clearly in the studies published between 1931 and 1940 and those which have followed.

M. Rumilly is the sworn enemy of everything that can be injurious to the life of the past in all its complexity. By virtue of this principle he rejects the apparatus of sources, worshipped by university-trained historians. Not that he holds in contempt the necessity for first-hand documentation; on the contrary, the exactitude of the innumerable quotations interlarding the thirty-two volumes of the *Histoire* published between 1940 and 1959 are a guarantee of the strictness of his self-discipline. Moreover, M. Rumilly does not fail to draw attention to a text when it is considered to be of real importance. His disdain for well-arranged bibliographies and footnotes set out in battle formation at the foot of the page is in no way an affectation; it is simply due to the fact that he is a writer. For M. Rumilly is the only artist among contemporary historians. Because he counts on the effects of style to bring the past to life, this past can be felt only if it reaches the awareness of the reader without obstacle. Constantly drawing attention to research that has been done or documents which it would be useful to consult would hinder the historian in his most powerful means of communication.

So it is not surprising that M. Rumilly orders his material to serve the effect he is seeking, that of experience that has been lived. Instead of all-encompassing views of historical complexity, it is excursions into the very heart of events which he proposes to us. For an understanding of the religious conflicts which broke out in the second half of the nineteenth century, is a very short paragraph of such as the following not as good as a long analysis?

In Montreal there had been formed a group of resolute laymen more ultramontanist than the pope, claiming to own the Church, to interpret its words and, fearing nothing, if need be to teach a lesson to the bishops. In the dispute all were openly and firmly hostile to Laval. They were men of ability, worthy men in private life, sincere in their convictions and all the stronger on this account. Their head, Senator François-Xavier Trudel, well set up, clever, using his pen like a sword—striking with flat side and keen edge— was an outstanding personality. Very religious, he wrote nothing without first sinking to his knees in prayer in order to plead for light from the Holy Spirit. He would draw strength from this meditation and then, rising from his prayer-stool, he would deal out to his adversaries two or three vigorous columns which would be inserted in *Le Monde*. A tall statue of the Sacré-Coeur held the place of honour in his drawing-room. Naturally this lay monk had married a woman fond of clothes and a spendthrift who grew tired of such a life. She asked for a separation and pushed cruelty to the point of taking Joseph Doutre for her lawyer.[59] [*trans.*]

The danger of this method of historical writing is obvious: the result of too great an accumulation of pictures and of a desire to give an exactly true impression is that the total picture becomes less clear. To make up for this disadvantage in *Henri Bourassa* M. Rumilly for instance slows down his procession of sketches by means of explanatory headings of the kind found in school texts. This, quite simply, is to admit that a method is imperfect. It is significant that the references, the bibliographies, the general views which Robert Rumilly brushes aside as a matter of course, should be finally replaced by labels of this kind.

A comparison between Robert Rumilly and Guy Frégault is revealing. These two historians, different in every way, in temperament and in method, represent in their works the eternal debate that goes on between historians. Does the truth admit of glamorizing, in style for instance? Does the past live for us without life-giving art? It is of no use to try to reply since these problems cannot be solved by aesthetics. The critic, in his eclecticism, is permitted to recognize two valid forms of the historiographical art whose theoretical foundations matter less than their practical applications.

Gustave Lanctot (b. 1883)

As mistrustful of the "little facts of history" as of too vast syntheses, Gustave Lanctot has preferred to choose subjects which, while admitting of broad developments, run no risk of yawning chasms. And so we have two characteristic works: *François-Xavier Garneau* (Toronto: The Ryerson Press, 1926) and *L'administration de la Nouvelle-France* (Paris: Champion, 1929).

In the light of a century of research and a profound reorientation of historiography, Garneau's work called for re-evaluation. M. Lanctot's criticism—the best that has been made of Garneau's work —is fair on the whole and is not lacking in insight. It is true that Garneau made no attempt to see the *habitant* in his daily life. But can the historian of the first half of the nineteenth century be blamed for not having made a searching analysis of economic conditions?

In his doctoral thesis, *L'administration de la Nouvelle-France*, M. Lanctot treated his subject exhaustively and convincingly. His work, open to slight alteration but to no change in its broad outlines, will for some time to come be the last word.

In the *Histoire du Canada* (Beauchemin, 1960) we have the achievement of a lifetime devoted to understanding the French-

Canadian past. A remarkably exhaustive synthesis which takes in the legendary era of the first Asiatic migrations, proceeding from there to the Irish and the Norsemen who were the first Europeans to tread the earth of America, Lanctot's *Histoire du Canada* subjects the first century of French colonization to a new scrutiny.[60] In the light of the conclusions which Lanctot forms on the subject of myths of the French-Canadian past, it does seem necessary to give up the idea of making the century following Jacques Cartier's discovery the century of Christian evangelization. The clergy played a glorious role in the building of New France but most of the colonists were to leave France for secular reasons.

Among those embellishments of history which Lanctot reduced to more modest proportions, the most significant, the one which shows most clearly his contribution to the history of French Canada, is furnished by the Dollard story. It seems that Abbé Faillon was responsible for the error of which generations of French Canadians have been the willing victims. Dollard des Ormeaux does appear to have contributed powerfully to the saving of New France by his act, traditionally compared to that of Leonidas. But in falling with his companions at Long-Sault, Dollard had only sought like so many others to defend himself, without having any suspicion of the importance of his sacrifice. As we know it was for Abbé Groulx and his disciples to turn to such great account this episode of the war against the Iroquois.

Works: *Les Canadiens-français et leurs voisins du Sud* (in collaboration), Editions Bernard Valiquette, 1941; *L'oeuvre de la France en Amérique du Nord* (Fides, 1951); *Une Nouvelle-France inconnue* (Librairie Ducharme, 1952), etc.

Jean Bruchési (b. 1901)

The real contribution of Jean Bruchési to French-Canadian historiography is that he was one of the first to bring his attention to bear on the outside world.[61] A well-informed observer of European politics in 1929, M. Bruchési travelled across Poland, Austria, Hungary and the Balkans. It was the first time that a French-Canadian historian had taken an interest in that part of the world. The upheaval to which these regions have been exposed since 1930 make certain aspects of his intimate reporting out of date. Jean Bruchési had, however, an instinctive understanding of the centuries-old aspirations of the Poles, the stubborn dream of

Latinity of the Roumanians, the indomitable energy of the Magyars. And so, thanks to this alert eye-witness, one can get some idea of the particular situation of Western Europe around 1930.

Aux marches de l'Europe is also the testimony of a man belonging to the last generation of French Canadians who will have been able, by leaving Canada, to benefit from the inestimable advantage of knowing a Europe and a Near East bearing the mark of French culture. Thanks to the 1914-1918 victory, French language and culture, precisely at the time when M. Bruchési made his trip, were enjoying a last burst of international favour. In world councils, particularly in the League of Nations, the language of Rivarol was clearly ahead of its rival, English, which was soon to be called to take first place. The moral and intellectual security which France, by the prestige of its arts and arms, had never ceased to obtain for French-Canadian intellectuals from 1763, brought Jean Bruchési to this conclusion: "The place that French language and culture have in these parts will help to make us forget the indifference with which both are often treated not too far away."

Jean Bruchési's example, unfortunately, has found only very few imitators. The dilemma of French-Canadian historians is only too evident: it is impossible everlastingly to go back to the material furnished by the history of New France. Jean Bruchési understood very well the ethnic problems of the Balkan countries because, as a French Canadian, these problems were not foreign to him; and French Canadians are obviously even better placed for a good understanding of the Americans! They have the privilege of belonging to two worlds: to America, where their roots go deep, and to Western Europe, where their particular spiritual form is centred. Here they are, placed in the middle of the American world whose enormous power of penetration extends to the most remote countries. Without at any time neglecting their own history French-Canadian historians must obviously turn to the United States. It is at this price that they will escape provincialism and be able to make known abroad the unusual qualities of mind which are at once Canadian, American and French.[62]

Marcel Trudel (b. 1917)

Since 1947 Head of the Department of Canadian History in Laval University, Marcel Trudel[63] began with the publication of his thesis, *L'influence de Voltaire au Canada.* The historian gives proof in this work of considerable confusion in his thinking. People who make a business of comparisons know how tricky a matter it is to unearth the direct influence exerted by one writer on another. It is all the more risky to try to discover that influence in the case of a politician or a private individual. To impute to Voltaire alone the numerous instances of resistance to which the French-Canadian clergy have been subjected is manifestly unjustifiable. It is the whole problem of anti-clericalism which M. Trudel takes up, without indicating its complexity.

Less debatable is his *Louis XVI, le Congrès américain et le Canada.* Might there have been an inclination on the part of France to take back Canada at the time of the American Revolution? Marcel Trudel brings forward his reply based on a thorough study of the texts. It does seem indeed, that, pushed by Vergennes, the aim of French policy may have been to keep Canada for England. Like England, which in 1760-1763 had thought of giving Canada back to France to hold the Americans in check, the France of Louis XVI judged that it was a matter of self-interest to perpetuate the Anglo-American quarrel. That is why France did not contemplate taking part in a possible conquest of Canada by the Americans.

Attracted, it appears, by religious problems, in his *Chiniquy* M. Trudel has recalled the figure of the only founder of a dissenting sect that French Canada has produced. Instead of explaining M. Trudel disproves, at times on a note far from serene.

In *L'esclavage au Canada français* the historian has corrected some statements of Garneau, who would have congratulated the French-Canadian clergyman for his anti-slavery sentiments. Proof is furnished of the existence of slavery in Canada, which was everywhere acceptable in the eighteenth century, and of the participation of different classes of French-Canadian society, including the clergy, in the traffic in "ebony wood." At the same time M. Trudel, with the help of impressive documentation, establishes in convincing fashion the evident contribution of black and Indian blood to the French-Canadian community.

Principal works: *L'influence de Voltaire au Canada* (Fides, 1945); *Louis XVI, le Congrès américain et le Canada* (Quebec: Publications de l'Université Laval, 1949); *Le régime militaire dans le gouvernement de Trois-Rivières, 1760-1764* (Trois-Rivières: Editions du Bien Public, 1952); *Chiniquy* (*ibid.,* 1955); *L'esclavage au Canada français* (Quebec: Les Presses Universitaires Laval, 1960).

DONATIEN FREMONT (b. 1881): Born at Erbray (Loire-Inférieure), Donatien Frémont studied in Nantes. Because of the anti-clerical feeling that reigned in France at that time M. Frémont thought of leaving the country, as Georges Bugnet and Robert Rumilly were to do later on. He reached Canada in 1904. In the Canadian West M. Frémont played an important role in the defence of French language and culture. Editor of the *Patriote de l'Ouest* (Prince Albert) and then managing editor of *La Liberté* (Winnipeg), M. Frémont made himself historian of the French settlement in the West: *Mgr. Taché et la naissance du Manitoba* (Winnipeg: La Liberté, 1930); *Pierre Radisson* (Montreal: Lévesque, 1933): *Monseigneur Provencher et son temps* (Winnipeg: La Liberté, 1932); *Les secrétaires de Riel* (Montreal: Chantecler, 1953).

OLIVIER MAURAULT (b. 1886): Born in Sorel, Olivier Maurault became a priest of Saint-Sulpice. After studying in France at the *Institut catholique de Paris,* Olivier Maurault held different teaching positions, becoming in 1934 rector of the University of Montreal. The Sulpiciens having played a distinguished role for three centuries of history in the City of Montreal, it was quite natural for him to become historian of his order and of his adopted city: *Le petit séminaire de Montréal* (Montreal: Derome, 1918); *La paroisse: histoire de l'église Notre-Dame de Montréal* (Montreal:Carrier, 1929); *Marges d'histoire* (Montreal: Librairie d'Action canadienne-française, 1929-1930), 3 vol., etc.

GERARD FILTEAU (b. 1906): With a doctorate from Laval University, and the Prix David in 1937, M. Filteau, after the fashion of Lionel Groulx and Guy Frégault, traced the evolution of national sentiment among French Canadians. *La naissance d'une nation* (Montreal: Editions de l'Action Canadienne-française, 1937), 2 vol.; *Histoire des patriotes (ibid.,* 1938-1942), 3 vol.

CRITICISM

How is it to be explained that the best contemporary critics tend to specialize? An initial explanation comes from the fact that the field of French-Canadian letters is progressively being occupied by the laity. Would Camille Roy have been able to devote an important part of his leisure to criticism had it not been for the advantages that went with his calling? If only a few rare novelists can hope to earn their living by their literary production alone, the critic must abandon any such ambition. Another factor is that French-Canadian literature has grown very much richer. Of course the number of great poets and novelists with international appeal is not such that a team of specialists would be required to make an inventory of them. Nevertheless, if there is to be a balanced judgment everything has to be read. That is why critics who are often found in journalism, radio, and television, through necessity as much as inclination, restrict themselves to the literary present or the recent past.

Jean Le Moyne (b. 1913)

There are not many pages of literary criticism in *Convergences* (Editions HMH, 1961). A few short essays on Henry James, Scott Fitzgerald, Saint-Denys-Garneau and an analysis of the role of woman in French-Canadian literature are enough, however, to make Jean Le Moyne the most penetrating of contemporary critics.

Having taken into account everything that Europe has contributed to his training, Jean Le Moyne is seen to be affected at the same time by the United States, from which he is separated, however, by the fact that he is French-Canadian. Thus his thought becomes a meeting place (*un lieu de convergences*) of which he is the first in French Canada to make conscious and systematic use. The demonstration is convincing to the extent that one may wonder if his pessimistic conclusion about the lack of any possibility for the French-Canadian writer to confer a valid artistic form on his experience is not contradicted by his own example.[64]

Two brilliant essays on Henry James and Scott Fitzgerald are no doubt a slender contribution to American literature. But when the soundings are taken one is allowed a glimpse of what freely possessing the whole self would permit future French-Canadian critics to accomplish. The French Canadian has never hesitated to claim the right to his European heritage. But because, at the same time, he has not dared to exploit his American qualifications, he has always remained cut off from life.

Most critics, from Camille Roy to the Parisian reporters who contribute regularly to the literary pages of today's French-Canadian reviews and newspapers, are still essentially provincial. Le Moyne is their superior precisely because, imbued with French thought, and particularly with the lofty Catholic speculation of Maritain and Teilhard de Chardin, he has been further enriched by reading American literature, which he has enthusiastically made his own.

The direction that French-Canadian literature will take appears clearly indicated in *Convergences*. Neither French nor American but Canadian, this literature with Le Moyne is on the road to a promising future.

Le Moyne was too intimately associated with Saint-Denys-Garneau to give us a perfectly true picture of him. With his complexes and inhibitions, Saint-Denys-Garneau is becoming a national poet. Sociological criticism, based on the archetype of the French Canadian woman, allows Le Moyne to make a lucid explanation of the prevailing anaemic condition of the principal French-Canadian novelists. On the other hand when sociology justifies holy fits of anger, the result is the strident and almost barnstorming note which comes out of the otherwise suggestive study of Saint-Denys-Garneau.

Gérard Bessette (b. 1920)

Gérard Bessette is the first French-Canadian critic whose work is not entirely dependent on Paris. All that nineteenth-century criticism handed down to us—concern for biographical detail, examination of sources, psychological studies in the manner of Havelock Ellis—is in his case subordinated to the necessity of an honest scrutiny of the text and an explanation of its success or failure. He has set forth his method in a doctoral thesis, *Les images en poésie canadienne-française.*[65] It is by means of a renewed tropology that Bessette attacks the poetic mystery. Drawing attention to the fact that tropology, abandoned because it has become associated with Scholasticism, is nevertheless capable, when well understood, of exposing the mechanism of creative art in poetry by the light it throws on the poet's technique and the substratum of his ideas, Bessette traces the tropological evolution of French poetry in order to be able to subject the principal French-Canadian poets to a close examination.

The critic raises a number of problems at the root of French versification. Is it true that French-Canadian poetry, which is like French poetry in this regard, is unsuccessful in truly describing reality—in the way that English and German poetry does—unless it has first transmuted it? Is it also true that the present lends itself badly to poetry and that, for this reason, Crémazie, who half-way succeeded in the genre, furnished indirect proof of the spontaneity and "contagious dynamism" with which a French-Canadian poet can infuse his work?

These fundamental questions are an indication of the suggestiveness of a study which suffers, however, from one too-evident weakness: it depends on a method which is of little use in explaining that portion of contemporary poetry which is most alive.

Gilles Marcotte (b. 1925)

While Le Moyne makes use of the image of woman to explain French-Canadian literature, Gilles Marcotte has recourse to the "exile" theme, which takes him back to the sources of the collective subconscious (*Une littérature qui se fait*, Les Editions HMH, 1962). Since Crémazie, several of the most representative French-Canadian poets have borne witness to their feeling of exile. By this it must be understood that, psychologically divided between Europe, of which they are not a part, and the American continent, in which they feel imperfectly integrated, French-Canadian writers have an indwelling sense of imperfection and malaise. Their reaction takes shape in the morbid introspection in French-Canadian literature of which Crémazie gave a first example in his *Promenade de trois morts*. Exile, which has become a method of analysis, leads Marcotte to an unexpected rapprochement between Crémazie and Anne Hébert. The demonstration is not lacking in subtlety and constitutes an excellent example of the new element that this kind of criticism is bringing to French-Canadian letters. At the same time, criticism based on archetypes has dangers which Marcotte does not escape. Whatever he may say, Alfred Garneau remains a mediocre poet. A thematic X-ray picture of him would be unable to hide the poverty of his poetic imagination. Further, if there is any connection between Alfred Garneau and Alfred Lozeau, it belongs at least as much to sociology as to literature.

Notwithstanding these weaknesses, the archetypal critic, of whom Marcotte is one of the best representatives, is clearly of service to French-Canadian criticism in ridding it of continual references to the literature of France.

Guy Robert (b. 1933)

The most systematic exploitation of the resources offered by thematic criticism has been undertaken by Guy Robert, in *La poétique du songe* (Association des Etudiants de l'Université de Montréal, 1962). Taking his inspiration from Bachelard, Robert attempts to communicate with "the creative consciousness of the poet" by subjecting the work of Anne Hébert to an experimental thematic study. Twenty-two themes, from love to the concept of time, are compared by means of connections between them suggested by an attentive reading of the texts.

For the critic, the most apparent advantage of this approach is to be found in the necessity of creating his own references and in this way of escaping, at least in appearance, the immense weight of the criticism done before him. The difficulty Robert has been unable to avoid comes from the ponderous inventory that results. By a strange contradiction the critic who proclaims the sacred value of the poem, its irreducible mystery, sees himself obliged to break up into a thousand pieces the components of its fascination.

As a critic, Guy Robert has already given proof of a rare ability to reproduce the work he is examining in apt verbal equivalents.[66] The technique, still imperfect, would have only to be joined with intuition to make a decisive and convincing combination.

The fine study, *Pellan, sa vie et son oeuvre* (Montreal: Editions du Centre de Psychologie et de Pédagogie, 1963) along with *Connaissance nouvelle de l'art* (Librairie Déom, 1963), has confirmed the critic's growing authority. Robert's curiosity extends to all the arts for which, in *Connaissance nouvelle de l'art*, he proposes a simplified formula of understanding. The enterprise, which is too ambitious, allows him, nevertheless, to stir up a good many ideas, some of them original. Guy Robert is already conspicuous for the seriousness of thought that bestrides continents and eras. In the history of French-Canadian literature no critic has been better prepared, so early in his career, to undertake an objective and elegant analysis of the artistic production of his time.

Pierre Angers (b. 1912)

Of all the critic-priests it is Pierre Angers who has given the broadest definition of his profession: "What seems to us to be the first task of criticism is to look for the full meaning of a work, to go down into the very source from which it springs, in order to understand it in its abundant richness as well as in its failings, and to appreciate it according to the norms which have reference to the different planes of existence."[67] For Pierre Angers, catholicism well understood takes in every aspect of reality, the proof being that the critic who is prompted by real charity comes to the work of art without prejudices. If all critic-priests had interpreted their role with the same ecumenism, French-Canadian writers would have benefited more from their co-operation. It is to be observed, however, that even in the case of a mind inspired with generosity, the theoretical statement can be very different from the practical application. Does Pierre Angers not attach more importance to the Index than the members of the Papal Concilium who met in Rome in 1962?

DOSTALER O'LEARY (1908-1965): His *Roman canadien-français* (Montreal: Le Cercle du Livre de France, 1954), closer to polite conversation than to scholarship, avoids the pitfalls of the genre. Before him, Berthelot Brunet (1901-1948) had come to uncomplimentary conclusions about French-Canadian literature in *Histoire de la littérature canadienne-française* (Montreal: l'Arbre, 1946). O'Leary, on the other hand, seeks before everything else to do justice to each novelist. As a critic he is above all reasonable, his verdicts being what the majority can agree with.

HARRY BERNARD (b. 1898): Literatures of the two Americas have had to free themselves from Europe. Fruitful rapprochements between literatures present themselves quite naturally to the critic seeking to analyze the rapidity or the slowness with which American, Brazilian or other American literatures are brought into being. Before Harry Bernard, French-Canadian criticism, taken up with French and French-Canadian literature, did not take a serious interest in the literature of the United States.

In his *Essais critiques* (Montreal: Librairie d'Action canadienne-française, 1929), Harry Bernard had already expounded the importance for French-Canadian literature of a vigorous regional tradition. Starting with the idea that a literature lives and reaches the world only in proportion as it is firmly anchored in the soil and people to which it belongs, Harry Bernard wanted to show in *Le roman régionaliste aux Etats-Unis* (Montreal: Fides, 1949) that the Americans have been successful in creating an original and universally admired literature because they have knowingly practised regionalism.

The theoretical build-up of Harry Bernard's study is weak. What exactly is a regional work? To say that Flaubert wrote regional novels because Normandy figures largely in his work and that for like reasons Maupassant, Daudet, Tolstoy and Dostoievsky were also regional novelists, is to empty a definition of all meaning.

M. Bernard's patient research—which extends from 1913, the year when *O Pioneers* by Willa Cather was published, to 1940—makes a useful catalogue of the American regional novel, that is to say, of the novel which either historically or geographically or simply in its examination of man, to any extent takes into account different parts of the United States.

At the end of the inquiry one could ask: "What is it that separates the rare novels which have survived from the some three thousand regional works published between 1913 and 1940?" Is it not precisely that indefinable ingredient which, for want of a better word, we sometimes call genius? If the lesson is good for the French-Canadian novel—and this is indeed the critic's idea—should we not have to reproach French-Canadian writers for a lack of genius rather than for failing to write regional novels?

JOURNALISTIC CRITICISM

It is by way of newspapers and literary reviews that most critics express themselves. Among those who illustrate best the good qualities and defects of a criticism which essentially tends to lack unity and especially a comprehensive view of criticism itself, are Pierre de Grandpré and René Garneau.

More sophisticated than their predecessors, better informed and more receptive to the latest innovations in the novel, poetry or the theatre, their reviews in *Le Devoir* or in *Mercure de France* can stand comparison with journalistic criticism in the three great capitals of the West, Paris, London and New York.

Their weakness is seen in the theoretical basis. In the case of Grandpré, who, of the two, may be taken as the theorist, the substratum is borrowed. One learns that authentic poetry is a harbinger; it increases and sometimes precedes awakening in a people.[68] The general effect of a literature is always the expression of a collective destiny.[69] Art is truth.[70] And so on. The fact remains that his criticism, which takes in the current literary scene in France, raises the tone of *Le Devoir*, which is the best-edited French-Canadian daily of the present day.

René Garneau, before being considered as a critic, is first of all an excellent prose writer. Everything leads one to suppose that, placed in the centre rather than on the periphery of French-Canadian literature, René Garneau could have found a better use for his talent than occasional criticism. This has the serious disadvantage of being done while officially he is cultural attaché in Paris. To make French-Canadian literature known in France is the most laudable of missions. It is a sign of the times, in which older nations have their sensitive side as well as younger ones, that every study of French-Canadian literature destined for French readers must end with a touching peroration on Franco-Canadian affinities. René

Garneau has had no difficulty in conforming to this kind of criticism since, to French Canadians themselves, he proclaims that the French-Canadian writer must aim at reaching not the French-Canadian public but readers of the French language "everywhere in the world where they are to be found." To accomplish this objective works must be conceived with the idea of responding to "the demands and habits of French taste."[71] On the one hand to pray for the coming of an original French-Canadian literature and on the other to conceive of that literature only as something already familiar, such is the most characteristic attitude of this critic. It is for similar reasons that he sees the literature of the United States as an offshoot of English literature.

It must be admitted that it would be unfair to point out the fragile theoretical bases of newspaper criticism. Normally critics of the *New York Times, Le Monde* or the (London) *Times*, whose first function is to put their readers in touch with the publications which seem to them most significant, do not have to reveal the guiding principles of their art. How many of them, driven to this necessity, could do better than Pierre de Grandpré? When Grandpré and Garneau keep strictly to the text of what they are writing about, their criticism is always honest and sometimes distinguished.

The present critics of *Le Devoir* give their attention to all manifestations of literary life and are found to be closer to French-Canadian reality than their predecessors, who were too much inclined to cast an envious eye in the direction of Paris. Jean Hamelin, Jean Vallerand, Jean Ethier-Blais keep writers on the *qui-vive* with their alert and biting reviews, unjust at times but useful, all things considered.

THE THEATRE

After more than a century of uninterrupted existence, literary life in French Canada today is reaching its theatrical phase; so French-Canadian literature will have grown by imitating the course of the great literary traditions of the West. Poets and chroniclers precede dramatists and producers, the creative activity of the first depending almost entirely on a large and enlightened public. The United States, whose literary evolution is so often in advance of that of Canada and other countries in the two Americas, had to pass through the golden age of New England before coming to Eugene O'Neill and Tennessee Williams in the twentieth century. Now it is only since the last war that French Canada, confident at last of being able to preserve its essential character, dares find any satisfaction in self-contemplation.[72]

From the establishment in 1937 of Emile Legault's *Compagnons* down to 1963, French Canada has passed from amateur theatre to permanent companies. At the beginning of Legault's career everything was yet to be created or discovered: a homogeneous company of actors, an auditorium and particularly a loyal public. This public has taken shape, numbering about fifteen thousand spectators. Permanent and occasional companies of actors come to about ten in number. Auditoriums, conceived for the theatre, are at their disposal. Finally, playwrights, nonexistent in 1937, have made their appearance.

Emile Legault
and the Compagnons de Saint Laurent

A dynamic director, Emile Legault, by his example proved that Montreal was ready for good theatre. Starting in 1937 Legault at first, as much from prudence as necessity, limited himself to the religious theatre of Ghéon; but gradually this dedicated cleric was to lead his public, lay and religious, to the audacities of *Viol de Lucrèce* (André Obey), prudently re-baptized *Lucrèce*.

The revelation of Anouilh's *Antigone*, in 1947/48, particularly surprised those who, having been present at the first staging of the play in Paris at the time of the German occupation, were in a position to compare the Paris and Montreal casts, and furnished undeniable proof that a French-Canadian company could, under certain circumstances, hold its own with the best Paris theatre. More important still, a French-Canadian point of view was revealed.

Two centuries of coexistence with Anglo-Saxons have made French Canadians less extroverted. The evocation of passion or intensely lived feeling by the actors of principal theatrical companies of Paris can appear overdone and sometimes even ridiculous to a French-Canadian audience. It is undeniable that in France the tradition of Racinian tirades, justifiably preserved in the *Comédie Française*, has not been without influence on the playing of more than one very able contemporary actor. Following the imperatives of his own nature the French-Canadian actor will howl more softly and recover his composure more quickly than his Parisian counterpart. And it is good that it should be so since in both cases the authenticity is there.

In 1952 the *Compagnons* disbanded. The French-Canadian public, grown accustomed to shows worthy of the French cultural centre of America, was ready to welcome the two permanent companies founded by former Compagnons: the *Théâtre du Nouveau Monde* and the *Théâtre-Club*.

Montreal
Centre of French-Language Theatre

As of 1952 theatre was recognized at last as part of Montreal life. The *Théâtre du Nouveau Monde,* founded at the end of 1951 by Jean Gascon, Jean-Louis Roux and Georges Groulx, was so successful that it was possible for it to play Molière *(L'avare, Tartufe, Don Juan, Le malade imaginaire)* in the principal cities of English Canada and in Paris to take part in the International Drama Festival. The interpretation given to Molière drew mixed reactions from the critics, but no one disputed the vigour and individual style of these French-Canadian adaptations which proclaimed the universal appeal of the greatest of comic writers.

With fine strength of purpose, the *Théâtre du Rideau Vert* (founded in 1948) was meanwhile making ready to become the only permanent theatre of Montreal. Mesdames Yvette Brind'Amour and Mercédès Palomino, after some groping about, found their formula for success: to compete with the cinema by offering to the Montreal public various types of shows calculated to please all tastes. While popular plays were liberally employed in making up the programmes, great contemporary dramatists were not neglected either. The *Théâtre du Rideau Vert* was to play Anouilh, Garcia Lorca, Montherlant, Sartre and Claudel. Finally a few Canadian authors (Félix Leclerc, Maurice Gagnon, Roger Sinclair) profited from the selective hospitality of the company and enriched the young French-Canadian theatre with their respective styles.

The *Théâtre-Club*, for its part, from 1954 adopted a policy which put it half-way between the *Théâtre du Nouveau Monde* and the *Théâtre du Rideau Vert*. Its directors, Jacques Létourneau and Monique Lapage, were to present each season two or three shows of very different persuasion, such as J. B. Priestley's *Le virage dangereux* and Musset's *Le chandelier*. The French-Canadian repertoire, in its beginnings, was to be represented by Marcel Dubé's *Le barrage*.

In the ten years between 1952 and 1962 more modestly endowed groups contributed to the creation of an atmosphere favourable to the theatre. The little theatre attempted a few interesting things.

La Poudrière, founded by Janine Beaubien in 1958, added a note of cosmopolitanism to Montreal's equatorial summers by giving its public plays in English, French, Italian and German. In 1959, the creation of *Egregore* rounded out the Montreal theatrical scene with the addition of this avant-garde theatre, made up particularly of young people who wanted to undertake the most audacious experiments.

The *Comédie-Canadienne,* whose goal is to encourage the birth of a national theatre, opened its doors in 1958. To the auditoriums already in existence has been added the municipal theatre of Montreal. Having little to envy on this score in London, Paris and New York, Montreal is confident about the future. Young playwrights, still too often deserters from television, will feel more and more drawn to a form of art which, for the first time, offers great possibilities for the expansion of an indigenous culture.

Paul Toupin (b. 1917)

The finest promise of contemporary French-Canadian literature was published in 1960 with the title *Souvenirs pour demain* (Le Cercle du Livre de France). Four plays[73] had preceded *Requiem,* a stylized "in memoriam," frightful in its experienced intensity and orchestrated in masterly fashion.

The revolt of writers of the period after the war seems to have provoked the most varied reactions—fierce irony in some, anticlericalism in others. Toupin keeps his distance and will seek his own emancipation, perhaps having judged the milieu to be unworthy of or unsuited to reform. The writing profession seemed to suit his temperament and to be the only really noble one in that it sanctions the search of self.

A pilgrimage to Spain (*Au delà des Pyrénées,* 1949) put Toupin immediately on the road where he belonged. The dignity of the Spanish people and the frankness of their self-expression were a revelation to him of the nature of his anxiety, which was to belong entirely to himself. Through all his work one can feel this yearning for the complete possession of personality through systematic rejection of the false values inherited from French-Canadian society. This is why he quite naturally writes praise of Berthelot Brunet (*Rencontre avec Berthelot Brunet,* Fides, 1950), whose bohemian life, the unexpected positions he takes, fascinate the young man looking for absolute freedom.

In the course of the next ten years Toupin wrote three plays which represent stages in the conquest of self. Largely egocentric, his theatre is organized around the meaning that must be given to one's inner freedom. For this reason there is a static quality to *Brutus, Le Mensonge* and *Chacun son amour*. Toupin talks about himself in a tone that is playful, mocking, sometimes serious, half-way between the confidences of a Sacha Guitry and the amusing affectation of a Giraudoux.

The Caesar in *Brutus,* like the Stéphane in *Chacun son amour*— two incarnations of the author—exposes the imposture of men who, in order to live, have need of false ideals, precisely those of which Toupin has rid himself. "I have believed," Caesar says to Brutus, "in more things than exist. There is a time for believing and a time to stop believing in what you believed." This is a thought which will be repeated in another key by Stéphane: "I have no theory about anything. Everybody lives with the nature he has and tries to make the best of it."

Having made the rounds of beliefs and sensations, Toupin has come now to a philosophy of the immediate. Love is only a vain word, friendship also. But bodies exist. When a woman offers herself and there is an affirmative response in the blood, a single act is imperative, an act to which no particular importance need be attached.

A theatre which ends in a commentary on life risks being weakened by declamatory speeches and witticisms. *Le Mensonge,* which brings to light the paradoxical element in truth, clearly indicates the rather narrow limits within which Toupin sees himself obliged to practise his art. *Brutus*, in its first version, though brilliant at times, was too much like a monologue and the writer felt the need of making it more alive in the second version, which appeared in 1960.

It was logical that Toupin should furnish a commentary on his theatre, that is to say on himself. *Souvenirs pour demain* are powerful in their immediate evocation. In looking back on his father's death, Toupin bequeaths to French-Canadian literature some of its most compelling pages. In them one perceives no pose in Toupin and his disenchantment, as bitter as it is real, puts him in a place far removed from that of the feeble iconoclasts who abound in French-Canadian literature today.

Toupin's plays will not appeal to a wide audience, but the living sound of them guarantees him first place in the literature for theatre now being born in French Canada.

Gratien Gélinas (b. 1909)

Tit-Coq (1948) in the history of French-Canadian theatre occupies a place analogous to that of *Bonheur d'occasion* in the novel. A long tradition of theatrical presentations had been established with some scattered French-Canadian creations which were short-lived. In the same way a few great novels had been published before *Bonheur d'occasion* but each of them had remained an isolated phenomenon. Before Gélinas there did not exist in Montreal an audience sufficiently large for a dramatic author to depend on it, while before Gabrielle Roy a collective movement in the direction of the novel had not yet taken shape.

Shortly before the war Gélinas had won over a following with his *Fridolinades*, sketches in which the public was apparently delighted to see itself caricatured. Gélinas' method, though polished later on, has never varied. The superstitious atavisms, the hopes and fears of the French-Canadian people expressed in language both racy and picturesque, became his infinitely variable hero. The plot, always melodramatic, is only a pretext.

Tit-coq takes up again the perennial experience of the ex-serviceman, deceived while he is away by his wife whom he counts on finding upon his return. Created during World War II, *Tit-Coq* makes too broad an appeal to political contingencies of the time to be taken up again today with any success. The New York failure was foreseeable. Written just for French Canadians· at a given moment in their history, this play, very important by reason of the possibilities in the new and different theatre it revealed, remains a mediocre work.

Bousille et les justes (Quebec: Institut littéraire du Québec, 1960) is of a superior order. Portrayal of the popular instincts is no longer mixed with political considerations or any others. A vague lawsuit puts members of one family at loggerheads with Bousille, a dim-witted fellow whose heart is in the right place. Comedy and tragedy are combined to make *Bousille* the most vital play in contemporary French-Canadian theatre.

The superiority of Gélinas, when his talent is compared with that of Toupin, is in his experience of crowds. Gélinas avoids by instinct the static element found in Toupin. With Gélinas everything becomes action. And because Gélinas seeks to express the soul of the people, his cast, better allocated, gives an impression of homogeneity and balance lacking in Toupin, who entrusts the fate of his plays to the magic presence of a mouthpiece.

Marcel Dubé (b. 1930)

While Toupin has established himself in the theatre of ideas and Gélinas in the humorous and somewhat caricatural reproduction of the face of French Canada, Marcel Dubé is still looking for a formula which will allow him to develop his view of the world. Four principal plays[74] reflect a very clear determinist slant and an imperfect technique.

For Dubé there is calamity in the end for the family that is poor, with inevitable antagonisms at work in the midst of it. Three of his plays show different facets of the drama of wounded pride, brought on by the act of living together.

Tarzan, the hero of *Zone*, head of a little band of near-delinquents, is the incarnation of the virtues and weaknesses of youth gone wrong in spite of itself: Joseph, the army private, engulfed in a mess that a disastrous family life and the sudden end of the war make it impossible to escape; Florence, who rushes to meet her seducer, urged on by the repressions of a life where she has been held down too long.

Dubé's plea for understanding—somewhat over-simplified in *Zone,* in which inherent good in the delinquents, underlined by their previous records, is taken up by their justice-loving defender—is less conspicuous in *Un simple soldat,* which is his best play. Joseph is touching in his downfall because his father, as weak as he is, by wanting to come to his rescue only brings final catastrophe.

Dubé's theatre suffers from being too close to television. The family nemesis—a perfectly legitimate conception in the drama— does not go well with the sensational turn of events, always found at the end of his plays. Joseph's ruin we accept because it has been inevitable from the beginning as a result of the ancestral forces which destroy him. But the ending of *Temps des lilas,* which belongs to a third-rate detective story, makes the odd life of the main characters even more improbable.

Suffering and disgrace from time immemorial have belonged to the repertory of the playwright, but he must lead up to them honestly. It is within the competence of any dramatic author to make us see wounds and hear cries. But real emotion is awakened only if there has been a skilful building up to those wounds and those cries.

With the disappearance of obstacles in the means of execution, to which Dubé has recourse for the interpretation of French-Canadian life, a powerful theatre might result. The canvas is vast, the palette is one of quality. All that remains is for the colours to be clear so that the picture can stand out.

Jacques Languirand (b. 1930)

Unlike Toupin, Gélinas and Dubé, who accept the theatrical norms of the past, Languirand makes a spontaneous decision in favour of avant-gardism, composed of symbol and anxiety. The play which defines him best is without doubt *Le gibet* (Le Cercle du Livre de France, 1960). The hero, Perplex, represents modern man in revolt against the pressures on him of a society which has little concern for individual values. A stylite monk of the twentieth century, Perplex establishes himself on top of a "post" to try to live there as long as possible. His act is the equivalent of a challenge to society. Perplex "dares" for others. His example influences a few neighbours who, if it were not for him, would have allowed themselves to be diverted by the unimportant little events of life, without ever being able to raise their eyes to the "gibbet." But men do not permit the individual to assert himself. Perplex will be abandoned even by those for whom he has procured a momentary rift in the cloud of monotony in which they live. That is the fate reserved for the men of vision and the benefactors of mankind.

The symbolism of *Le gibet* is imposed somewhat bluntly. More successful are the plays which, relieved by a smile, make Languirand's conclusions more easily acceptable. *Les violons de l'automne* (Le Cercle du Livre de France, 1962) produced an undeniably comic effect in presenting two old people, "Him" and "Her," on the threshold of a wedding night and making them pretend that they believe in the illusions they have in fact lost. *Les insolites* (*ibid.*, 1962), performed for the first time in 1956, makes it possible to estimate Languirand's progress in his search for dialogue suited to the stage. The repartee and a certain sadness, too, which account for the success of *Violins de l'automne*, are to be found also in *Les insolites*. But the playwright's lack of experience, the fact that he had not yet found quite the right key, were responsible for making his characters appear more preposterous than amusing and their retorts too obviously purposeful.

PHILOSOPHY, ERUDITION

Philosophy has yet to be born. There is nothing comparable in French Canada to the rise of an American philosophy, which is a philosophy of action relying on the methods of the natural sciences. After close consideration of this question it becomes very doubtful that French Canada will ever arrive at the establishment of a philosophical school of thought distinguishable from the great currents of world philosophy. Charles Sanders Peirce, William James, Josiah Royce, John Dewey, George Herbert Mead, in their optimistic anti-cartesianism are a reflection of that dynamic and profoundly original society that is the United States of America. French-Canadian society has its originality too, but this, instead of being in opposition to Europe, looks to it to find its stability in Catholicism. It is naturally possible, even probable, that with time French Canada may produce thinkers who will not owe everything to Thomism. To the extent that they move away from it they will become less representative of the French-Canadian community.

Is Thomism flexible enough to admit of redefinitions which take into account the future evolution of mankind? To this question Catholicism replies with a most affirmative "yes" and modern speculative thought with a categorical "no." That is to say that French-Canadian Thomism has no chance of issuing forth to the outside world and will always remain the expression of the philosophical particularism of the French Canadians.

It must be recognized that the riches of Thomism are far from having been fully exploited in French Canada. The Thomist doctrine, *essentiellement progressive et assimilatrice,* according to the formula of Jacques Maritain, can be so only if the great problems of the modern world are posed "first" and Thomist philosophy is brought to bear on them subsequently. Now, in French-Canadian universities the opposite procedure is often followed. *Philosophia perennis est.* The world in which we live fits into this framework as it can, and this is the origin of that air of Byzantinism which clings to the study of philosophy in French Canada.[75]

As for erudition, it is faring better. The two things wrong with it and which were noticeable at its beginnings, dilettantism and partiality, seem to be disappearing. Very fortunately, too, erudition today extends to domains other than those of history and national literature. The first significant French-Canadian contribution to French literature was the study by Roméo Arbour, *Henri Bergson et les lettres françaises* (Paris: José Corti, 1955). That a French-Canadian priest should be able quite serenely to approach French literature without attaching declarations of doctrine to aesthetic considerations and the history of ideas, is the best proof that French-Canadian society, without denying its spiritual origins, can and must participate in the peaceful battles of the modern spirit.

The *Dictionnaire canadien* (McClelland and Stewart, 1962), the work of a group of eminent linguists, will help in the years to come, when it is finished, to accredit the specifically French-Canadian lexicon. At the same time as the inevitable confirmation of the French-Canadian version of the French language is being accomplished, complementary works are being undertaken, works intended to confirm the close relationship which French Canadians have with French-speaking people the world over. When J. Vinay and J. Darbelnet published a *Stylistique comparée du français et de l'anglais* (Paris: Didier, 1958), in which the often complementary resources of the two languages are shrewdly analyzed, writers found themselves the first beneficiaries. English, which all French Canadians must come to terms with instead of letting it seep into their minds in fraudulent fashion, becomes more familiar and enriches, when all is said and done, the word possibilities of the writer who is aware of the two linguistic currents which are at the service of his thinking and feeling.

On a more immediately practical level the numerous works of Pierre Daviault, devoted to the problems of translation, have contributed effectively—from *Expression juste en traduction* (Editions Albert Lévesque, 1936) to *Langage et traduction* (Ottawa: The Queen's Printer, 1961)—towards maintaining the maximum number of contacts with the outside world.

French Canada has not yet produced a language school comparable to the one connected with Geneva and French Switzerland. Linguistic co-existence, which is debilitating for many French Canadians, should one day make it possible for linguists to arrive at original interpretations of their relatively privileged situation.

NOTES TO CHAPTER FIVE

1. By reason of the industrial growth in Montreal, particularly marked from the second half of the nineteenth century, the city of Quebec will progressively see its place taken by this rival as the pole of attraction of the French-Canadian elite. The Librairie Garneau, founded in Quebec in 1844, will nevertheless play an important role in the spread of French books. Some provincial publishing houses, still functioning, are worthy of mention: the Librairie Richer (Saint Hyacinthe, 1872); the Librairie Ayotte (Trois-Rivières, 1881). In Montreal the Librairie des Ecoles (1849) and the Librairie Granger (1885), will all share in the creation of a French-Canadian book business by their publication of religious and academic texts.

2. Cf. *The Canadian Catalogue of Books Published in Canada,* Toronto Public Libraries, 1940. Of this number sixty-five books (twenty-four per cent) are on religious subjects and thirty-nine (fourteen per cent) on the humanities.

3. Founded in 1934 by Robert Charbonneau, Paul Beaulieu and Claude Hurtubise.

4. Review edited by Guy Sylvestre.

5. M. Claude Hurtubise is its president (1962). The most active members are: Fides, Le Cercle du Livre de France, Beauchemin, Institut littéraire de Québec, Ecrits du Canada Français, Editions de l'Hexagone,

Presses Universitaires Laval, Editions de l'Université d'Ottawa, Editions du Jour, The Queen's Printer. The former *Société des Editeurs canadiens du livre français* was changed into the *Association des Editeurs canadiens* in 1961.

6. The French-Canadian exhibit comprises about 200 books chosen from those produced in the last ten years.

7. The Salon will bring together, outside of the twenty-five French-Canadian exhibitors, fifty French, five Belgian, two Swiss, two Italian and one from the Netherlands. The *Salon du livre* held at Quebec in October of 1962 showed noticeable progress over that of Montreal, which was held, however, only a few months earlier, as the participation of French and Belgian publishers has increased twofold.

8. In 1961, 1,100 books were published in French, that is, more than twice the number of the rapid-growth period from 1942 to 1946. (This statistic did not take into account Canadian government publications.) For a number of years the French book business has remained steady at between 12,000 and 15,000 books. The rhythm of growth in French-Canadian publishing makes it possible to envisage in about ten years time an annual production of 2,000 books. So, taking into account the French-speaking population (one-tenth of the population of France), the French-Canadian publishing business has attained a comparable level of productivity. Before the last war the majority of books published in French Canada belonged to three main categories: religion, national history (considered at times as illustrating the truths of the first) and belles-lettres. In our day publications are growing in diversity to take in the applied sciences and the humanities. From one generation to the other the proportion of publications of a literary nature has scarcely varied, between ten and fifteen per cent. Literature intended for religious enlightenment occupies an important place; while tending to level off in recent years it still represents between fifteen and twenty per cent of the book trade.

9. Cf. Appendix Two. To this important document should be added *Projections libérantes* (1949), a mimeographed pamphlet bearing, among others, the signature of Borduas, and published by Mithra-Mythe.

10. It seems that it was Alfred Pellan who, after his return to Canada in 1940, started Borduas on the path of surrealism, and that *Prisme d'yeux,* published by Pellan in February of 1948, influenced Borduas when he brought out *Refus global* some months later. Cf. Guy Robert, *Pellan, sa vie et son oeuvre* (Montreal: Editions du Centre de Psychologie et de Pédagogie, 1963), p. 52.

11. *L'Académie canadienne-française* (Montreal, 1955), p. 11. In Appendix III will be found a résumé of the activity of the Academy as well as the main clauses of its *Règlements* and a list of its members.

12. It is during a luncheon which takes place every autumn at the restaurant Au 400 that the jury chooses its prize-winner. In 1962 the jury was composed of the following members: Roger Duhamel (president), Mlle. Jeanne Lapointe, le R. P. Gay, MM. Jean Béraud, Jean-Charles Bonenfant, Pierre Daviault, Paul l'Anglais, Jean Simard, Guy Sylvestre.

Cercle du Livre de France prize-winners: 1950: Bertrand Vac (*Louise Genest*); 1951: André Langevin (*Evadé de la nuit*); 1952: Bertrand Vac (*Deux portes, une adresse*); 1953: André Langevin (*Poussière sur la ville*); 1954: Jean Vaillancourt (*Les Canadiens errants*); 1955: Jean Filiatrault (*Chaînes*); 1956: Eugène Cloutier (*Les inutiles*); Maurice Gagnon (*L'échéance*); Jean Simard (*Mon fils pourtant heureux*); 1957; Jean-Marie Poirier (*Le prix du souvenir*); 1958: Claire Martin (*Avec ou sans amour*); 1959: Pierre Gélinas (*Les morts, les vivants et les autres*); 1960: Claude Jasmin (*La corde au cou*); 1961: Diane Giguère (*Le temps des jeux*); 1962: (No award); 1963: Louise Maheu-Forcier (*Amadou.*)

13. Would there not seem to be an interesting comparison to be made, if we are to understand the special quality of the French-Canadian temperament, between Giroux's hero and Saint-Denys-Garneau, since the latter, in one of his most beautiful poems, describes a quite similar state of mind?

> *Après les plus vieux vertiges*
> *Après les plus longues pentes*
> *Et les plus lents poisons*
> *Ton lit certain comme la tombe*
> *Un jour à midi*
> *S'ouvrait à nos corps faiblis sur les plages*
> *Ainsi que la mer*
> *Après les plus lentes venues*
> *Les caresses les plus brûlantes*
> *Après ton corps une colonne*
> *Bien claire et parfaitement dure*
> *Mon corps une rivière étendue*
> > *et dressé pur jusqu'au bord de l'eau*
>
> *Entre nous le bonheur indicible*
> *D'une distance*
> *Après la clarté du marbre*
> *Les premiers gestes de nos cris*
> *Et soudain le poids du sang*
> *S'écroule en nous comme un naufrage*
> *Le poids du feu s'abat sur notre coeur perdu*
>
> *Après le dernier soupir*
> *Et le feu a chaviré l'ombre sur la terre*
> *Les amarres de nos bras se détachent*
> > *pour un voyage mortel*
> *Les liens de nos étreintes tombent d'eux-mêmes*
> > *et s'en vont à la dérive sur notre couche*
> *Qui s'étend maintenant comme un désert*
> *Tous les habitants sont morts*
> *Où nos yeux pâlis ne rencontrent plus rien*
> *Nos yeux crevés aux prunelles de notre désir*
> *Avec notre amour évanoui comme une ombre*
> > *intolérable*
> *Et nous sentions notre isolement s'élever*
> > *comme un mur impossible*

(*Poésies complètes* [Fides, 1949], pp. 139-140.)

In an analysis of Saint-Denys-Garneau, Lévis Fortier, on the subject of this poem, makes the following comment: "A debasing and sinful experience, the poet did not dwell on it and gives up every memory of sensual pleasure. He shows us in the same poem how imprudences of the carnal self sow disgust, loneliness and death. Instead of inexpressible joys what has he found? A terrible dismay." *Le message poétique de Saint-Denys-Garneau* (Ottawa: Les Editions de l'Université, 1954), p. 102.

14. *L'abatis* (Montreal: Fides, 1943), pp. 150-151.

15. A sensitive interpretation of the Acadian country, *La folle* (Fides, 1960), in the form of a lyric drama, completes *Le barachois.*

16. Quoted by Robert Charbonneau, *La France et nous* (Montreal: Editions de l'Arbre, 1945), p. 65.

17. *Mondes chimériques* (Montreal: Bernard Valiquette, 1940), p. 91.

18. *Neuf jours de haine* (Montreal: Editions de l'Arbre, 1948), p. 46.

19. Pseudonym: Bertrand Vac.

20. Pseudonym: Claire France.

21. Works: *Canada* (Paris: Flammarion, 1945); *Laframboise et Belle-humeur* (Paris, 1939); Eva Charlebois (Paris: Flammarion, 1944).

22. Paris: Plon, 1952.

23. *Répertoire*, p. 38.

24. Cf. pp. 229-230.

25. *La bagarre*, p. 56.

26. Pseudonym: Claire Martin.

27. Collaborators: Michel van Schendel, Gilles Hénault, Jacques Brault, Wilfrid Lemoine, Yves Préfontaine.

28. *Les poésies complètes,* with an excellent introduction by Robert Elie, was published by Fides in 1949. The *Journal,* with preface by Gilles Marcotte, was published in 1954 by Beauchemin. At the end of *Message poétique de Saint-Denys-Garneau* by Lévis Fortier (Les Editions de l'Université d'Ottawa, 1954), there is a bibliography of books and articles which have been devoted to the poet and his work. In *Ecrits du Canada français,* 1957, pp. 137-231, there is an interesting study by Gilles Marcotte.

29. *Poésies complètes*, p. 41.

30. *Ibid.,* p. 63.

31. *Ibid.,* p. 96.

32. *Ibid.,* p. 139.

33. They are: *Quitte le monticule impossible au milieu* and *Je te prierai ta grâce de me crucifier.*

34. *Les îles de la nuit* (Montreal: Lucien Parizeau, 1944), p. 66.

35. *Ibid.,* pp. 75-76.

36. *Rivages de l'homme* (Quebec: Charrier & Dugal, 1948), pp. 37-39.

37. *L'étoile pourpre* (Montreal: Les Editions de l'Hexagone, 1957), pp. 68-71.

38. *Mémoire sans jours,* p. 23.

39. Guy Robert has subjected the poetry of Anne Hébert to a suggestive analysis in *La poétique du songe* (Association Générale des Etudiants de l'Université de Montréal, 1962).

40. *Poètes de l'Amérique française* (Montreal: Editions Albert Lévesque, 1934), pp. 96-97.

41. *Suite marine* (Montreal: Paul Péladeau, 1953), pp. 186-187.

42. *Ibid.,* p. 248.

43. Works: *La fiancée du matin.* This first collection, published in Montreal in 1953, is out of print. *Les cloîtres de l'été* (Éditions de l'Hexagone, 1954); *L'homme et le jour* (*ibid.,* 1957); *La mouette et le large* (*ibid.,* 1960); *Recours au pays* (*ibid.,* 1961); *Pour saluer une ville* (Paris: Seghers, 1963).

44. Editions de l'Hexagone, 1958.

45. *Ibid.,* pp. 31-32.

46. Extracts from *Soleil sous la mort* (Ecrits du Canada Français, 1963), Vol. XVI, pp. 221-228, reveal an astonishing compactness, perfectly appropriate to the sorrowful subject of Hiroshima.

47. *Les belles au bois dormant* (Editions de l'Hexagone, 1960).

48. Works: *Le temps de vivre* (Les Editions Cité Libre, 1955).

49. Works: *Les armes à faim* (1955); *Le ciel fermé* (Editions de l'Hexagone, 1956).

50. Works: *Faire naître* (Editions Erta, 1949); *Yeux fixes* (*ibid.,* 1951); *Images apprivoisées* (*ibid.,* 1953); *Les armes blanches* (*ibid.,* 1954).

51. Editions Erta, 1954.

52. Cf. *Liberté,* March-April 1961, May-June 1963. If he were to write nothing else but *La braise et l'humus,* this poem of unhappy love would merit survival in the production of these last ten years.

53. *Docteur ès lettres* of Loyola University (Chicago), professor at the University of Montreal, then at the University of Ottawa, M. Frégault since 1962 has been a member of the new Department of Cultural Affairs of the province of Quebec.

Works: *La civilisation de la Nouvelle-France, 1713-1744* (Société des Editions Pascal, 1944); *Iberville le conquérant* (*ibid.,* 1944); *François Bigot, administrateur français* (Les Etudes de l'Institut d'Histoire de l'Amérique française, 1948), 2 vol.; *Le grand marquis* (Fides, 1952); *La guerre de la conquête* (*ibid.,* 1955).

54. M. Frégault carries his concern for accuracy to the point where he takes historians to task in the very text of his works on such items as dates of little importance (which he will place a few days later), the kind of correction which would find its place in a marginal note. As to the thousands of marginal notes, properly so called, with which these two works are furnished, one may believe that M. Frégault's reputation would not have suffered had he thought it useful to suppress some of them.

55. *La civilisation de la Nouvelle-France,* p. 280.

56. The deportation of the Acadians, it is learned, without the accident of history could have been carried out by France ("Was the only merit of France to be that, in spite of herself, she was in a physical position which made it impossible for her to perpetrate the misdeed which would redound to the shame of her rival nine years later?"). Vol. I, p. 240. Montcalm would seem to be only a narrow-minded colonialist, very much the inferior of Vaudreuil, the "Canadian." Does the demonstration of Montcalm's fundamental lack of ability run any risk of obscuring his reputation? It is enough to reflect on how impossible it was for witnesses of the last two world wars to come to any agreement on the unfolding and significance of the main events which marked their course to make one doubt that it would be possible to reconstruct the stratagem of battles which took place in the eighteenth century.

57. *La guerre de la conquête,* p. 459.

58. Born in Fort-de-France, Martinique, M. Rumilly studied at the Lycée Buffon and the Lycée Louis-le-Grand. His law studies having been interrupted by the war, he went into the infantry. When the First World

War was over he was attracted by *Action Française* and became associated with the *Camelots du Roi*. Despairing of the future of France, M. Rumilly seems to have come to Canada in search of a France nearer to his heart.

Works: Besides his *Histoire de la Province de Québec,* whose publication by different publishers came to thirty-three volumes in 1961, M. Rumilly has written studies on Sir Wilfrid Laurier, Mercier, etc., the main elements of which are to be found in his *Histoire.* His *Chefs de file* (Montreal: Editions du Zodiaque, 1934) are elegantly written interviews. *Le Frère Marie-Victorin et son temps* (Montreal: Les Frères des Ecoles Chrétiennes, 1949) is a reconstruction of the struggles French Canadians had to go through in order to have scientific training. M. Rumilly is the author of a *Histoire du Canada* (Paris: La Clé d'Or, 1951).

59. Histoire de la Province de Québec, Vol. III, pp. 82-83.

60. The second volume (1963) contains an interesting retrospective account of the economic activity and social state of New France for the years 1663-1713. With the third volume (1965), the whole *ancien régime* has been reviewed by Gustave Lanctot. The gap which the historian very early in his career had pointed out in Garneau's work, that is, the lack of sufficient economic and sociological data, has now for the most part been filled.

In Appendix Four one may consult the declaration which M. Gustave Lanctot at our suggestion consented to draw up to explain his conception of history.

61. A graduate of the *Ecole libre des sciences politiques,* M. Bruchési was Professor of International Politics at the University of Montreal (1929) and Editor-in-Chief of *La revue moderne* (1930-1937). Several times a delegate from the University of Montreal or from Canada to different international meetings, M. Bruchési has sought to be of service to French-Canadian letters by making himself the apostle of a broad French culture. M. Bruchési was appointed Canadian ambassador to Madrid in 1961.

Principal works: *Aux marches de l'Europe* (Editions Albert Lévesque, 1932), *Rappels* (Editions Bernard Valiquette, 1941); *Histoire du Canada* (Beauchemin, 1951); *Témoignages d'hier* (Fides, 1961).

62. It would be unfair to omit Edmond Boisvert [Edmond de Nevers] (1862-1906) whose two works—*L'avenir du peuple canadien-français* (Paris: Henri Jouve, 1896) and *L'âme américaine,* 2 vol. (Paris: Jouve & Boyer, 1900)—are by way of a precursor. Having lived in Berlin where he had studied with Theodore Mommsen in 1888, he came to think that in the United States only two nationalities would escape the American steam-roller. He even imagined a string of French-speaking towns stretching from Louisiana to Quebec. The Middle West was destined to be subject to Germanic influence. These extravagant prognostications are accompanied by what are occasionally very wise observations on the American temperament, expressed in a language superior to that of French-Canadian historians of the period.

63. Principal works: *L'influence de Voltaire au Canada* (Fides, 1945); *Louis XVI, le Congrès americain et le Canada* (Quebec: Publications de l'Université Laval, 1949); *Le régime militaire dans le gouvernement de Trois-Rivières, 1760-1764* (Trois-Rivières: Editions du Bien Public, 1952); *Chiniquy (ibid.,* 1955); *L'esclavage au Canada français* (Quebec: Les Presses Universitaires Laval, 1960).

64. *J'avoue ne plus croire que nous puissons jamais rendre compte de nous-mêmes en français à cause d'un fait primordial: l'invention et la forme de l'Amérique ne sont pas françaises (Convergences, p. 27).*

65. A doctoral thesis presented before the Faculty of Arts of the University of Montreal in 1950 and published by Beauchemin in 1960.

66. Cf. "Présence du poète Alain Grandbois," *Le Devoir,* October 20, 1962.

67. *Foi et littérature* (Beauchemin, 1959), p. 16.

68. *Le Devoir,* November 9, 1957.

69. *Ibid.,* November 16, 1957.

70. *Ibid.*

71. *Les arts, les lettres et les sciences au Canada* (Ottawa, 1951), p. 94.

72. Jean Béraud's study, *Trois cent cinquante ans de théâtre au Canada français* (Le Cercle du Livre de France, 1958), deals necessarily with the plays from the Classical and Romantic repertory which have been given in Canada since the beginning of the seventeenth century, with actors and impresarios who have not despaired of the future of theatre in the country. For the contemporary period see: Jean Hamelin, *Le renouveau du théâtre français* (Les Editions du Jour, 1961).

73. For the publication of his *Théâtre* (Le Cercle du Livre de France, 1961), Toupin did not retain *Le Choix,* his first work. The three plays that were republished are entitled: *Brutus* (1950); *Le Mensonge* (1952); *Chacun son amour* (1955).

74. *Zone* (created in Montreal in 1953) and published in Vol. II of *Ecrits du Canada français*; Le temps des lilas (Quebec: Institut littéraire du Québec, 1958); *Un simple soldat (ibid.,* 1958); *Florence (ibid.,* 1960).

75. The controversy which arose on the subject of the introduction of the French *baccalauréat* in Canada is very instructive in this regard: *L'introduction du baccalauréat français au Canada* (Montreal: Fides, 1946). The author, Jean de Stavelot, concludes that the French philosophy programme is clearly positivist and contrary to Thomist philosophy. To this statement Julien Peghaire, a French priest, replies that this programme can be treated in Christian and Thomist fashion and that the two conceptions in fact, the Christian and the French, complement rather than exclude each other. Julien Peghaire makes this remark which is essential to an understanding of the difference between an *a priori* and an *a posteriori* Thomist theory:

> . . . The philosophy programme in secondary schools in France contains problems which are not posed in Scholastic philosophy: that these problems are important in themselves and for the training of young men of today; that, consequently, the Scholastic programme would complete and perfect itself by posing these same problems and solving them according to the fundamental principles of St. Thomas. [*trans.*] Jean de Stavelot, *op. cit.,* p. 231.

M. Jacques Brault, Professor of Philosophy in the University of Montreal, is in substantial agreement with our opinion in the following declaration:

> In French Canada philosophical research has scarcely begun and we must admit that we have lived our Middle Ages before our Antiquity . . . Thomists or not, too many of our philosophers have

practised philosophy like a haughty, snarling, niggling religion, ready to lay the ban, or like a high-voltage exercise in ideas whose precise and rigid rules required a total absence of initiative and imagination. I think, nevertheless, that some day there will be given to us a philosopher who will deal with man as no other and in accents unheard up to that time. What he says will be valuable because it will have put its roots down into our soil so deep, so close, that when all is said and done what is individual in it will have the most universal values. [*trans.*] (*Livres et auteurs canadiens,* 1961, p. 77).

For a more favourable interpretation of French-Canadian Thomism see: Edmond Gaudron, "French-Canadian Philosophers," in *The Culture of Contemporary Canada,* published by Julian Park, Cornell University Press, 1957, pp. 274-292.

CHAPTER VI

FRENCH-CANADIAN LITERATURE
IN ITS RELATIONS WITH
FRANCE AND FRENCH CULTURE

Since its origins French-Canadian literature has developed symbiotically with French literature. While in a condition of absolute dependence in relation to the parent literature at first, French-Canadian writing has taken on a look of its own which becomes more pronounced every day. That this literature, born of a people whose destiny it is to expand in the middle of an American and Anglo-Saxon continent, should owe but little to the mentality surrounding it says much for its spiritual foundations. In a reflex action, of which French Canada is not the only example in the history of conquered peoples, these writers have made use of the foreign elements which have seeped through and which, with time, have become a part of the national consciousness.

For any real understanding of the direct relationship between French-Canadian and French literatures, the deep-seated reasons for it, and its present and future effects on the course of French-Canadian writing, it is necessary to recall the conditions in which it has been possible for Franco-Canadian relations to develop since the Conquest.

If it had not been for the Treaty of Paris, New France, in what has since become standard procedure, sooner or later would have proclaimed its independence. As an American-based people, the French Canadians afterwards exerted constant pressure on England for recognition of their collective personality. At the height of this struggle France was regarded as trustee of the genius of the *race*. In proportion as Canada, by means of population and political and social organization, became *anglicized,* the French-Canadian elite redoubled its efforts to escape the Anglo-Saxon hold on it, at the same time multiplying its contacts with France. Concurrently with this re-emphasis of French personality, renewed with each generation, a change was taking place in the people—slowly in the nineteenth century but accelerated since then—in the direction of a society increasingly influenced by the United States.

It was in 1855 that diplomatic relations could be officially resumed for the first time between France and Canada.[1] The way had been

251

paved for this event by the French Canadians themselves who, in 1853, had sent Guillaume Barthe to France as their emissary. "The idea of kissing . . . this soil of France," he declared afterwards, "caused a veritable ecstasy in me."[2] Having come to France with no support other than feelings of veneration for the country of his ancestors, this French-Canadian patriot was able to interest a number of outstanding and highly placed persons of the Second Empire in his plan to create permanent links between France and French Canada. Villemain, in his capacity of perpetual secretary to the French Academy, undertook to interpret to his colleagues the hopes of the French Canadians. Elie de Beaumont, perhaps because of his Norman origin, called on Barthe to invite him to attend the Monday sessions of the Academy, granting him one of the seats reserved for honorary members.

By the time that Barthe was ready to return to Canada, doubtless without realizing difficulties that it had been possible to ignore only because of the fact that he was a French Canadian, he had obtained permission for the *Institut Canadien* to be associated with the *Institut de France*. When he was given this news he was told, "You, sir, have obtained what our provincial academies have never been able to get and do not even dream of asking for any more."[3] Later on Thiers made a gift of his works to the *Institut Canadien* and the comte de Nieuwerkerke, "surintendant" of fine arts, obtained from Napoleon III the gift of some *objets d'art* to decorate the lecture room of the new French-Canadian institution.

It was under these happy auspices that the voyage of Commander de Belvèze occurred in 1855—a voyage which has remained famous in French Canada.[4] There was great excitement when a frigate bearing the French flag was seen coming up the St. Lawrence towards Quebec City. On hearing the news crowds of people hurried down, crying, "Our people have come back!"[5] A keen observer, Belvèze was astonished to find in the outlying country a population that had remained entirely French in language and customs. In his report to Napoleon III he called attention to the fact that "this French race is still numerous, lively, full of memories and affection for France, and it holds the first naval and military position in Canada. It can be only to our advantage in the future to foster and to revive what remains of our nationality, not with any intention of absorbing it or conquering it but in the interest of our political and commercial relations."[6]

The nature of French-Canadian feeling for France in the nineteenth century was clearly shown during the Franco-Prussian War and particularly after the downfall of France. The event produced an explosion of sympathy in French Canada and was the first occasion on which no longer just a few but a good many Frenchmen came to realize that across the seas lived a friendly population.[7] The relations between France and French Canada which, up to that time, had been only occasional, became increasingly close. The humiliation of France and, consquently, that felt vicariously by numerous French Canadians, contributed to the strengthening of Franco-Canadian friendship.[8] "In peoples as in families," declared a Consul of France in Quebec in 1877, "blood tells. Let us hope that France will see herself in this daughter, cut off from her for more than a century, a daughter piously treasuring in her heart love for the mother country. Now, in our present misfortune, the French-Canadian nation brings us consolation for she is the living declaration of national rights as opposed to conquest. . . ."[9]

Perhaps never in the history of Franco-Canadian relations have French Canadians felt closer to each other than in the last quarter of the nineteenth century. André Siegfried, who wrote a book on Canada at the beginning of our own century which received wide attention, made himself the mouthpiece of his countrymen when he qualified the interest which France was beginning to take in Canada as *passioné.*[10] Siegfried added: "Those of our politicians who have visited the shores of the Saint-Lawrence . . . as Frenchmen, in the broad meaning of the word, have met a reception there which they can never forget."[11]

There was a cooling-off period as a result of the anti-catholic politics of the Third Republic. Several French monks took refuge in Canada where—like those priests before them who had thrown in their lot with Canada at the time of the Revolution—they helped to underline the shift in the religious feeling of the two peoples.

Then came the First World War. The Franco-English alliance did not have the result that was expected. The French Canadians, from instincts of self-preservation, preferred on the whole to serve the cause of French culture by staying at home.

The years between the two wars were to see the upset of the very foundations of the French-Canadian society as it had endured for centuries and which, from being an agricultural society, had begun to be proletarian. Progressively less influenced by the Church, the majority of the French-Canadian people was rudely catapulted into a world which sought ideals other than its own.

In 1940, when France bowed to Germany again in conditions which endangered the very idea of French culture, French Canada's reaction was weaker than in 1870. Meanwhile, Canada has grown. In our own time the survival of the French Canadians, long in doubt, is assured. The traditional bitterness between Canadians of the two original nationalities is lessening and French Canadians hold high positions in the country. In our day there is no longer a Fréchette or a Faucher de Saint-Maurice anxious to identify himself in every way with France, since French Canada has discovered a political dedication and is beginning to create a literature of its own. As for the people at large for whom the busy modern world has an increasing attraction, it is the American ideal they understand instinctively. Is this to say that the cultural and sentimental bonds which exist between France and French Canada are destined progressively to loosen? The answer is no, because the emancipation of Africa is creating a new dimension in the relations between the two countries. Very rich when compared to the new French-speaking states, French Canada is aware that it is in a position to share in their development. France, which would be unable to provide for all the needs of its former colonies, asks nothing better than to benefit from the disinterested co-operation of French Canada. Thus, among Frenchmen, Africans and French Canadians is being formed a linguistic and cultural community beneficial to them all. Moreover, whatever may be the ups and downs of the French-Canadian people, in the future the writers whose situation in America is so exceptional will for a long time be like a living hyphen between France and Canada.

French-Canadian literature, imperfect as it may be as the expression of the conscience of a young people, has always been something of a gamble. All French-Canadian writers, without exception, in addition to the difficulties inherent in the art of writing have had to surmount those peculiar to their linguistic and spiritual isolation. But even in the heroic period of French-Canadian literature, when the timid efforts of its writers ran the risk of sinking into oblivion forever, it always found a friendly voice in France to encourage the birth of an indigenous literature in French Canada.

The first collection of poetry to be published in French Canada was that of Michel Bibaud. Now this event did not pass unnoticed in France where Isidore Lebrun[12] wrote a favourable review of this poetry in the *Revue encyclopédique de Paris*, while reproaching the poet for failing to describe French-Canadian customs.[13] Garneau's historical work was summed up in the *Revue des deux mondes* and brought its author numerous favourable notices; *Jean Rivard*, notwithstanding the fact that his was a work lacking in polish, appeared serially in *Le Monde*; samples of Etienne Parent's writings were published in *La Gazette de France*; Chauveau's *Charles Guérin* found reviewers also. If it is true that this literary product awakened the benevolent curiosity of only a very limited number of Frenchmen, it would be impossible to exaggerate the

importance of even the slightest word of encouragement for French
Canadians of that era. Etienne Parent had copied by hand a work
that he had been unable to purchase for lack of money, so much
did he wish "to keep up with France and to find in its doctrines and
lofty inspirations the secret of our emancipation."[14] In the almost
complete silence into which the literary product of so many of the
first French-Canadian writers was to fall, those voices from the
other side of the Atlantic, however scarce, were of inestimable value
in French Canada. In these conditions one can understand that
when the French Academy in 1880 for the first time awarded a
prize to a French Canadian, this fraternal gesture produced such
an impression that nearly half a century later the critic Henri d'Arles,
in evoking the presence of Fréchette in the Académie Française,
cried out:

To find himself here under this cupola, face to face with the Im-
mortals, in the midst of all that Paris holds to be most distinguished
in letters and in the arts . . . to hear his name proclaimed, his work,
published far off, praised . . . ah! what a divine moment . . . What
infinite compensation for the neglect of which one has been the
object at home! Intellectual France dispensed justice . . . Fréchette
was thus the first Canadian crowned by the French Academy. Such
a distinction was a great event. In the history of our literature it
is epoch-making.[15] [*trans.*]

It is true that those about to receive these honours, and many
French Canadians along with them, have not always made a distinction between the homage paid to literature on such occasions
and that, often more decisive, paid to fidelity to France.[16] Louis
Dantin regrets that the Academy in this way has encouraged
"ridiculous illusions."[17] For once he was too severe. The tradition
begun by the Academy in 1880 is in conformity with the spirit of
the institution. And, all things considered, the numerous literary
prizes awarded since that time to French-Canadian authors by that
illustrious company have had a salutary effect on French-Canadian
literature.

Along with this official honour, the less public recognition
accorded to French Canada and French-Canadian historians by
French critics and men of letters constitutes a little-known chapter
in the history of Franco-Canadian cultural relations.[18] It is, nevertheless, on this level that French-Canadian writers and their opposite
numbers in France have become acquainted, at least through correspondence, and that France has exerted a subtle and very useful
influence on French-Canadian letters.[19] Many are the French-
Canadian writers who have felt better understood by a few French
friends than by their compatriots.[20]

French criticism, too, has played an important role by contributing to the shaping of taste in French-Canadian critics who are inclined either to go into raptures or to attack with systematic savagery.

In this regard Charles ab der Halden deserves quite special mention. This man, unknown as a critic in France, has left his mark on the difficult beginnings of French-Canadian literature, as Quesnel has done. At a time when real criticism was confined to the works of Camille Roy and Dantin, Halden, by his *Etudes de littérature canadienne-française* (1904) and his *Nouvelles études* (1907),[21] gave distinguished proof of the use that a professional critic can make of a peripheral literature. He rendered a service to French-Canadian writing in making known the results of his research on the Garibaldian phase of Buies' life and indicated what remained to be done to rescue from obscurity one of the very exceptional French-Canadian writers who had had real wit. Finally, by his review of Chapman, Charles ab der Halden furnished a model of the unmerciful attack that objective criticism may be permitted to make.

In short, all through the century following its long and arduous expansion, French-Canadian literature has benefited from the moral support that official France at one time or another has accorded and from the benevolent way in which some of its men of letters have stood behind it. French Canadians and Frenchmen in these cultural exchanges were following what has always been a natural inclination. It is easy for the Frenchman to call up the touching picture of a small people of his own nationality continuing, in adverse circumstances and against all expectations, to speak the language of France, and for the French Canadian to see it as his duty to perpetuate in America the noblest tradition of a supremely civilized nation.

Will this latent and reciprocal sympathy, still noticeable in our day in the two peoples, withstand the increasingly numerous contacts which are being established between them? Ready-made notions entertained on both sides of the Atlantic risk disappearing into thin air before the reality of two centuries which have been lived apart. Nevertheless, supposing that the last illusions do fade away, there will always remain the powerful bond of language.

It is French-Canadian writers who can best tell us how necessary it is to build up strength from the common source of the French language. It is true that certain voices have been raised in vindication of the rights of a French-Canadian language sufficiently removed from French to be distinguishable.[22] Yet French-Canadian literary tradition is proof that this outcome is unlikely.

Arthur Buies was one of the first to launch a campaign to purify the language.[23] His diagnosis of the chronic malady from which the French language suffers in Canada is not entirely inapplicable even today:

There is one thing in our case which will be eternally detrimental not only to our correct use of French but to the familiarity and intimacy of our feeling for it, and that is the fact that we live in an English milieu, that we are surrounded by the English. . . . I put it to you that the majority of public men, professional men, all those who have some professional career or other, know less French than English, that unconsciously they are habitually using a quantity of English words and expressions. I shall go further, and though the whole legal profession fall on me and skin me alive, I will say that in general our lawyers . . . speak neither English nor French, but a crude jargon that can be understood only because one is accustomed to it. . . . It is not their fault; it is the milieu in which we live. . . . Here business, industry, finance and the arts and trades, even education, even habits, even the way we say *bonjour* or blow our nose, everything is English. How is it possible for our language to resist all these outside influences which act on it all the time, enveloping it, strangling it?[24] [*trans.*]

A century later this theme would be taken up again by Roch Valin:

For about fifty years writers in this country have been using language that is an instrument of increasingly doubtful purity, spotted with anglicisms, which insinuate themselves increasingly as they grow in number. Even the educated public is becoming less and less sensitive to these anglicisms, the growing practice of bilingualism having flouted its vigilance, allowing it to think English in French words.[25] [*trans.*]

Close contact with France would be the only solution:

There is only one last hope: to turn our attention more than ever to France and to set ourselves resolutely to learning its language all over again. . . . The only positive chance of survival at hand is in the closest possible linguistic adhesion to the French-speaking peoples of Europe.[26] [*trans.*]

These remarks call for a few additional considerations. If it is indisputably true that many French-Canadian writers are expressing themselves in an impoverished and frequently incorrect French, must the conclusion be that they are the victims of their Anglo-Saxon milieu as Buies would have it? This, no doubt, is partly so. It does seem, however, that the most convincing explanation has scarcely held the attention of the critics.

As a North American the French-Canadian writer moves in a world where action takes precedence over abstract thought. The French Canadian, whose Catholicism would normally incline him towards non-worldly preoccupations, is accustomed from his school days to being confronted with few obstacles of a speculative nature and comes to maturity with a North American (rather than a French) intellectual outlook. The lack of elegance and of correctness in French-Canadian prose is explained only by the author's incomplete cultural background. The obstacle is not so much the omnipresent English as a French that has been poorly learned.

For the French-Canadian writer there will always be one sovereign remedy against the foreign language all around him, to keep in touch frequently and closely with French literary tradition. For more than a century, out of necessity, this is indeed the path that the majority of these writers have followed. But it is for not having been sufficiently persevering and tenacious in their acquaintance with the best authors that most of them have left us unpolished works.

Having admitted this we must recognize that it is easy to exaggerate the importance of language and that the linguistic dispute has often hidden some essential literary truths in French Canada.

Grammatical correctness is not in itself an element of beauty. In the history of French literature most great prose writers—Flaubert at the head of the list—have committed numerous offences against the language. Genius has its own laws and has no need of the hobbles invented by professors and critics. If the artist attains his goal what does anything else matter? For the writer this goal is to transcribe, by means of the written language, the meaning of the world as he sees it. The unfortunate thing is that language is an inheritance which no single writer can significantly alter. And this is the reason why most of us, in order to be understood, are obliged to express ourselves according to tradition, that is to say according to school grammar. In other words we are to be blamed for "offences" only in so far as they stand like obstacles between the original creative idea and the reader's comprehension. When the writer—and literary history gives us examples of it—succeeds in forging a style of his own, somewhat outside the established linguistic norms, this freedom is more often the outward sign of a profound knowledge of the inherited language. In the twentieth century such is the case of Marcel Proust who rethought the French language to make it serve an exceptional sensibility.

Now this is precisely where we have the quarrel between the supporters of Canadian-French and French-French. Should the greatest possible use be made of French-Canadian archaisms, even the anglicisms and solecisms which abound in the spoken French of the average French Canadian? Or, on the other hand, must there be an effort to follow as closely as possible the language of the classical authors of France, ancient and modern? Each school in each generation has its supporters. There is no doubt, however, about the solution to these problems. The debate has lasted so long only for lack of great writers who would have settled the question once and for all by their example.

Clearly it would be impossible to lay down the law in one direction or the other on what is the ideal literary language. The Americans, like all young peoples, have struggled with the same difficulties. Their literary tradition includes Henry James, whose language is indistinguishable from that of the best English writers, and it has as well Mark Twain, whose works are filled with regional expressions.

The present generation of French-Canadian writers is only beginning to free itself from the pseudo-dilemma of language. The glorious and overwhelming example of French literature, a literature of prose writers *par excellence,* has hidden one obvious fact that is evident in other traditions, particularly in the Russian. Life comes before style. Doubtless the pinnacle of art is reached when these two elements merge harmoniously. But how many of the great writers of literature known throughout the world are models of linguistic perfection? The fact is that language, if it is to be living, calls for life. And life can indeed be there in its natural state and burst into a text without the help of the Academy.

Much more significant for the historian of French-Canadian literature than the linguistic question is that of French Classicism.

In its infinite variety, which admits of the most contradictory forms of art, French literature, as compared to other great Western literatures, remains Classical. At the very core of Classicism, as it is understood in France, there is the idea of *clarity*. In the short history of French-Canadian literature the most eminent critics, like Dantin and Camille Roy, have sounded the refrain of clarity. So it is important to see precisely what French-Canadian literature owes to the Classical tradition.

Although the idea of clarity has varied in France through the centuries, customarily it extends to precision of vocabulary, clearness of ideas, care in making transitions and, finally, to the harmonious arrangement of the elements that make up literary works.[27] This is the highest ideal of the seventeenth century, an ideal to which most of the great writers who brought fame to French literature in that era adhered. Romanticism did seem able for a certain time to upset the established aesthetic order. But in the last analysis it is the Classical tradition that is shown to be the stronger. In the twentieth century philosophy, poetry and the novel have found in Bergson, Valéry, Gide and Mauriac writers who are the proof that, in France, Classicism in the broad sense can be endlessly renewed and corresponds to what is most original in the French genius.

In the nineteenth century, at the time when European nationalisms found a profound echo in national literatures, it was relatively easy in France for *la clarté française* to become a kind of patriotic dogma preached by the critics. The number of earnest critics who have been led to discover that there are elements of clarity in French literature of the Middle Ages, in which the salient feature is *desmesure* (immoderation), is astonishing. Even in our own day it is not uncommon to read that French Classicism goes back to the *chansons de geste*.[28]

In Canada where the French elite turned to France after the Conquest it was inevitable that the critics should adapt for their own a dogma which lent itself to their hopes all the more readily in that it was of the Christian century of Louis XIV. In the history of French-Canadian criticism one would look in vain for a single voice raised to put the debate on a plane of aesthetics or of the history of Western criticism.[29] Influenced by French criticism and especially by that of the universities, French-Canadian critics from the end of the nineteenth century have made themselves the faithful disciples of French professorial criticism. Through them the younger generations of French Canada have had set before them the same ideal of clarity which has been drilled into French school boys for generations.

It was Camille Roy more than anyone else who constituted himself defender of the French virtue of clarity. During his reign he never stopped preaching to future writers the absolute necessity of studying the writers of French Classicism.[30] In Dantin also one can observe a conception of aesthetics which has its origin in this same clarity. These two critics with their followers have contributed to making French-Canadian literature veer away from its Romantic sources.

Contemporary literature includes prose writers like Robert Elie who fall little short of the Classical ideal in the simplicity of the means employed and the moderation of the vocabulary. Others, Giroux among them, are close to the masters of the French novel of analysis, dependent also on an essential element of Classicism,

since clearly marked boundaries of the passions are always styliza-
tions of reality. Others again, like André Langevin and Roger
Lemelin, show a more specifically native mood which is characterized by an overflowing energy that is impatient of restraints of
style and language. In all these writers there is an indication of what
the future of French-Canadian letters will be.

Taken altogether French-Canadian literature seems destined to
find its equilibrium and its true originality in what will be a
combination of the two spirits, French and Anglo-Saxon. France,
by means of its literature, will offer to future French-Canadian
writers the always fruitful example of what thought can accomplish
when joined with form and eloquence. The Anglo-Saxon world
by its political genius and powerful social organization will direct
French-Canadian minds towards a sense of human solidarity, but
perhaps also towards sentimentality. These divergent influences will
be reconciled in the French-Canadian literature of tomorrow by
that powerful religious sentiment which ensures the survival of
French-Canadian culture in America. Brought to a high human
standard, this literature could in time join proudly those other
literatures growing all across the world today.

NOTES TO CHAPTER SIX

1. Eight years earlier the government of Louis-Philippe had given to a
representative named Vattemare the responsibility of stirring up the
book trade between Canada and France. From 1763 to 1855 relations
between France and Canada had never been completely broken.

2. *Le Canada reconquis par la France* (Paris: Ledoyen, 1855), p. vii.

3. Guillaume Barthe, *ibid.,* p. 349. It appears that the association on
which Barthe depended was reduced to modest proportions since the
Institut de France seems to have ensured the sending of only certain of
its publications (cf. Jean Bruchési, *Témoignages d'hier,* Fides, 1961, pp.
191-195).

Since the publication of our first edition, M. Auguste Viatte has been
good enough to consult the *Archives de l'Institut* to verify the nature of
this "association." In a letter dated November 6, 1960, he writes:

    I have verified since, in the *Archives de l'Institut,* that he never
    obtained anything, actually, unless it was the sending of some
    academic publications, nothing in any case having any resemblance
    to an 'affiliation.' Three out of seven of his proposals had been kept
    for study; I find no trace of this study after he left France and I
    have a strong impression that the presentation of the statutes of
    the *Institut Canadien de Montréal* put an end to this study by con-
    vincing the members of the Academy that there existed no common
    measure between their learned Companies and an Association open
    to all, which took in without any election beforehand anybody
    interested in its activities, a little like the *Sociétés d'Emulation* which
    were growing rapidly in France in the same period.

4. Paul-Henry de Belvèze (1801-1875). Descendant of an old Montauban family, Paul-Henry entered the Polytechnique in 1820. Joining the Royal Navy two years later, he was named *enseigne de vaisseau* in 1825 and *capitaine de frégate* in 1837. He was charged with various diplomatic missions to Spain, to Greece and the Holy Land. *Commandeur de la Légion d'honneur* in 1852, he undertook his last and most important mission when he re-established, in the name of the Emperor, diplomatic relations between Canada and France.

Belvèze was a good letter-writer (*Lettres*, Bourges: Typographie Pigelet & Fils et Tardy, 1882). Having retired to Toulon, he wrote to his friend Rohault de Fleury in 1869: "If I were alone, with no family, and younger, I should be inclined to cross the sea to that North America where the society of the future is growing and to put myself in a front seat to watch this old European society break down . . . . " (*Lettres,* p. 234).

5. Paul-Henry de Belvèze, *Mission de la Capricieuse au Canada en 1885,* p. 49. Library of the University of British Columbia, Vancouver.

6. *Ibid.,* pp. 84-85.

7. Here is the description by Faucher de Saint-Maurice of the reaction of the French-Canadian crowd to the announcement, made by Germany, of the surrender of the French army:

> That evening . . . the offices of *L'Evénement* were still open. An enormous crowd, silent, were in the way as they lined up at the door. . . . Some—says an eyewitness—were dismayed and looked thunderstruck. Others laughed out loud at the foolishness of people who could believe in King Wilhelm's message; they were being mildly merry so as to leave no place for despair. They were all waiting anxiously for the publication of the despatches, divided between a painful belief and a vague hope, when suddenly the crowd made way respectfully for M. Gauthier, Consul-General of France. There was silence at once; all eyes turned to him. From his solemn mien which seemed to convey emotion and that unmistakable air which reveals a broken heart, there was no doubt in anybody's mind and all eyes were set with tears. For a long time people stayed there, weeping silently, surrounding the French representative with the keenest sympathy, the deepest respect. . . . France vanquished will receive more resounding expressions of respect but never a more sincere testimony of affection. [*trans.*] *Le Canada et les Canadiens-français pendant la guerre franco-prussienne* (Quebec: A. Côté, 1888), pp. 41-42.

8. To understand the evolution of French-Canadian feelings for France it is useful to recall Louis Fréchette and so many other writers of the nineteenth century who considered themselves *Français d'Amérique*. When in Chicago in 1870 Fréchette and his friend Alphonse Leduc pounced on four Germans who had just been singing too heartily the praises of Germany in front of the offices of the *Chicago Tribune*. A little later in the same city Fréchette fought a duel with a German guilty of having written disparagingly of France.

Cf. Marcel Dugas, *Un romantique canadien* (Paris: Editions de la Revue Mondiale, 1934), p. 38.

9. J. Guérard, *La France Canadienne* (Paris: Charles Douniol & Cie, 1877), p. 45.

10. *Le Canada puissance internationale* (Paris: Armand Colin, 1937), p. 41. This book, with the one that had preceded it in 1907, *Le Canada, les deux races*, has not lost its timeliness. In this regard Siegfried will have played a role for Canada similar to that of Tocqueville for the United States.

11. *Le Canada puissance internationale,* p. 143.

12. Born in Normandy in 1786, Isidore Lebrun entered the university in 1808. In 1816 he was holding a chair in Fine Arts when he resigned because education seemed to him to be passing into the hands of the religious bodies. Works: *De l'instruction publique sous Napoléon et de l'Université* (1814); *Tableau statistique et politique des deux Canadas* (1833); *Miscellanées maritimes et littéraires* (1858).

13. Bibaud reproduced the article in his *Magasin du Bas-Canada* (1832), pp. 21-22.

14. Guillaume Barthe, *Souvenirs d'un demi-siècle* (Montreal: Chapleau & Fils, 1885), p. 283.

15. *Louis Fréchette* (Toronto: The Ryerson Press, 1924), pp. 14-15.

16. Xavier Marmier (1809-1892) had written a book, which attracted wide attention at the time, on his travels in America: *Lettres sur l'Amérique* (Paris: Arthur Bertrand, 1851), 2 vol. He had shown a keen interest in French Canada and seems to have done what he could to make it possible for the Academy to designate one of its prizes to a foreigner:

> It was M. X. Marmier who, as a traveller, we think, discovered French-Canadian poetry and made himself the patron of M. Fréchette. For the first time the Academy awarded one of its prizes to a work written in the French language by a foreigner. It considered that the author belonged to our race and seized the opportunity to strengthen the oneness of origin and to draw tighter the bonds of friendship between France and Canada. [*trans.*]

The above commentary appeared in *Polybiblion* (June 1881). Quoted by W. Chapman, *Le lauréat* (Quebec: Léger Brousseau, 1894), p. 315.

17. *Gloses critiques* (Montreal: Lévesque, 1931), p. 71.

18. After Isidore Lebrun, mention should be made of Louis-Etienne Dussieux (1813-1894), professor of history at Saint-Cyr who, through his *Canada sous la domination française* (Paris: Librairie Victor Lecoffre, 1883), first published in 1855, wished to interest his compatriots in Canada: "Canadians [French Canadians] thank me for being the first Frenchman to give an account of their efforts to escape English domination and keep New France for the mother country" (p. vi). For Rameau de Saint-Pierre (1820-1899) Canada became a passion to which he devoted a good part of his life. Even before he was able to visit the country for which he had such a special predilection he wrote *La France aux Colonies: Acadiens et Canadiens* (Paris: A. Jouby, 1859, a book which aroused enthusiasm among the French-Canadian elite of the era (cf. Jean Bruchési, *Témoignages d'hier* [Fides, 1961], pp. 141-181). Jules Claretie encouraged Evanturel with the preface he agreed to send him for his *Premières poésies* (1878). The young Rémy de Gourmont wrote two inaccurate books which were, however, full of sympathy for his *compatriotes,* the *Canadiens: Les Canadiens de France* (Paris: Firmin-Didot, n.d.); *Les Français du Canada et en Acadie* (*ibid.,* 1889).

19. A kind of tradition was soon established by virtue of which the French Canadian interested in literature, arriving in France for the first time, was almost sure of benefiting from a fraternal welcome through some French writer or statesman recognized as the official friend of Canada. Isidore Lebrun and Dussieux were among the first "Canadophiles"; in the second half of the nineteenth century Xavier Marmier and Jules Claretie were happy to welcome French-Canadian writers passing through Paris. Joseph Marmette, who was able to see

something of the two just mentioned, devoted some very informative pages in *Récits et souvenirs* (Quebec: C. Darveau, 1891) to the relations between French Canadian and French writers.

20. In 1933 Dantin wrote to Jean Bruchési with regard to his *Marches de l'Europe:* "I am happy at the success of your *Marches* and to know that criticism overseas has given it favourable treatment. It is more than enough to make up for a few venomous attacks from this side of the water." G. Nadeau, *Louis Dantin, sa vie et son oeuvre* (Manchester, New Hampshire: Editions Lafayette, 1948), p. 220.

21. Published in Paris by Rudeval.

22. There has always been a great temptation for peoples sprung from European colonization to free themselves from the imaginary yoke of the inherited language. The Americans, in the era of the War of Independence, seem to have thought of a Draconian solution, which was to make their mother tongue Greek. On further consideration they felt that it would be better to impose this solution on the English.

In Canada, among the defenders of the French-Canadian language, it does not appear that any of them has ever thought of anything but legitimizing local words and sayings. The reasonableness of such a programme is sometimes lost sight of because of the outlandish way it is presented. To quote Albert Pelletier:

"How can we be sure of expressing our feelings, and expressing them well in a vivid and original way, in academic language that we do not speak, that we have never practised except in books? This is to oblige our writers to render what they see and feel and experience, what is new and strange to them, in a bookish manner." Then our defender of French-Canadian language concludes: "And if our *patois* is too difficult for the academicians, well, so much the better—we shall have our own language. . . . If the French want to read us they will translate us as they translate Provençal literature." This conclusion being simply in fun, Pelletier adds: . . . "There is no question of putting the pick and shovel into the very genius of the French language. . . . We simply ask of French-Canadian writers that they exercise common sense and taste and art in their use of French-Canadian vocabulary in order to make a literature that may be less bookish, more personal, more human and closer to life." *Carquois* (Montreal: Librairie d'Action canadienne française, 1931), p. 23ff.

23. In 1855, in *Le Pays* of Montreal. He was followed in this path by Hubert La Rue, Tardivel, Oscar Dunn and, in 1885, by Fréchette and Lusignan. *See*: Arthur Buies, *Anglicismes* (Quebec: C. Darveau, 1888).

24. *Anglicismes*, pp. 47-49.

25. "A Few Linguistic Aspects of the Teaching of French," *Nouvelle Revue Canadienne* (June-July, 1953), pp. 336-337.

26. *Ibid.,* 340.

27. Cf. Daniel Mornet, *Histoire de la clarté française* (Paris: Payot, 1929).

28. Daniel Mornet, after showing what French classicism owed to the teaching of Latin rhetoric, which became the traditional manner of teaching in France as early as the beginning of the seventeenth century, and after declaring that clarity was not to be looked for in some hidden *race* impulse but to be acquired through careful effort, nevertheless felt free to state:

> French writers have not forced themselves so long and patiently to be clear only because French writers had always been capable of clarity, effortlessly and instinctively. From the *chansons de geste*

to the Renaissance, innumerable writings bear testimony to this art of narrating, of explaining and even of debating with brilliant facility. The clarity of Villon, of Charles d'Orléans; the clarity of our chroniclers, of Villehardouin, Froissart, Joinville; the clarity of our farces; in a certain sense the clarity even of our *chansons de geste* or of our mystery plays. The tradition was not lost in the sixteenth century when . . . there had to be a struggle to maintain, recover, organize and establish it. [*trans.*] (*op. cit.*, pp. 260-261.)

29. Alexis de Tocqueville, certainly one of the keenest minds of the nineteenth century, observes that it was in the eighteenth century that men of letters had a position of preeminence in France that was unique in the history of Europe. Rivarol's famous work on the universality of the French language and the French mind came at the right moment. The sentence, "what is not clear is not French," fell on fertile ground. "I have heard it stated," declares Tocqueville, "that the taste or rather the passion that we have shown for general ideas, systems, and high-flown language in political matters was due to some special attribute of our race, to what was grandiloquently called *l'esprit français*, as if it would have been possible for this so-called attribute to appear suddenly towards the end of the last century after being in hiding for all the rest of our history." *L'Ancien Régime et la Révolution* (Paris: Gallimard, 1952), pp. 200-201. If the Romantics rejected the Classical ideal it was above all a reaction against a tradition which seemed to them to be sterilizing. Few of their writers were equal to the task of subjecting the Classical ideal to critical examination based on a thorough knowledge of the evolution of literature, and on the fruitful German speculation which followed Baumgarten's aesthetics (1714-1762). Ernest Renan, who felt that he was a prisoner of clarity, doubtless because of his Celtic blood, put on record these reservations about the virtues of clarity:

The French requirement of clarity and discretion, which admittedly force one at times to say only part of what one thinks and which are a hindrance to profoundness, seemed tyrannical to me. French would express only those things that are clear. Now, the most important laws, those which have to do with the transformations of life, are not clear; they are seen in a kind of half-light. [*trans.*] Preface to *L'avenir de la science* ("Oeuvres complètes," Vol. III [Paris: Calmann-Lévy, 1949], p. 719.)

30. Cf. p. 100.

APPENDIX ONE

Albert Lozeau (1878-1924) occupies a place apart among poets of his generation and is not to be linked with any of the groups which took shape in French Canada in the first twenty-five years of the twentieth century. He belongs neither to the group known as *artistes*, nor to that of the "native soil" poets, nor even, contrary to general belief, to the *Ecole littéraire de Montréal* (Lozeau was not a member of the School in 1900 and succeeded in contributing to the *Soirées du château de Ramezay* only through the good offices of his friend Charles Gill, who intervened in his favour to bring him recognition. He was actually a member of the literary group, because of friendship for Gill, only from 1904-1907 but took no part in it, the School in this period not being in operation). Albert Lozeau is a lone soul.

Speaking of Albert Lozeau's loneliness one thinks immediately of the infirmity which crippled him from adolescence. But this infirmity which kept him away from the world did not in any way hinder him from mingling in the literary movements with which most French-Canadian writers of the time threw in their lot. The truth is that Lozeau preferred remaining aloof. His long illness, by the psychological effect that it had on him, made him constitutionally a solitary and led him to seek only within himself the guiding principles of his poetic work.

His beginnings were slow and extremely modest. Lozeau wrote his first verse in 1898, before discovering in himself the source of real poetry. His affliction, from the fact that it lasted, lost its sting until he no longer suffered too much physically; but on the other hand he was still too young, or too appreciative of the care with which he was surrounded, to grasp the full horror of his condition, to have an inkling of the sadness in life awaiting him. He read the French poets with delight and understanding but seemed to have nothing to say when he took up the pen himself. At the beginning his verse was rather mediocre, expressing in a style full of padding and even solecisms at times, artificial feelings with a predominant and insipid sentimentality.

266

It was love which was to make Albert Lozeau a real poet. In 1902 the invalid fell in love with a girl who was drawn to him first of all merely out of pity and sympathy. It was not a question here of any dream love, unreal and illusory, but of an authentic love that was shared. For from 1903 Lozeau believed that he was going to recover, while his sweetheart and everybody around him thought so, too. (As a matter of fact the doctors did undertake a series of treatments which, in their opinion, were likely to get the patient back on his feet.) The two young people gave themselves up to loving each other and to their hopes; they had any number of plans, they talked about marriage. Unfortunately the treatments did not have the expected result. The invalid left his bed and was able to sit up, but he could not use his legs and would never again be able to walk. The happiness of the lovers turned to uneasiness, then anguish. There were no more plans for marriage; gradually the girl withdrew. In 1909 she married another suitor.

From 1902 to 1909 the drama of Lozeau's life was one of extreme poignancy. In this period when he knew the purest joys of love as well as the cruelest torments and disappointments, he applied himself to fathoming the secrets of his heart, to finding a direction in the destiny of man, to penetrating the mystery of things. These seven years were years of an extraordinary poetic experience. There is no doubt that at that moment it was Lozeau who was the most authentic French-Canadian poet, the most inspired and the most prolific. The finest pieces in *L'âme solitaire* (1907) date from 1902 to 1906; *Le miroir des jours,* which was to appear only in 1912 and is one of the most perfect collections of verse of the period, was written almost entirely between 1907 and 1909.

Literary criticism on the whole has never been willing to believe in the authenticity of Lozeau's love poetry; it has pushed into the background that entire portion of the poet's work and has created the myth of a Lozeau who was above all a nature poet. This is a basic error. Lozeau is essentially a love poet. He was the first poet in French Canada to produce an amatory work worthy of the name, the first to venture without shame or effrontery on that path which is considered in this country to be so perilous. To this day Canadian literature has few works about love which are as sincere and as beautiful as that left by Albert Lozeau.

Certainly Lozeau did write numerous poems inspired by nature and which are, generally speaking, well written. But he was wrong when he made up these collections to separate them from those about love. Criticism fell into the trap. In reality, the nature theme in Lozeau had its origin in the other two which are of first importance and closely linked together—love and solitude. Lozeau rarely considered nature objectively. On the contrary, he could see it only with the eyes of his soul, which was by turns trusting and tortured. An analysis of the poems in which Lozeau speaks of nature, if we place them in his work chronologically, is enough to make it clear that his feeling for nature was only another expression of what he felt as a lover and a solitary.

One fact which is inescapable and extremely revealing is that after 1909 Albert Lozeau almost entirely stopped writing in verse. It was as if with love lost to him, poetry had deserted him. More than ever he was alone but the intensity of what he was suffering blasted his creative faculties. From that time on he devoted himself almost entirely to prose. After 1914 the war furnished subjects for a number of different pieces, but for the most part they were poems written for special occasions and are without any great interest. Later on, thanks to his friends, Lozeau would be able to travel a little and see the country around Montreal. These circumstances were to bring back to life somewhat and briefly renew his poetic inspiration. The spectacle of vast landscapes, new for him, was to awaken in him a profound love for the motherland and become the object of fine bits of verse scattered over the seven or eight last years of his life.

This sketch would be incomplete without this addition: Lozeau knew a fate which was particularly cruel. Almost all the joys which normally belong to a man by right were refused him. For a few short years life seemed to smile on him but that brief period of hope was followed by terrible disillusionment. However, few men have been as valiant as he was in facing life. Always, by means of a patient process of spiritual and artistic growth, by a courageous and clear-thinking examination of his inner life, Lozeau forced himself to dominate his misfortune and to conquer his destiny. He offers the touching spectacle of a poet wounded, very sensitive and extremely vulnerable, who, by dint of struggling with fate and with himself, recaptured happiness, found joy again and peace of mind. Numerous poems in *L'âme solitaire* and *Le miroir des jours* make us live over again the ups and downs of that grievous struggle.

It is difficult to understand the obscurity into which Albert Lozeau has fallen. His work is easily among the finest of the period. Our literature has rarely produced anything as appealing. It has particular worth in the sincerity of the feeling and the depth and intensity of the emotion which stand out in it so clearly. As to form, Lozeau's work has neither the brilliance of Emile Nelligan's *Poésies* nor the Parnassian beauty of Paul Morin's work. Lozeau never allowed himself to be tempted by stylistic contrivances, never wanted to be a virtuoso of verse. But he had a profound acquaintance with all the resources of his profession. Nearly always with a touch that was deft and unerring, and often—especially in *Le miroir des jours*—with consummate art, he put them to the service of a very pure inspiration. He is often compared to certain French poets like Sully Prudhomme. But the resemblance is superficial. He is one of the most personal and original of our elegists.

Yves de Margerie
June 1, 1962

APPENDIX TWO

Offspring of unassuming French-Canadian families, workmen or lower middle class, from the beginning of the country to our own day still French and Catholic by resistance to the conqueror, by arbitrary attachment to the past, by preference and sentimental pride and other necessary things.

A colony in 1760 pushed down inside the smooth walls of fear, customary refuge of the conquered; abandoned there for the first time. The privileged class takes to the sea again or sells itself to the stronger side. It will go on doing it every chance it gets.

A little people pressed close to the cassocks of the priesthood which remained the sole trustees of faith, knowledge, truth and national wealth. Kept apart from the universal evolution of thought, which was full of risks and of dangers, brought up without ill will, but with no supervision, with a false estimation of the great facts of history, when complete ignorance is not feasible.

A little people, descendants of a Jansenist colony, isolated, defeated, with no defence against the invasion of religious communities from France and Navarre, desperately anxious to perpetuate in these places blessed by fear (the beginning of wisdom!) the high reputation and the benefits of Catholicism which was ill treated in Europe . . .

A little people that in spite of everything multiplies generously in the flesh if not in mind: in the North of immense America, with youth and vigour of body, with heart of gold but with the spirit of a monkey, spellbound by the annihilating magic of the memory of European masterpieces, contemptuous of the authentic creations of its oppressed classes.

Our fate seemed to be stuck fast.

Revolutions, wars in the outside world nevertheless break the imperviousness of the charm, the efficacy of the spiritual block.

Drops that cannot be checked trickle out through the walls. Political struggles become sharply partisan. Contrary to all hope the clergy commit some indiscretions.

Revolts follow, succeeded by a few capital executions. The first ruptures are passionately effected between the clergy and some of the faithful.

Slowly the breach widens, narrows, widens again.

Trips abroad multiply. Paris exerts every attraction. Too far out in time and space, too restless for our timid hearts, often it is only the opportunity for a vacation used to perfect a retarded sexual education and to acquire, from the fact of having lived in France, an easy authority with an eye to better exploitation of the crowd, once home again.

Revolutionary works, when by chance they come to hand, seem to be the bitter fruits of a group of eccentrics. In our lack of judgment academic authority has a different prestige.

Travel, too, sometimes offers the rare occasion of an awakening. Everywhere there is infiltration of what is not viable. Prohibited reading spreads. It brings a little balm and hope.

There is enlightenment in the fresh life that comes from contact with poets who were anathema: those men who, while not monsters, dare to express loud and clear what the most wretched of us choke down in a stifled whisper out of shame and terror of being swallowed alive. A little light comes as a result of the example of those men who are the first ones to recognize the present anxieties that are so sad, so hopeless. They bring responses that have value in the disturbance, the accuracy, the freshness, that differ from the endless old stories offered to this country of Quebec and in all the seminaries of the globe.

The boundaries of our dreams are no longer what they were.

We are overtaken with vertigo at the disappearance of the cheap tinsel hanging heavy over the horizon not long since. The shame of hopeless bondage is giving place to pride in a liberty that may possibly be won if we fight for it.

The devil take the holy water sprinkler and the tunicle. They extorted a thousand times over what they ever gave in the past.

Out beyond Christianity we touch the burning human brotherhood to which it has become a closed door.

The reign of fear in all its forms is ended.

In the mad hope of effacing the memory of them, I enumerate them: fear of prejudice, fear of public opinion, of persecution, of general censure; fear of being alone without God or society which unfailingly isolate; fear of self, of one's brother, of poverty; fear of the established order, of justice; fear of new contacts, fear of the supernatural, fear of the necessities; fear of the floodgates wide open to faith in man, in the society of the future; fear of all things capable of releasing a transforming love; a blue funk, a red, a white; fear, the link in our chain.

From the reign of debilitating fear we go on to that of anguish.

One would have to be made of stone to stay indifferent to the sorrow that is in the determined false gaiety, in the most cruelly extravagant psychological reflexes: cellophane coveralls for poignant present despair.

After this overwhelming reign of anguish comes that of nausea.

We have been sick at our stomachs before man's apparent helplessness to correct evils. Before the futility of our efforts, before the vanity of our past hopes.

For centuries the generous aims of poetic activity have been doomed to inevitable failure on the social level, violently rejected from the compass of society with an attempt at using them afterwards in the inevitable collapse of integration, of false assimilation.

For centuries splendid revolutions, their breasts overflowing with sap, have been crushed to death after a short moment of delirious hope, in the landslide scarcely interrupted in its irremediably downward course.

Not to be sickened at the spectacle of rewards given to blatant cruelties, to liars, to falsifiers, to manufacturers of objects stillborn, finishers of things, tired-out self-seekers, computers, false guides of humanity, poisoners of living springs.

Not to be sickened at our own cowardice, our powerlessness, our frailty, our lack of understanding.

At the disasters of our loves. . . .

In the face of constant preference for the cherished illusions instead of the objective mysteries.

Where is the secret of that efficacy in misfortune imposed on man by man only if not in our relentless eagerness to defend the civilization which presides over the destinies of the ruling nations.

The United States, Russia, England, France, Germany, Italy and Spain: sharp-toothed heirs of a single decalogue, of a single gospel.

The religion of Christ has dominated the world. Look at what has been done with it: Sister "faiths" have passed on to little-sister exploitations.

Suppress the precise forces of competition in raw materials, in prestige, in authority and they will agree perfectly.

Give supremacy to whom you will, complete control of the earth to whom you will, and you will have the same actual results if not with the same arrangements of details.

All things point to the end of the Christian civilization.

The next war will see its collapse in the suppression of the possibilities of international joint action.

It will be in a state of rigor mortis before eyes that are still closed.

Decomposition which began in the fourteenth century will nauseate the least sensitive.

Its execrable exploitation, kept in a state of efficiency for centuries at the price of the most precious things in life, will be revealed at last to the multitude of its victims, docile slaves all the more relentless in its defence when most wretched.

There will be an end to the quartering.

In the thirteenth century, the limits set to the evolution of the moral structure of merging relations having been reached from the beginning, intuition yields first place to reason. Gradually the act of faith gives place to the calculated act. Exploitation begins in the bosom of religion by the selfish utilization of existing feelings that are at a standstill: by the rational study of holy texts to maintain the supremacy that had been obtained spontaneously.

Rational exploitation is slowly extended to all social activities: a maximum return is exacted.

Faith takes refuge in the heart of the crowd, becomes the last hope of turning the tables, the ultimate compensation. But here, too, hopes are blunted.

In high places mathematics succeeds the metaphysical speculation which has become useless.

The spirit of observation follows that of transfiguration.

Method brings on imminent progress within limits . . . Our reason permits invasion of the world, but of a world in which we have lost our unity:

The separation of psychic powers and reasoning powers has almost reached a climax.

Material progress, reserved for the class of people who possess, methodically held in check, has permitted political evolution with the help of the religious powers (then without them), but without renewal of the bases of our sensibility, of our subconscious, without allowing the full emotive evolution of the crowd which alone would have been able to get us out of the deep Christian rut.

Society born in the faith will perish by the weapon of reason which is "Purpose."

The inevitable regression of collective moral power into strictly personal and sentimental power has woven the screen which was already a wonder of abstract knowledge behind which society hides in order to devour comfortably the fruits of its contracts.

The two last wars were necessary for a realization of this absurd state. The terror of the third will be decisive. H-hour of total sacrifice is almost touching us.

Already the European rats are trying to make a bridge in desperate flight over the Atlantic.

Events are breaking in a wave over the greedy, the luxurious, the calm, the blind, the deaf.

They will be knocked down without mercy.

A new collective hope will be born.

Already it is demanding the ardour of the exceptionally clear-sighted and is the single unnamed factor in the new faith in the future community.

The magic booty, magically conquered from the unknown, is waiting right there. It was brought together by all true poets. The measure of its transforming power is in the violence exerted against it and in its resistance afterwards against attempts to make use of it . . .

All things making up the treasure are revealed to be inviolable by our society. They remain the incorruptible reserve of tomorrow. They were ordered spontaneously outside and against civilization. To become active (on the social level) they await the release of present necessities.

Meanwhile our duty is simple.

To break definitively with all conventions, to break away from their utilitarian spirit. Refusal, knowingly, to fail to live up to our psychic and physical possibilities. Refusal to close our eyes to vice, to deception, perpetrated under cover of knowledge, of service rendered, of gratitude due. Refusal of quarters in the one plastic village, a fortified place but too easy to bypass. Refusal to keep still . . . Do what you will with us but you must listen to us. . . . Refusal of glory, of honours (the first granted): signs of prejudice, ignorance, servility. Refusal to be servants, to be used for such ends. Refusal of all PURPOSE, evil weapon of REASON. Down with them both to second place.

MAKE WAY FOR MAGIC! MAKE WAY FOR OBJECTIVE MYSTERIES!

MAKE WAY FOR LOVE.

MAKE WAY FOR NECESSITIES.

To global refusal we set up in contrast complete responsibility. Self-interested action remains bound to its author; it is stillborn. Acts of passion fly off from us by reason of their own dynamism.

Gaily we take entire responsibility for tomorrow. With the rational effort once turned back, the present is freed from the shades of the past.

The past had to be accepted with birth, it could not be held sacred. Anyway we are not in debt to it.

It is naïve and unhealthy to consider men and things in history in the magnifying light of reason which credits him with qualities unattainable to present-day man. Most certainly those qualities are beyond the reach of the clever antics of the academics but they are out of reach each time that a man obeys the deep needs of his being, each time that a man consents to being a brand new man in a new time. A definition of any man in any time.

An end to the wholesale assassination of present and future at the hands of the murderous past.

It is enough to take out of yesterday the things we have to have today. At best tomorrow will be only the unforeseeable consequence of the present.

We do not have to worry about it before it comes.

Nice people smile at the small monetary success of our collective expositions. So they have the charming impression that they are the first ones to discover their small market value.

If we hold exposition after exposition it is not in the silly hope of making a fortune. We know that the people who have money are on the other side of the world from where we stand. They could never risk with impunity these incendiary contacts.

In the past only involuntary misunderstandings made such sales possible.

We think that what we have written here is of a nature to dispel all of these in the future.

If our activities are becoming urgent it is because we feel violently the urgent need of union.

There now! Success all of a sudden!

Yesterday we were alone and undecided.

Today a group does exist, with ramifications that are deep and courageous; already they are spreading across frontiers.

So a magnificent duty is ours to accomplish: to preserve the precious treasure that falls to us. It, too, is in the direct line of history.

As tangible objects, they require that connections between them should be constantly renewed, faced, questioned. It is an impalpable connection, exacting, demanding the strength of action. This treasure is the poetic reserve, the emotive renewal which the century to come will draw upon. It will not be a case of transmission but of transformation without which the result will be a warping of the truth.

Let those who are tempted by adventure join with us.

In foreseeable time we catch a glimpse of man freed from his useless chains, realizing at last in the unlooked-for and necessary order of spontaneity, in splendid anarchy, the fullness of his gifts as an individual.

In the meantime, without rest or halting, in sympathy with those thirsting for something better without fear of long periods of failure, in encouragement or persecution, we will joyfully pursue our wild need of liberation.

Paul-Emile Borduas

(This manifesto was reproduced in the review *Art et Architecture,* No. 26, April, 1960.)

APPENDIX THREE

A few regulations of the
French-Canadian Academy

History and Object

ONE: The French-Canadian Academy was founded December 7, 1944, and was set up as a public body by letters patent of the federal Government, January 23, 1945, at the request of Victor Barbeau, Marius Barbeau, Robert Charbonneau, Marie-Claire Daveluy, Léo-Paul Desrosiers, Rodolphe Dubé, Guy Frégault, Alain Grandbois, Lionel Groulx, Louis Lachance, Philippe Panneton.

TWO: Its object is to serve and defend the French language and culture in Canada.

THREE: Its motto is: *Feu qui dure.*

FOUR: It rewards works which are worthy of it by the presentation of a medal.

FIVE: The headquarters of the Academy is in Montreal.

Composition

ONE: The Academy is composed of twenty-four members.

TWO: Of this number two-thirds represent poetry, the novel, theatre, criticism, essays, linguistics and history, and one-third, the moral, religious, philosophical and legal sciences.

THREE :The Administrative Council is free to change this proportion.

Elections

ONE: Any Canadian subject of French language, man or woman, is eligible on the sole condition of having published at least two works of value.

TWO: Sitting in open session the Academy examines the candidatures submitted, confirmed by letter from the applicants to the secretary and recommended by three sponsors.

THREE: An interval of two months must elapse between an official candidacy and the subsequent vote.

FOUR: Election is by a majority of votes in secret ballot.

Reception

ONE: The successful candidates are presented in a public session by one of the sponsors.

TWO: They must read here, with the consent of the Council, a work relating to the field of work which they represent.

THREE: The reception speech is obligatory.

Members of the Academy

Victor Barbeau, Marius Barbeau, Roger Brien, Robert Charbonneau, Robert Choquette, Marie-Claire Daveluy, Léo-Paul Desrosiers, Guy Frégault, Alain Grandbois, Lionel Groulx, François Hertel, Louis Lachance, Rina Lasnier, Robert Rumilly, Simone Routier, Roméo Boucher, Germaine Guèvremont, Roger Duhamel, Marcel Trudel, Paul Toupin, Pierre Angers, Jean-Louis Gagnon, Gustave Lamarche.

Publications

Cahiers de l'Académie. Since 1956 *Les Cahiers* have been published yearly.
Bulletin de linguistique. Published by the French Language Bureau of the Academy.

APPENDIX FOUR

Marginal Notes

A work of research, of criticism and of selection, history falls into the category of social science. It sets up for itself the task of presenting a clear picture of the past, but without the shelter of final confirmations it is open to all the winds of individual and collective subjectivism. In addition, whether it wants to or not history constitutes an inescapable instrument of ethnic and national formation, primordial buttress of minority racisms. This dual role imposes on it an obligation to rise to the highest level of excellence. Its practitioner must be at one and the same time honest, documented, objective and impartial. What he writes will be valid according to the validity of his conscience even more than of his learning.

Until the beginning of the century French-Canadian historiography was the product of clever amateurs rather than of technical experts. It was compartmentalized into political, military or religious sections. But, soon falling under European influence, it abandoned its provincialism to adapt itself to contemporary demands. It was only in 1935, however, that the University of Ottawa set up, under Gustave Lanctot, the first university course in historical methodology. Three brochures by the same author (*Historiens d'hier et d'aujourd'hui* (1941); *L'histoire et ses exigences* (1943), and *Regards sur l'histoire canadienne* (1948), are a condensation, so to speak, of the essential precepts of the profession. In short they recommend the refusal of conformism, an examination of sources, narrative realism and wide use of economics and sociology. Finally they call attention to the necessity of seeing events in the perspective and in the way of thinking of their time, nothing being more false or disastrous than measuring the past with the yardstick of the present.

As to editing, the author of *Histoire du Canada* has been unwilling to choose between the chronological style which reels off the facts without putting order into them, and the topical style which takes them out of the order of their efficient concomitance.

279

He has preferred to use these two styles in order to preserve for his story the movement, the crisscrossing and the reactions of events, but by intersecting them at the right points with sketches, flashbacks and conclusions which permit a grasp of the forward movement of the sectors and of the accomplishments in each period.

Gustave Lanctot
The Royal Society of Canada
October 24, 1963

PRINCIPAL PSEUDONYMS

REAL NAMES BRACKETED

Alonié de Lestres (Lionel Groulx)

Arles (d') Henri (Henri Beaudé)

Conan, Laure (Félicité Angers)

Dantin, Louis (Eugène Seers)

Delahaye, Guy (Guillaume Lahaise)

Doutremont, Henri (Georges Bugnet)

Dreux, Albert (Albert Maillé)

France, Claire (Claire Morin)

Gallèze, Engelbert (Lionel Léveillé)

Guèvremont, Germaine (Germaine Grignon)

Hertel, François (Rodolphe Dubé)

J. Guérard (Albert Lefaivre)

Le Normand, Michelle (Marie- Antoinette
    Tardif-Desrosiers)

Mabit, Jacqueline (Mme. Pierre Baillargeon)

Martin, Claire (Claire Faucher)

Nevers, Edmond de (Edmond Boisvert)

Rainier, Lucien (Joseph-Marie Mélançon)

Ringuet (Philippe Panneton)

Vac, Bertrand (Aimé Pelletier)

Valdombre (Claude-Henri Grignon)

INDEX

281